Transcultural Writers and Novels in the Age of Global Mobility

Comparative Cultural Studies
Steven Tötösy de Zepetnek, Series Editor

The Purdue University Press monograph series of Books in Comparative Cultural Studies publishes single-authored and thematic collected volumes of new scholarship. Manuscripts are invited for publication in the series in fields of the study of culture, literature, the arts, media studies, communication studies, the history of ideas, etc., and related disciplines of the humanities and social sciences to the series editor via e-mail at <clcweb@purdue.edu>. Comparative cultural studies is a contextual approach in the study of culture in a global and intercultural context and work with a plurality of methods and approaches; the theoretical and methodological framework of comparative cultural studies is built on tenets borrowed from the disciplines of cultural studies and comparative literature and from a range of thought including literary and culture theory, (radical) constructivism, communication theories, and systems theories; in comparative cultural studies focus is on theory and method as well as application. For a detailed description of the aims and scope of the series including the style guide of the series link to <http://docs.lib.purdue.edu/clcweblibrary/seriespurdueccs>. Manuscripts submitted to the series are peer reviewed followed by the usual standards of editing, copy editing, marketing, and distribution. The series is affiliated with *CLCWeb: Comparative Literature and Culture* (ISSN 1481-4374), the peer-reviewed, full-text, and open-access quarterly published by Purdue University Press at <http://docs.lib.purdue.edu/clcweb>.

Volumes in the Purdue series of Books in Comparative Cultural Studies include <http://www.thepress.purdue.edu/series/comparative-cultural-studies>

Arianna Dagnino, *Transcultural Writers and Novels in the Age of Global Mobility*
Elke Sturm-Trigonakis, *Comparative Cultural Studies and the New* Weltliteratur
Lauren Rule Maxwell, *Romantic Revisions in Novels from the Americas*
Liisa Steinby, *Kundera and Modernity*
Text and Image in Modern European Culture, Ed. Natasha Grigorian, Thomas Baldwin, and Margaret Rigaud-Drayton
Sheng-mei Ma, *Asian Diaspora and East-West Modernity*
Irene Marques, *Transnational Discourses on Class, Gender, and Cultural Identity*
Comparative Hungarian Cultural Studies, Ed. Steven Tötösy de Zepetnek and Louise O. Vasvári
Hui Zou, *A Jesuit Garden in Beijing and Early Modern Chinese Culture*
Yi Zheng, *From Burke and Wordsworth to the Modern Sublime in Chinese Literature*
Agata Anna Lisiak, *Urban Cultures in (Post)Colonial Central Europe*
Representing Humanity in an Age of Terror, Ed. Sophia A. McClennen and Henry James Morello
Michael Goddard, *Gombrowicz, Polish Modernism, and the Subversion of Form*
Shakespeare in Hollywood, Asia, and Cyberspace, Ed. Alexander C.Y. Huang and Charles S. Ross
Gustav Shpet's Contribution to Philosophy and Cultural Theory, Ed. Galin Tihanov
Comparative Central European Holocaust Studies, Ed. Louise O. Vasvári and Steven Tötösy de Zepetnek
Marko Juvan, *History and Poetics of Intertextuality*
Thomas O. Beebee, *Nation and Region in Modern American and European Fiction*
Paolo Bartoloni, *On the Cultures of Exile, Translation, and Writing*
Justyna Sempruch, *Fantasies of Gender and the Witch in Feminist Theory and Literature*
Kimberly Chabot Davis, *Postmodern Texts and Emotional Audiences*
Philippe Codde, *The Jewish American Novel*
Deborah Streifford Reisinger, *Crime and Media in Contemporary France*
Imre Kertész and Holocaust Literature, Ed. Louise O. Vasvári and Steven Tötösy de Zepetnek

Transcultural Writers and Novels in the Age of Global Mobility

Arianna Dagnino

Purdue University Press
West Lafayette, Indiana

Printed in the United States of America.

Library of Congress Cataloging-in-Publication Data

Dagnino, Arianna, 1963-
Transcultural Writers and Novels in the Age of Global Mobility / Arianna Dagnino.
pages cm. — (Comparative Cultural Studies)
Includes bibliographical references and index.
ISBN 978-1-55753-706-5 (pbk.: alk. paper)
ISBN 978-1-61249-375-6 (epdf)
ISBN 978-1-61249-376-3 (epub)
1. Fiction—21st century—History and criticism.
2. Multiculturalism in literature.
3. Literature and transnationalism.
4. Cultural fusion in literature.
5. Comparative literature. I. Title.
PN3352.M85D34 2015
809.3'9355—dc23

2014040755

Cover image: *Metamorphosis no. 3* by Stefano Gulmanelli (Milano).

I dedicate *Transcultural Writers and Novels in the Age of Global Mobility* to my parents and to Giacomo, Leonardo, Matilde, and Morgana.

Contents

Acknowledgments

An intimate thank you goes to my husband and companion, scholar Stefano Gulmanelli, with whom I was able to share not only the more prosaic house chores and parental/family responsibilities (thanks for all those school lunch boxes and those carefully prepared dinners!), but also lengthy, stimulating, and at times eye-opening conversations on our respective research theoretical territories. I would also like to offer my thanks to our children, Morgana and Leonardo, for filling our life with laughter and wonder at the end of a long draining day of writing. I would like to thank Steven Tötösy de Zepetnek, series editor of Books in Comparative Cultural Studies published by Purdue University Press, for his suggestions and editing. I am grateful to Giancarlo Chiro and Enza Tudini (University of South Australia) and to Sneja Gunew (The University of British Columbia), who contributed to enhancing the quality of my inquiry and the consistency of the overall structure of the work. A special thanks goes also to Diana Glenn (Flinders University) for her help. I thank Inez Baranay, Brian Castro, Alberto Manguel, Tim Parks, and Ilija Trojanow, who allowed me to conduct interviews with them about their life experiences and ways of writing. The interviews not only corroborated and further expanded my initial ideas on transcultural orientations and creative expressions, but also challenged the transfer of their knowledge within the parameters of academic discourse. With the writers' permission, I have included excerpts of the interviews in various parts of this book. I would also like to thank Dianna L. Gilroy, the copy editor at Purdue University Press, for her careful and accurate work of revision.

I am particularly grateful to all those generous friends and colleagues who, at a time or another, were so kind as to read or discuss sections and whole chapters of the book (either in English or Italian), always providing useful feedback, suggestions, and insightful comments. In particular, I thank Maurizio Ascari (University of Bologna), Jane Ball, J. M. Coetzee (University of Adelaide), Dorothy Driver (University of Adelaide), Brian Fox, Simonetta Ghirlanda, Janett Jackson, Russ Jackson, Meredith McAvaney, Kathryn Pentecost (University of South Australia), Gabriella Saba, and Susanna Iacona Salafia (Fatih Unversity). I also thank Ghil'ad Zuckermann (University of Adelaide) for having provided the correct spelling of the Yolŋus's Aboriginal language. Finally, I thank my parents, my sister, my aunt, and the rest of my family in Liguria, who have always made me feel their warm presence and support even from afar.

Parts of this book have been published previously in learned journals and conference proceedings. In all instances these published articles and papers have since been rewritten and updated. I also thank the editors and the anonymous reviewers of these articles and papers for their interest in and support of my work. In all cases the copyright release of texts published previously are granted, as follows. *CLCWeb Comparative Literature and Culture* (Purdue University Press), *Proceedings of the Annual Conference Cultural Studies Association of Australasia 2011* (University of South Australia), *Proceedings of the Border Crossings Conference 2012 at Kangaroo Island* (Flinders University), *Proceedings of the Intercultural Research: Looking Back, Looking Forward 2014 Symposium of the Centre for Intercultural Language Studies* (The University of British Columbia), *Transcultural Studies* (University of Heidelberg), *Transcultural Studies: A Series in Interdisciplinary Research* (Charles Schlacks), *Transpostcross* (University of Bologna), and *Transnational Literature Journal* (Flinders University).

The meditations on the Australian versus Mediterranean winds on page 54 have been inspired by the comment "Venti d'Australia" posted on 17 November 2009 in the blog *Three of Us*. I am grateful to Serena Bongiorno for allowing me to reproduce, with some alterations, a few sentences drawn from her post.

Introduction

We are living in an age of increasing interconnectedness, where political borders and cultural edges tend to blur and growing numbers of people throughout all layers of society are "on the move" across the planet, experiencing the effects of dislocation, deterritorialization, and cross-cultural acculturation (or transculturation). Hence, we have the growing influence of views and approaches related to transnationalism, flexible citizenship, neonomadism, neocosmopolitanism (in its rooted, situated, or vernacular variants), or transculturalism. These views and approaches constitute an attempt to grasp and theorize the dynamic nature of our "global modernity" in its various social, anthropological, political, and cultural aspects. As Arif Dirlik maintains, "Modernity may no longer be approached as a dialogue internal to Europe or EuroAmerica, but is a global discourse in which many participate, producing different formulations of the modern as lived and envisaged within their local social environments" ("Modernity" 17).

Within a more specific literary context, I theorize that this contemporary scenario is also giving birth to growing numbers of culturally mobile writers, whom I call "transcultural writers" (Dagnino, "Transcultural Writers"). That is, imaginative writers who, by choice or because of life circumstances, experience cultural dislocation, follow transnational life patterns, cultivate bilingual or plurilingual proficiency, physically immerse themselves in multiple cultures, geographies, or territories, expose themselves to diversity, and nurture plural, flexible identities. Thanks to this specific status, and through a related process of "creative transpatriation" (my term; Dagnino, "Transculturalism" 13), these mobile writers have found themselves at the forefront in capturing and expressing an emerging transcultural sensibility—what Mikhail N. Epstein calls "the freedom of every person to live on the border of one's 'inborn' culture or beyond it"—that appears better suited to the needs of a rapidly globalizing society ("Transculture" 334). Challenging visions of the "clash of civilizations" (Huntington) with their apparently irreconcilable divides on the one hand, as well as complete cultural relativism on the other, transcultural writers—whom I also call "transpatriate writers"—are disposed to reclaim an inclusive vision of culture/s, one which stresses the power of confluences, overlappings, and interactions rather than of polarities. In this way, not only do they contribute to the development of a transcultural literature which in its narrative choices transcends the borders of a single culture and nation, but they also promote and engage with a wider global literary perspective and, possibly, a new way of imagining and living identity. Needless to say, transcultural writers are not new on the landscape of literary history. However, it is only now that the pattern of modern (im)migrations and the phenomena of globalization generate transcultural experiences and develop transcultural sensibilities. This translates into an increase in the numbers not only of transcultural writers, but also of those scholars and artists who are promoting a transcultural perspective in literary studies and in the humanities in general (see, e.g., Dagnino, "Comparative"; Brancato, "Transcultural"; Gilsenan Nordin, Hansen, and Zamorano Llena; Helff, "Shifting Perspectives"; Schulze-Engler, Introduction).

In *Transcultural Writers and Novels in the Age of Global Mobility*, I explore the identity and cultural metamorphoses inherent in the transcultural process of "transpatriation" that may be triggered by moving—physically, virtually, or imaginatively—outside one's cultural and homeland or geographical borders. This process allows individuals, including writers, to adopt new ways of self-identification and, consequently, new creative approaches or modes through the development of a transcultural lens, "a perspective in which all cultures look decentered in relation to all other cultures, including one's own" (Berry and Epstein 312).

Examples of writers who underwent a creative transpatriation can be easily found. Just keeping to the twentieth century, the US-American writer Paul Bowles, with "his imaginative assimilation and interpretation of Moroccan culture" (Patteson 182), the Belgian-born French novelist living in the United States Marguerite Yourcenar, or, in his own way and with his multifarious cultural experiences, the Argentine writer Jorge Luis Borges may be considered among the forerunners of a phenomenon that only now, at the beginning of the twenty-first century, is acquiring greater impetus and resonance. It is through this process of transpatriation that writers such as Pico Iyer, Alberto Manguel, Amin Maalouf, Michael Ondaatje, and Ilija Trojanow—just to mention a few—have acquired their transcultural perspective, developed their orientation towards the world at large, and shown us the path towards a transcultural disposition and mode of being. This more or less consciously acquired orientation affects their writing in a way that contributes to the creation of transcultural literature and, more specifically, of transcultural novels, whose "fuzzy" nature I discuss.

Theoretical frameworks of transculturality have been deployed and engaged, especially in the Latin American region, since the late 1940s, after Fernando Ortiz coined the term "transculturation" to describe the process of mutual—even if asymmetrical—cultural influences and fusions between so-called "peripheral" and colonizing cultures (see, e.g., Canclini; Rama; Spitta; Tötösy de Zepetnek, "Configurations"). The concept of transculturation has been further developed, among others and within a postcolonial framework, by Mary Louise Pratt in her book *Imperial Eyes*. In the present study I refer to the subsequent conceptualizations of "transculture" and "transculturality" developed by Epstein (*After*, "The Unasked," "Transculture") and Wolfgang Welsch ("Transkulturalität," "Transculturality," "On the Acquisition"), respectively. These conceptualizations are intended to overcome the binaries of dominant versus subordinate and colonizer versus colonized cultures inherent in the original and postcolonial interpretations of "transculturation." Expressly drawing on these latter theorizations, transcultural literary studies are now gaining currency among those scholars and writers who feel the need to supersede the perceived existing limits—without denying their innovatory inputs and their validity as models of interpretation in analyzing the diversified influences of imperial power and the importance of cultural diversity—of postcolonial and multicultural approaches (see Brancato; Huggan, *Australian*; Orton and Parati; Sturm-Trigonakis, *Comparative*). These are being seen as far too attached either to an excessively essentialized vision of national/ethnic identities or to "an anti-colonial politics that seems increasingly unsuited for coming to terms with cultural, social, and political conflicts in a world transformed by processes of rapid globalization" (Schulze-Engler, "Theoretical" 26).

But who are contemporary transcultural writers and how do they differentiate themselves from other kinds of writers? And how and in what way do their transnational experiences and transcultural attitudes affect their creative outputs? Drawing from the broader theoretical framework of "transcultural studies" of which "transcultural literary studies" (Pettersson, "Introduction," "Transcultural"; Schulze-Engler, Introduction, "Theoretical,"; Helff, "Shifting," "The Missing") are a niche, my study engages with these two main questions and fulfills seven objectives:

1) To explore, identify, and outline the social and cultural contexts of globalization exemplified by neonomadic lifestyles and patterns of critical thinking conducive to the modes of expression of a transcultural orientation and imaginary (part 2, chapter 1).

2) To develop—drawing on the existing literature but also adding my own contribution to literary criticism—a suitable conceptual (part 2, chapter 2) and analytical framework (part 2, chapter 3) which allows the study of texts through the interplay of socio-techno-economic realities, cultural constructs (ideologies, worldviews, language patterns), time (the historical dimension), and the lived transformational experience of their authors.

3) To clarify the nature and the role of transcultural literature within the domain of contemporary world literature(s) (part 2, chapter 3).

4) To develop an understanding of those writers who have acquired a transcultural orientation and identity through their cultural border crossings and their transnational experiences (part 2, chapter 4).

5) To identify the common cultural elements which characterize the current creative outputs (transcultural novels) of these writers under the influence of their creative transpatriations (part 2, chapter 5).

6) To develop a taxonomy for transcultural theoretical and analytical frameworks (see "Glossary of Concepts for the Study of Transculturality").

7) To write a creative artifact (part 1) as a contribution to the field of transcultural prose literature with "unreliable" forms of narration (Helff, "Signs" 75), the fusion or transcending of genres (fiction and nonfiction, auto/biography, and novelistic

narration), and the transcultural "fictional(izing) nature of memory in the face of our 'moving world'" (Butt 293).

I address the above outlined objectives by analyzing and comparing the lived experience and imaginative works of five writers—Inez Baranay, Brian Castro, Alberto Manguel, Tim Parks, and Ilija Trojanow—selected according to a set of criteria which identify them as transcultural writers. To do so, I conceive a creative artifact (a work of creative nonfiction, part 1) through which I am able to recount in an imaginative way the in-depth interviews with the five selected authors. Further, I use the accompanying critical exegesis (part 2) to investigate systemically and theorize the impact of creative transpatriation on transcultural writing within a transcultural comparative framework. While doing so, I am careful to let the two pieces—creative artifact and critical exegesis—reflect on each other thematically, critically, and stylistically. By creative transpatriation I mean the combined process of defamiliarization with one's primary culture and the de-ethnicization, detribalization, deterritorialization, and denationalization (or dispatriation) of one's sense of identity, belonging, or allegiance. I prefer to give to this process of becoming transcultural the term "transpatriation" (rather than dispatriation) in order to emphasize the importance of moving beyond (physically and imaginatively) one's own culture, as well as of overcoming—or, better, "unlearning"—ways of identity formation which rely too heavily on ethnicity, nationality, geographical or cultural locus, or religious affiliation. I am aware that the term in itself—a combination of "transcultural" and "dispatriation" (on this see James; Palandri; Sinopoli and Tatti)—may be linked to traditional concepts of patriarchy and established hierarchies, but in this case the concept of "creative transpatriation" is my attempt to go beyond the notion of patriotism (let alone nationalism). I explore how the process of "creative transpatriation" affects the creation of transcultural fiction, how border-crossing novels dialogue between cultures, and how cultural transformations produce cultural encounters worldwide. I would like to point out, however, that to outgrow one's primary culture and affiliations does not mean to disown them and their foundational role, rather, it means not to be or feel limited by them.

As I discuss in detail in part 2, chapter 3, Epstein's concept of the transcultural "continuum" may be understood as an all-inclusive space of subjective consciousness and cultural possibilities which does not deny the formative importance of native/national cultures—and, to some extent, their accompanying worldviews—but at the same time allows an openness to the reception, integration, inclusion, negotiation, and permeation of other cultures, languages, and worldviews. Epstein acknowledges the essentiality of origins or primary groups of reference—as well as the deconstructionist attempt to demystify them—but sees them just as points of departure which should not thwart subsequent, perhaps more extended or more complex, forms of cultural development, enrichment, and identity formation. Similarly, within literature writers, readers, and critics can step out of their native cultures and detach themselves from national or ethnic allegiances, not only to challenge their collective dominance as paradigms for literary production, consumption, and analysis, but also to evoke new cultural imaginaries, visions, and vocabularies, thus increasing their (and our) sensibility and empathy towards other people and their perhaps unfamiliar lifeworlds. As Richard Rorty reminds us, "this is not a task for theory but . . . especially, the novel. Fiction like that of Dickens, Olive Schreiner, or Richard Wright gives us the details about kinds of suffering being endured by people to whom we had previously not attended" (*Contingency* xvi).

The interviews with the five selected authors which represent the core of the creative artifact have inspired my own writing and scholarship and, by revealing recurring patterns and similarities in the writers' lives as well as in their creative outputs, have helped me to elaborate a theory of transcultural writing and outline a general profile of transcultural writers. The interviews have also represented a source for the analysis of plural identities, belonging, memory, bilingualism or plurilingualism, and the relationship with the Other which inform a transcultural writer's orientation. All this does not necessarily mean that I focus on biography, or, even worse, on the kind of "biographical furor" despised by Milan Kundera that tends to annihilate the art and the meaning of a novel in favor of a voyeuristic propensity to detect and reveal in it the real or alleged events and details of an author's life (*Testaments* 266). Although, as Kundera himself concedes, "every novelist, intentionally or not, draws on his own life" (*Testaments* 265; on Kundera see, e.g., Steinby); this statement seems to echo Borges's claim: "All literature in the end is autobiographical" ("A Profession" 23). What interests me is the cultural orientation of transcultural authors and how this factor might influence their creative outputs. More poetically put, I am curious to explore the "magical link" between cultural dispositions and imaginative texts.

For over twenty-five years I have traveled, lived, and studied in several countries (France, England, the former Soviet Union, the U.S., South Africa, Australia, Canada) as a foreign correspondent, travel writer, and sociocultural analyst, and thus in writing this book I have drawn extensively on my personal experiences of writing and living abroad. My biography, intellectual interests, and creative endeavors have had a cumulative effect in prompting me to explore the processes of transpatriation in order to investigate transcultural fiction. More than specific stylistic solutions, which can obviously belong to a range of different literary genres, subgenres, and approaches, it is cultural attitudes and dispositions of transcultural authors while writing their imaginative texts which count most and should be taken into consideration when studying transcultural fiction. As Berthold Schoene maintains in his investigation of the emerging cosmopolitan novel, "What matters in the end is a particular stance towards the world, which must come to be shared by author and reader, but whose manifestation and effect obviously rely first and foremost on the author" (16). In other words, I accept Nick Couldry's suggestion "to shift our starting point from specific texts to the wider *textual environment*—the flow of texts around us and our movements within that flow—but retaining a sense of the important role which analysing specific texts can have under certain conditions" (136).

With this in mind, I investigate how the process of creative transpatriation experienced by transcultural writers in their transnational and culturally errant status might effectively lead to specific attitudes and, consequently, to specific literary outputs across cultures or with an interest in a dialogue between cultures. As Couldry states, "Each person carries with them an individual history of reflection which cannot be reduced to shared cultural patterns. Partly pure accident, and partly structured, this history is the trace of that person's perceiving, absorbing, interacting, reflecting, retelling, reflecting again, and so on, a sequence endured by that person alone. This very particular 'structure' is what we mean by 'experience'" (51). It is not just a question of literary definitions, genres, and technical solutions, rather, it is a question of changing mindsets, different cultural approaches, heterogeneous identities, deterritorializing dynamics, and, subsequently, of emerging new imaginaries which are created in the process through the interaction between transcultural writers and their globalizing—possibly transcultural—readership. Anthony D'Andrea goes to the core of the question when he critiques a certain limited conception of cosmopolitanism which does not delve sufficiently into the analysis of how new forms of reflexive subjectivities—with their embodiments, desires, perspectives, social dispositions, and imaginaries—are engendered under conditions of cultural, spatial, geographical deterritorialization and complex global environments: "This conception virtually ignores the impact of affective and visceral engagements with radical alterity in reshaping personhood" (*Global* 16).

Although it is impossible to measure and thus to quantify aspects such as sensitivities, imaginaries, or outlooks, these can be made manifest (and thus detectable) in a literary work, for example, in the choice of themes, characters, voice, setting, but also in the use of dialogue, plot construction, or language that is performed by individual authors (see in particular part 2, chapter 5). Already in 1977 Raymond Williams underlined the fact that "in denying the active relationship and interrelationship between literature and other social experiences and practices, we are cut off from considering what in fact are real relations, the primary relations, between literary practice and other kinds of individual and social experiences and practices" ("Literature" 25). Thus, schematically, we can infer that a certain life trajectory, supported by a process of creative transpatriation, may, but not inevitably, lead to the production—and the subsequent reception by an attuned readership—of a transcultural creative work (among earlier attempts to link a transcultural lived experience and transcultural subjectivity with a transcultural literary output, but still under a postcolonial or diasporic perspective, is Coral Ann Howells's "Not Belonging").

Transcultural studies stem from a particular interest in "literature as a cultural practice": according to Lars Eckstein when talking specifically about English literature, "while not neglecting the aesthetic realm . . . literary texts [are conceived of] as embedded in social, economic, and political realities which . . . are inevitably marked by processes of 'transculturation'" (14). Similarly, discussing Epstein's theories on transculture, Anesa Miller-Pogacar expresses the view that "literary analysis inevitably sheds light not only on the works under immediate discussion, but on the larger cultural system as well . . . One might well ask, Is the aim of a given research project to discover facts about culture or about literature?" (10). These claims corroborate William H. Sewell's historic overview of how literary studies, together with disciplines such as anthropology or sociology, have increasingly incorporated—if not become—the study of cultures (36). A similar viewpoint was expressed by Mikhail Bakhtin: "Literature is an inseparable part of culture and it cannot be understood outside the total context of the entire culture of a given epoch. It must not be severed from the rest of culture, nor, as is frequently done, can it be correlated with socioeconomic factors, as it were, behind culture's back. These factors affect culture as a whole, and only through it and in conjunction with it do they affect literature" (*Speech* 2). All this does not deny or diminish the fact that, as Castro notes, "there is such a thing as a literary universe, an environment which exists only within books, not within societies—a *biblio-pantechnicon*, a total library. I am thinking of Borges here, a writer I identify not only as Argentinian, but as one who is dispatriated in books, dispersed through them" (e-mail correspondence, 6 September 2012).

It is important to note, however, that through a transcultural lens cultures are not seen as mutually exclusive absolutes as in the past; rather, they are increasingly being perceived as hybridizing organisms in continuous dialogue with one another, fluctuating in the ongoing transmutation of cultural "permeations," amalgamations, and confluences (Welsch, "Transculturality" 197). As Ulf Hannerz states: "Rather than being easily separated from one another as the hard-edged pieces in a mosaic, [cultures] tend to overlap and mingle. While we understand them to be differently located in the social structure of the world, we also realize that the boundaries we draw around them are frequently rather arbitrary" ("Cosmopolitans" 239). One might say otherwise that transcultural comparative studies are particularly interested in the "worldliness" of literary texts (Said, *The World*). In Edward W. Said's view, texts are cultural products situated in the world and in the worldliness of the literary critic or theorist (see Ashcroft and Ahluwalia 18). In other words, texts and their creators have an effect on the system of culture that does not depend only on the paradigms of the literary canon itself, but also on the way texts are situated historically, culturally, socially, ideologically, and economically. The same may be said for those who analyze them with all the biases inherent in any specific position and viewpoint and despite the fact that scholars and critics cannot proceed in their interpretations and infer conclusions simply from context. As Said clarifies, "the real intellectual is a secular being" and as such is situated in society whereby his or her "morality" is influenced by "where it takes place, whose interests it serves, how it jibes with a consistent and universalist ethic, how it discriminates between power and justice, what it reveals of one's choices and priorities" (*Representations* 120). Fernando Coronil is among those scholars who, together with Said, assume that there is an ongoing dynamic and dialectic interaction between "cultural texts and historical contexts" ("Transcultural" 140; see also Meyer-Kalkus 117-20). This is one way of interpreting what scholars have defined as "the cultural turn in literary studies," acknowledging together with Jan Walsh Hokenson that "culture [has] moved from margin to center of literary study" (60). Said also points out that he does "not believe that authors are mechanically determined by ideology, class, or economic history, but authors are, I also believe, very much in the history of their societies, shaping and shaped by that history and their social experience in different measure. Culture and the aesthetic forms it contains derive from historical experience" (*Culture* xxiv).

The concept of the "transcultural" not only describes a type of writer and a kind of creative output, but also qualifies the mode of inquiry (not an ideology: note that in this I do not follow one of the basic premises of cultural studies and comparative cultural studies), the set of critical tools and vocabularies which are adopted to analyze transcultural literary texts and their creators' ideas within a comparative cultural studies paradigm. In the same way, scholars from the Nordic Network for Literary Transculturation Studies use the term "transculturation" not as a theory but as "a matrix through which a set of critical tools and vocabularies can be refined for the study of texts from a localized world, but institutionalized globally." All this to say that if, in this contemporary global scenario, we study literature in a culture-sensitive environment, we benefit by doing it through a transcultural lens. This approach may be better sustained by adopting the methods and conceptual frameworks drawn from the latest developments in comparative literary studies (in particular those identified as "comparative cultural studies"), which in their "fragmented and pluralistic, non-self-referential and inclusive" nature have already demonstrated their ability "to facilitate the cross-cultural and interdisciplinary study of literature and culture" (Tötösy de Zepetnek, "From Comparative" 2; see also Tötösy de Zepetnek and Vasvári).

The importance of the role of comparative literary studies in shaping a transcultural approach by "challenging monologic concepts of culture and emphasizing 'interference' and 'translation' between local and global, national, and transnational" can be found in the following statement by Marcel Cornis-Pope: "By comparing and interfacing cultures, [they] can help us rediscover and consolidate the middle ground between Eastern and Western, Northern and Southern, dominant and peripheral that we have neglected because of our polarized worldviews" (198). It is through this combination of comparative literary studies and transcultural studies that researchers might be better able to distance themselves from the perspective that focuses too strictly on national literatures, which "represents anew an entrapment in the national paradigm" (Tötösy de Zepetnek, "From Comparative" 6). As Kundera points out, "open any textbook, any anthology: world literature is always presented as a juxtaposition of national literatures" (*The Curtain* 36).

In the present research, a comparative approach through a transcultural lens—what we might call "transcultural comparativism" (my term)—seems to be endowed with the kind of dynamic open nature and flexibility most needed in dealing with the fast-changing contemporary movements and trends in culture and literature. It also promotes a new type of comparativism truly without borders, using "transculture/ality" (my term) as a model and theoretical framework to connect works which are no longer identifiable with only one culture or one national landscape. By virtue of this approach, we are able to move away more easily from the paradigm of the nation-state with which until recently literary studies have mainly been associated and embrace instead the latest theoretical developments in the field of contemporary comparative world literature(s), especially those emerging from the trans-Atlantic regions and, more generally, in the Anglophone world (Connell and Marsh; Damrosch, "Toward," "World Literature as," "World Literature in"; D'haen, Damrosch, and Kadir; Gupta; Spivak, *An Aesthetic*, *Death*, "Rethinking"; Thomsen, *Mapping;* Tötösy de Zepetnek and Mukherjee). These latest developments promote a new definition of world literature as a non-Eurocentric literary system made of texts coming from different cultural and linguistic traditions able to cross national borders. They induce us to understand and approach contemporary world literature as "a mode of circulation and of reading" applicable to "established classics and new discoveries alike" that takes into account the complexities of the present cultural and economic globalization (Damrosch, *What Is* 5; see also Walkowitz, *Cosmopolitan*). In this respect, seconding a more pluralist notion of world literature as in "world literatures," growing numbers of scholars now prefer to talk about "world literatures" in the plural (see Boruszko and Tötösy de Zepetnek; Juvan, "Worlding"; Wang). As such, the necessity arises to mark out a partially new field of discourse that is inherently deterritorialized or, at least denationalized and, most of all, fluid and transcultural. On the other hand, it is hard not to share Ellen E. Berry's point of view when she posits that she is "much less ready to believe that any one system of explanation—however subtle or powerful—can be the whole answer or can provide a fully useful model of analysis" ("Nomadic" 303).

By privileging a transcultural perspective, a form of "*movable praxis*, a constantly shifting and dynamic approach," paraphrasing Alastair Pennycook when describing critical applied linguistics, we thus acknowledge its ability to promote, emphasize, and consider vital a flexible and fluid manner of enquiry particularly suitable to the present context of global mobility, global writing, and global languages (*Global* 37; see also Dagnino, "Global"). As Pennycook implies, this means treating languages (and, among them, the more globalized ones) not as discreet entities as in the old categorizations where languages, as well as identities, "are assumed along lines of . . . location, ethnicity, culture," or within national or international framings, but rather as social activities (practices) that "incorporat[e] the local, agency and context in their complex interactions" and that are "always in translation . . . always under negotiation" ("The Future" 682-85). It is in this context more than anywhere that the "constant processes of borrowing, bending and blending of cultures . . . the communicative practices of people interacting across different linguistic and communicative codes, borrowing, bending and blending languages into new modes of expression" are mostly felt and experienced (Pennycook, *Global* 47).

With regard to the creative artifact, I experiment with the techniques of creative nonfiction as a means of proposing in a less formal and more dynamic way what might emerge from the in-depth interviews. On a general level, we can conceive of creative nonfiction as "the written expression of, reflection upon, or interpretation of observed, perceived, or recollected experience" (Root 46). Andrew Bourelle describes creative nonfiction as the work of "an author writing about real events or topics through her own personal, creative approach" (11). Despite this generic definition, scholars and writers agree that marking out the territory of creative nonfiction is not an easy task. It is a vague and blurred genre, a form of writing that tends to confound the boundaries between personal essay, narrative reportage, social commentary, literary journalism, memoir, biography, and fiction. But it is also a way of narrating the reality that exists independently of the writer in which creative liberties, small fabrications, and considerable changes seem to be allowed in order to obtain a sense of mystery, a symbolic meaning, or just a better aesthetic result. According to Lynne Van Luven, by combining "a private understanding with an accurate portrayal of the external events," an accomplished creative nonfiction writer "brings inner and outer worlds together in a piece of prose which illuminates a larger issue, enables readers to understand a larger truth, or sparks a series of epiphanies from which new awareness comes" (vii).

Thus I adopt the voice of the storyteller treating participants as actors or characters in an unfolding drama. I build the creative work organically in different streams, each stream being the fictionalized account of one of my encounters with the selected authors, except in the case of Tim Parks, whose thoughts are diffused throughout the text. As we shall see in the course of the present study, the water metaphor connected to visions of rivers, flows, confluences, streams, and bridges is a recurrent theme. Also in the transcultural writing of the writer Tawada Yoko there is a strong accent on water metaphors. As Francesco Barbieri remarks, analyzing the transcultural elements in her collection of short stories *Where Europe Begins*, "The border among the different cultural realities is nothing more . . . than a liquid entity in constant becoming" (74; unless indicated otherwise, all translations are mine). Interspersed among the interviews are pools of still water, formed by memories and recollections of my past experiences in different countries, cultures, and languages, as noted in my diaries. As Ryszard Kapuściński writes about his travel notes in the preface to his book *Imperium*, about the former Soviet Union, in my case the travel diary entries also "arose in the margins of my journeys" (x). Taken together and linked to each other, these pools flow in a fictionalized narrative stream of my own transcultural development and becoming. In the specific case of this creative work, the context of the encounters with the five selected authors and the broader framework of the dialogues have been greatly fictionalized, while the writers' answers to my questions adhere strictly either to our taped conversations or to what they wrote or said in other contexts on different occasions.

Chapter 6 works as a sort of afterword and as a moment of transition between the creative part and the critical exegesis. By mixing or interpolating literary and scholarly modes of writing, it also tends—in a transcultural confluential spirit—to blur the line between the assumed binary natures of theory/practice, content/form, and fiction/criticism. The creative artifact helped most of all to give an account of the impact of transpatriation on the cultural, linguistic, and creative attitudes of the selected authors as well as my own. The underlying theme of the artifact is thus the subconscious or implicit process of cultural and imaginative metamorphosis that leads the writers—and hence their fictionalized characters—to go beyond the culture in which they were born to transcend their ethnic, national, racial, or religious self-referentiality.

As an imaginary setting for the literary conversations with the five selected authors I use the city of Istanbul. In its complex cultural genome, as well as its plurilingual and multiethnic fabric, the modern development of ancient Constantinople represents the nexus point between two continents (Europe and Asia), two religions (Christianity and Islam), two empires (Byzantine and Ottoman), and an unparalleled plurality of cultural influences (Greek, Roman, Arab, Persian, Hebraic, Russian, Armenian, etc.). As Elif Şafak reminds us, evoking the transcultural heritage of the city in which she sets most of her novels, "In Istanbul you understand, perhaps not intellectually but intuitively, that East and West are ultimately imaginary ideas, ones that can be de-imagined and re-imagined . . . East and West are not water and oil. They do mix. And in a city like Istanbul they mix intensely, incessantly, surprisingly." Thus, the harbor city facing the Marmara Sea might hopefully become once again an expression of that spirit of confluence that was once masterfully represented by the ancient city of Alexandria and that has been recently evoked by Trojanow and Ranjit Hoskoté: "Confluence does depend on a certain mobility of people, ideas, goods and services, as it relies on the presence of meeting places, junctions, nodes where everyday interaction with the Other is a fact of life, and you cannot ignore difference because you are surrounded by it, you live, eat and breathe it. It requires an interweaving of mercantile complicity, where each side needs the Other to complete itself economically. A third precondition is an element of freedom from complacent dogma, and a basic curiosity and intellectual generosity: an interest, over and above the motives of gain and advantage, in that which is not the same, shared, or identically conditioned. In one word, we are describing an open system; the typical example of which is a harbour-city, none more famous than ancient Alexandria" (14).

In the translingual spirit of transculture/ality and since my native language is Italian, I first wrote the creative work in Italian and then translated it into English. I was cognizant of the difficulties and limitations inherent in any literary translation, especially when provided by a nonmother-tongue speaker. I was also aware that translation is another discipline altogether with its own complexities, theorizations, and analyses. Nonetheless, I felt it was important to give the creative work and the critical exegesis, which I wrote directly in English, a wider audience. Undeniably, within the academic world "global English"—meant as a flexible, polycentric world idiom used from a multilocal, multilingual, and non-nation-based perspective—is the recognized *translingua franca* (Pennycook, "The Future" 677, 685). In this way, I also allowed the authors I interviewed (among whom only Parks and Manguel know Italian) the opportunity to check the accuracy of our conversations and, if needed, provide further feedback. In light of this, the present translation of my creative work is not meant to be considered for its literary merits, but for its pragmatic purposes.

I selected the writers for the interviews on the basis that they would need to share at least three common traits: 1) a composite and variegated cultural identity made of different ethnic or cultural backgrounds: Bulgarian, German, and Kenyan for Trojanow, Argentinian, German, and Canadian for Manguel, Chinese, Portuguese, and Australian for Castro, Hungarian and Australian for Baranay, and English and Italian for Tim Parks; 2) an extended and ongoing transnational or transcultural experience in different countries, in different continents, and at different latitudes. In other words, I was looking for those lived experiences which give "a different slant on the world, a different accent in your thoughts, a different kind of narrative you've identified with" (Baranay, "Multiculturalism" 127); and 3) a creative transcultural literary work or body of work. Drawing on Eckstein's definitions of transcultural literature, I focused on the selection of texts "in which processes of transculturation are particularly prominent and relevant," which call attention to "issues of transculturality" or which are the product of the "contact zone," understanding the contact zone in "an extended sense which includes all kinds of cultural encounters from colonial days to the ubiquitous exchanges in today's globalised world" (Eckstein 14).

In looking at the authors' biographies, bodies of work, and—no less significant, for obvious practical reasons—geographical locations at the moment of my research, I was cognizant that my selection was not an attempt to reproduce a worldwide representative sample of transcultural authors. Nonetheless, I was also aware that the biographies of the chosen writers needed to have a high degree of cultural and geographical mobility, while their creative works needed at least to adhere to the parameters relating to transcultural literature and prose fiction as outlined by Sissy Helff ("Shifting") and Eckstein. Furthermore, it is of note that the task of deciding who is a writer was left to the publishers, reviewers, scholars, and critics who guard the gateway to the contemporary international literary establishment and assign writers to one or other rung of the ladder. In other words, the writers chosen for the interviews are fairly significant writers who have negotiated their access to the Western (Anglo-American dominated), competitive, and concentrated metropolitan arena of publishing houses and reviews. This means that—notwithstanding their undisputed transnational dimension and knowledge of several languages and cultures—their writing style and their use of genre is still profoundly Western. In my choices I was also bound, as we all are, by the constraints of my own cultural upbringing and orientation.

As mentioned previously, the panel of selected writers is not meant to be exhaustive or representative, but paradigmatic. Given also the space constraints of the critical exegesis, I could not assume that I could cover more than a limited range of authors. Nonetheless, I sought authors who not only have been exposed to a variety of cultural landscapes, but also whose texts achieved a significant transnational and transcultural readership. Most importantly, in my selection process I tried not to fall into what I consider the trap of ethnicization and did not seek at all costs to achieve in the chosen panel an ethno-cultural representation of contemporary transcultural writers. After having scanned at an international level the possible representatives of transcultural writing according to the above-mentioned criteria, I shortlisted twenty authors who fit the initial definition of a transcultural writer. Here is the initial list of the twenty possible candidates for my interviews from which I then selected the five authors of the present study: Inez Baranay, Brian Castro, J. M. Coetzee, Edouard Glissant, Amitav Gosh, Abdulrazak Gurnah, Milton Hatoum, Alberto Manguel,

Janice Kulyk Keefer, Oonya Kempadoo, Pico Iyer, Pap Khouma, Nicola Lecca, J. M. G. Le Clézio, Amin Maalouf, Michael Ondaatje, Tim Parks, Salman Rushdie, Miguel Syjuco, and Ilija Trojanow. In order to personally interview them, I then had to reduce the number to five. My selection also had to take into account the accessibility and availability of the writers, travel logistics, and financial constraints. In the course of my research, I found other writers—such as the Pakistani novelists living in the US, Kamila Shamsie and Bapsi Sidhwa, the Turkish writer living in London, Elif Şafak, and the Japanese writer Tawada Yoko, who majored in Russian literature in Tokyo, received a doctorate in German literature at the University of Zürich, and is currently living in Berlin—who would have suited my panel and that is why, in most cases, I quote them directly or indirectly, as is also the case with Iyer and Maalouf. Sadly, Glissant died before I could contact him for an interview, while in other instances, for example with Rushdie or Coetzee, although many of their works may be considered transcultural and may be alluring to a transcultural readership, their immense fame and the fact that they have already been extensively studied as examples either of exile, (im)migrant, or postcolonial writing made me hesitant in chosing them as examples of transcultural writing. Overall, I am satisfied that each of the selected writers fulfills the criteria as they have been set out.

I met the authors for the interviews at different times and in different locations in Europe and Australia. Instead of being structured, the interviews followed a thematic development and worked more as extended conversations while exploring a range of preselected themes. On a broader level, I dealt with the cultural transformations of the authors through their transnational experiences and interactions with different cultural landscapes. I was also able to explore in a more detailed way issues related to identity, hybridization, deterritorialization, and defamiliarization. I focused on questions of belonging, cultural approaches, consciousness, relation to the Other, worldviews, bi-multilingualism and also on genre, thematic patterns, and narrative techniques. My aim was that of identifying and theorizing how their creative and cultural attitudes manifest themselves in their literary oeuvres drawing forth interesting observations on dispatriate transcultural writing and its belonging to the big cluster of the "literatures of mobility" (my term; see glossary; Dagnino, "Global," "Transcultural"). Then I divided the topics in my interviews into four thematic blocks: 1) cultural or social environment and cultural roots, the sense of belonging, the relationship to place, globalizing processes, feeling at home, the use or idea of specific places (the hotel, the ship, the stream of water) as metaphors of transcultural lifestyles and writing modes; 2) identity and the ability to adapt, multiple selves, metamorphic or chameleonic attitudes, fluid perspectives, self-revealing biographies, the sense of memory, the slowness versus speed in human relationships, the refusal to be rigidly defined or categorized, and the sense of impermanence and transitoriness; 3) ethical stances and the relationship with the Other, racism and hybridization, multi- and interculturalism, the emergence of a global readership, cosmopolitanism, the spirit of resilience, and the morality of style; and 4) literary or narrative transcultural orientations and the relationship with foreign languages, polyglossia, translingualism, the choice of multiple national settings, mobility, and transnational characters.

Manguel was born in 1948, Baranay in 1949, Castro in 1950, Parks in 1954, and Trojanow in 1965. There is an age difference of 17 years between the oldest and the youngest of them. It was thus interesting to discover the similarities, but also the differences, which characterize their individual creative transpatriations, not only because of their distinct personal experiences of geographical and cultural dislocation, but also because of their generational disparities. In comparing their dispositions towards literary creativity, cultural approaches, and narrative strategies, I focused on finding common elements which contribute to and inform their transcultural writing, although the five of them write in different languages, about different things, and in different national, cultural, and geographical contexts. The writers' voices need to be prominent in my approach, thus direct quotations have been embedded in the creative output and to a lesser extent in the exegesis. Thus, when referring to transcultural writers either in the critical exegesis or the creative artifact, I refer specifically to the five authors chosen for the interviews and, in a more general way, to the twenty authors whom I identified in my initial preselection and the three authors (Shamsie, Şafak, and Yoko) whom I discovered in the course of research.

From a theoretical point of view, the exegetical study supports the creative component of the study. In accordance with the conventional parameters of scholarship, it formulates in a more structured way the most significant elements of the research topic, thus reinforcing its contents and clarifying in a more systematic way its results. It is informed by research from a number of fields, including (comparative) cultural studies, postcolonial studies, and (im)migration studies as they relate to narrative forms. More specifically, it is based on those literary and critical theories which address or characterize the key terms of the research and which refer directly to the most recent conceptualizations of the transcultural. I emphasize that this is not ideological as might be the case with the notion of transculturalism, but is meant as a mode of inquiry, of thinking, and of identity formation. By "transcultural writers" I refer to early twenty-first-century authors who do not belong in one place or one culture—and usually not even one language—and who write between cultures and are interested in the complex dynamics of cultural encounters and negotiations. Namely, authors who are more connected to the transnational patterns and modes of expression of our contemporary globalized condition than to the more conventionally intended (im)migrant literature of the late twentieth century (on transnational writers and literatures see Seyhan; see also Thomsen, *Mapping*).

This choice of terminology is owing to the fact that these writers' cultural orientations tend to be reflected in their creative works, thus fostering the emergence of a transcultural mode of writing through which cultures are seen as vastly fluid, confluential, and collective identity networks. In trying to find a suitable definition for these writers' paradoxically indistinct, almost unclassifiable literary identities, it is relevant to retain the root-word culture, acknowledging its potency and ubiquitous presence in human relations and social engagement. As Blaine J. Fowers and

Barbara J. Davidov remark, "A serious approach to culture recognizes that cultural ideals, meanings, and practices shape individuals profoundly" (705). If seen in this light, the term "transcultural" proves to be preferable to such terms as "cosmopolitan," "diasporic," "transnational," or "postnational," although these adjacent concepts and categories may share several common aspects and stir similar resonances in the way they have been theorized by those literary scholars keen to find new interpretive frames to capture the sea changes of global dynamics and find new ways at looking at texts.

In the specific case of the term "cosmopolitan" within literary discourse, it is hard to disregard the fact that this concept is highly charged and over the course of its long history has acquired political connotations to the extent that "cosmopolitics" is now one of the most en vogue neologisms (see, e.g., Ghosh, *When*; on the cosmopolitan outlook applied to literary studies see also Schoene, *The Cosmopolitan*; Driver, "Zoe"; Walkowitz, *Cosmopolitan*). Hence, one might be open to the feeling of unease of those scholars, critics, and writers such as Kundera who are reluctant to confound literary aesthetic efforts with the assumed hopes, ideologies, and often normative implications of political activism or political agendas. There may be inherent dangers, for example, in sharing Gayatri Chakravorty Spivak's view that comparativism—especially if approached in extremis as a "political gesture" when there is no acknowledgement by the political other, the colonizer, of the equivalence of different languages and literatures—incarnates "the double bind between ethics and politics," which for many scholars tends to be inevitably conducive to essentializing, authoritarian, or moralistic stances ("Rethinking" 616; see also Spivak, *An Aesthetic*). As Kundera states, "I have always, deeply, violently detested those who look for a *position* (political, philosophical, religious, whatever) in a work of art rather than searching it for *an effort to know*, to understand, to grasp this or that aspect of reality" (*Testaments* 91). In short, being aware that every artistic product, every act of literary writing, every aesthetic effort is in itself also a political act or is also immersed or situated in a political dimension does not mean that it must be necessarily interpreted through the restrictive lenses of a political or ideological standpoint. As Maurizio Ascari remarks, "it is thanks to their ability to trigger the imagination, opening us to alternative worldviews, that narratives exert an action on reality and translate into political acts" (13). On the other hand, this does not mean either that a comparativist should not use world literature, as David Damrosch assumes in his discussion with Spivak, "to shake comparative literature out of its dogmatic slumber, to critique its nationalist self-involvement, and to really push back against the market at every opportunity . . . a good research project challenges the reigning doxa, pushes against the euphorias of national self-satisfaction" (Damrosch and Spivak 463). Paolo Bartoloni points out that, thanks to the growing influence of cultural studies, "the need to support the contemporary field of comparative literature should arise not "from . . . maintaining narrow discipline boundaries and specificities" but rather "from the far more significant cultural and social necessity to engage globalization through a cross-cultural, transnational, and interdisciplinary approach" (*On the Cultures* 7). Further, in more than one case the term "cosmopolitan" has been associated with the attitudes of a well-heeled class of international globe-trotters or of competent and perhaps not less privileged "consumers" of cultural folklore (mainly in terms of food and music): "Especially . . . understood in this attitudinal way . . . [many cosmopolitanisms] ignore or downplay the underlying structural, as well as the wider social, political and economic, forces at work in all cultural relations" (McDonald 373). Taking as a paradigmatic example the situation of Australian society's monocultural shortsightedness despite its claims of a multicultural consciousness, Mary Besemeres and Anna Wierzibcka argue that "although Australia prides itself of being multicultural, there is actually little awareness of what it means to live between cultures . . . It is not enough to be tolerant, to have good will, to be curious about other people's folk dances, costumes, and culinary traditions" (xiv).

In the context of my study, not even the term "intercultural" would pass the transcultural test, since according to Welsch it also stems from the epistemological framework of national cultures, where cultures are seen as separate, well-defined, and self-referential entities instead of metamorphic, confluential, and intermingling processes (see "Transculturality"). In *Other Others* Steven Shankman examines why we should now privilege the term transcultural to intercultural or multicultural within a literary context. It must be noted that while questioning the traditional conceptual meaning of interculturalism (especially in the way it is still used by the Intercultural Institute of Montréal), which together with multiculturalism "start[s] from the assumption of distinct and separated cultures," Peter D. McDonald attempts to overcome this conceptual hurdle by proposing the adverbial phrase "thinking interculturally," which acknowledges that the world "could more productively be understood to be in a continual process of intercultural transformation and exchange" by prioritizing "this movement across cultural borders of various kinds" (372). A further perspective on the concept of interculturalism which recognizes the interdependence of people, their interconnectedness, and the fundamental importance of "community cohesion" is proposed also by Ted Cantle in his book *Interculturalism*. The reasoning by McDonald and Cantle is similar to that proposed by transcultural theorists.

The terms "diaspora" and "diasporic" still retain a tight connection to a more or less displaced minority and certainly a close identification with a community or collective group of reference, be it ethnic, religious, national, or cultural. This happens even when one refers to the voluntary diasporic conditions of late modernity without any physical connection to a geographical locatedness and from the perspective of a postnational constellation (instead of the nation-state). This means that diasporic subjects (and writers) are seen to be linked to a strong collective sense of identity or belonging while transcultural subjects are more prone to develop an individualized (or personalized) sense of identity or belonging. The term "transcultural"—not yet mired by any controversial or limiting sociopolitical interpretations and connotations—thus appears to be more easily and freely usable within a theoretical framework in which social or even political issues tend to acquire an aesthetical or imaginary dimension or are transcended aesthetically or imaginatively. Being more open and less restrictive in its meaning, it faces fewer risks to be transformed into a new ghettoizing category for writers and works which do not seem to adhere to nor comply with any specific national canon nor with the (im)migrant or postcolonial paradigm. As Sneja Gunew argues after having analyzed concepts of cultural hybridity and *métissage*, "this exercise has resulted in taking increasing care to understand rather than reify the complexities and specificities of the terms and debates in each of their historical and material contexts" (*Transcultural Translations*).

It is important to highlight the fact that contemporary authors who move outside their own native cultures or homelands tend to defy conventional pigeonholing: as with their works, their complex and fluid nature seems to dispel any attempt to pin them down, to fit (or restrict) them into any kind of defining box, even the most flexible and sophisticated one. As Rosi Braidotti says of her metaphoric polyglot nomads, they are "usually beyond classification" (*Nomadic* 22). If I group them together it is only on the basis of their cultural attitudes and their ethical and "imaginative affinities" (Rushdie, "Commonwealth" 70). Like the cosmopolitans mentioned above, transcultural writers may represent another tiny, often well-heeled minority. If we also take into account that they are well educated and hardly belong to the category of economic or forced migrants, although they may be the children of migrants, they might be seen as privileged middle-class citizens. Thus, some scholars and critics might consider even this choice of subject and its correlated arguments too elitist, relying upon too socially narrow a conception of mobility, "celebrating the ability of elite migrants to move between locales and ignoring the quite different experience of working-class or subaltern migration" (Apter, "Literary" 150). On the other hand, we should not lose sight of Couldry's remarks, at least within cultural studies, about the "downplaying of the "middlebrow" (let alone of the highbrow) and "the lack of attention to the cultural experience [and, I would add, to the counter-discourses] of elites" (3).

In light of the above, even the study of a perceived privileged group of people—whose biographies show that their backgrounds, or their parents' backgrounds, are or were not so privileged after all—acquires its meaning and relevance. In Couldry's view, more studies are needed not only of the "popular," the "marginal," and the "deviant," but also of the better off if we really want to recognize culture "as a space of multiple voices and forces" with its plurality of self-reflexive attitudes and its creative forms of resistance to mainstream narratives (3, 4). More importantly—although at present their creative transpatriation and transcultural attitudes may be seen as a niche phenomenon—through their literary texts transcultural writers may also affect imaginatively and at the same time reflect and express the specific sensitivities and collective imaginaries of growing numbers of readers of transcultural fiction. At least this is the case if we adhere to Rorty's view that "a whole lot of people can suddenly undergo a gestalt switch as a result of reading a novel" (*Take Care* 123). I do not intend to celebrate what some might perceive as privileged lifestyles, transcultural modes of being, literary attitudes, and theorizations, but analyze the combined effects of these phenomena in the development of a specific form of transcultural writing. In light of contemporary "cultural globalization" and at the dawn of what Peter Burke sees as a "new form of cultural order," what mostly matters is the need to find new interpretive keys and theoretical frameworks, together with a new terminology, that may prove better suited to the analysis of an emerging transcultural literature (*Cultural* 115). As Helff remarks, "it seems problematic to approach transcultural texts with a narrative theory that does not consider the extra-textual world and transcultural practices as their main sources of information" ("Signs" 279).

Given the objectives of the book, I employ Franco Moretti's approach of "distant reading" ("Conjectures" 56). Within the growing and hardly manageable terrain of comparative world literature(s), with distant or "second hand" reading Moretti proposes the analysis not of particular texts, but of the aggregated data coming from others' studies and analyses of those texts (57). This approach does not substitute close reading, but integrates it strategically in order to identify unexplored connections or define elements within and among genres or to establish broad literary patterns—what Moretti calls literary "waves" (66) and Mads Rosendahl Thomsen calls "constellations" (*Mapping* 3)—through time and space. The argument is that such patterns might not be discernible in any other way. Thus, I proceed with a conventional close reading and a systematic textual analysis of at least one work by each of the five selected authors. Adopting a sort of comparative bird's-eye view across the latest published works of my chosen writers, at the same time using the comments and insights of differently located scholars and critics on these and other perceived transcultural writers, I seek to detect the common elements in their writing which could identify, at a broad level, the general characteristics of a transcultural work of fiction. If I have drawn examples from a broad variety of writers who have written or commented on transcultural fiction and I have not given preeminence to the authors I have interviewed, it is because these authors have been given pride of place in the creative component of this work. As well, it seemed important to draw into the conversation a wider spectrum of authors who could inform the bird's-eye view model I employ.

Supported by a comparative process, this mode of "distant reading" makes it possible to interpolate a loose formalist analysis of the texts with a sociocultural exploration of the writers' lifeworlds. According to Ian MacRae, the strategy of "distant reading" proposed by Moretti is able to "house or frame" the "contrapuntal perspective" suggested by Said because it "serves as a means to read texts across a wide array of cultures and languages," as a way "to think through and interpret together experiences that are discrepant" ("American" 13). The choice of this approach has been determined by the nature of the objectives of my study, namely to develop a notion of the transcultural, as well as a deeper understanding of transculture/ality as an emerging literary phenomenon that does not require a fine-grained analysis of individual works. I am interested as much in transcultural writers as subjects who have already developed a transcultural sensibility as in their creative outputs. Thus, the "structures of feeling" (Williams, "Literature" 37) and the cultural or identitarian understanding of these authors are as important as the works themselves.

This way of proceeding has opened the dialogue with the adjoining creative product and also provided the production and articulation of a wider interpretive pattern. In both cases (the creative part and the exegesis), in fact, the goal was the same: to capture and better define the emergence of another literary wave (transcultural writing) and with it, possibly, of another kind of novel (the transcultural novel). In this bird's-eye view approach, where, to paraphrase Moretti and his theory of distant reading, "the reality of the text undergoes a process of deliberate reduction and abstraction," distance should be understood as "a specific form of knowledge: fewer elements, hence a sharper sense of their overall interconnection" (*Graphs* 1). This panoptic way of reading would allow meaning to occur in a plurality of modes and would allow us, by being in the historical contextual flow of literature, to capture something confluentially new. Williams had already emphasized the need to find "a mode of reading" that would acknowledge both the collective conventions of literature in a given time and the "irreducible practice" of "individual projects," which attest to the reality of "the pre-emergent": "The sense that one often has in some of the very newest literature is that it is articulating something which one has already felt but felt without this articulation . . . perhaps the most interesting part of [an] enquiry [about the significant relations of literature *in* society] will be into this pre-emergent phase in which new structures of feelings are creating new practices of writing" ("Literature" 36-37). Thus, following Scott McLemee's reasoning on Moretti's distant reading practices, my study contributes more to contemporary literary history than to literary textual analysis: "Moretti is not asking 'What does [insert name of famous author or novel here] mean?' but rather, 'How has literature changed over time? And are there patterns to how it has changed?' These are very different lines of inquiry, obviously. Moretti's hunch is that it might be possible to think in a new way about what counts as 'evidence' in cultural history" ("Literature"). All this is possible if we adopt the notion of history applied to art expressed by Kundera that art "has nothing to do with progress; it does not imply improvement, amelioration, an ascent; it resembles a journey undertaken to explore unknown lands and chart them" (*The Curtain* 15).

What follows is a description of how I develop the contents of the critical exegesis. In chapters 1 to 3 I define and explain the different concepts, theorizations, and categories taken into consideration and in chapters 4 to 5 I exemplify the literary figure of transcultural writers and sketch the nature of their creative output, the transcultural novel. In chapter 1 I outline the contemporary social and cultural environment which, with its transnational dynamics and globalizing phenomena, fosters the emergence of a generation of transcultural writers. In chapter 2 I present an account of the history of the notion of transculturation and of theories of the transcultural (in particular Welsch's formulation of "transculturality") in which cultures are not seen as monolithic entities or as mutually exclusive absolutes, but as hybridizing organisms in constant relation to each other, fluctuating in the ongoing flux of cultural transformations, amalgamations, and confluences. I employ Epstein's concept of "transculture" as a means of cultural self-identity and development and propose transculture/ality as an expanded theoretical framework for the study of early twenty-first century transcultural literature. In chapters 1 and 2 I also explain in which context terms like culture, cultural identity, globalization, transnationalism, cosmopolitanism, neonomadism, and transculturalism are used in the course of the study. In chapter 3 I offer a brief overview of the growing importance of a transcultural perspective in cultural studies and literary studies and develop a framework of transcultural literature in relation to the "literatures of mobility" within the wider domain of world literature(s). In the final section of chapter 3 I explain the five-dimensional nature of "transcultural comparativism" as an analytical framework for the study of transcultural literature. Drawing on the life stories and comments gathered during the interviews with the selected authors and with the support of other scholars' and creative writers' arguments or ideas, in chapter 4 I analyze the results of the research and outline a sort of "liquid"—fluctuating, never rigidly determined—profile of transcultural writers and theorize their role in the development of transcultural fiction. In chapter 5 I present a short historical account of the expansion of the novel—with its tendency to borrow from and cross over different genres and cultures—at a planetary level. Then I sketch the main, albeit "fuzzy" features of transcultural novels and their role as "harbor novels" (my term), that is, as transcultural works of fiction able to open new cultural imaginaries and at the same time reconcile different cultural perspectives. In the conclusion I present a summary of my analysis emerging from the study including a sketch of the main elements of a transcultural orientation followed by closing remarks and my personal reflections on the role of transcultural fiction and transcultural writers in a world of globalization.

The bilingual writing (Italian and English) of the study with its double nature (creative in the first part, scholarly in the second) provides me with a "schizophrenic perception in two different dimensions": in a different context, this allowed Kapuściński to watch and consequently write about the fall and fate of the Soviet empire "on the screen of a television set . . . as well as on the screen of the country's ordinary, daily reality" (*Imperium* 320). In sum, my study proposes the formulation of an extended transcultural conceptual and analytical reference frame (namely, "transcultural comparativism") together with the application of a specific form of "distant reading" for the exploration of early twenty-first century transcultural literature. Altogether, my study follows and supports the framework of comparative cultural studies "based on tenets of the contextual (systemic and empirical) approach in the study of culture" as outlined in the aims and scope of the monograph series of Books in Comparative Cultural studies (see also Steven Tötösy de Zepetnek who developed said framework).

Part One

Writing and Transcultural Life

Chapter One

Trojanow's Drive toward Mobility and Cultural Confluences

My father played jazz in his twenties, in postwar Italy, no money in his pockets, but echoes of America in his ears. Together with his cousin he tried to migrate to Australia. His problem was that during the war, barely fourteen, he had been wounded and lost an eye: in 1951 the Australian Department of Immigration accepted his cousin but rejected him as disabled. When I was born, I inherited his restlessness, his longing for the elsewhere. I grew up listening to him singing in English and reciting passages of novels in English, and accepting his reading suggestions: Conrad first of all, then Hemingway, Steinbeck, Dos Passos, Fitzgerald—all writers on the move, expatriates open to the world. A man paralyzed by fate, my father passed on to me the gene of permanent mobility and the lust for the frontier. Only now, after almost four decades from the child that I was, do I realize that I have unconsciously made my life his dream. All my choices, my studies, my interests, my professions have taken me away from my roots, in a never-ending search for other territories, other horizons. For him, I have crossed borders, opened new life trajectories, and immersed myself in cultural streams away from my origins. Even the man who would become my life and road companion needed to fulfill those requirements of impermanence and derootedness. My husband, S., was born in Jeddah, after his migrant father left Eritrea (when Italy lost the war and its colonies) and crossed the Red Sea instead of repatriating. Thus S. grew up in Saudi Arabia, speaking Italian at home, Arabic with the locals, and English with the expatriates: a foreigner by birth, a cosmopolitan by vocation, and, like me, a neonomad by choice.

I was on a train, a long-distance train. One of those trains that even at full speed speak to you of the slowness of past times, when moving from one corner of Europe to another would take days of railroad, not a few hours of flight. *Slowness*—the Czech émigré Milan Kundera wrote a whole book, directly in French, on this disappearing state of grace, synthesized in the first rule of his "existential mathematics": "The degree of slowness is directly proportional to the intensity of memory; the degree of speed is directly proportional to the intensity of forgetting" (39). I got on in Venice, would change in Budapest and get off in Istanbul: the same route as the Orient Express, but without its luxury. Ahead of me I had all the time in the world. Trains have always had this effect on me. Like books, they act as temporal tunnels: in an instant—in a page, in an eternity—traveling through physical or mental landscapes the past passes in front of you together with the present and all your possible futures. No wonder that to explain his space-time concept Einstein resorted to a train metaphor. Or that, to conceive the universe, Borges thought of a perpetual traveler lost in an infinite library. And are they not the Inuit who tell us that every imagined and recounted story already contains in itself the past, the present and the future, since "it is the story—not time—that travels" (Manguel, *The City* 79)? Trains, libraries, labyrinths, fantasies, myths, transitions: my destiny on earth. My name is Arianna—Ariadne in Greek, like the daughter of Minos king of Crete who helped Theseus kill the Minotaur and escape from the lethal maze with a thread. Ungrateful, Theseus abandoned her on a beach in the island of Naxos. Dionysus found her, drank her tears, and married her. Wife to an itinerant god, since then.

I was travelling alone, but not for much longer. As we were entering the central station in Sofia, the couple of French tourists with whom I shared the compartment said good-bye quickly before making for the exit. I had not encouraged any conversation between us; instead, as I waited, I had withdrawn into my book. It was Italo Calvino who wrote that books can be "a defense" that shut out the external world, "a dream" to sink into like a drug, or "bridges cast toward the outside" (*If on a Winter's* 142). I use them in all the three ways, depending on the circumstances. The screeching of the train's brakes covered the sound of my footsteps as I was heading towards the carriage restaurant: we had agreed to meet there. I looked out of the window trying to capture the soul of that Eastern European capital from the history of its station. I quickly reinterpreted what I had been reading in the guidebook: built in 1888 with the help of Italian workers; demolished and rebuilt in 1974 to give way to the brutalist architecture of the Soviet era; recast in 2000 to shape the new times by adding questionable tensile elements that badly mimicked the canopies of acrylic glass of the Olympic Stadium in Munich. Some people had defined it "a Kafkaesque nightmare." That is how they mask the past, I thought—without elegance. The train set off again with a slight jolt; before reaching a level crossing it emitted a long whistle, a warning that it wouldn't stop. I tore my gaze away from the grey uniformity of the umpteenth urban outskirts and met the eyes of a man standing in front of me, a backpack slung over his shoulder, a book in his left hand. I took a peek at the title and smiled faintly, more to myself than to him.

In my fiction of my conversation with Trojanow: "Does it amuse you?" the stranger asked me in English, following my glance. I held up the volume that I was holding in my lap, to show him the cover: *Istanbul*, by Orhan Pamuk. Same author, same title, different editions. I introduced myself, stretching out my hand, as if wanting to catch the rattling of the train over the railroad switches while we were leaving Sofia: "Arianna Dagnino." "Ilija Trojanow," he replied, holding out his right hand and scrutinizing me with a serious expression, as if he were trying to connect the mental image of me that he must have been forming during our repeated email exchanges and the woman of Italian origins (but living in Australia) who now was facing him, outside the virtual dimension of a computer screen and so distant from the Latin stereotype: no trace of Mediterranean abundance, of dark and obscure sensuality. But he had already gone beyond that: "I guessed it was you." A passage from Trojanow's travel diary came to mind. In it he recounted his verbal exchange with two Arabs outside a mosque, during his pilgrimage to Mecca. They asked him where he came from. He replied, "India." "It cannot be," they retorted. "Why?" he asked. "You are too fair." "You have an obsession with skin color," he shied away. The older one smiled at his quip but then insisted on knowing where precisely his family came from, reassured only when Trojanow invented some distant ancestry from a central Asian tribe, though this was not far from the truth. Now that same pilgrim-writer stood in front of me and, after raising his book, talked to me as if we already were travel companions. "An obvious reading given where we are headed." I nodded and again detected a slightly foreign inflection in his English. Clearly a man accustomed to travel, I thought—I would have sensed it anyway, even if I had not known who he was.

Trojanow showed that relaxed way of filling a space, without encroaching; of bringing into focus people and situations without making himself noticed; of adopting a neutral language without imposing one of his preference or of obvious belonging. As if he knew there was no point in revealing oneself straight away. After all, this is what I had experienced wherever I had been: the émigrés, the eternal wanderers, the new and old nomads know how to smell and recognize each other; they are aware they speak a common language able to go beyond whatever lingua franca or secret idiom. It is a universal language that some value and others barely sense: the great privilege of wayfarers who travel the routes of the world—physically, mentally, or through a book. Calvino had also mentioned it, writing how, by night, around the campfires of Euphemia, city of barterers and merchants, people came from "seven nations" to tell their stories of "wolves, sisters, treasures, scabies, lovers, battles" and weave their memories "at every solstice and equinox" (*The Invisible Cities* 36). It was their way of trading memories before setting off again for new horizons. But it was also their way to preserve memories, to place them where they could rest like stratified sediments of past humanities. Only then one might use those memories to weave wefts of meaning, longings, regrets that do not want to be silenced—in this world of ours where everything is transient and nothing seems to last. Calvino knew what he was talking about, having lived himself as a wanderer—he was born in Havana, Cuba, had grown up in Sanremo, Italy, married the Argentinian translator Esther Judith Singer, lived with his family in Paris for thirteen years, and spent his last years in Rome.

After taking a seat Trojanow pointed at the position of my bookmark. "You are almost at the end." Speaking in English, I realized, we had neutralized the linguistic formalities of the Italian *lei* and of the German *Sie*. From now on he would simply be

Ilija, even though I would keep referring to him by his surname. "Will you also meet Pamuk?" "I'd love to, but presently he is in the U.S." And I thought of the transitory quality of our biographies, mine and those of the other authors I was about to interview—moving biographies, shaken by chance, destiny, or stubborn willpower. Only a few years before, for example, the writer who was now sitting in front of me had lived in Cape Town, South Africa, and before that had lived for five years in Mumbai, India. These were just a few scraps of information about Trojanow that I had been able to gather in anticipation of our interview. In accordance with his character, his bio-notes seemed to be rather scanty.

We were both hungry. We skipped polite conversation and instead agreed to scan the multilingual central European menu. He ordered for both of us, after having inquired after my tastes, addressing the waiter—a native from Innsbruck, as it turned out—in soft German, a language in which he appeared perfectly at ease even though it was not his mother tongue.

"Here, if I had to write the biography of someone like me, I would start in 1971," Trojanow began answering my first question over the digital audio recorder before the waiter served us our lentil soup with *Knödel*. "In this one year, between the age of six and seven, I ascertained that everything important in life changes, and it can change at an incredible speed. In this one year, I moved from communist Bulgaria to a refugee camp in Italy, from another refugee camp to the normality of capitalist life in Germany, and, then, from the cold winters of Northern Europe to equatorial Kenya." Trojanow had his transcultural baptism of fire at a tender age but not so tender that he would not be able to remember: "I was a normal Bulgarian kid living in a Bulgarian family in the same room with my parents, another was occupied by my uncle and my aunt, my grandmother slept in the living room. I was attending kindergarten and probably nothing much would have happened with my life if my parents hadn't decided to flee Bulgaria." Instead, in that fateful year, one night the young Trojanow found himself smuggled across the Yugoslavian border into Italy by wading a river on his father's shoulders with the help of certain Arab students in Zagreb (an odd way to pay for one's studies, I thought).

After that, the Trojanows found themselves locked in a refugee camp near Trieste, on Italian soil. "They served us spaghetti," said my companion, retrieving another memory. "At the beginning, I found it exotic and a great treat, until we realized it was the only item in the menu, both at lunch and dinner, and that the only way to get out of there and change diet would be to accept the visa for one of the countries in their list: Argentina, South Africa, Canada, Australia—but nothing in Europe." "I guess after that you hated spaghetti." "Not at all, it's all forgotten," he said with a smile. After several weeks of pasta-only meals, the Trojanows were on the run again, crossing other territorial borders and finally landing in another refugee camp in Germany. "After six long months, we obtained political asylum and my father—being an engineer—found work at a small consultancy. Only a few months had passed, though, before the company sent him off to Kenya. I still remember when he came home and said: 'We're off to Africa.'" "We had just settled down," Trojanow said in a low voice, absentmindedly rotating the spoon between his fingers, engrossed in his memories. I watched the scene from the outside, as if at the movies. He paused slightly, almost imperceptibly, but just sufficiently long to produce the necessary rhetorical effect before concluding the first chapter of his life: "After two weeks we were in Nairobi." Then he kept quiet, as if he wanted to leave me the time to retrace his child's journey and relive, together with him, that further change of scene. As the silence fell between us, I was suddenly aware of the light chatter that had started to liven up the carriage restaurant, but I did not look around. Instead, I stared out at the desolate sunset plains, imagining dusty acacia trees engulfed in purple light before his voice started again, this time in an even lower, more intimate tone. "Everything was different: the language and the climate but also the colors, the smells, the landscape, even the bird calls—a cacophony of sounds to me incomprehensible, then. Of course I'm embellishing here, because it's impossible to analyze yourself in recollection." I knew he was right: every time we remember our past we become novelists of our life books, we keep inventing and reinventing our stories, trying to fill in the gaps in the elusive nature of past events, eroded or augmented by the dysfunctional time of memory.

The train was running fast now, in the extreme oblique light of a dying sun. I realized that I had not even started to decipher the man in front of me, and that probably I would never be able to do so, even by reading him. But that was as it should be. Nothing in him seemed out of the ordinary, as if he purposely tried to go unnoticed, to blend in. Of average height, with grey-speckled hair cut short but not too short, at 46 he could happily pass for a youngish, carefree globetrotter or a more mature academic. He seemed quite fit but not in an obvious way; his skin might have become darker in the open sun but it did not stand out among the pale northern Europeans among whom he had returned after living under sunnier skies. All in all, he was a chameleon, ready to transform and adapt (deliberately or naturally?) according to his environment, be it a carriage restaurant rattling through the European East, a coffee house in Vienna, where he now lived, or any hangout in Sofia, where he had boarded to reach Istanbul with me. One might see him as a *moveable man*, in the same way that the nineteenth-century traveler and explorer Sir Richard Burton would have appeared to his contemporaries. For years Trojanow had imagined himself in the shoes of that great orientalist, translator, polyglot, and master of cultural metamorphoses, following his tracks in India, Africa, and even Mecca, before writing his "biographical novel" (*The Collector of Worlds*)—rather than his "novelistic biography," as he was keen to underline—the book that in 2006 would grant him international exposure. His "love and hate" relationship with Burton, as he himself had described it, had lasted seven years (five for pure research—readings, travels, experiences—two for writing). Seven years spent with the aim of staying true to Burton's character, to safeguard his personality and his mystery, without "caging" him in a point of view. "For this reason I detest biographies—he remarked in a previous interview—which claim to tell the definitive truth of someone's life, to contain a person's existence" (see Trojanow, "Le identità"). In collecting the early memories of the first writer in my list, it occurred to me that my resilience—that capacity of recovery and persistence in the face of adversity—was also born from my childhood experiences: in my case not for a sudden transnational adventure (how fascinating it would have then appeared to me, aside those dramatic circumstances), but simply because I could hardly draw breath.

From my travel diaries (Sestri Levante, Genova 11 January 1995)

> I suffered from asthma. How many nights had I endured the huge weight that pressed against my chest. How many days had I been confined to bed while all the other children went to school. It was a different kind of forced paralysis from my father's one, but it would lead me all the same, as if by reaction on my neonomadic path. Something similar had already happened, I would later discover, to the asthmatic Robert Louis Stevenson, who was born and bred in Scotland and died in the Samoan Islands: 'During the long night of his childhood, when, gasping for breath . . . he had sat up in his bed . . . waiting for what they called the Night Hag to finish her ghastly business and go, he had told himself that if ever he had enough strength, he would use it to lead his body to the edge of any possible adventure; he would take to the road or the sea, he would set off like a new Ulysses in the hope of strange encounters but, above all, he would travel for the sake of the journey itself" (see Manguel, *Stevenson* 35). My native Liguria, that thin strip of land wedged between the Apennines and the sea, felt restrictive. The perceived limitation of its spaces and views was stifling. I had realized that even before I left in search of my elsewhere, before reading of Stevenson's wanderings or Rushdie's words: "He had spent five years, five springs, away from home . . . Now, returning, he saw through travelled eyes. Instead of the beauty of the tiny valley circled by giant teeth, he noticed the narrowness, the proximity of the horizon; and felt sad, to be at home and feel so utterly enclosed" (*Midnight's Children* 11). Thus, at fifteen, I already knew what I wanted: to be a foreign correspondent; to be sent far away; to be paid to travel and write. I wanted to be put on an airplane and find my "interviews with history" over many borders, as my undisputed role model—the war reporter and journalist Oriana Fallaci—had been doing for years. At that time, when she published her shocking personal report on Vietnam War, *Nothing, and So Be It*, and *Interview with History* (after having met and intellectually wrestled with powerful figures such as Henry Kissinger, Indira Gandhi, the Shah of Iran, Muammar Gaddafi, Yasser Arafat, Golda Meir, and Deng Xiaoping), she was at the zenith of her career, long before her controversial about-face and the reductive anti-Islamic fervor that would characterize her later years. In a nutshell, it was the lack of air and intellectual stimulation that pushed me out of my provincial cocoon.

Who knows how Trojanow as a child had taken what was happening to him, the several moves, the new places, the different people. I was curious. "Never had any problems, if you listen to my parents. They always said I was easy-going and very calm," he answered quickly, before dwelling upon his consequential line of reasoning: "But why are we what we are? My Indian friends in Mumbai, for example, say that they have never met anyone more culturally flexible than me. They'd take me along and I'd blend in: but I can't tell you why I'd do that; it's not a choice, it's not that I belong to a religion and I wake up in the morning determined to blend in. It has to do with something beyond my own choice and feeling. I have a friend in Buenos Aires who used to be a diplomat and, looking back at the reactions of his three children, has developed his own theory. According to him, there are two kinds of people: those who have no difficulty whatsoever and actually find moving around the globe exciting and intriguing, and those who really suffer in this kind of situation. This friend of mine has a daughter who is like me, to whom all the changes are like a blessing, certainly beneficial; and he has a son who has been traumatized by the reiterated moving—even now that he is an adult he can't get over this sense of existential loss which happened at a certain point in his life."

"A drive toward mobility, the other toward a sedentary state," I proposed. "Mobile or rooted, longing to leave or eager for territorial stability: these are the yin and yang of our human existence. In *Lila,* the philosophical novel in which he expounds his value-based Metaphysics of Quality, Robert Pirsig talks about them dialogically, in terms of 'static quality' and 'dynamic quality.'" Trojanow took on a quizzical look and bent over his forearms, ready to listen. "The way I understand it, the first one is the fundamental structure of culture itself," I started to explain, "It is the asset that comes from fixed rules, from the tradition and values that have expressed them." The second one is an asset external to any individual culture and cannot be caged in any system of precepts but needs to be constantly rediscovered according to cultural development. Dynamic quality, the quality of freedom, creates the world in which we live, but only the configurations of static quality, the quality of order, keep it functioning. According to Pirsig, the two qualities need each other to exist and prosper, in the same way that—paraphrasing—the mobile person, the nomad, needs her sedentary counterpart. If we look at it this way, it's a win-win situation.

"At this point one might ask," Trojanow said following my reasoning, "whether or not becoming a transcultural author—multipolitical, multisocial, multisocietal, or whatever—is an artistic choice. And if it's not a truly artistic choice how has it become part of my artistic expression?" "That's precisely what I'd like to know," I replied, smiling at him, and then I tried to spell out what I meant: "Probably, one does not become like that out of choice: simply, it happens. One does not say: right, I want to become a transcultural writer, thus I have to write this kind of fiction, with these characteristics. Probably, in some way or another, the way one experiences the world, one's transnational biography, or simply some hereditary genetic trait (if we are willing to take into consideration the innate nature of certain psychological specificities) have an effect—although subliminal—on one's writing, on what one decides to tell and the way one chooses to do it. There hardly seems to be anything artificially constructed, calculated, or self-imposed about it. Every time I read a certain kind of book, every time I perceive strong resonances and affinities in its pages in terms of themes, sensibilities, or stylistic choices I also discover that their writers' lived experiences—as migrants, travellers, exiles, diasporic, stateless, transient, neonomadic subjects, or whatever has prompted them to translate or transpatriate themselves—have something in common."

"Transpatriate?" asked Trojanow. He seemed intrigued. "Yes, in the sense of physically and psychologically—better, ideologically—letting go the grip of one's homeland. Or, at most, as the Italian writer Nicola Lecca told me when I met him in Innsbruck, where he was currently living (after his stints in England, Sweden, Spain, and Hungary), choosing one's own homeland, "without having it imposed on you by birth or by incidental circumstances" (Dagnino and Lecca). "Actually, I don't think that many writers feel the urgency of having a homeland," Trojanow stepped in. "I mean, this year we celebrate the bicentenary of the death of Heinrich von Kleist, the great German writer. Here is someone who actually believed in the German concept of *Heimat*, the fatherland, but in my opinion that's an exception. I find that even the idea of having one form of allegiance to a country is a form of idiotism." "It may be so," I said, a bit doubtful, "nonetheless, there seems to be, in some cases, even amongst intellectuals, a reassertion of that attachment to the territory where a shared language and a specific set of cultural heritages and values are seen as the essential binding agents." "If we take into consideration Italian authors," he replied, "I have no doubt it might be so. In my limited experience, I have the feeling that they don't change even when they go abroad. The worst books I have read on India are by Italians. I mean, Pasolini wrote about India: a disaster. And Moravia wrote about Africa: another complete disaster—he looks out of the window and all he sees is Italy; he compares Accra with pasta: it's so funny, but also so parochial. In a way, when you read their books you feel an unwillingness to be transformed by India or Africa, which I find very typical of these men. It's as if they wanted to measure it, ethically measure India or Africa, but they don't actually want to slide into it, live it." I caught myself slightly smiling, thinking instead of Trojanow, who claimed he "wore" the four languages he knew best (Bulgarian, German, English, Hindi) as if they were clothes in a wardrobe: "I put them on whenever I need." But I also realized I was smiling out of a slight embarrassment (why, then? because of national pride?), thinking—even more than of Pasolini's India or Moravia's Africa—of what Lecca had told me only a few days before, when I had asked him why in his opinion there were so few Italian writers living and working abroad: "It's not worth it. Every time you go to a dinner party in Rome you meet someone from RAI who then invites you to put on a TV show; when you are in Milan, you go to a certain author's house, or invite someone to your literary festival, who then will reciprocate by inviting you to his. This kind of mentality—I do something for you, you do something for me—goes with the territory. Going away, as the Italian writer Cesare De Marchi did (he now lives in Germany), is suicidal from an economic point of view. And, anyway, even abroad, this is what the market wants from Italian authors: books about the mafia or the camorra" (Dagnino and Lecca).

"Some prefer to guard the territory, to play the role of the provincial writer," I thus said, "in the same way that, although in a different epoch and circumstance, the Austrian writer Thomas Bernhard decided to do." Trojanow nodded in agreement then said: "Bernhard stayed only in one place and studied it deeper and deeper. At the end of the day, he himself was a provincial petit bourgeois who had a very keen sense of the hidden horrors of the petty provincial bourgeois life. He was never able to overcome that, he was stuck in this world that he hated but was also the only one he could imagine. He needed this kind of hatred as the gas that fuelled his narrative engine. He exaggerated reality, constructed it, and transformed it into a caricature of the existing world." "Done with the fatherland, the nation, the province," I thus remarked with ill-conceived irony, picking up the thread of our interview, "only home remains, feeling at home. . . ." Trojanow finished his cup of Turkish coffee and peered intently at its grounds before looking me straight in the eye with a serious expression: "I don't believe people when they say, 'my home is Germany.' Either they haven't thought about it thoroughly, or they are lying, because I'm sure their home is where their loved ones are, where mother is, or where their children are, where they grew up. It's the soccer pitch where you have spent your youth, the ice-cream parlor where you kissed a girl for the first time, stuff like that. I think people are being intellectually dishonest when they dispute that belonging is extremely subjective, extremely intimate, extremely personal, and extremely limited in space."

I kept quiet, thinking back at what the playwright Michael Schindhelm had told me in a recent exchange of emails about his book on his Dubai experience (*Dubai High*): "It is the concept of feeling 'at home' that has changed. Expatriates in Dubai (or Shanghai, Rio de Janeiro, Melbourne) live it as a chapter in their life more than anything else. To them, Dubai is a safe and easy environment where to live, work and communicate. I believe that this makes a city your home. Not forever, of course, but 'forever' doesn't exist any more." Life lived in chapters: it was like that now, wasn't it? You end a chapter, you start a new one—increasingly complying with the artifices, and the unlimited possibilities, of a narrative without borders. "And what about you? Do you ever feel the need to belong to anything? Even if not to a fatherland or a nation. . . ." I asked him at this point. "I actually think that I belong more than many other people do," Trojanow answered without thinking. Then he took his time to elaborate: "I've a very strong sense of belonging to planet Earth, which sounds a bit esoteric but it has to do with my continuous awareness that we need a paradigm shift in the way we relate to nature. We are reaching a stage where we really have to readjust our form of civilization or there will be huge cataclysms. Thus, I actually sense a real urge to belong there, I mean, belong to an intellectual development. But, apart from that, I feel I have many other forms of belonging." "What do you mean exactly?" I prodded. "That I am just as nostalgic and sentimental and defining as anybody else," he replied. "For example, I sense a very true belonging within the German language, despite the fact that my mother tongue is Bulgarian and that I grew up playing and joking in Swahili. I sense a belonging when I'm walking through the streets of Sophia, when I'm in Mumbai, or when I'm in many countries in Africa. I miss Africa in general, with its sounds, its smells, its lights."

"Thus, however feeble, you also acknowledge a connection between belonging and territory," I insisted, "like those who maintain that it is there, in that particular region, in that particular spot on the map, that their roots lie." "I never use the word roots, I'm not a tree," Trojanow replied in a determined tone, as if he had provided that same sort of answer many times. "Nonetheless, this confirms what I have already said. That is, the way one identifies oneself with the territory has a very personal connotation and concerns a very limited space. For example, if you are a wine grower, the boundary is your vineyard. Metaphorically speaking, 'the vineyard' could be any small piece of land: a mountainside, a valley, a bend in the river, a beach. Nothing bigger than that."

"The border ends there, it cannot be extended to encircle a nation, an ethnic group, let alone a state," I concluded on his behalf. At this point, as if we wanted to mark the resonance in our way of thinking, we both let our gazes wander beyond the window screen, there where the landscape flowed free and undisturbed in the early crepuscular lights. After all, for the two of us the territory was like that: one of the places in which we had lived, which we had crossed by foot, bike, bus, or train. In transit. The territory was everything and nothing—what might unexpectedly emerge on the wave of a memory, an emotion, an accent. Simultaneously we belonged to everything and nothing. Following the thread of his—of our—thoughts, my interlocutor continued: "I am well aware of a certain criticism formulated against people like myself: that is, our lifestyle is a luxurious postmodern existence that allows one to hop from one country to the other, to juggle around and jet-set; a kind of chic cosmopolitanism; a form of elitist pastime." "A deplorable irresponsibility, one might argue." "Since it's a criticism leveled quite often, of course I've thought about it a lot." "And you have reached certain conclusions, I presume." "Exactly. First of all, this criticism doesn't acknowledge the fact that I've no other choice, that being cosmopolitan for me is an existential blessing but also a challenge and a necessity, as much as there would be no other choice for someone who had a strong sense of belonging or who had a very strong sense of —yes, let's use here the German word—*Heimat*." "And the second conclusion?" "It's as though there were a reinforced chronology in all these discussions about sense of belonging and cosmopolitanism; and that this chronology, which must adhere to a kind of Darwinian evolutionary linearity, is supposed to start with belonging and end with uprootedness and cosmopolitanism."

"Nonsense," he continued, "I actually think that in order for them to be so clear-cut and regulated, these definitions of belonging had to be invented by an enormous industry, an enormous machinery working through politics, science, and the arts. You can see that any kind of definition of belonging—whether it is regional, national, or extremely local—happens because an enormous amount of energy went into it: this is the proof that this is not a natural state. We might therefore argue that the transcultural consciousness is the natural state and that the other guys are unnatural because they have been bogged down in some kind of box of belonging. In these people's minds, cosmopolitanism, or what you call transculture, cannot be a natural state." As night was slowly falling, I pondered upon the apparent unnaturalness of our shared way of feeling and living. The train darted ahead illuminating its way towards the south like a comet and I wondered if the transcultural might be reduced to the banality of a fashion, or to the pressures of the market. Right at that moment, my mobile phone, sitting on the table between us close to the audio recorder, silently vibrated, signaling that I had just received a text message. I touched its screen and read quickly: "Depot Dans Cafe, Cihangir, Istanbul, Saturday 8 October 9:00 pm." I raised my eyes and Trojanow, who must have read the message furtively, couldn't hide a half-smile tinged with amused suspicion. "My secret lover . . ." I said, playing along with his half-smile. Trojanow looked at his watch for the first time since we had met—it must have been past midnight—then looked at me with a conspiratorial expression: "There is still time for another batch of questions." I smiled at him gratefully, while the phone, changing to stand-by mode, dimmed with a vague halo of secrecy. The train was running faster than ever in the night, across the steppe without apparent limits, as it had done, a quarter of a century before, on my journey to Moscow.

From my travel diaries (Moscow, 11 November 1985)

> I was a student then, but I was already in transit. Three nights and two days rattling on the rails: Milan-Venice-Budapest-Kiev-Moscow. Tolstoy kept me company with his *Karenina*, along the tracks of a foretold destiny. The year before I had met a young man who had struck me with a sentence: "I will become a famous writer." He eventually became one. He had the right stuff. He talked of gods. He thought of himself as a god. He had "il senso della frase," the sense of the sentence, as he used to say, and a remarkable sense of humor. Physically he was a disaster: he stank of beer, wore a moustache (at 21!), smoked a cigar. But he was coming from the historical Milan and he frequented its literary circles while I was still moving about with the cautious gait of a provincial girl, although inside me, with all my reading, I already felt a worldly wise woman. It was that same writer who, one year later, accompanied me to the Central Station in Milan and hoisted my luggage on the train that would take me beyond the Iron Curtain. In Moscow I plaited my hair in a single braid fastened with a black bow, wore a black fur busby and a long black woolen overcoat. It seemed I had just come out from a nineteenth-century novel—instead I was in the middle of the Soviet crisis. People queued in the streets at minus ten degrees to buy flour, soap, toilet paper, boots, whatever they might be selling clandestinely from the trucks at that moment. There, at that time in history, my way of dressing was not considered late Romantic but simply gloomy, if not openly offensive, as I would discover too late. One day, in a street coffeehouse (only standing places, sitting down was considered bourgeois)

> a *babushka* (an "old woman") spat those words at me: "Aren't you ashamed, *devushka*? ("girl," that's how elders addressed young women in Soviet times; the courtesy, but also bourgeois, pre-revolutionary titles Mr., Mrs., and Miss had disappeared from the daily vocabulary). You are wearing the Nazi color." Instead, I suddenly felt pride: because that old woman, despite having harshly addressed me, had done it in Russian, mistaking me for a young Russian. I could pass for one of them: to me only that counted, then. I read Dostoyevsky, I read about the miseries of the Russian people, then as much as ever. I sent letters to my family, writing with a pencil on the coarse paper that they used as tablecloth in unauthorized basement taverns. For six months I was almost cut off from the outer world. To phone abroad from a public place was an enterprise that demanded long hours of waiting among hundreds of ethnic proletarians assimilated by the empire: Turkmens, Kazaks, Georgians, Kyrgyzs. The news from abroad was metered out with a dropper. My missives were full of growingly bleaker tones—at least that's what my mother told me, worried, when I got back home. But then I was not aware of it. I had adapted to that humid subterranean world of mechanics who read Gogol, of poet-engineers, of incognito intellectuals, of non-declared Jews. Vodka, Marina Tsvetaeva's poems, and cigarettes without filters. I was right in the belly of the Russian devil. I was exactly where I wanted to be, on the other side of the barricade, the Wall, the Curtain, there where few ventured.

Tearing myself away from that well of memories, I returned to our carriage restaurant. At dawn we would reach Istanbul and I realized that, following my thread of thoughts instead of his, I hadn't yet asked Trojanow to tell me about his concept of cultural confluence that had also become part of my vocabulary. "Let's start from its geographic meaning," Trojanow started to explain, quoting from the book he had written with Ranjit Hoskoté. "No great river would reach the ocean without being fed by tributaries: the brooks, streams, and rivulets that join its flow, often bringing with them more water, alluvium, minerals, or fish than the source stream" (*Confluences* 4). "And this, you are telling me, applies to cultures as well," I said. "Exactly. As we wrote in our book, the river's official name conceals the truth of its composition; while the nametag passes into legend and lexicon, the ancestry of confluences becomes invisible. Our history, regulated by concepts of singularity and pure origin, is as much of a cartographer's invention as the great river. By taking a certain tableau of it to represent culture's form and essence, it mistakes a snapshot of the river for its whole course. In the same way, the confluences of every culture are concealed, and homogenizing foundational myths are installed in their place. Thus, the timeless stability of our culture guarantees the security of our identity. Therefore, we have to preserve the purity of our culture against contamination by the Other" (*Confluences* 4-5). I added, "While you and your friend Ranjit maintain that, on the contrary, individuals and communities interact among each other creating a culture that is never monolithic but changeable, never pure but always hybrid." "That is, confluential, as culture has always been." "As you have been saying, 'No confluence, no culture'" (*Confluences* 7), I said, quoting him. Trojanow gave me a wink, a little pleased with himself, and kept talking enthusiastically, rolling the words like a mountain torrent, reading again from his book *Confluences* (7, 11-12): "When culture is alive, it alters itself through inspirations from near and far, it changes course. Culture is the eternal shape-shifter. Only by interacting with the Other, can a culture keep itself alive."

"Thus," he continued reading, "the greatest civilizations were built on confluence, and not always through a pacific process. Cultural transformation has been effected just as much by peaceful encounter as by the tumults of war, invasion, slavery, inquisition, pogrom, and exile" (*Confluences* 7, 11-12). "The process of confluence not as a utopia but as a reality that at times may be dramatic, even undesirable," I remarked. "It's a matter of fact," Trojanow replied. "Confluence may happen through dialogue but also through oppression. The best example is African American music: it starts with slavery in the plantations, it develops in the ghetto, and now the whole world is crying because Michael Jackson has died. This music came from the most subjugated and subjected culture of the United States and in 150 years it has become the mainstream export of the most powerful nation of the world. I mean, confluence has nothing to do—and that's what most people misunderstand—with ideals or people being nice to each other; it's not a feel good story, it also happens when people kill each other. There is no way to stop it and that's what puts conservatives off. You may try, you may even construct walls: it's not gonna help you, because there is no other cultural energy, no other law than the one to form new confluences. At the end of the day, culture always strives towards confluence: it is always greedy for new input, it always wants to be provoked and inspired by something that it didn't know, didn't have, didn't acknowledge."

I checked my list of questions and asked Trojanow who he thought his readers were. "I don't have a clue," he answered, "and I don't even want to know about it. The only thing that I'm aware of is that most of them are multilingual and, even if they do not have German as their mother tongue, they don't even wait for the English translation to read my books. For example, I've an Indian friend who can read German; thus, I would get early feedback from a Saraswat *brahmin* living in Mumbai or from my Dutch translator rather than from a group of intellectuals gathered at Café Schottenring in Vienna, at walking distance from where I live." "Times are definitely a-changin'," I agreed without originality, mainly to show him I was following his reasoning. "In the old days," Trojanow continued, "if you published a novel in Vienna you would get the first feedback from the local authors in coffee houses, then you would be reviewed in Viennese newspapers, and later on your book might appear in Berlin, so that you would get feedback also from the cultural circles in Berlin and then, progressively, from a more extended German language audience. Only perhaps ten years later, if you were so lucky to be translated, you would get feedback from France or England. These concentric circles were quite well defined."

"It's as if, like people, languages were now losing their territorial borders," I said, thinking of Tim Parks, the writer of British origin who had studied at Harvard and had been living in Italy for the last three decades. It was he who had claimed in our interview that if for certain authors style was still deeply inscribed in a national tradition, for others it was already affected by a transnational future, as it happened with him: "At the beginning," said Parks, "living away from London, I was very concerned that my intimacy with contemporary English was going, that I didn't know of new words that were being invented and I was anxious about that, I was anxious about the sound of contemporary English. But then I also realized that my books sold better in Germany than in England, some of them sold better in Italy and some other sold better in Holland. Thus you become aware of an international public and, even without thinking, as you write you begin addressing a different audience and because you are addressing a different audience the kind of stories you are telling begin to shift a little and I think to a certain extent the style you use begins to shift. And then all of sudden I thought, 'No, this is much better, my English is becoming quite personal but also lexically is becoming quite pure.' In other words, I was eliminating all the idiomatic phrases that are invented in the London scene, so that now my language perhaps is more easily projected towards an international scene. The most interesting fact is that this is not peculiar to English: the same is happening to many other writers in many other languages."

"It seems it's becoming more and more difficult to stand still, to adopt a permanent configuration. Everything—people, ideas, goods—is on the move, circulates anywhere, physically or in the virtuality of cyberspace," I commented to Trojanow, introducing my next question. "I thought that perhaps for a transcultural writer the hotel—maybe a historical one, with its patina of past times—might represent a good metaphor for a certain idea of 'place,' of stability within impermanence. In his book *Shanghai Dancing* Castro writes [and I read from my notes]: 'The . . . hotel is much more than anonymity, for its constant changes, flux, turnovers create the intimacy of an extendable world, a transit point, a confluence of lives'" (334). "Yes, it's a good metaphor," said Trojanow, "because what defines the difference between living in a hotel and in your flat?" "I guess the sense of always being a guest, never really at home . . . or at home anywhere, in any hotel of the world." "That's very good, that's one aspect . . . but there is another aspect: objects are no longer that important," Trojanow said after gesturing to the waiter that he needed another cup of coffee.

"Let me tell you another story," he continued, "When I was in Buenos Aires I met a famous curator of big art exhibitions. This man lives in a hotel in Rio de Janeiro. If I'm obsessed with what I'm writing in that moment, he is completely obsessed with his current curatorial project: that exhibition defines his life as much as that novel defines mine. Because of that—if one takes the metaphor seriously—the objects that he puts together are only valuable to him for the duration of the exhibition; the moment the exhibition closes and the objects are disbanded, he starts a new cycle of collecting in the same way as I start collecting new stories and material for my next book." "Hence, this sense of transitoriness," I noted. "I'm speculating here, of course,"

Trojanow said. "I'm treating him as if he were my literary alter ego, while he might have something different to say, but as a literary figure he would feel uncomfortable with objects remaining the same around him. Now I think," he continued, "the mistake would be to assume that this kind of person doesn't feel a sense of belonging because he distrusts the idea of having always to deal with the same objects. On the contrary, he might have a very astute, pronounced sense of belonging but that would not hinder him from expressing it—as you said—through this transitional ideal of objects (as much as stories) being assembled and then dispersed." "Which we might consider a nomadic kind of attitude," I remarked. "Only to a certain extent," Trojanow replied, "because unlike the nomads, who are still so close to nature that they wouldn't leave any signs behind them, both the novel and the exhibition leave footprints. I mean, when a bird has passed through the sky it's gone and the sky doesn't know about it. By the way, do you know how many years a footprint lasts in the Antarctic, before completely disappearing?" "One hundred years?" "Right," Trojanow said, slightly astonished by my quick answer. "It was a guess," I then explained. "It takes the same time for a cigarette butt to be metabolized by the desert; that's what the ranger that led me into the Kalahari among the last Bushmen told me." "This is the great difference," he noted, "we can no longer pass through any space without leaving traces." But it's also the first time in our human history, I thought, that—by choice or by necessity—we can be nomads again. The latest digital technologies free us from the territorial roots implicit in any process of sedentarization and allow us to access and add to the knowledge historically accumulated. For the first time we can leave traces of our acquired knowledge—the only ones we should actually leave—even in permanent or temporary mobility.

"Going back to your initial question," Trojanow said, resuming the thread of our conversation, "Nabokov lived in a hotel most of his life, and the ship is the setting of many of my favorite authors, starting from Conrad and Stevenson. My last novel as well is set on a ship, one of those vessels for scientific research that host people from different backgrounds and nationalities and thus become microcosms of cosmopolitan and intercultural realities." Ships made of paper, imaginative and multilingual vessels pushed towards an elsewhere that tends to confound the reality of the world and that of the book. Who taught me that?

From my travel diaries (Moscow, 28 December 1985)

> Dimitri was my guide to the Russian underground. He kissed me and sang Vysotsky to me—the songs of this anti-establishment singer-songwriter ostracized by Soviet authorities spoke truth in their own oblique way. One night, he led me where no foreigner—least of all a fortuitous tourist—would ever get to: a street, a nineteenth-century building, a front door, a cold entrance hall, one landing. In the silent darkness that smelled of bygone affluence, my poet lit his cigarette lighter and brought it closer to the wall. Then, through our condensed breaths, I saw, at first indistinctly, then more and more clearly: tens, hundreds of writings

> running up those walls encrusted by time and memory. Dimitri read out loud some of them, interpreting them with his warm actor's voice. They were all passages from Mikhail Bulgakov's *The Master and Margarita*. He told me that the authorities regularly covered those writings under a layer of whitewash but—relentlessly—those surreptitious traces kept reappearing. The magic of the initiated. The words that lived on, at all costs. "Manuscripts don't burn" (Bulgakov, *The Master* 287). It was an exemplary lesson. Then and there I understood that being a journalist, a mere reporter of reality, would not be enough. More than that, what I deeply desired was to live in books, with books, for books—in a paper-made world even more than in a physical elsewhere; not in the static dimension of a library, though, nor in the musty self-referentiality of the academy, but rather in the generating and regenerating current where lived experience and imagined life continuously flowed into each other. I wanted to flirt with books and their authors, as if each one of them had been written for my own intimate pleasure. I wanted to take the risk of never being myself in order to live all the other imagined lives (including mine) in a game of cultural rather than biological transmutations. As if I could undergo infinite metamorphoses, not in the skin but in the mind; as if I could live many more lives than I would ever be able to do by living only mine, away from the familiar everyday existence, from undisputed loyalties—away from the loss of desire. I wanted to be without roots: a mere dispatriate; a woman of the books, in a sea of books; a muse; a siren (or a selkie); a vestal; a vagabond—always shifting, from page to page, culture to culture, idiom to idiom. I wanted not just a life of writing, but a life of reading, possibly in the original, interpreting the signs on the page, translating them into other languages, other sounds of the mind—literary polyglossia as art de vivre, as if books were really made to live inside them."

By now the train was approaching the Golden Horn. Before the darkness surrendered to a new daylight and our voices became too tired, I asked Trojanow what till now I had held back: "You showed your displeasure in being pigeonholed, you didn't like it when they talked of you as a migrant, exile, or ethnic writer. Would the definition of transcultural writer also sound to you like an unbearable label?" "It depends on what you mean by this term," he said. I explained, "I mean a writer ready to adapt to the different contexts in which he finds himself; who is always on the border between cultures and conceives them not as static elements but as flows, as changing organisms that mutate through endless hybridizations. A writer who transcends his own culture not to deny it, but to expand the color palette with which he can paint and modify his identity and his way of imagining the world." "We should then assume—and I understand what you mean—that the author you describe has in himself a sense of origin, an awareness of where he comes from." "No doubt," I said thinking of how important the sense of memory—the purely biographical one as well as the deeper historical one—was now that we were all becoming wanderers on the move along unusual routes.

It was almost as if we wanted to plunge ourselves into the invisible roots of time, now that our geographic roots were progressively vanishing; as if, in this way, we might find a solid anchor for our fluctuating liquid lives. "That is why I see this transcultural writer as a very clear-cut kind of persona," Trojanow resumed talking after finishing his second coffee, "someone who has had an immigrant, transformational, or transnational experience (either the family came from somewhere else, or they reached another place) and a lot of the dynamics of his narrative are centered around these experiences." "Getting to transcend them, though," I answered. "I understand," he replied, "You are implying that there must be something else, the willingness to go one step further; otherwise, according to your definition, even Franz Kafka might already be considered an example of a transcultural author. Then let's use the metaphor of the yoga class here. Now, Kafka was defined by the multiplicity of his upbringing, that is the Jewish-German-Czech track, but he was also in a way caught up in that identity. I can hardly envisage him going to Prague and saying: 'Hey, these guys are offering yoga classes, let's try them out.' And then actually doing a few years of yoga, thus developing a completely different kind of relationship to his body, acquiring a different kind of morals and ethics. I guess that being transcultural means a certain willingness to take that further step." "You said it yourself: letting oneself be transformed," I hinted, thinking back at his comments on Pasolini and Moravia. "This aspect would have to be added—wouldn't it?" he said, "to distinguish, let's say, the Kafkas from the Rushdies, if one wanted to distinguish them." "Otherwise there would be nothing new," I added, "the history of literature is already studded with writers who, before and after Albert Camus, were nourished by the outsider's gaze. One needs that *quid*, that something more, as you say, really the ability to think of the mind as an open system, a harbor city like the ancient Alexandria." "Today with the crisscrossing of cultural impulses across the physical world and the internet, every individual is a potential Alexandrian," Trojanow said, as if he had followed my thoughts, "so that when the custodians of national, civilizational, or religious purity proclaim the end of the multicultural society, they are proclaiming the end of culture itself."

"Do you really think that we can self-determine our cultural identity?" I asked. "Yes, I believe one can get to build for oneself a fluctuating identity, from an imaginary homeland to the next, through a chameleonic existence lived in temporary communities." "Chameleonic," he said, "because the chameleon does not wear a single color but chooses the one that better adapts to the situation; and what counts most, it produces *aus sich heraus,* from within itself, the colors of its transformation. It certainly couldn't buy them, who knows, from Benetton." "*Aus sich heraus,*" I repeated under my breath. By switching from English into German, Trojanow had seemed to remark the importance of that expression, to underline to what extent each individual, although influenced by experiences and external circumstances, in fact has the freedom to autonomously build a culture and identity—from within himself or herself. "Only in the realm of white elephants and black widows," my interlocutor continued, "the chameleon would seem a mere outsider, flashy in its colors but liminal to the context" ("Adelbert von Chamisso"). "In other words," I said, trying to interpret his reasoning, "only where cultures are still worshipped as if they were inalterable stone monoliths the chameleon is perceived as an unnecessary—often disturbing—transient element. It's always a question of mobility, isn't it? In this case, of cultural mobility." Trojanow thought it over for a while, passing his fingers over the cover of *Istanbul* before replying: "One of the things that defines my writing—if you asked me that question—is the sense that I can write about anything. Earlier on, we talked about Thomas Bernhard, and the feeling that he knew how to write only about one thing, I mean, for better or for worse, I'm not being judgmental here. I have just met a friend of mine, a poet, who has finished reading my new novel: he is astonished to find a new Trojanow in each new book although, at the same time, he feels that it's always Trojanow. He's right, there's only one Ilija, but in different shades of color, in different places of the planet and the mind." "Living through a constant game of cultural metamorphoses," I murmured as I scribbled on my notebook, almost sure that my words were swallowed up by the sudden clattering of the train. "To a certain extent," said Trojanow instead, nodding, "There is no infringement to the freedom of my choice and voice and this allows me a great narrative flexibility. For example, since in my new novel on climate change I was interested in introducing a series of philosophical metaphors and considerations drawn on my experience in India, I have invented an expedition in the Himalaya region, to which my Bavarian expert in glaciers also takes part. It is obvious that I wouldn't want my character to be a provincial guy who has only seen Bavaria. I wouldn't want to write about a man like that. I would always invent characters who, for whatever reason, have opened up to the world, so that through their own sense of the world I can make a series of other connections. Although I'm always looking for ways to convincingly fit these other worlds into my novels."

"Hence, even the choice of setting is representative of a certain transcultural sensibility," I remarked. "No doubt," Trojanow replied. "It's not by chance, for example, that Rushdie would go back time and again to Kashmir, which is an incredibly confluential place in India, rich in cultural mixture. It is clear that authors like that use settings and epochs (the Moghul Empire, for example) that conform with their own cosmopolitan ambitions and ideals." "You yourself maintain that," I said quoting him, "'Most of the writers I care for, that I admire, are authors who depend on several languages . . . Even though they might write in only one language, the stories they pick up, the narratives in their work, come from different languages and different worlds'" (Trojanow, "Location"). "Yes, I believe that this kind of flexibility needs to be included in the equation, when one talks of transcultural authors," he said. "Thus you agree with that definition," I assumed without trying to conceal a slightly cunning smile, remembering that indeed he had not yet answered the question that had led to this concatenation of arguments. "Again this urge to categorize everything, isn't it?" he said twisting his mouth in a sad and at the same time bitter grimace. He continued, "Academics and politicians can't do without it. While I find that, at the end of the day, all these categories have very little to do with my life experience, which is very multidimensional and where things that I thought to be true yesterday suddenly turn out to be false and the other way around. If, as I understood it, being transcultural implies this ability to adapt, transform, and change continuously, then the moment you try to fix an identity into a category, this identity has already changed. Hence, the first step would be to acknowledge that there are people who can't be pressed into one mould. The whole idea of transculture, I guess, is not to be defined by one model. If you have opened up to so many different forms of thinking, to so many different horizons and perspectives, this invariably means the willingness to live at the crossroads of paradoxes, ambivalences, and contradictions—without a model. If, like myself, you have been very seriously immersed in other philosophies (the old Indian, the Buddhist, or the Sufi philosophy) and accept that paradoxes are instrumental for enlightenment, then you see how the whole thing starts to become very complicated." Was this not the same thing that Parks would tell me only a few hours later, when I would meet him in his little studio facing the Galata Bridge? "The idea that I would assume a very carefully argued and very fixed position, as if I was standing outside the world saying what's going on, is wrong," Parks had started off, "It's really not like that. The point is that we are in things. We are fictionally in Istanbul but in reality in my office at IULM (Independent University of Modern Languages) in Milan, and here I am operating in an Italian mode, in an Italian faculty, in a university system in crisis, in a country where there are cuts being made, in a language which pushes me in a certain way, and this is my life, my moment, my ethos, my present. When I go to the UK, I'm immediately aware of little metamorphoses going on, of a different world I'm moving in."

Here I was, back to the labyrinth, I thought, dismayed but also excited. Here I was, back to where I had started, rolling up the ball of thread around the rings of an infinite library that did not provide answers. The circle—without beginning or ending—remained the most ancient and sacred symbol, as the *mandalas*, the wheels of *dharma,* the concentric signs of shamanic medicine, the whirling dervishes, the aboriginal paintings still reminded us. "Fate takes on shapes that keep repeating themselves," Borges wrote in one of his letters to Estela Canto, "there are circling patterns; now this one appears again: again I'm in Mar del Plata, longing for you" (qtd. in Manguel, "Borges" 50). In this ecstatic and circular movement inside and outside me, I would see again the Theodosian walls, the Galata Tower built by my Ligurian ancestors, with different eyes or, perhaps, with the same eyes. Surely with a new perspective.

Chapter Two

Castro, the Other, and the Complexity of Belonging

I was in Istanbul at last, in this metropolis of twelve million inhabitants that deserved a lifetime to explore instead of a few days, that would need to be lived and tasted—as not even twenty years earlier I had been able to do—in little sips, in the interstices of time and memory, and through the intricacies of its ancient streets and multiple idioms. I was no longer facing the desolate autumnal steppe running along the train rails nor the ascetic walls of the seventeenth-century study where Parks had received me on my first day in Istanbul, while the sun bleached the minarets of the old town. Instead, I was surrounded by the Middle Eastern opulence of a historical grand hotel, opened in 1892 among the consulates and the residences of the European district to host the wealthy passengers of the Orient Express. Beyond its walls the city traffic roared in an eternal rush hour like a crazed beast—unrestrainable. It reminded those who now chose to stay at the Pera Palas that they did not do it simply to enjoy the luxury of a four-star accommodation but most of all to succumb to the mere sin of nostalgia, tempted by the recall of another epoch: the slow—for some, enervating—age of steam trains and ocean liners. Many of those who in the past had lodged there had left a mark, beyond any border, in the collective imaginary and in the lives of many others: Alfred Hitchcock, Greta Garbo, Mata Hari, Sarah Bernhardt. Among the most assiduous guests of the "Pera" there was also Mustafa Kemal Ataturk, the father of the Turkish Republic, the authoritarian and charismatic reformer who—by abolishing the caliphate, secularizing the state, banning the wearing of the fez, acknowledging the parity between the sexes—had forced the West into the heart of Islam. Ataturk would spend all night in the halls of the Pera Palas dancing the Argentine tango; but, to me, what counted most was that in that same grand hotel Agatha Christie had written *Murder on the Orient Express*, perhaps the first transnational (although not yet transcultural) crime novel of its kind. It was there—precisely in room number 411, now maintained as a small memorial to the author—that, thanks to the kind benevolence of the hotel director and to my inner satisfaction, I was going to have my cup of *çay* (tea) with Brian Castro.

Before our meeting I had intently looked at one of his rare portraits found on the internet. I was searching for traces of *his* Orient, the primary source of his writing. At least, that is what I sensed in reading his novels: each one of them sounds like a distant litany, an invocation to an extreme, possibly baffling, elsewhere—*Far East, Far East, Far East*. Castro's pen rasps against the page as if trying to unearth the seal skin that has been smothered under a thick layer of Anglo-Saxon soil—Castro's first skin, perhaps his real skin: China. His literary sensibility comes from the most peculiar composition of cultures, genres, and genes. His father, as he himself recounts in one of his books, "represented everything that was Western." His parents were Portuguese but he was born and raised in Shanghai and moved to Hong Kong just before the war (*Looking* 41). His mother, on the contrary, daughter of a Chinese man and an English missionary woman, "symbolised everything that was Eastern. Serious and concerned, she was dedicated to survival." (*Looking* 42).

Castro writes in English, but feels in Cantonese, I thought. He follows the brush like a calligrapher, "calibrating both the ruminations of the heart and the rhythmic heart of the language," in the flow of an inner writing similar to an exercise of Zen discipline (*Looking* 17). He lives in his writing as if it were a monastic retreat—a call that cannot be ignored, under pain of losing himself. This I sensed. I found Castro mostly in his paper women, the female characters of his books: women seen as absences—or vanishing essences—knots of silence, muffled steps, shadows. Women as rustles of silk, tears that leave no trace, butterflies under glass. To me Castro was Swan, the poetess of *The Garden Book*, the miscegenated Anglo-Chinese woman growing up during the White Australia policy (officially repealed in 1975), who yearns for an elsewhere without borders and writes her poems on the back of leaves. So that everything would pass—like autumn leaves, that belong to the world and nothing else: not certainly to a state, a nation, a race, a culture, a language. At least that is how I imagined, and possibly constructed, Castro before meeting him: an almost asexual being—or containing both sexes in equal parts—who fed on filigree words, ideograms, metaphors, oneiric fragments, gaps of the indescribable. As if one could only express oneself in the blank spaces left between words, lines, genders, meanings—in the pauses between thoughts. As if the accent were always on the not written, on what could only be sensed, grasped by a sudden beating of wings, even when reading what had been written, what had not flown away.

But I must be more precise: one does not read Castro, one learns to decipher him, I thought. Each sentence is a cross reference, by itself it does not exist: the correlations are infinite, as well as the chains of metaphors, symbols, evocations. I imagined Castro each time he entered the crypt of his study, faintly smiling over the shoulder to the ectoplasm of Borges, the master of intertextual and multilingual references. I imagined him through his writing, which was smoothed and refined with Carthusian methodicalness, and as such was to be read in low gear, on a long-distance train, with the meditative placidity with which one would taste a vintage wine, so as not to lose any nuance, any subtle aftertaste. But unlike the tormented, withdrawn, stubbornly unsatisfied characters of his novels, I soon discovered that Castro, quick of tongue and mind, was also quick to open himself in a smile and share his humanity. If we had been in Adelaide he would have received me in his anonymous city office in the university campus where he taught and that he reserved for his intentionally slim public life. We would have met in that city at the end of the world, of a former empire, and at the edge of the outback. In that case, we would have been right in the middle of a luminous southern spring, in a world in dazzling light that, at first glance, seemed unconcerned with life's inevitable shades and undertones. Instead, we were there, where the Bosphorus met the Sea of Marmara, in a warm and spicy autumn that struggled to forget the past summer and its never-ending nights. They served our *çay,* a strong black tea, in small glasses in the shape of tulips supported by a silver structure that reminded me of that more humble vessel used, twenty-six years before, to serve tea on my train to Prague. A year had passed since my Muscovite stay. In the capital of old Bohemia where Kafka had written his works in German, we were still beyond the Iron Curtain but it did not take me long to realize that it was still advisable to adddress someone in the street with an *Entschuldigung* in German rather than with an *Izvinitie* in Russian—the heavy weight of the past Austro-Hungarian Empire still easier to digest than the present-day Soviet monolithism. It was in Prague, the quintessential literary city, where I lived a love story made of words of another epoch.

From my travel diaries (Prague, 12 December 1986)

> Ah, Prague under the first snow! And the evenings at the Golden Tiger, the tavern where Bohumil Hrabal kept writing till the end. Till he let himself fall from the fifth floor of a building (so they said) while feeding pigeons. It was as if he had enacted one of his stories, where—inevitably—someone decides to put an end to one's life flying out from a window, soaring forever over mankind's brutalities. I watched the old Hrabal writing a few tables away while Joseph, his German translator, kept me company and fed me stories. For months this young man with his wild eyes and disheveled hair led me into and behind those Czech books that read like sad picaresque fairy tales. To outwit the censors, Hrabal had invented clowns who in their clumsiness exposed to ridicule communist Czechoslovakia and drunkards who tried to save from destruction the books of great philosophers by literally drinking their words, "until the thought dissolve[d] . . . like alcohol, infusing brain and heart" (*Too Loud* 1). But how could we laugh reading those stories that, as the critic James Wood remarked, began with "Baron Munchausen-like adventures" and ended "in tears and solitude" ("Bohumil Hrabal")? For months Joseph and I lived a parallel love story, inventing a magic seventeenth-century Prague. We imagined ourselves as supporters of independence on the run from a Bohemia once again under the Hapsburg yoke, separated by destiny but united by the baroque letters that we sent each other from our desks overlooking the roofs of the Malá Strana

> district. He knew that he had ensnared me—but not for long—with his imaginative way of offering me alchemies of words. We left each other in the silence of a still magic Prague. Before the train left, taking me away forever, Joseph slid a piece of paper into the palm of my hand. I kept it close to my chest for a long time, my gaze chasing after the foggy contours of far away synagogues. When at last I read it, I did not find him but Borges: "Time drifted away like sand. Love flowed, secular in the shadows, and I possessed for the first and last time the image of Ulrica" (qtd. in Manguel, *A Reader* 54). For the first time I understood myself through the eyes of someone who had been able to read me. And I realized that, from now on, I would prefer to focus not on what was being said but on what was being evoked. On the keyboard of a typewriter and, ever more often, of a computer, I would look with tenderness at those space bars worn down by the thumbs' work, eroded by the necessity of letting words, sentences, ideas breath. In any significant book, in any memorable encounter, I would look for this: for any other possible meaning hidden between words, suspended somewhere over the page or around the conversation. It was the last time I was behind the Iron Curtain before the fall of the Berlin Wall. I would never go back, as Joseph had sensed. Life was pushing me elsewhere.

From Istanbul to Prague, chasing the memories induced by a glass of *çay*, and back. "When I was eleven they sent me to Australia," the voice of Castro the raconteur finally arrived, now that I had him in front of me, at ease on his damask armchair, in the soft light of a mild Levantine October. With his grey-speckled moustache, thinning hair, and interlaced hands on his lap, he seemed to have always belonged to the decor of that period hotel. Thus Castro was sent to boarding school, alone, I gathered, drawing also from all I had been reading about him. He had been raised in 1950s Hong Kong, at that time one of the most cosmopolitan cities of the world, in an extended family characterized by its lively mix of quaint acquaintances and imperial languages: the Chinese spoken by his mother, the Portuguese of his father, the English that reigned supreme in the British colony, the French learned at school. But in 1961, according to his father's wishes, Castro was sent to face an Australian "whites only" policy still in full bloom, conceived to admit within the nation's boundaries only immigrants with the right skin color, save rare wealthy exceptions.

"When I came to Australia from Hong Kong I really thought the world was like where I came from, where everybody spoke all sorts of languages and you had a mixing of different cultures," Castro said while I focused on the suddenly sad turn at the corner of his mouth, "At that time—and this may sound a bit kitsch, I suppose—on Sundays my father would take me to Indian, Chinese, or French restaurants, where we'd meet his colleagues, who were mostly Portuguese and English; while at home I met my mother's friends, who were all Chinese and wouldn't speak a lot of English." "Do you still speak Cantonese?" I asked. "Yes, but obviously not as well as when I was a child. Unfortunately for me, that language flow suddenly stopped when I left Hong Kong. You know, I was kind of time warped." While Castro told me the story of his youth spent in the fiercely white Australia of the 1960s, I had no difficulty envisioning him as a child, and then an adolescent, of short stature, with dark thin hair and faintly Oriental features. I saw him stand up to the sneers of his Aussie peers and the scorn of those who in the street would call him *chink*. Castro would eventually emerge from his ten-year immersion in the Anglo-Saxon culture of the 1960s Australia thanks to his writing. Reading him I had the impression that for the rest of his life, in his writing and reading, he would do nothing but try to regain that idealized state of childhood, that constant hybridization of chromosomes, sounds, ways of talking, gestures, rituals, dress codes, points of view, *tagli di vita* (life snaps). His books were like that—polyhedric, polyglot, polysensory. And he, at least as an author, was like that—transculturally "time warped," caught in an imaginary dimension of enriching coalescences and refined cultural sensibilities. I thought of Castro's Australia. And I thought of my Australia, the one that I would find—self-satisfied with its myth of the luckiest and easiest country—many years later, at the beginning of a new millennium.

From my travel diaries (Adelaide, 10 January 2008)

> On my first day in Adelaide, numbed by the twenty-hour flight and still wrapped in my wintery cocoon, I watched what surrounded me as if I were in an aquarium, with all those muffled sounds and gilled humans that seemed to float in the hot air, going about in placid slow motion, apparently content with their overheated, oven-like environment. Sailing along the multiple, immense parks in the city center and the miles-long beaches facing the ocean, I kept having that strange feeling of unreality. As if all of a sudden I had plunged into a scene of *Pleasantville*, the movie in which everything is apparently perfect. I was in Adelaideville, then, where the lawns are manicured, the children play in happy harmony, people greet each other with a smile, the elders do their stretching on the grass and the barbecues turn instantly hot by pressing a button—for free. But there must be a snag—my cynical European inner voice kept on nagging me—somewhere, in that unruffled version of suburbia without clouds, right behind that canvas of light, under that sheet of cobalt blue sea, in that yellow soil that turned red as soon as it reached the external borders of the outback, its dry heart. That was my Australia—the one I would experience as an expatriate, a luxury immigrant, an Italian arrived by jumbo jet in the twenty-first century instead of by ship in 1950 with a cardboard suitcase; an Italian who no longer stank of garlic but, it was presumed, had the "Made in Italy" label stitched even in her panties.

For Castro the first fundamental training in adaptation happened then, at the watershed between eleven and twelve years, in a time when children were not spared opportunities to develop their resilience. "You had to be tough, work your way into the new culture," he resumed, "although the loss was immediate, I suppose. I was immediately homesick. But in those days you were told that as a boy those things were not thought about. You didn't feel anything. You were not supposed to feel anything." The young Castro soon adjusted to the reality of rural Australia, in the northern fringes of New South Wales. He even learned to be a *jackeroo*, as Patrick White did following his father's will before he could eventually dedicate himself to his writing. "Most of my classmates were from farms and country properties, so sometimes on holidays I would go with them and do all that farm stuff, you know. I learned to ride horses, muster sheep, build cattle yards. I have always been a bit of an amorphous kind of person. I was not actually a city boy, you know, even though not many people are aware of that." Especially now, I would say, with his ten published novels and a teaching position in Creative Writing at the University of Adelaide. "I can replicate perfectly the way people talk in the outback, I know their way of thinking, possibly better than a citizen from Melbourne or Sydney can." Castro was now referring to the sharp, concise way of speaking, imbued with dry humor, typical of the drovers. Indeed he had grown up with that, after having left the bustling human activity of Hong Kong for the remoteness of unknown rural settlements.

Somehow, Castro's biographical and professional trajectory (among other things, later on he would become an overseas reporter in Hong Kong for *Asiaweek* and a teacher in France), reminded me of Mark Twain, who went from master riverboat pilot on the Mississippi to gold miner in California, from reporter in San Francisco to lecturer at American universities. I tried to imagine an adolescent Castro, with his stories already germinating in his head, drawn into the outback. Who knows then if, despite his skin being almost that of a "whitefella" and his ancestors from elsewhere, he had also felt the spiritual power of the "Aboriginal Dreaming," the freedom of a never-ending pace, the slow rhythm and the secret fascination of a ritual journey across the desert and into a mythological dimension beyond time and space. Who knows if Castro had been forever lured by the oneiric map, the labyrinth of invisible paths sung by those elders who still cared or dared.

From my travel diaries (Uluru, 15 July 2010)

> We were in the land of the Anangu. For tens of thousands of years their ancestors had roamed the desolate and inhospitable expanses of the Australian Red Centre singing the nomadic essence of man. In front of us stood one of their most sacred sites—Uluru, the mesmerizing and mysterious rock that the British settlers had preferred to rename Ayers Rock. Since time immemorial, powerful taboos forbade its access to men in specific sites and to women in some others. Nowadays, tourists

> are kindly requested not to climb the gigantic sandstone dinosaur that has been so often profaned by the white man. Acknowledging the will of the ancients, we just followed its ten-kilometer long perimeter. But what would we see, I wondered, if we instead had climbed to its top, as many tourists still did, impervious to the wishes of those who had never had a voice? I imagined an immense dome of cobalt blue and a red expanse stretching beyond any limits of the eye and of the heart. It was a vision to drown in, forever. That time we averted the temptation to dominate the world from above and violate ancestral grounds. But would this do any good, I wondered?

I watched Castro looking at the small desk where Agatha Christie had written her murderous pages. I cleared my throat and asked him the next question, thus cutting the thin thread of our mutual wandering: "There is a scene in *The Garden Book* that struck me, for the vivid way in which you describe it and for what you infer by imagining it. Norman Shih (the son of Swan, the Chinese poetess, and of her U.S. lover) is in Paris and one morning inadvertently drops his Australian passport into the gutter flushed with water." "Yes," he responded, "I remember it." "I'd like to quote exactly what you wrote: 'By the time I recovered it [the passport], the pages were soaked with slime and dogshit and the plastic was starting to peel away, deconstructing visas and birthplaces and all the fancy laser logos they use to guarantee selfhood. I am nothing but a plastic sheet'" (*The Garden* 285). "That was written from the voice of a character, but ironically the critique there was of nationalism," Castro explained. "When I read this passage," I said, "I was reminded of what Zygmunt Bauman wrote, that is, that the representatives of the new mobile power elite of the world—together with the asylum seekers, the refugees, the economic (im)migrants—'are shifty and unpredictable, they have no tie to any place' (*Liquid* 48). This, in his view, implies a lack of loyalty towards the countries in which these people temporarily live." "If you ask me and if we speak in essentializing terms, no, I don't feel any sense of allegiance," Castro replied, "I now have an Australian passport and obviously I have certain duties to perform for my host country. But I don't feel that kind of nostalgic patriotism that you see on television. Moreover, I find a lot of that very false." "You once said," I went on with the second part of my question, "'I try to reduce myths, particularly national ones, to rubble'" (qtd. in Barker, "Theory" 243). "And I still believe it," he said, adding, 'It is unfortunate that some people are choosing the advent of the twenty-first century to hark back to old ideas of nation-states and static identities'" (Castro, "Writing" 150). "I am curious to know, then, how you personally interpret, as a citizen and writer of the world, the concept of culture and its contemporary relevance." "Well, again," he responded, "I'm skeptical of any kind of identitarian motif. All kinds of things we have been talking about are evolving, changing constantly; actually, cultures are so amorphous. . . . Bauman probably speaks of cultures as liquid forms, to the extent that sometimes they disappear entirely."

"The culture of Shanghai in the 1920s, for example," Castro continued, "has completely disappeared; and that of Hong Kong is also probably disappearing; as it happened to Alexandria, which used to be such a cosmopolitan place and now is no longer except in terms of tourism [Alexandria, again, I took a mental note, another recurring reference]. So I really think cultures change and take on new forms and move around. Culture is seasonal and cyclical: I don't think that, culturally, you can see a graph depicting progress. It's perhaps less intellectual matters that retain their so called identitarian qualities, such as food, music—but obviously even music evolves—religious rituals, certain memories." "Do you really think it's possible to outgrow that initial imprinting, that sort of ethnic narcissism, that sort of religious or national self-referentiality?" I thus asked him, watching his hands, which might easily be Portuguese, Chinese, French, or Australian hands. And I thought again of Castro's poetess, Swan: "Am I Chinese before I am a woman or am I woman first?" (*The Garden* 272). "If I had to answer in a single phrase," he said, "I would say that it's possible to 'transcend' in the practice of art. I think that one's writing is far more identified with a style, with an education, with writers that you admire and who have gone before you than with a national, ethnic, or religious belonging. It's not necessarily where you come from, it's where you read from."

Castro the intellectual, who writes about far away yet intimate worlds: he writes in English, feels in Cantonese but thinks, and aesthetically lives, in French—his third language, his third skin. "I find rather paralytic this constant repetition, this incessant reinforcing of national emotions and concepts," Castro said, interrupting my muted meditations. "'Identity is multiplicity, made possible by a constant movement . . .'" I read from my notes, quoting Castro, and introducing my next question, "'We are always becoming somebody else, crossing thresholds, testing boundaries.'" Then I raised my eyes to meet his, vaguely puzzled: "You have written this, in one of your books." "I don't remember where," he said. "In *Looking for Estrellita*," I told him, "While in *The Bath Fugues* your main character says, 'I realized how quickly I had become another.' I wonder if you really think that one may keep true to oneself, that is, keep a certain integrity, a certain inner coherence, although through the prism of a multifaceted, always adapting, always becoming, identity. In other words, I wonder if being chameleonic, learning to play with one's multiple selves can also have a positive connotation; or if instead, as the Western tradition implies, the chameleon remains the symbol of the hypocrite who never expresses his or her real self but always hides behind a mask."

"Polyglossia: that's where I come from," Said Castro, "that's probably the primary thing. The secondary thing is again where your literary education comes in: when I first read Gabriel García Márquez he had these different voices, different perspectives; William Faulkner did the same thing. So it's a technique to grant different viewpoints and that's always refreshing and original. And then, I confess, I think I'd just get bored with one voice, I can see myself boring myself, so I switch. To adopt multiple selves, in life as in writing, is not a pathology, rather a methodology. It's not something new, by the way. As I said before, many writers have done it." I did not remind him, but Castro also wrote that when one interlaces two or three voices and moves through several different spaces, rather in the manner of a hologram, that is the moment "when one sees things in depth, and when one abandons the notion of a fixed, two-dimensional reality" ("Writing" 150).

This also brought to mind something Trojanow had told me about the multiplicity of voices as an ethical and, by reflex, stylistic necessity: "You cannot talk about encounters between different people and about the dynamics of these encounters if you don't give the different participants (or characters) a voice. So in a way most of the novels from the European tradition that claim to be about encountering the Other are fake, because the Other doesn't have a voice." Trojanow had pointed out that in many of the English novels about Africa, Africans don't really figure, "they appear only through the lens of the English narrator." Therefore, he had made the claim that "there is no deep knowledge of Africa and of its people at all. The only thing there about Africa is the way English people saw it or, as in the case of Hemingway, Africa is seen just as a fascinating backdrop—the Kilimanjaro is a beautiful sight in front of which to discuss American subjects." He had concluded his reasoning by explaining what it meant when people started telling him stories, as happened when he did research for his new book on Bulgarian gulags: "The moment they tell you their stories you owe them something, especially if these are traumatic, terrible, frightening stories. They don't tell them for fun but because they believe that in a way you will pass them on. If you engage in such a dialogue, in such a form of communication, you take on a responsibility on how these stories must be told and how many voices they need to have."

At least this is how Trojanow saw things. "If we relate this to your other questions," Castro said, resuming his train of thought, "probably being transcultural means to have the ability to put yourself in other people's shoes, and thus live also their lives the way you perceive them. I remember Elias Canetti saying that when you met Herman Brock and shook his hand, it was as if he was breathing you in, examining your psychic self, your spirit. It was a way of actually not just making contact with another human being but understanding, even though imaginarily, what it meant being you. It probably doesn't happen any more because the world is so vast, so brutal, so material and . . ." "So rushed," I suggested. "Yes, there is no time for this kind of contact, this slowness of the afternoons, of meetings, of conversation and understanding friendship, of knowing where you are coming from and what you are working on without asking—the pure understanding of human to human. Those things have to be cultivated, they are not just natural, they are a form of education, a form of erudition, I would say." Then for a while we were both quiet, both listening to the rumbling sound of the city muffled by the double windows. We should have been out there, I thought—to live; to immerse ourselves in other people's lives; to slowly and creatively absorb Istanbul. "In regard to your question on the chameleon," Castro said regaining a lighter tone, "maybe I didn't think too much about this word, but if I happened to use it in a novel I would use it with two edges: so that it is a critique as well as a positivity. I myself can change like a chameleon, as I told you. If for example in Australia two *ockers* addressed me in the street not too politely, I could immediately replicate their broad Australian accent. As soon as I spoke they'd go back into their shells without any longer perceiving me as a foreigner. They would both laugh and say: "He's an *ozzie*! He's one of us." It's funny how powerful a language and an accent can be."

It's all a question of language, I thought. You never know which idiom will guarantee your survival. Or which language, by promoting other interpretations of the world, will better nurture what you feel you are, or have become. "It seems that the use of foreign words, although never predictable, is instrumental to your writing," I went on. "On the other hand, you are also careful not to use words in other languages—be they Cantonese, Portuguese, or French—in a way that may color your works with unwanted ethnic overtones." "Yes, I'm particularly conscious of that," said Castro, "because I read such a lot of so-called ethnic fiction. Again, it depends on how schooled your author is. I can read Rushdie, for example, and he doesn't have to explain a lot of those Indian terms or whatever, he simply contextualizes. When I write I'm always listening—maybe it's a form of musical ear, or inner ear—I'm listening for the awkwardness, the clumsiness, the clanking sounds when something doesn't work. Obviously, certain foreign words reveal different things depending on the readers. For instance, when I read Thomas Bernhard [again the provincial Austrian writer evoked by Trojanow! I thought without interrupting Castro], when the translator leaves a German word in without translation or explanation, even though I have no German and I may be totally wrong about its meaning I can still get the feeling of that word, and understand that that word is essential in that context. Again, I think that if you are linguistically aware sometimes you just get it, as if you had developed some sixth sense."

"I guess that," I elaborated, "in a world where a growing number of people are raised bilingual, trilingual, or even polyglot, the idea of books where you find words in different languages will no longer be perceived as snobbish or elitist. Probably this kind of book, especially if written in English, replicates or slightly anticipates the new global pidgin being progressively spoken all over the world, where terms in Hindi, Arabic, or Chinese are mixed with those in English, Spanish, French, or German. Like in *Code 46*, that British sci-fi movie set in a dystopian near future world divided between those privileged ones who live 'inside,' in hi-tech, high-density cities, and those dispossessed who live 'outside,' in desert areas, united only by their highly hybridized global lingua franca." "That's interesting," Castro said, "although I don't see that phenomenon happening in Australia, a country that, despite all its immigrants, remains strongly monolingual. I mean, you go into any bookshops and there are no foreign language books—it's all English, mostly not even in translation. Generally, around the world among anglophone countries the translation industry is very poor. Certainly in Europe more people tend to read across their borders. I was in Amsterdam and I looked at the bookshops there and it was amazing: there were books in Dutch, German, and French way before they were being translated into English. Let's put it this way, the arrogance of monolingualism in Australia is still a problem."

From my travel diaries (Adelaide, 15 May 2010)

> The first time I arrived in Australia I was still taken by the modern mythology of this continent. I really thought I had landed in the model nation of multiculturalism. Anywhere I looked, I could see positive confirmation of that. Only with time I would become aware of the unsaid, the weak signals of a distortion that had never been removed. And once picked up, those signals started resounding within me as if coming from a bell tolling without respite. A visit to the Art Gallery of South Australia was an eye opener. I had gone to listen to the Ngarrindjeri Women's Choir, an event within a show dedicated to Aboriginal culture. With a sense of expectation, I thought I was about to listen for the first time to the chanting of those seven women with their wide hips and different shades of skin color. But when they started their first piece I was dismayed to hear they were singing in English. In English! Not in Ngarrindjeri, as I would expect. Sure, it was easier like that, I understood what they were singing: they were talking about their land, of Aboriginal pride, of being there to tell their story. But I felt for those women, daughters of parents who had been forced to forget their own language without being able to pass it on, forced to erase the memories enclosed in the sounds of their childhood (only later on I would discover that there are other choirs formed by members of the Ngarrindjeri people who still sing in their traditional language). "We speak English here." Apparently, the British settlers had succeeded in their efforts: by forcing Aboriginal people to grow as whites, study and speak in English, and pray by crossing themselves they had cancelled a whole galaxy of meanings, codes, and knowledge. There were dozens of languages that no one, except a small bunch of elders lost in the most impervious parts of the interior, spoke any longer—dozens of buried languages that now researchers were hopelessly trying to save from extinction. By eliminating a language you contribute to wiping out another way of looking at the world, of being in the world, of interpreting yourself and what surrounds you. But who cared, now that the mining companies tried to wheedle out the exact location of the different clans' sacred grounds, which strangely enough coincided with immense veins of gold, silver, zinc, iron ore, and uranium. I looked around and saw an audience of decorous, mostly white, elderly spectators, gratified by their current liberalism, their being there now to honor the Aboriginal culture, after having systematically annihilated it. The choir finished their performance—nothing remained but this, the performance—and I went back into the sun, there at the end of the world, of their world.

We allowed ourselves a pause, in order to taste the various fancy cakes that had been served with our *çay* (Castro just nibbled, I noticed, as if he were able to live only on air and light), then I charged again into the fray with my battery of questions: "Trojanow says that by now he prefers to reveal the bare details of his biography and of his interests: 'Otherwise, they cage you into a definition and from there you can no longer escape.'" "He is right," hinted Castro, "people want to know about 'the curious'—your face as it were metaphorically—where you come from. But they do it only to satisfy their own stereotypes. You see, once they have pigeonholed you, they are comfortable. While instead, as a writer, you should always make them feel a little bit more uncomfortable. When I first started out writing, my publishers tended to present me in a certain light, underlining the exoticism of my biography. So that people could say: 'Oh, we get you now.' In fact, they didn't. They would classify me as a Chinese author because I set my early novels in China or among Chinese immigrants. They wouldn't know that, at any new novel, I would change. So, you know, the next novel might be set in Europe and have no Chinese characters in it. Although I keep coming back to that side of things, so there'd always be an element of quote-unquote 'Asia' in that." "And that puzzled your readers," I interrupted him, "each time you presented a different setting at each new novel: Vienna and Freud's neurotic patients (including the one who eventually moves to Australia); Tasmania and the clash between whale hunters and First Australians; Japan and the Russian spies right before the Second World War. Your settings—as well as your characters—seem as mobile as your life." "I think it has to do with the way I am," he said, "As matter of fact, I keep shifting. I constantly have to move, not just for the inspiration but even psychologically there is some motivation to say I don't want to be stuck in one backwater for the rest of my life. So, from many points of view, I think the best thing is to be transient, to have different places one can go to and feel comfortable. I feel as much at home in Hong Kong as in the Blue Mountains, in the Dandenong Ranges as much as in the French Dordogne—actually, it's there that sooner or later I would like, perhaps with some other academics, to buy a farm. I feel so comfortable speaking French, being with French country people." "You have always wanted to be outside the Australian canon, even in your writing . . ." "And I have paid a price for that," he replied twisting his mouth in a sad smile, "I have never gone out and tried to be a Tim Winton, you know. I don't go out and describe the desert (and with his hand he gestured towards an elsewhere of red soil 20,000 miles away from where we were at that moment) and say, 'This is mine.' No, it's somebody else's. So I'm looking in that place that is always illusionary or delusionary. I think it's a place elsewhere, in my mind rather than in some natural landscape."

From my travel diaries (Adelaide, 10 April 2010)

> Uuaaa aahh aahhh aaahhh uuuaahh ahhh ahh: in the austral land where I lived now you didn't need an alarm clock to wake up in the morning: around six o'clock the cries of the laughing kookaburras pushed the

world out of its bed by mocking it. In the evenings, the breeze of an extreme south flowed through the open windows veiled by mosquito nets: it brought with it the scent of the ocean and of gum trees, with their memories of resins, lemon zest, and moldy clothing. Further down there was only Antarctica. Even when it rained, the air turned immediately dry, incapable of letting itself be soaked by a humidity that did not belong to it. Unseen, the aridity of the outback enveloped Adelaide in its vast embrace. I breathed, at last. I listened to my breathing, sunk into my breathing, and rejoiced at how effortless it was. There were nights in which it seemed that the winds running along the creased flanks of the hills were racing among themselves, trying to blow a little harder than the time before, and the previous one, in an escalation that seemed to have no limits. In the semidarkness, I watched the tree branches put on their crazed dances while the intensity of the gully winds grew stronger and stronger. "Is this wind normal?" I asked our neighbor after my first experience, the foliage of the eucalyptus and of the palm trees already whispering in the swelling breeze. "Absolutely," he answered with the phlegm of those who learnt not to be upset by the inevitability of the elements—or of life. Getting there, but still engrossed in the nostalgia of other latitudes, the English settlers had not associated the winds' names with poetic references nor had they looked for them in those native idioms they were so doggedly trying to get rid of. They had not listened to the Yolŋu when they spoke of the *bärra' yindi*, the northeasterly powerful wind, or when they felt on its way the *bärra' nyumukuniny*, the delicate breeze that touched you as lightly as a maiden's (*dhuykun*) breathing. No, we were in Australia, the continent-island, the country forced to build its new identity on supposed historical absences, on the vacuum created in history. This despite the fact that, it was now estimated, at least 250 different Aboriginal clan groups, each with its own culture, language, and religion, were present on the continent at the time of the contact with the first European settlers. Tramontane, gregale, levanter, sirocco, ostro, libeccio, ponente, mistral recited from time immemorial the Mediterranean sailors plucking the petals off a wind rose that contained the echoes of never too distant lands; but not down under, where the winds did not convey Homer's verses, the song of the sirens, the war cries of the Norman warriors, nor the call to prayer of the muezzin. As my girlfriend had written in a bout of fresh nostalgia for her native Syracuse, those southern winds never carried with them the fragrances of Siculan bread, the spiced aromas of Algerian cuscus, the scent of the Corsican *maquis*. Down there, the tramontane never blew from the north bringing with it frozen memories of Siberian steppes and tales of Mongolian raids. Along the austral shorelines the sailors never perceived a god and a fate behind each breeze. But even

> there where I lived now, so far from that Istanbul absorbed in a whirl of Mediterranean impressions, the wind stopped all of a sudden, interrupting the flow of memories. In that sudden quiet, only the old Aboriginal man at the station was left to dream the wind, to slowly walk along the platforms imagining his ancestors' world: footsteps on a desert beach, women busy opening mussels with stone knives, the ocean roaring in a boundless solitude—a reminder that the Dreamtime was disappearing and did not care about our regrets.

But, again, I was wandering. . . "Your writing might thus be interpreted as a challenge or a point of resistance to the collective Australian identity," I thus went on with my interview, "It's the freedom to narrate, to fictionalize what needs to be interrogated and that cannot be done otherwise." Castro's answer reached me: "Having to create something makes you think about how you are creating, who you are creating for, how it is going to be received, and if it has to have all these contradictions and ambiguities. That is supposed to be the way that I question myself all the way through. I'm still doing it: I think the constant questioning, the constant thinking in those terms makes you actually not find solutions to problems but, as you were saying, transcend those problems, because you see them as so minor after all. When I was in my early twenties and starting as a writer I was very paranoid and self-conscious, very touchy about racial issues, totally disturbed about how I was seen on television. I was actually upset when they were putting this kind of hyphenated thing on me, you know, Australian-Chinese or whatever (in British and Canadian English it is, e.g., German-Canadian, Australian-Chinese). Some people would even call me ABC, which means Australian-born Chinese, while I wasn't even born in Australia. Now I don't bother anymore, in some way you become confident in yourself, and not necessarily because you took on a specific identity." "As a matter of fact, you are not the only one tired of being a hyphenated writer," I said, "Rushdie, the 'Indian-born English writer' or, if you wish, the 'British-Indian novelist,' has also mocked this trend. Trojanow ascribes this attitude to the need for people to jump to easy conclusions. For example, he told me that when he introduced himself to an audience in Germany and explained that he was of Bulgarian origins there would always be someone who would come up and say: 'Oh, now that you mention it, I can detect a slight accent!' when in fact, as he says, his German is perfect, has no inflection whatsoever, and he wouldn't have any problem being a speaker on the German national radio." "It happens the same to me," Castro sneered, "When I'm in Paris I'm immediately Vietnamese because I speak French. The French can be very shallow in their use of categories; I remember a hairdresser in the Rive Gauche cutting my hair and saying, '*Mais vous êtes un type vietnamien*!' not believing that I was Australian."

"What you told me earlier about being a chameleon among Australian ockers and what you have just stated," I went on, meeting the attentive, never distant gaze of my writer, "reminds me of the contrasting feelings of attraction (mixophilia) and repulsion (mixophobia) towards the idea of mixing with the stranger described by Zygmunt Bauman and which apparently, more or less consciously, we all harbor within us." "In particular," I tried to better explain, "we tend towards mixophobia when we are looking for 'islands of similarity and sameness' (Bauman, *Liquid* 90), or what Richard Sennett defines 'the "we" feeling' opposed to the Other (qtd. in Bauman, *Culture* 90)." "Sometimes having to deal with strangers is problematic," Castro replied, keeping his hands crossed on his lap, "because there is a certain trauma in hospitality, you see, so if you want to be hospitable you have to take on some kind of trauma and not many people realize that 'Hey, my trauma is actually my gain: if I open up my house I'll obviously lose certain things but at the same time what it's doing is making me confront my own face.' Thus, yes, I feel there is always a sense of danger and loss to accept and a lot of people are closed to accepting anything. I also think that appearances are on the surface and yet so deep in certain ways. For example, when I went to certain parts of Southern China, because of my looks, I was considered Siberian: the Chinese were very astute in recognizing that 'I am not' Chinese. That was very interesting and confronting at the same time."

Even to acknowledge who is really a stranger, who is really the Other is never easy nor banal, I thought, remembering what Trojanow had told me on the train: "In the political arena the representations of strangeness are always superficial: a *burka* is enough, because with a *burka* you have a very clear sense of difference. But just by getting on a train things already get more complicated: how would I then be able to identify—unless for the one wearing the *burka*—the groups I think I belong to? I open the door of the first compartment, the people speak German and I think: 'Hey, I belong in here.' But then I listen to them talking and there are six dumb heads who are going to a sex party, who speak horrible German and are talking only nonsense. I go to the next compartment and I find a group of Italians going to a homosexual party: 'Not for me.' In the compartment nearby there are five English soccer fans already drunk. What is stranger to us is not necessarily 'visible': only if you first travel together for a while with people you may realize who is different or who is similar to you. My experience in life has taught me that, if I meet a person who is from a completely different country and religion, within half an hour I might find out that I share with this person many more things than with my neighbor. It has happened to me many times: you are sitting there, waiting for the bus, drinking a *chai* . . ."

Only then did I interrupt my mental notations on Trojanow's interview and address Castro, to whom they had served, by chance, another cup of black tea: "Let's go back to what you were saying about the hyphenated writers," I suggested, "Perhaps this emphasis on ethnic, cultural, or national traits imposed on certain authors may be explained by the marketing strategies connected to the boom in what Parks defines as 'global literature.' He has publicly criticized this trend." "What did he say precisely?" Castro asked. "That a writer is not famous 'unless internationally famous . . . Even the recognition extended to him in his home country is significantly increased if he is recognized abroad'" (Parks, "The Nobel"). "The problem, according to Parks," I continued, "is that this acceleration in the internationalization of literature has a perverse effect on the way writers now tend to write. In other words, we've got a real paradox: as much as one's individuality, one's autonomy from the national culture is being appreciated, it seems that, now more than ever, it is more advantageous to have a typical 'national' product to offer on the international scene: it may have to do with Scandinavian sado-pessimism, Irish parody, South American magic realism or Italian mafia/camorra. This means that instead of getting free from the national, ethnic, or cultural identification this process of internationalization contributes to reinforcing stereotypes. Parks takes as an example the Chinese writer Xiaolu Guo, who started writing in English with the explicit purpose of being able to access a wider market. Despite the fact that she has now been living in London for several years, her publishers only want to buy the rights of her Chinese stories, not the ones set in England. Unfortunately, Parks remarks, 'reading her short stories, one can see at once how much would be superfluous to the Chinese reader; a great deal of the material is only there to explain things to us, the international audience'" ("The Nobel"). "I agree with him," Castro said, slightly turning to face the window, as if he wanted to rebuke that deafening cacophony of car horns, screeching tires, and scooters' exhausts that came from the outside, "It seems to me that this thing that they now call 'global writing' or 'world writing' is taking out all the densities and complexities to make everything uniform so that it is recognizable everywhere. That to me is a deterioration and despoliation of literature. You can tell it straight away from the first page: they are trying to get you in but it's cheap."

"What is China to you?" I asked Castro, changing the subject. "You have written about it in so many ways . . ." and I quoted him: "'China, my woman, my familiar fiend, my heavenly demon'" (*The Garden Book* 36). "It's an imaginary China, of course," said Castro, "It's an imaginary China that has long since disappeared. It's the China of my childhood but also a constantly changing phenomenon. Every time I go back I'm always surprised how it has changed, how everything is changing, not only physically because skyscrapers are different or the population has tripled. It has more to do with the fact that anything can happen in China. In fact, the strangest things happen in this terrible dense mass of humanity where at every corner you can see the difference between those who are still in the fourth century and those who already live in the hypermodernity of the twenty-first century." "From medieval times to the near future in a blink of an eye, by crossing a street, or by taking the right (or wrong) turn," I said, while memories of China were pressing to gush out from my travel diaries, from the dead silence of intimate pages without readers, "as if it were still possible to experience a different form of humanity."

From my travel diaries (Beijing, Pamir, Hong Kong, July-August 1994)

> The Chinese countryside for us, then. It was one of our first long trips together as a couple. We were two solitary travelers, while the authorities preferred to have only groups of more easily controllable tourists just happy to visit the Forbidden City and a small segment of the Great

Wall close to the capital. Those tourists did not ask, as we had done, to go into the interior, follow ancient caravan routes, ride through the Xinjiang Province and reach the Islamic communities of the Uighurs, at the border with Pakistan, there where the Han became a minority. Ancient melodies played on a flute resounded in the air while I was writing in the sun. S. was taking pictures, I was taking notes. One day, absorbed in my writing, I did not notice that a small knot of people had gathered around me: there were men, women, children, young and old. When eventually I raised my eyes from the page, I saw them, watching me in respectful silence: they were watching how a Westerner, what's more a left-handed one, writes. When we reached the Pamir plateau I had a high fever. S. helped me to lie down on the veranda of the only nearby tavern facing the Karakul Lake. Then I persuaded him to leave me there and wander about. I thus found myself there, at almost four thousand meters of altitude, unable to take one more step, drenched in my sweat. I watched the surroundings as if it were a mirage, slipping in and out of my deliriums, absorbing the landscape—I myself made landscape. Around mid-morning a painter installed his easel a few steps away from where I was lying, in front of the snowy mountain caps being reflected by the crystal clear waters as in a perfect mirror. On the plateau where we were, the mountains did not seem so high after all, although I knew they were all over 7,500 meters above sea level. We remained like that for a long time, in front of that scenery, in an uninterrupted silence, while he painted and I returned to my feverish trance. Only when he took his leave and exchanged just few words in English with me, I found out that my improvised travel companion came from Japan. In fact, as I wrote later on once I felt better, not even those few words would have been necessary, since what we shared that day, in that rarefied beauty, was a gift from our precultural—or if we wish, postcultural—humanity, where even language no longer matters. When after Kashgar, the oasis of Turfan, and the silences of the Pamir we reached the coast, it came as a shock. In my notebook I wrote that to see the outskirts of Hong Kong was like witnessing the reality of life but also the defeat of that humanity I had experienced up there at 4000 meters. From the train window I watched the multitudes closed in 40-story hives, imprisoned in nuthouse-skyscrapers. I imagined the 130,000 souls per square kilometer of the Mong Kok district and my breath caught at the thought of the new China: mountains of concrete and steel instead of dragon clouds and paper lanterns; venomous mushrooms growing in a monstrous haste. Mine were nothing but travel notes, and their brevity made them sound too radical and judgmental, as they should never be . . . because, let's face it, is not it the density and the physical contiguity typical of the metropolis—as history teaches

> us—that generate the best examples of intercultural exchange, the diffusion and fertilization of ideas? And who knows where the balance point is between one's freedom, the harmony inspired by a landscape, and the intellectual vivacity, the shared intents, the hybridization of minds that nestle in a forest of skyscrapers?

"Tell me, Brian, how do you perceive China in relation to European culture? You wrote: 'While the West seems to have run out of ideas in the creative and cultural fields . . . the Asian region is alive with opportunities for a new hybridization'" ("Writing" 154). "When I generally look at what's coming out of Europe," he quickly replied, "I'm seeing what other people call the 'museum culture.' For a long time, because I read French, I felt that the French culture, the French literature had died. Who are they producing these days, apart from Michel Houellebecq, who just wants to shock in that awful way? I think it shifted towards, you know, postmodern discourse, that aura of the 1960s and 1970s, Jacques Lacan, Jacques Derrida, and all those people. So that kind of intellectual thrust seems to me to be taken out of the creative narrative, if you like, and made into this kind of intellectual discourse that is going around and around and around. Anyway, that's Europe." "What about China?" I asked. "Because of the vastness of its population," he said, "the talent that is hidden and actually suppressed is vast—that maybe comes back to the idea that when there is suffering and you are not allowed the freedom to narrate then great experiments come out of it. You can't stop the human spirit and the creative artist's experience, thus I think there is great hope for that as China liberalizes more."

"Who knows, then," he mused, "what wonderful novels might come out, say, from the Muslim population of China, the Uighurs or the Siberians, from those who come from such dramatic backgrounds and material trauma. If there is an aesthetic of suffering, and I don't want to make of it some kind of feat, even though it's always something to admire, then it's from there that we can expect to see interesting experiments with the text, with the language." Or if there exists an aesthetic of population density, I would have added, thinking again of the Mong Kok district . . . but I kept quiet and instead I stretched my hand to switch off the audio recorder and free Castro from the golden cage of the Pera Palas. During our interview he had told me how for him the period grand hotel enclosed the nostalgia of a lost time: "My father used to tell me of our rented penthouse at the Cathay Hotel before he lost everything. He was a bit of a playboy, so he deserved what was coming. But I guess that kind of idea of the grand hotel came always from his stories. I felt it was in my blood too: this kind of living in these grand hotels is something that a certain class of people did, you know, and you had all the valets, the waiters, the servants . . . and it was constantly exciting, and when he lost everything and became quite poor he would still take me to the lobby of these grand hotels in Hong Kong and he would just have this cup of tea, to reminisce. And he would pass all these stories on to me, and I would sit there, absorbing all these stories and memories." If for Castro the grand hotel enclosed the mysticism of memory ("this ocean that you can swallow and imagine") and the metaphor for his writing ("the place that has seen all the movers, those guests who come and go, with all the imagined stories that come with them, leave with them"), it was also true that, as a writer, Castro did not want to be cocooned off from the world, "to look into the abyss of our humanity—as one French wrote in the past—from my comfortable armchair in the lobby." As he himself claimed, "there is no complexity to the extent of just playing with technique, no complexity without the encounter with the world": the world out there, out of the books, out of the Pera Palas, there where life and the Other started, where Istanbul started. I was travelling with hand luggage only. In my bag I had a small bottle of eau de parfum and a pair of shoes of fine red suede with high heels: these were the only things that never changed while all the rest—cities, languages, employers, continents—kept changing. In the Bosphorus the evening was setting in and I had a meeting, out there, in few hours.

Chapter Three

Baranay's Transient Life in Writing

No, there was no need, not now at least, to say where I went last night; nor to tell how lively the ancient district of Cihangir becomes after sunset, when the veiled women withdraw from indiscreet eyes and the big brand shops, the department stores, the businessmen and the bureaucrats leave the scene to the street sellers, the film crews, the companies of actors, the gay couples, the young travelers, and the expats looking for local color and bohemian undertones. Where now antique dealers, small art galleries, and vintage shops are, once forests grew—the forests where Cihangir, the son of Suleiman the Magnificent, went hunting. I would tell all about that, but another time. Now I needed to concentrate on my next interview. Taking my time I undressed, as if enacting a ritual, although the attendant at the Cağaloğlu *hammam*—a big muscular woman whose thick eyebrows met over the nose—seemed to discourage any sense of spirituality or religious observance in her strictly practical and distracted way. Before she gestured for me to enter the changing room, she gave me a checkered cotton cloth, the classical *peştemal*, to wrap around my hips. I took everything off, including the glasses for my short-sightedness. Then, following her sharp orders given in a rough English, I clumsily entered a hall suffused with vapor, where I lost any sense of bearing, as if fog were inside and outside me. It didn't seem like twenty years had passed since an almost identical despotic fat attendant, naked and shuffling around in her rubber slippers, had given me the same orders, gesturing or using the same basic English expressions: "stand up, turn around, wash yourself." Then it was my first time in Istanbul and my first time in a real Turkish bath.

"I am here, at your left." "Inez?" I peered, looking without seeing. "Yes. Please, take a seat here." As I drew closer to the source of the voice, I made out the silhouette of a woman sitting with her legs crossed in Lotus position, her back straight against the marble-clad wall of a bathing niche, her breasts still blooming and steady in her middle-aged Adamitic state. It did not surprise me: it was she who compared the practice of writing to the practice of yoga—"Think of the body as a text written by yoga, and the self as a text written by your writing" (Baranay, *Sun* 58). Yes, Inez was also a teacher of Patanjali yoga (following the tradition of B. K.

S. Iyengar); and no, that was not the only thing that had been left with her after her time spent in India. "I told the attendant that you would find me here," she said. "She made herself understood," I answered, shaking the hand that had reached me through a veil of steam. I saw droplets of sweat on her arm and, for whatever strange association, I remembered the condensed humidity trickling from a block of sandstone at the borders of the Amazon rainforest, together with the words of the poet Aimé Césaire: "Many people are weak because they don't know how to become stone, or tree." As I squatted by her side, on the low seat, I gazed up at the dome above us, barely discerning the circular small openings that filtered the daylight, multiplying it in a kaleidoscope of beams. I thought about the audio recorder in my bag in the changing room—it was useless. "Don't worry," Inez said, reading the involuntary apprehensive look on my face, "we won't do our interview here but in the relaxation area." The *hammam* was an unusual place indeed for an interview, I had thought when Baranay proposed that we meet there; unusual elsewhere but not in Istanbul, where even politicians and businessmen prefer to settle the thorniest matters among the mists of an ancient tradition. There I was, getting acquainted with Inez's dripping body even before knowing her thoughts.

As we were chatting away, I realized that we talked as if we had always known each other, as if our skins had instantly recognized each other and got rid of a long series of preliminaries. Inez tended to express herself in a vibrant, sympathizing way, as if at that moment only you counted, ready to absorb your humanity as far as she was allowed to—and even beyond, to where her intuition led her. I noticed that she spoke about her past experiences in a succinct but meaningful way, by which I sensed that she had already extensively pondered over them. I found myself listening to the woman sitting by my side, her hair wrapped in a toweling turban, as if in a trance, taking in her warm, hypnotic, self-confident voice. Her English had a slight Australian inflection, softened by the cohabitation—although not in-depth, as she admitted—with other languages (the Hungarian of her early childhood, the broken Malay of her adolescence, the Indonesian of the young traveler, the mix of foreign languages captured in her maturity), by listening and repeating words from ancient liturgical idioms (the Sanskrit of her yoga practice) and, most of all, by the habit of adopting the ways of talking of her interlocutors, be they academics or underground artists, *brahmins* or villagers from rural India, tranquil mothers from the city suburbs of Sydney or neurotic business women from New York.

"In the presentation of your research project," she said, mixing her words with the bath vapor, "you talk of 'dispatriation' and how this state may lead to forms of 'creative transpatriation': they are both expressions that I hadn't encountered before and that I'd like to adopt. I've never felt I had (or belonged to) a homeland. Everyone in my family was born in a different country, though both my parents were Hungarian. I felt as much that I came from Italy, where I was born as from the Hungary of my ancestry, or the Australia where I grew up. Puzzled by questions of where I came from and what nationality I was when young, later on I found out that my official identity at birth was 'displaced person' and that definition seemed to make something clear. It seems to me that dispatriation is the condition into which I was born, the condition I had to understand to make sense of myself in the world. Quite likely, its gift has been a complexity of vision, and that has inevitably informed my writing." As other thousands of *reffos* (refugees) or *wogs*, as immigrants were disparagingly referred to by the Anglos, Inez too had to endure the trials of immigrant children: "We've all got a black-bread-and-salami story, we *wogs*," she joked about it now, "Our smelly stinky reffowog lunches. All the other children had white soft sandwiches filled with stuff we had to find out about—vegemite, peanut butter, devon—and they swapped half of this for half of that. But we had coarse thick black bread with spicy garlicky sausage and we threw it away or we hid it or we ate it with shame, defiance, resignation; we flavored it with revenge, secrecy, pride . . . we couldn't swap with them, all we could do was share Latvian bread, Polish sausage, Serbian pickle, Italian ham, Greek cheese. That was our 'one Europe'" (*The Saddest* 20). "Your writing was born from there," I said. "Right, my dispatriation became a creative transpatriation, as you have defined it, when it began to inform my creative work. What the Anglos might delicately refer to as 'my background'—my black bread and salami childhood—gave me a different slant on the world, a different accent in my thoughts, a different kind of narrative I've identified with" ("Multiculturalism" 127). I thought of Inez's distant *reffo*-style version of Europe and compared it with the wild Australian interior and its own heart-of-darkness dynamics, which I first discovered roaming across the bush through books and films rather than by 4x4.

From my travel diaries (Adelaide, 3 March 2010)

> It has nothing to do with the poetic mythology of the outback, with the inspiring uplifting freedom of vast open spaces: *Wake in Fright* is a punch in the stomach. This film has been retrieved from oblivion, painstakingly restored and given back to Australians. When it came out in 1971 with the title *Outback* it was indigestible to most Aussies. It is a ruthless portrait of how they were (and, in some cases, of how they still are). It would be difficult, after all, to feel at ease with what they would see in that reflection: a mass of boozers (it is impossible to keep count of how many beers are knocked back in the film) and frustrated machos who keep gambling, are not able to make a complete sentence, and roam the plains in their Land Rovers brutally shooting kangaroos as their pastime. If there has been a wild wild West, there has also been a wild wild Outback. The film is based on the 1961 novel *Wake in Fright* by the Australian journalist Kenneth Cook but is not the work of an Australian (although the coproduction is Australian). The film director is the Canadian Ted Kotcheff, the scriptwriter is the Jamaican Evan Jones, the main producer is an American subsidiary of Westinghouse. As the film critic Paul Byrnes (an Australian) writes, "There has never been a more savage and scabrous film about

> Australia. Unfortunately, it was also uncomfortably true" (Review). It is Byrnes again that makes the connection between *Wake in Fright* and John Milton's *Paradise Lost*. The same kind of question hovers in the hot air: "If men and women are able to live freely, what freedoms will they choose?" The answer that emerges watching the movie is not encouraging: all the possible sins and incivilities are contemplated. Just imagine a version of *Lord of the Flies* with adult characters. Although the small town of Bundanyabba (a thinly disguised Broken Hill) is presented as a kind of Sodom burnt to the roots by a scorching sun and lost in the dreary emptiness of the far western plains of New South Wales, its inhabitants don't consider it as such. "The Yabba is the best place in Australia," says a taxi driver to the newcomer, a young schoolteacher at the beginning of his odyssey into hell. Later on in the movie, "Doc" Tydon, a chronic alcoholic, will rephrase it this way: "All the little devils are proud of hell." A film not to be seen, perhaps, but to know that it exists, that's for sure.

I squinted, attempting to focus on Inez's image without the help of my lenses, reviewing her features—a fair, almost milky freckled skin, aquamarine eyes, locks of blondish hair slipping out from the turban's coils—hardly fitting the stereotype of the southern European but certainly in keeping with that of an eastern European, although the two were judged by the same standard in the Australia of the 1950s-1960s. "Yes, I have blond hair and I'd pass for a white Anglo-Saxon," she replied to my remark, "but my name was what-was-that-again/different/what kind? and my childhood was saying to my mother, 'please, don't talk so loud; please, talk English; please, don't wave your hands about. It took us longer to be proud of our mothers'"(*The Saddest* 20-21). "As long as it took for the *wog* food, as you have written, to be nationally acknowledged," I said after having found her quote: 'Wog food becomes exclusive food becomes trendy food becomes city food becomes food" (*The Saddest* 21). As long as it took for multiculturalism to take root, at least in the kitchen. And in spite of the fact, I thought, that the newly arrived Italians were now devoting themselves to the art of barbecue.

From my travel diaries (Perth, 30 January 2008)

> It was my first barbie. Barbie for barbecue, in that Australian breezy way to shorten words: "sunnies" for sunglasses, "arvo" for afternoon, "hubby" for husband. As if language reflected that simplified attitude towards life that does not require too much effort nor, possibly, too many syllables. That evening, with the smell of sizzling meat in the air, I found myself wandering under the gum trees and among the dry-tolerant native plants of a private garden. I still felt the sentences of *Eucalyptus*, the novel by the Australian writer Murray Bail, dancing in

> me like dew drops on the tip of a leaf, revealing the unexpected of a continent and its meaningful consistency, even there where nothing but aridity seemed to thrive. The literary critic Danny Yee had described Bail's novel as "a splendid celebration of landscapes both natural and cultural" ("*Eucalyptus*"). The host introduced me to the cook for the evening. Even before I stretched my hand to greet him, Claudio Montisi had already burst out laughing, addressing me in Italian with his indomitable Tuscan accent, sucking in all the "c" letters, as if Australia had kept passing over him like the waters of the Arno river. "Every time it strikes me: one can always tell an Italian apart, even from afar," he said with a smile, "The same unmistakable look: you new expatriates have plenty of it . . ." "And you? When did you arrive?" I enquired. "Oh, seven years ago . . ." "How much easier for us now than fifty years ago," I remarked plainly. "Sure," he agreed putting more sausages on the sizzling slab, "but 'Maremma maiala,' I have fucking struggled. What do you think? Another language, another culture, another way of thinking. And I'm lucky I have an Australian wife!" "You stayed, though. Still better here than in Italy." "You bet," he replied, turning around a mass of chicken thighs and lamb ribs, "that doesn't mean I don't miss Florence, you know. You can't forget your roots. I called my son, who's born here, Michelangelo." Claudio stopped talking to intercept one of the guests and pass on to him a plate full of cooked meat—"Here Mike, for the boys"—before introducing a new topic into the conversation: "The problem is no longer us *wogs*, anyway. Now the problem is them." "Them who?" "The Chinese of course," he answered brandishing his large fork, "Have you seen the cover of the latest issue of Bloomberg Businessweek? . . . There it is, the Sydney Opera House, with one of its sails painted in red and five yellow stars shining on its left-hand side, to replicate the flag of the People's Republic of China. Underneath, the caption reads: 'Here is the deal: You take the money, we take the country.'"

"None of this matters anymore and it shouldn't," Inez commented in a slightly ironical tone, "It's a new Australia and you don't whinge. We live in a cosmopolitan city and watch American TV on satellite. Everyone's sick of the debate on national identity. I love the English language and hope the world heals and renews. We forgive ourselves and forget our childhoods. I meet my friends for cappuccino and some days they say I'm still just trying to pass for white" (*The Saddest* 24).

"Then, at fifteen, it was Malaysia," I said, prompting her to go on. "It was a profound experience," she said quickly, going along with my wishes, "Unlike many or most of the Australian and English military families, my parents enjoyed eating local food and my mother regularly played bridge with Chinese women she stayed friends with. It was so long ago now but those two years abroad did give me a taste for experiencing other places and eating chili." And sweating in the tropical heat, I would add, watching our moist bodies and imagining Inez in that physical and cultural elsewhere that since then kept attracting her through a never-ending series of comings and goings. The first leg of Baranay's moveable feast was Bali, then came Southeast Asia, Morocco, Europe, later a year as volunteer in Papua New Guinea, along the lines of one of her characters: "I imagined I was starting to live the way I'd planned to: foreign situations, foreign possibilities" (*Pagan* 29). Why then should not she enhance those opportunities, I thought, reading her biographical notes? They would invite her to spend some time among the community of artists at Saratoga Springs, in the US; to live and write (for at least six months) at Madras University as well as the BR Whiting Library in Rome and the Binger Film Lab in Amsterdam; to teach creative writing in Spanish academies; to publish her novels in India before in Australia, her putative homeland. Thus I reconstructed, sometimes by mere recollection, sometimes by checking the notes I subsequently took, our informal conversation (preamble to the real interview) among the hot steam of the Cağaloğlu *hammam*, whose architecture had practically remained unchanged since it was built in 1741 by Sultan Mahmut I.

After the vigorous massage and scrubbing on heated marble slabs we received at the hands of the big attendant woman, we finally landed, wrapped in dry towels, on a pair of resting chairs in the relaxing area. In front of us there was a coffee table with two lemon sherbets and my audio recorder. To introduce my first question, I quoted the description Inez had given of Nora, the main character of her novel *Pagan*: "She belonged to the exiles and her roots were laid in a mixture of memory and fable and forgetting . . . She was a woman who was born into one world and who would live her life in another; who lived in a tiny colonial town and felt she should be in Paris; who would be homesick wherever she was, always, even over the sea" (53). Then came my question: "Where is home for you?" "Wherever I am sleeping that night," she answered impulsively, "wherever I am staying at the time." Then, thinking it over, she added: "At times I share Nora's feeling—feeling homesick wherever she is. Being in one place means missing somewhere else." "At home everywhere or nowhere," I remarked, "Perhaps even your sense of belonging is as 'mobile.'" "If I have allegiances they are to people and ideas, not to places, countries, or nations," Inez replied, gazing around at the other guests softly chatting, reading, or dozing off in their resting chairs, "but that's not the same thing as belonging, isn't it?" "I guess," I nodded briefly, not wishing to lay bare my own thoughts on the matter at this point. "I know, those who think like that are considered unreliable," Inez went on, "but this doesn't mean that they don't have ties anyway, strong ties, the ties of being identified that way. Is it only ties to 'a place' that make someone the opposite of shifty and unpredictable?" "Trojanow claims he has no roots, since he is not a tree," I reported. "Yes, I am apt to say that as well: roots are for trees," she said smiling, chuffed by this complicity among alikes. "Or even better I agree with Rushdie," she said, "at least I think it's he who said that we do not put down roots, we put up aerials."

"Still in another sense one might feel rooted, or anchored, not in a place but in a practice or a way of life—one's daily habits carried out everywhere: to read, drink coffee, do yoga . . ." I remarked. "From what I understand you consider even the English language as a practice—in this case a supranational practice—and means of communication stripped of too stringent pressing ethnic-cultural traits, or in any case free from the necessity to adhere to any specific national canon—be it British, American, South African, Canadian, or whatever." "Right," she said, "That's why I'm all for a cosmopolitan Australian English full of variations, a mongrel English, and a happily mongrel nation" (see "Multiculturalism" 124). "An English like the one they might speak in India," I inquired, thinking of what Baranay's Meenakshi says in *Neem Dreams*: "Yes our life is about back to India, and reclaiming tradition, and no, not all foreign influence is bad—we know our history, how swiftly the foreign becomes the traditional—and yes we say let's be proud of being Indian and no we don't want to ban the English language, the English in the English language is not the English of people from England. The world speaks English, we've spoken English all our lives, English is an Indian language . . . an English in which the English are an unremembered historical stain" (*Neem Dreams* 19, 142). "Well, that's what I've in fact tried to point out in the novel by employing various Englishes in the characters' speech," she confirmed, "Meenakshi went to an English medium high school in India and embraces the mongrel English of her student days in New York; Andy is middle-class English; Jade an urban Australian whose speech is inflected by her own time in New York; Pandora, also an Australian, was brought up in the country and, although from a half-Greek family, speaks a more unembellished standard Australian. Jolly is an Indian teenager in a rural area with scant but enthusiastic English. Dinesh's English has not been much employed outside of his rural south Indian region but is a matter of necessity and pride" ("Multiculturalism" 124).

"With *Neem Dreams*," I went on, "one enters pluralistic, multivocal worlds, rich in lexical crossbreedings and bastardizations. It is a real—not faked—multiplicity that, from what I gathered, you would like to see replicated also in Australia, in the country that boasts it is the most multicultural in the world." Inez knew well what I was referring to, that is, the criticism that various intellectual quarters of Australian society level at Australian multiculturalism. In short, that *Anglos* still favor a monocultural (Anglo-Saxon) framework which acknowledges a single national language (English) and magnanimously grants its kaleidoscopic ethnic minorities the freedom to parade their costumes, traditions, foods, and tastes in the same way as street vendors exhibit their merchandise in a country fair. It has a lot of color and it is okay as long as it slightly rhymes with folklore but, for god's sake, do not ever let these languages (and their underlying cultures) undermine the indisputable dominance of the *Queen's English* and of what it still represents down under (see Hage). "India has multiplicities of culture, ethnicity, language, religion, and that's before you try and work out caste and class and their relation. There have been enormous successes in this: migratory movements and mixed marriages resulting in content and stability," Inez started to answer, shaking with one hand her still damp thick and curly hair,

"The tolerance of difference in India is so deep and widespread and natural that it is an effort to bring it to conscious attention, but this is not always noticed by the outsider's gaze upon India, with the domination of the daily news of communal violence, caste wars, ethnic tensions. These tensions, and the ways they are manipulated for political purposes, are part of the material of *Neem Dreams*. As an Australian author including this phenomenon in a novel set in India, I might have been looking for a way to understand the manipulation of these tensions in my own country and in the world, to expose it, to register my own refusal to ignore or endorse it. Setting a novel elsewhere gives a writer the possibility of the necessary perspective that enables the creation of fictive truth" ("Multiculturalism" 28).

Mimicking Inez, I too sipped my lemon sherbet before introducing my next question: "You have set your novels in so many different places—India, Sydney, Bali, Venice—and while you were writing them you were in other places again: in New York, Amsterdam, Rome, Brisbane . . ." Inez nodded, signaling that she got the sense of the question. "It is normal in my world for people to be in such places. People do move around a lot these days. I choose to set my novels in places that I want to investigate in reality and in imagination; even though, to transform them into settings for my stories, I have first to be away from those places." I remembered how she had explained her modus operandi: "For example, I began the first draft of my new book while living in Rome for six months, but I couldn't finish the chapters about Rome until I left Rome," and with Sydney she said it was the same thing: "For the Sydney setting to work in the novel, it had to become a place in imagination. If I had remained in Sydney I would have been part of it, it part of me. The daily interaction would preclude the perspective, the sense of distance and separation" (Baranay, "Writing"). "I guess this has also to do with the way you interpret the creative process," I said, "in particular the connection between memory and writing. I quote you: 'To write a story is to make a memory or displace a memory'" (Dagnino and Baranay). "Well," she answered, "to stay in a place is to constantly change your experience of that place. Leave it, and you can fix the place in your memory by composing that memory. As I understand the way memory works, an event is remembered once: the next time you remember it, that memory has already changed. So the memory of any particular event is always a bit different, even if you don't realize it" (Dagnino and Baranay). "The performance artist and storyteller Laurie Anderson has beautifully described this same phenomenon, that is our propensity to unintentionally alter and edit our stories through the lens of new perspectives," I briefly interrupted her, running through my notes, "here, this is what she writes: 'You got your story and you hold onto it and every time you tell it you forget it more'" (Anderson, *A Story*). "This must be true," Inez nodded in agreement, "because your mind has changed since you last remembered an event. If I write something based on something true, I will only ever be able to remember it the way it was written. To write is to stop the memory from changing."

Two young Italian women (tourists, I gathered) had started chatting not far away from us. While my interviewee was taking a sip from her sherbet, I couldn't help but briefly overhear their conversation. I half-smiled and, noticing Inez's questioning eyes, I translated for her: "They have found out that the dervishes they saw performing last night were not real monks but Bulgarian dancers hired by a theatre company to lure tourists in search of authentic cultural experiences." "We have all fallen for it, haven't we?" she said sympathetically. "No doubt," I answered, thinking of when in *Neem Dreams* the Australian Pandora enters for the first time the house of Meenakshi in rural Southern India and is surprised to find that in her living room there are a CD stack tower, a hi-fi stereo system, and a TV set mounted on a metal stand: "Here in this remote estate in a remote area. So you'd expect something more, well, local. Preconceptions, get rid of them" (*Neem Dreams* 6). In fact, I was thinking about my own sentimental journeys . . .

From my travel diaries (Manaus, Amazonas, 23 August 1995)

> I was in Manaus, in the Amazon of Herzog's *Fitzcarraldo*. But it was not enough. I wanted the real experience, the authentic one. I wanted to feel the place mine, live, not mediated by the last, although alternative, tourist guide. Thus, after several negotiations, I boarded (together with a good supply of bottled water) the boat of Paulo the fisherman. He would take me upstream, where his family lived, just a little further from where the Rio Negro meets the Rio Solimões, giving birth to the Amazon River. During our crossing, I saw the two confluents flowing parallel to each other for a long stretch without mixing their waters. The one dark and clear like strong tea, the other fair, almost café au lait, but muddy—each determined to keep its own density, speed, temperature; each content with (or proud of?) its own identity. It was a reminder, I thought 15 years after that experience, that cultures also tend to go along side by side for quite a while before merging into new blends and mixtures, more bountiful and richer than they would ever presume. Paulo took me fishing with his children, invited me to bathe (which I did) in waters infested with piranhas ("If there is no blood around they don't attack," he assured me), showed me how to catch young crocodiles with bare hands, how to drink sap from enormous trees by nicking their bark with a knife. I was content to be in nature, with nature—as he apparently was. Till when, on the third night of my stay, I discovered another reality, less romantic but certainly not less real. That evening, as usual, after having dinner with the whole family I went to my room-hut (built on stilts and connected like the others to the central body of the house by a small pier). By candlelight and with the only opening window barred by planks to keep the mosquitoes away, I jotted down some notes in my diary before lying down in my hammock. It was only after quite a while that I heard a slight vociferation, an unusual commotion coming from the heart of the house. I put my

> sandals on, opened the door and headed towards the source of those sounds. When I reached the spacious room where the family gathered to share their meals, I could not believe what I saw: at least twenty persons had gathered there (who knows from where, who knows how they got there) to watch a telenovela. A telenovela! No one paid attention to me, they all had their eyes glued to the small screen and were laughing, crying, having a good time, and suffering as if they were themselves the main characters of the story, as if they had forgotten where they were, in the middle of a jungle, along a river infested with crocodiles and piranhas, on a palafitte, in front of a TV set working with the electricity produced by a young boy pedaling briskly on a bike connected to a transformer.

This story, which I retrieved from my scrapbook of memories, was not too dissimilar to what Inez had written of her life in Bali: "We [my grandson and I] pick a huge banana leaf for shelter from the rain on a long walk and pass a village woman in sarong-kebaya holding a nylon umbrella. There is a white guy wearing a sarong, the Balinese wear jeans. We find a coconut to drink; the boy who opens it sucks on a bottle of Coke as he watches us" (*The Saddest* 28). But I could have revived many more other episodes of my itinerant life in search of authenticity—be it local, ethnic, or cultural; as when, on the Southern border of the Gobi desert, I had insisted on spending the night in a Mongol *yurt.* Once inside the old circular tent S. and I had taken refuge from the biting cold under a felt blanket that in its long life most probably had never been washed, only to find out the following morning that its owners now comfortably lived in a small brick-and-mortar house just behind the hill. What is authentic and what is not? What has ever been? I now asked myself. Where does their modernity start and where does our Western world end? Who/what is the Other and who/what is not? These are questions with no real answers, except perhaps the one provided by the architect Rem Koolhaas: "The 'Western' . . . is no longer our exclusive domain . . . It is a self-administered process that we do not have the right to deny—in the name of various sentimentalities—to those 'others' who have long since made it their own" (qtd. in Iyer 144).

I looked away from the two couples and addressed Inez again, seizing the opportunity to introduce the topic of India, "the point of greatest attrition between modern and traditional, the melt line, or confluence," as Parks defined it in *Dreams of Rivers and Seas* (50). Confluence: here again the echo of this word with all its symbolic power. "India is the place where one is allowed to experiment at its highest level with the complexity emerging from a pressing contiguity of nationalities, ethnic groups, faiths, idioms, religions. After India how do you relate to these categorizations?" I asked her. "It seems far more will be revealed about who we are if we say, for example, that even identical nationality means very different things to different people," Inez started her reasoning. "To some people the nimbus of nationality, ethnicity, race, and so on seems scarcely to extend beyond the boundaries of discrete bureaucratic acts, to others it enfolds them. Similarly, dichotomies such as Western/Oriental, Indian/foreigner seem to me insufficient and even absurd in many contexts; especially if we take into consideration a globalizing planet with its growing numbers of NRIs (nonresident Indians, I mean), neonomadic souls and middle-class people emerging from the developing world. If we need dichotomies to understand other people, we can find more meaningful ones than the standard national/foreigner, black/white, ethnic/Anglo . . ." "Such as?" I asked. "Perhaps provincial/cosmopolitan, parochial/global, English-speaking/not English-speaking: these seem to matter more, or matter differently, in today's world" (Baranay, "Writing").

"As if in our contemporary world the social class," I added, "a shared vision of the world, or a common lifestyle could count more than nationality, race, ethnicity, religion." "I think that the middle classes have a culture that overlaps several other categories of cultural identity such as nationality and ethnicity," Baranay said. "This gives me an entrée into a sense of familiarity with some of the dynamics of Meenakshi's family. Meenakshi is closer to me in some ways than, say, an Australian woman from a very different background and life experience; Meenakshi comes from a middle-class, or bourgeois, family that valued education, conversation, travel abroad, and had long rubbed shoulders with people of various national backgrounds. It is to cosmopolitanism, our being citizens of the world, finally, that Meenakshi and I give the highest value: this is what made her feel at home in the mongrel city of New York; and it was what made me able to imagine her there, and follow her home to India" (Baranay, "Writing").

"The word cosmopolitanism doesn't irritate you then?" I asked, returning obstinately to my questions. "On the contrary," she asserted, "cosmopolitanism to me has always had a positive sense. In my writing as well I feel I don't belong to any national canon. I have always opposed—although back then no one was taking any notice when I would say these things—the idea that an Australian writer needs to show her level of Australianness, something that now (and I like to believe it) is a dying-out imperative" (Dagnino and Baranay). Also Kundera, Inez reminded me (she would email me the right quote, she assured me), had expressed his uneasiness in being enveloped by the ties of national literature, which are stronger the smaller the nation of reference is. "If it's true that," I continued in my fictional conversation with Baranay, "as you yourself maintain, people tend to use the term culture in different ways depending on the context, to suggest in a superficial way the nationality, language, or ethnicity of a group (rather than referring to 'a constellation of acquired and shared beliefs and practices,' as you have described it), do you think it's still possible to be free of all those identity-making hyphenations that others, even more than ourselves, label us with?" "Not sure why one would get rid of a hyphenated self. Add a few hyphens maybe . . ." she said (Dagnino and Baranay). "Be it Anglo Indian, Australian Chinese, Argentinian Canadian, or any other kind of hyphenated self," I concluded, following her reasoning. Not by subtracting but by adding: that is how one grows transculturally, I thought, taking mental notes of what I should write, emphasizing differences but, at the same time, combining all of them, even when they lead to banal categorizations. "I mean, nationalism's a dinosaur, right?" she said (Dagnino and Baranay): "Multi, that's for today: multicultural, multiple options, multinational" (*The Saddest* 29). "That is how one can overcome one's national, ethnic, racial, or religious self-referentiality," I said, trying to put my thinking into the form of a question, "expanding one's complexity, in an accumulation of multiple selves." "To overcome . . ." Inez repeated, adding a challenging or at least slightly annoyed tone in her voice, "sounds like vanquishing a foe! What is the foe here? What is one overcoming? For what purpose?" She kept silent for a little while, perhaps waiting for a reaction, which did not come. Thus she continued: "Well, I suppose endless self-referentiality is undesirable. And yes, it's possible to transcend certain categorizations. It's a matter of temperament and will, I think, perhaps also of opportunity." I thought about Inez's life, and her elasticity in grabbing opportunities as they emerged. Some time before, in one of her emails, she had hinted about an invitation to the Istanbul International Book Fair and the chance of taking advantage of that trip to spend some time in that part of the world.

A few weeks later, I received a message from her in which she announced that she would be living in Istanbul. Her life seemed to be as flexible as her body and her writing, which had been instructed by years of geographic impermanences and steady yoga practices. "How can we talk of truth and real selves in a post-modern world of uncertainty, relativism, unstable identity?" (*Sun* 58) she concluded her reasoning in my mind. "The self, even the one determined by cultures, is an illusion, and actually all we are consists of several piles—or, as the Buddhists call them, *skandhas*—of associations and memories and so on" (*Sun* 30, 19). Our egos, personalities and our sense of self, conceived as distinct and permanent, would be no more than the illusory effects of the *skandhas.* It is all so impermanent, I thought, closing our interview mentally, thinking also about the autobiography she had been working on, *Local Time.* She was transient herself, like most of her characters—a mobile Inez, drawn to keep moving by her curiosity but also by the necessity to transform real places into imaginary settings for her novels. Apparently this was, briefly outlined, the formula of her transcultural writing: a search for proximity (familiarity) with people (and the characters), and a distancing of herself from the sites and the characterizations of the Other imposed by different cultures, including the academic one.

From my travel diaries (Istanbul, 3 July 2012)

> There are no coincidences, rather temporal clogs, lumps of coagulated meanings, intuitive knots ready to be dissolved at the slightest distraction: unless one sticks obstinately to them, tries to interpret them, frame them in significant patterns before they flow away again undisturbed, disregarded. What happens once our life stories find the slightest opportunity to mesh with each other is up to us. It is a matter of trained concentration—an excessive form of insight, if you wish; an inability to pass lightly over the facts of our existence, our and others' words,

feelings, dreams. As though we were attracted by the same light, by the same desire to write, to live in writing, to search for the Other—that is for ourselves—through writing. As the writer Nicholas Jose wrote, "It is the human interest that makes the journey" (ix). This I thought while my literary guests mixed their reasoning among the choreographies of a symbolic harbor city. Their conversations showed an agility of emotional and intellectual interchange and an ease of mutual interpenetration that astonished me. Although, in the end, I was the director, the dea ex machina, the postmodern demiurge of these dialogues as they happened at different times, in different latitudes and often inverted seasons. This I thought while listening—and then relistening on the audio recorder—to Inez's voice, there in our imaginary *hammam*, interlacing her words, memories, and ideas with those of all the others.

Chapter Four

Manguel and the Paradox of Cultural Identity

I was in one of my dreams. Or perhaps still in my real life, but which had suddenly become a dream. I had boarded an old *caique*, its Latin sail displayed for merely aesthetic purposes, since the engine was running. I was facing the same view that swarms of merchants, mercenaries, diplomats, pilgrims, and writers had met arriving in Istanbul by vessel. Even the architect Le Corbusier had not escaped the fascination of a first encounter with the "city of the cities" by sea, in the classical way: "We have accessed the Golden Horn, between Pera dominated by the Tower of the Genoese and Stambul, pierced with minarets . . . and I was violently moved, because I had come to revere these things that I knew were so beautiful" (qtd. in Ronchey and Braccini 44). On the other bank, along the Anatolian coast, Alberto Manguel was waiting for me. I might have been the protagonist of an illicit love story, like the one that the French writer Pierre Loti had lived in his "Stamboul" fifty years before—the feeling of anticipation, the secret excitement were the same, at least for me. Although, if I had really wanted to feel the thrill of danger and passion that permeated the pages of Pierre Loti's semi-autobiographical novel *Aziyadé*, now it would be more likely to happen at the Russian market of Beyazit than outside the doors of an Ottoman *harem*. There, after the fall of the Soviet empire, the goods from distant Asian lands—Siberian caviar, miniated manuscripts, Uzbek fabrics, Turkoman prayer rugs, the immaculate faces of young *natashas* (by now the synonym for prostitute in Turkish)—were now back in full display.

I prepared for my meeting with Manguel with meticulous care: by reading his books, interviews, articles but also by paying attention to what I would wear, how I would arrange my hair—not to seduce him, but to meet his taste. I had a feeling that Manguel was a man of the world and an aesthete even before being a man of letters. Due to his age, I saw him as the patriarch of my quintet of authors. Having never met him, I perceived him as an erudite whose precious mind—as rare as an *incunabulum*, I would dare to say—after six itinerant decades at the service of reading had acquired an immense knowledge on the nature, history, and value of books. Because even before being a writer Manguel was—and spoke of himself as—a "reader." A reader who, to provide a proper home to the 30,000 volumes of his personal library, had gone to the point of restoring a fifteenth-century presbytery in the region of Poitou-Charentes, south of the Loire Valley, "in a village of fewer than ten houses" (he was keen to point out): "I knew that once the books found their place, I would find mine" ("A 30,000"). And who knows if the French countryside would really be the last leg of a life journey that had seen Manguel born in Argentina; raised for the first seven years in Tel Aviv, where his father was an ambassador; study in his youth in Buenos Aires and become one of the reading friends of an already blind Borges; live in London and Paris; work as an editor, journalist, and translator in Milan, Tahiti, in the British Surrey (where he founded a publishing house that, alas, was short-lived), and then in Toronto, where he acquired Canadian citizenship. As if it were the most natural thing to hop from one continent to the other, one country to the other, reading, speaking, and writing in more than one language—from the German learned from his nanny to the French studied at high school in Buenos Aires and the English cultivated around the planet.

In my fictional conversation with Manguel, when we docked at the pier and a refined white-bearded gentleman greeted me in courteous Italian, I understood that in front of me I had my polyglot writer. He had organized everything himself: my transfer by *caique* and the dinner in a small restaurant on the Anatolian coast where the Turks went to enjoy their *mezes* and fresh fish undisturbed by international tourists. Once we took our places at a finely set table, the shimmer of water being reflected on our glasses half filled with strong, aniseed flavored Yeni Rakı, Manguel explained to me, upon my invitation, what lured him to this city, where he kept coming back: "Perhaps it's the idea that if the fate of my ancestors had taken a slightly different bend I might be a Turk instead of an Argentinian." "How come?" "When he was 16 or 17, my grandfather on my mother's side left his Jewish village to the west of Moscow and came south, to the Black Sea and then to Istanbul. He did not want to enlist in the army of the Tsar, thus he preferred to change his name and flee, to make a fortune for himself in this vast bad world. Istanbul was not his final destination: his idea was to board a ship headed to Argentina, where gold was so plentiful—it was said—that it was used to pave the streets. Once in Istanbul, though, he fell in love with the city. 'Everything that a person may want is here,' he thought 'what is the point of pushing fate further?' Yet, he would do so and end his days in Buenos Aires. As you see, I could have been born here." "In one of the most transcultural places of the world," I winked, before turning my gaze to meet the scene of sails and minarets that opened in front of us. "The perfect setting for your interviews, no doubt," he agreed, opening himself in that wide, generous and profoundly human smile that more than once I had intercepted watching some of his portrait photos.

Only later on would I read what Manguel had written on Istanbul; it was a passage taken from his notebook that he would send me a few days after our interview. It was a pity it came so late, because I regretted not being able to share with him the aftertaste of those words: "I sometimes wonder how things would have turned out, who I would be, in what language and what kind of story I would now be writing if that black-eyed youth [his fateful grandfather] had decided to strike roots in that most fascinating of cities" ("On the Footsteps"). It was eight in the evening and the sun was enveloping the city skyline in a reddish-golden glow. We were in one of those fiery Istanbul sunsets that had fascinated so many foreign eyes. After a while, the quick steps and efficient maneuvers of the waiter turned us away from that contemplative moment: our *mezes* were on the way. Later on, after the supper and before they served our apple and cinnamon *çay*, Manguel encouraged me to switch on the audio recorder again and continue our interview. I skipped the questions on his biographical details, most of which I had gathered from various sources (including his autobiography, *Una vita immaginaria,* in the form of a conversation with his friend Claude Rouquet), and instead asked him about his relationship with languages, knowing that he considered not Spanish but rather English—which his mother did not speak—his mother tongue. "I was looked after by a nanny who was a German-speaking Czech; she taught me English and German and those were my languages until the age of seven; in fact, I didn't speak with my parents till that age: they spoke Spanish and French, so I got to know them when we returned to Argentina and I learned Spanish."

I kept quiet, puzzled by that intimate revelation, unable to prod him deeper, at this point, about the relationship with his mother, even more than with his mother tongue. I missed my chance and Manguel kept answering my initial question. "Even when we went back to Argentina I felt that with Spanish I was speaking and living in a language that wasn't fully mine, because it hadn't been there from the beginning. I think that there is a very early association between the experience of the world and the words we use to name it and that this is not going to happen again: afterwards, language seems to exist on another plane, a much more conscious plane. And so the quality of your first language is different, even if it's not—and I insist on this—the social language in which you live. What I mean by this is that my nanny's English was not perfect and had quite a strong German accent; but that imperfect accent to English was my first language. That is why when thoughts come unbidden they come in English, although I probably make certain mistakes in English that someone who is born and bred in England or the States would not make. Sometimes, however, the influence of the place I am in is so strong that if, for example, I am for a time in Germany I would wake up with thoughts in German, or if I am in Argentina it would be in Spanish." "What does one get, according to your experience, from knowing more than one language?" I asked. "When you speak different languages you realize that you don't think in the same way in the different languages; in other words, the same thoughts don't come to you in the different languages you know."

"Although I do not want to anthropomorphize language here," he continued, "I think that when a language is shaped and becomes defined in the course of its transformations it acquires a certain power, which enables it to name experience in a particular way. This has to do with everyday customs, cultural rituals, the place in which the language is spoken, the landscape and the characteristics of the politics and the economy of the place. The result of this is that a specific language allows you—more than that, it impels you—to focus in a certain way on a specific experience." "Are you thus suggesting that someone who was born and raised in the English language does not think in the same way than, let's say, someone whose mother tongue is Russian or Spanish?" I inquired. "Yes," he said, "because our knowledge of the use of the instrument and the use of the instrument go hand in hand: what we think—up to a large degree and more than we usually confess—is due to language itself. I've had that experience." After all, was this not the same thing that Parks told me, stretching his arms over his wooden desk, making his way through old books and manuscripts on the Florence Renaissance? "To really know another language, I don't mean simply to do it at school but to really become aware and operate in another language, inevitably relativizes language," Parks noted. "I mean, you become very aware of the extent to which your thoughts will fit into a pattern that language makes possible. You have different thoughts in English and you have different thoughts in Italian" (Dagnino and Parks). "Thus," I asked him, "you have different ways or patterns of reasoning in the two languages?" "Absolutely," Parks answered, "different languages give a different color and different nuances to the thoughts so it can be liberating, and eventually it can be imprisoning, when you realize that the liberation is just the liberation into another kind of prison but at least it's not the original prison, right? I do feel kind of privileged and in a sense proud that I have come out of the all-English thing. Not that there aren't wonderful English writers but really I wouldn't like to be locked into English literary culture" (Dagnino and Parks). As for Parks, also for Manguel the punishment of an eternal Babel in fact represented the gift of a multiplication of perspectives: "Like different readings, these interwoven tongues may illuminate our own circumstances . . . and also those of our neighbours" (Manguel, *City* 84-85).

There were so many other things I felt like asking my host that I could no longer linger on this subject. Hence, I introduced the next question, using a quote from one of his novels, *Stevenson under the Palm Trees*: "'For him [Robert Louis Stevenson] . . . nostalgia was the pain of missing places that he had never seen before' (40). Have you ever had the same hunger for foreign places, the kind of wanderlust that Bruce Chatwin talked about in *Anatomy of Restlessness*?" Manguel stretched against the backrest of his chair and started to answer: "I used to have great curiosity about foreign geographies, especially those that were connected with my literary incursions. I wanted to see the England of Dickens, the Milan of Manzoni, the Paris of Flaubert. And I was disappointed to find out that the written reality is always more interesting because it is more comprehensible. If once I had nostalgia for places I had never seen or if I was simply obliged to go to different places because of the circumstances of my life, today it is no longer the case. Now, at 63, if I could I would not leave my house. There comes a point when you feel satiated by the diversity, or by the sameness, and you want to stay in one place and brood. I think I've reached that point." I smiled, remembering how, despite his confessed need for sedentariness, it had been so hard to fit in our interview between his return from a trip to Mexico and a forthcoming departure for Southeast Asia. Where does "wanting" stop and where does "duty" start? But also, where does Manguel start and where does he finish? "If I asked you to visualize your identity," I continued, "your sense of self, what would you see? Perhaps an onion with different layers, a Rubik's cube, a patchwork, a puzzle, a stream of flowing water, a metamorphic entity, a mutant?" "None of the above," he said straight away, "because at any point in my life I would define myself in that moment, so not in a moment of change but in a moment of being a certain person and having a certain viewpoint. I suppose that at my age I might say I have an almost endless accumulation of such identities, but that at any given point I see myself in that moment, in that place. Moreover, even if I had a definite identity I would never know how to define it because as in physics the only place that you can't see is the place in which you are standing."

"Thus I am able to define myself," Manguel went on, "only through reflections, mainly literary reflections: when I sense that there is a page in a book that echoes something I feel I am, then I can say that that is part of my identity." "In *The City of Words* you tell the story of Cassandra, of how she, alone, 'must define herself and her attachments . . . all this not based on what she is told is hers but on what she chooses to identify as hers' (21). Does this process resonate also with your idea of how, more or less consciously, you are imagining your cultural identity?" I asked. "Any time I access a new cultural area my first impulse is to explore it independently. It's like a visit to the museum: I don't want to be guided, I may ask for guidance afterwards, but I want to see what is there, discover the narrative structure of the place on my terms and make my own choices. I think that this may be emblematic of my understanding of what a culture is in relation to the individuals who share that culture." "That is, in complete, assumed autonomy," I charged. "I think that a dynamic must be established in which the culture defines and the individuals redefine," Manguel replied, "and that when that dynamics stops, and the individuals simply take on what is offered officially by that culture, that culture dies. That is what happens in totalitarian regimes under fascism or communism but also under the consumer culture of capitalism: you are offered cultural points of reference that are not open for discussion." Also many tribal regimes suffer from the same authoritarian disease, I would have liked to add. But I kept quiet and just let my thoughts take me away.

Digested excerpt from my travel diaries (Harare, 29 May 1999)

> The stamps, the little bureaucrats in uniform at border posts—the symbols of postcolonial Africa. A desert of Tartars in its equatorial version, as though life were being consumed waiting for imaginary invaders, imaginary Others. In twenty days of foreign reporting I had entered and left four different countries—Tanzania, Mozambique, Malawi, Zimbabwe. I breathed a sigh of relief only when I heard that ta-tam, the sharp sound of the stamp hurled on my passport as a liberation, or as a punishment for my traveler's incontinence. Ta-tam. And another world of bare feet and misery opened up to my peregrinations. What was I looking for?

> I asked myself every time, at each checkpoint, at each difficult border, at each man in uniform—boorish and arrogant. Why didn't I stay home?—I asked myself every time—among the clean olive trees, the endearing people, the unread books, the fragrant focaccias. "This is the last time," I told myself. And, again, I found myself on the road. Thus, it ended up that all the lessons of all those years of constant travelling stockpiled one on top of the other, ready to crumble down on me when I was most vulnerable; when I was at the limit of myself and the world, with dirty hair, swollen feet in boots caked in dust, jeans soaked in sweat weighing on me like damp rugs, and a mass of children, with runny noses and flies sucking moisture from their eyes, yelling "Miss! Miss!" with their arms stretched out at me—already begging by the age of five. When I was completely worn out, the inconvenient truths came in English, and I reported them as such in my diaries. Did it hurt less, perhaps?

"It's difficult to resist the pressure of your group, your peers, the conformism radiating from the power structures," I commented, resuming the role of the interviewer in my fictional narration of my meeting with Manguel. But I might as well have kept quiet; Manguel already knew what he was getting at: "Our cultural identity exists in a paradox: in order to say who we are we have to simultaneously invent that which we are not and an area of allegiance to which we belong. These, though, are imaginary constructs that stand for material realities and can become so overpowering that they define all material realities. You were asking before what image best corresponded to my sense of identity and I spoke of defining it in each moment; but I should have added: within each moment knowing that that moment is no longer and that the minute I define my present identity that present identity belongs to the past. Obviously, a society cannot exist politically without the invention of a more constant definition of identity, and therefore allegiances are demanded on the basis of nothing but a kind of faith. There cannot be any rational argument to say 'I'm French' or 'I'm Canadian' or 'I'm Indian' beyond a bureaucratic definition." A pure and simple faith, which hung on to its Latin origins, I thought, noticing for example how the Italian language had its semantic roots of both words—allegiance (*fedeltà*) and faith (*fede*), in an ancient Latin *fides*. It might sound anachronistic, but clearly not for many people. I finished scribbling in my notebook and turned towards Manguel. "Because what you are implying with that statement," he went on, "is a recognition of political borders that are liable to change, of official histories that constantly vary, and of a population flow that constantly redefines who your fellow citizens are."

"With this in mind, then, how would one interpret the sense of belonging to a place, to a specific territory?" I asked him. "It is," he said, "something different from a sense of nationality: place is concrete. As far as regards us humans, we are in essence nomadic creatures. Nevertheless, or perhaps because of our nomadic nature, certain places become the Garden of Eden in which we want to be and from which we feel banished. For emotional and even physical reasons, we construct for certain places a specific narrative in which we insert ourselves and then those sites become our specific contexts. But that, as I said, is different from the social, political, and cultural aspects that are laid over the physical nature of a place." "Could you give an example?" I asked him, not sure I understood what he meant. "For example, I feel that where I live in now is one of those places that throughout my life I wanted to call my home. I have a very hard time imagining myself away from that house, with its garden and its library. Not because it's in France, though. Once again, if I could transport it to the Sahara or the Canadian Rockies it would be all the same to me. It's not the country in which I am and certainly not the France of Nicolas Sarkozy that attracts me, but the concrete physical specific stones and wood of that place." As Trojanow maintains, I thought: the place one feels to belong is limited to a bend in the river, a hill, a beach, a garden, a house in stones.

"I guess this attitude also affects in a peculiar way that assumed sense of allegiance which you were hinting at before," I said. "For a very long time up to my forties I felt that I didn't have a sense of allegiance to any country, partly because of that spirit of contradiction of which I spoke before. I didn't want to be forced to be attached to a country in which my mother had just happened to give birth to me: that always felt like an arranged marriage, where before you reach the age of reason you are told that this is where you belong. While, instead, I wanted to be able to make a decision by myself. But neither Argentina nor Israel nor any of the European countries in which I had lived felt as mine. Then in the early 1980s I arrived in Canada and discovered a country where certain ideas of citizenship seemed to be effectively possible. Thus I decided to become Canadian and that was a very conscious choice: I knew why I was doing it. Chesterton says somewhere that to say 'my country right or wrong' is like saying 'my mother drunk or sober.' There is no reason in that statement while instead I wanted my allegiance to be reasonable."

"And so I declared my allegiance to Canada," he continued, "but it is still a measured allegiance. That is to say, I do not swear allegiance to anything that Canada does or to anything that Canada sides in the form of its government, especially not with the current right-wing government, which is trying to undermine the open identity of Canada." "This seems to be a process more common than one would expect in these times of full blown globalization," I commented, "as if, all of the sudden, the world were afraid of this opening up, of this loss of steady and well defined identities." "If I were closer to an utopian thinking, I would say that we are witnessing a double trend or two trends that oppose themselves more than ever before. On the one hand, we are witnessing the dissolution of borders, the creation of zones of existence of societal areas undefined by political boundaries with the flow of migrations and the increase of transcultural migrations (let's think for example of the European zone or the Latin-American zone). On the other hand, we are seeing the closure of tiny societal regions that try to define themselves under the lowest possible common denominator—the Basque country within Europe, Québec within Canada, or even smaller areas than that—in order to assert some kind of imaginary identity outside those huge flows." "And here comes the real or imaginary Other," I suggested, hoping that his reasoning went in that direction. "Yes," he replied, "As I said earlier, every identity is based on the traits we see in the mirrors that are presented to us and the traits that we don't see. Through those which we don't see we build the Other.

"The Other is our negative in the photographic sense of the word, if you wish," Manguel concluded. "And it is by stressing this negative that conflicts often erupt," I said, introducing my next question: "In *City of Words* you write that 'sometimes . . . society must resort to exclusion; other times . . . inclusion may be the only way to put a stop to the conflict' (84). When you refer to the 'open identity' of Canada what precisely are you talking about?" "I'm talking about a society whose social policies enable it 'to measure . . . its own evolution' and that accepts the risk, by constantly redefining itself and finding new ways of inclusion and acceptance of perceived others, 'to be transformed out of all recognition'"(*City* 49). "From a merely theoretical point of view, then, how would you address the perceived question of Islam in Europe: as an inclusion or exclusion? Or, perhaps, we should accept the view of the writer Christos Tsiolkas, according to whom 'the tolerance of the radical artist cannot be a liberal tolerance. It is a radical, disturbing, dangerous tolerance; heretical, blasphemous, cruel . . . it also has to refute the silencing of the racist, the inhuman, the murderous and, dare I say it, even the fascistic'?" (49). "I will begin by questioning," said Manguel with a sudden irritated expression, as if annoyed by what he had just heard, "the word 'tolerance,' which I dislike profoundly. The idea of tolerance, the idea of picking up as a burden the question of the Other is of enormous arrogance because it places you in the position of he/she who can decide what is acceptable and what is not. So, first of all I do away with the idea of tolerance. It's not a question of tolerance, it never is. It's a question of redefinition." "And with this comment you have sidelined Tsiolkas and those who think like him," I said. "Let's move on to Islam . . ."

"It's impossible to look at these questions as if we could truly have a say on these changes," Manguel went on. "Could we really say: 'Well, let's decide: should we allow Islam to enter Europe or not?' We don't have that choice. Islam has entered Europe and will continue to enter Europe in a more noticeable way than before but the question as to whether we (whoever that 'we' is) should decide yes or no is a false question. Even in the case of perceiving realistically the noxiousness of this change—like when the First Australians saw the whites arrive in their land—effectively there is nothing we can do: it is happening; it has happened. The question is how to recreate society so that a new definition of itself can be built. A new wall, if you will, can be built, with other foreigners outside. There will be another other that won't be the Muslim community; it will be someone else who will always be outside. But the wall needs to be rebuilt. The absurd attempt of Pope Ratzinger to say that Europe must define itself as having Christian roots is both a historical absurdity and a political ineptitude. Why not define Europe as Greek, then—it would make much more sense." Another wall, I thought. Political reality/pragmatism and collective scenarios hinged on the constant renegotiation and redefinition of any kind of boundaries—social, geographic, cultural boundaries. There was no way out, it seemed, except in the artistic alterity, unreality, or surreal reality of individual creativity and personal resistance.

Digested excerpt fom my travel diaries (Jerusalem, 11 July 2001)

> Jerusalem, at the Wailing Wall. What was I doing there? Little agnostic creature in her mauve sheath dress, in that light that for hundreds of generations divides the truth in three monotheistic parts, like a ripe fruit. What was I doing behind those men dressed in black, moving their chest rhythmically to and fro while chanting in a gloomy repetition, and the other leaning their heads against the grieving histories of the ancient stones? What was I doing there, of all places? Contemplating the thousands of scrunched up papers squeezed between the cracks—who knows what kind of prayers, invocations, pleas they contained; in what kind of ardor, desperation, inspiration they had been conceived; in how many languages they had been jotted down. What was I doing there? Holding tight my own piece of paper, hiding a sudden anxiety behind my shaded lenses. I got closer to the wall and looked for an empty crack, which at my height was not available. I stretched up standing on the balls of my feet and pushed my piece of paper among many others between those stones that had seen all, heard all and knew all, even what I had just hoped for and could not confess to anyone, at least not until it became true. If it ever became true. The ritual had been accomplished, my "lay religiosity," as Umberto Eco would call it ("When" 20), had met the transcendence of an ancient faith, which did not belong to me, but of which I sensed the symbolic power, the invisible might. And this was enough for me. I was still in the novel of my life, without a prescribed ending, with no last words—still becoming, still waiting.

I turned to my dining companion and resumed my fictional investigation: "Would it be conceivable in our time," I asked Manguel, almost as if he were an oracle that had suddenly emerged from the waters of the Bosphorus, "to think of a universality without walls, devoid of Eurocentric stances, immune from that Western sense of ethical (and moral) superiority but able, ideally, to embrace everyone?" "What do you mean precisely?" he asked me. "I think of new forms of cosmopolitanism—or what Arjun Appadurai calls 'globalization from below'—of the possibility to strive for the common good of humanity instead of just one's tribe (be it an ethnic group, a religious community, or a whole nation)." "There is always a distinction between what is and what can be," Manguel started to explain patiently, searching for wisdom in the milky opalescence of his *rakı,* "what we imagine would be ideal to obtain and what we know perhaps we will never obtain. However, the fact that we suspect that something can never be obtained does not mean that we should not intend it. I believe that, as with any living species, there are certain basic tenets for us humans and that we have evolved those tenets in time. One of them is that we should try to preserve human life, we should try to avoid hurting others and we should try to live together in a balance between our rights and our obligations. This is despite knowing that we tend towards gratuitous violence, war mongering, greed, and rapaciousness." Manguel paused and brought the glass of *rakı* to his lips.

I waited, suspended on the thread of his reasoning. "In the same way that our cultural identity is constructed through that which we define and that which we reject, our human identity—that is our moral/ethical identity—would also be defined by what we accept and what we reject," he said, "In other words, we construct ourselves not only in the knowledge that we should not hurt another human being or another living creature but also in the knowledge that we can hurt another living creature and that we choose not to. I think that this is essential, because if we take the position of ignoring that we have that choice, we will be more easily led into the conviction that it is not a choice but a necessity and that we must wage war instead of that we can wage war. In the same way, without falling into a fairy tale communism or the fantasies of a Fourier or a Cabet, it is certain that we can share our life on earth more equitably and that is certain because those of us who have too much know we have too much, that the vast majority have too little and it would take a shift in our industrial and economic priorities to reset the balance both for human beings and for the rest of the planet." I knew we were straying from my interview, but I wanted Manguel to conclude his reasoning before steering him back to my set path: "If national industries shifted from the making of new materials to recycling"—he went on—"from chemically driven crops to naturally grown crops, from government budgets based on the arms industry to budgets devoted to education and culture, that kind of change would be possible but it would require a universally concerted effort and a couple of generations willing to wait for the change. This is not likely to happen but that doesn't mean that it's not a possibility. It's also not a probability." "This would also mean opening up to another kind of industrial culture," I said, "I wonder then, going back to the main thread of our interview, to what extent can we be open to the Other, to other cultures; and to what extent can we let ourselves be transformed by other cultures."

"Anyone transforms me up to a certain point in the sense that there is an exchange, even minimum, of ideas or impressions," he replied, "But the profound transformations that happened to me when I discovered, for instance, that there was such a thing as a Greek culture or the Middle Ages, no, I can't say that these contacts with other cultures transformed me. I lived for five years in the Pacific and I became interested in Polynesian culture and language but I don't think they transformed me. I learned things from them but they never became mine, and not because I stood, I think, in a Eurocentric culture but simply because I didn't feel an affinity with those other cultures. The fact that it simply is another culture, another important culture, another rich culture does not mean that necessarily I will take it on board and that I become more transcultural than before." Being transcultural has its boundaries too, I thought. The degree of openness is never absolute but—following Manguel's reasoning—always somehow filtered by our present self, the self of that particular moment. "I see," I continued, "Perhaps my question was simply meant to probe the existence, or the appreciation, of a certain disposition, a certain openness towards possible transformations, in the same way that the Canadian identity you have referred to earlier allows—

or at least has allowed so far—the individual to have and develop an 'open identity.'" "You can be open, of course you can feel that you are open, but that openness will vary according to the time of day (I mean, I feel far more open in the day than I feel in the evening, when I'm tired and I don't want to hear about anything) and the contingent situation (I feel more open if I am in a questioning state in a certain area and I come across something that feeds that questioning). This does not imply, however, the kind of cultural take over that seems to be suggested in your question: that happens very rarely and even when it does I'm quite wary of it. Some Canadian writers who come from cultures other than the Anglo-Saxon or the French one—say, for instance, Michael Ondaatje or Rohinton Mistry—are writers who have less assimilated European culture via Canada than brought into Canadian culture certain aspects of their own (Parsi and Sri Lankan in this case) culture. I distrust those sweeping conversions, like you suddenly convert to a new religion, like you arrive in India and become Indian."

"In other words, you are weary of those who, as the English say, 'go native.'" "Exactly," Manguel answered. "That embracing the culture you discover to me has the feel of a costume ball, where you put on the native dress and switch to the native food. I don't fully believe that. I find it much more interesting when there is a mutual feeding from one cultural standpoint to the other, for example when E. M. Forster writes about India, when Shisako Endo writes about European Christianity, when Borges writes about European culture. These are renovations for the discovered culture as much as for the discoverer. From here come the more effective, the more lasting results." "Your reaction," I said, "corroborates my thesis that there are more ways of living and interpreting a transcultural condition, which we might consider as an 'open mode' characterized by a great fluidity." "There are very meaningful examples that show to what extent you can embrace and enrich the culture while at the same time being conscious of that which has formed you up to that point," Manguel remarked, "It's the case of Joseph Conrad, who never lost his Polish accent even though he didn't write in Polish and didn't live in Poland. He was one of the greatest British writers, a quintessential contributor to and transformer of British culture of his time; still, he remained true to himself, whatever that is."

"What about Paul Bowles?" "Paul Bowles is another example in that sense. He is someone who writes from an American point of view, is interested in North African culture without pretending to be a North African. And so when he for instance discovers a talented Maghrebian storyteller, by transcribing and translating him he transforms that storyteller into the equivalent of an American writer. He doesn't abandon the tenets of the culture in which he was brought up but he opens it to the new cultures that he discovers." "As you say, he opens his culture to other cultures. He adapts to the different cultural environments he finds himself in to the point that he can no longer be related only to one culture. What about you? Would you personally feel comfortable in being defined as a transcultural author if that meant being on the border of one's culture, not belonging to just one culture or to any fixed culture?" "As I said before," Manguel replied, "as soon as you call me something I would say no, whatever that is. That can be a very unhealthy way of dealing with reactions from the outer world, but while I'm sure it has psychological reasons I've always felt uncomfortable with ready-made definitions. I believe that those definitions are always in the eyes of the beholder. So you are free as a reader of what I write to apply any label you like. One definition can be defended as much as any other, I suppose. I don't apply any labels to myself except under certain circumstances. When I've to choose a nationality then I will say I'm Canadian, when I've to choose a language in which I write, I would say I write in English. When I have to choose an allegiance it will probably depend on the place or person or object or subject that has the least allegiance, because I like to contradict." "After five interviews and five similar answers to that same question," I said sharing aloud my reflections, "I think that expressly because of this the authors that I would surreptitiously define as transcultural are, in fact, 'unclassifiable.' In the same way as I maintain that neonomads—the transient citizens of twenty-first century global mobility—cannot be constrained in a specific identikit."

I paused, to check Manguel's reaction, which did not come, as if he were waiting for more of what I had to say. So I went on: "Nonetheless, you are aware that for academic reasons sometimes it's necessary to find an umbrella term. I hope the definition of a transcultural author is sufficiently broad, open-ended, and less restrictive in its affiliation requirements than other previous categorizations." "Yes, of course I understand, and this can be useful if we want to think of certain aspects of contemporary writing," Manguel finally conceded, perhaps jaded by my persistence. "Let's take for example the case of nomadism, since you mentioned it. I have a chair in an Argentinian university and next year my subject is going to be nomadism and literature. I would like to bring in the idea of movement but through an interdisciplinary perspective: each area—sociology, economy, or physics—will contribute to the definition of the concept." And that is the point! I thought: even Manguel, in the end, had to acknowledge that, as soon as one steps out of the artistic dimension into the academic realm, one necessarily falls into the categorization trap, in search for the golden definition that can envelop the uncontainable complexity of being. I felt certain enough to ask him the last question, whose content was not dissimilar to that—intentionally and inevitably reductive—of the previous one. "I've noticed that many of the works that might be considered transcultural tend to have multiple settings, or that transcultural authors tend to radically change their settings, also from a geographical point of view, from one book to the other. Castro, for instance, set a book in Australia, one in China, one between Vienna and the New South Wales, and another one between the State of Victoria, Paris, Macao, and Queensland. Your novels are also set in different countries, to the extent that it's difficult to identify them from a national and cultural point view."

"Although in my novels there are many references to Argentina and Canada, I'd agree that, if you look at the whole of my work, there is that: it tries very hard not to remain nationalistic in any sense," Manguel confirmed with a suddenly detached tone of voice that I understood as exhaustion. Our interview was at an end. With a feeling of justifiable regret, I also understood that I had reached my goal: I had asked Manguel and the other authors all the relevant questions for my project and received all the answers I had hoped for. However, in doing so, I had forced Manguel and the other interviewees into my opportunistic, rather than opportune, academic realm and theoretical approach. Parks had been particularly sharp in this regard, boldly accusing me of searching for the impossible: "I have no problem with academic studies categorizing things and then seeking to show that each person has a particular position within it all. What I think is perverse is the invitation to have some kind of final opinion, particularly a prescriptive opinion on issues that are just vastly beyond any comprehension. Moreover, these issues are so deeply culturally related that I have just to accept right from the start, for example, that some of the writers growing up in China have a completely different vision of the world—and that's what we want—not because China is communist but because they grew up there." Parks was right, of course. But that was also what made a certain vision of art different from any other practice, including the academic one, as Kundera also remarked: "For me being a novelist was more than just working in one 'literary genre' rather than another; it was an outlook, a wisdom, a position; a position that would rule out identification with any politics, any religion, any ideology, any moral doctrine, any group; a considered, stubborn, furious nonidentification, conceived not as evasion or passivity but as resistance, defiance, rebellion" (*Testaments* 158).

The message was always the same: one cannot freeze art into a doctrine, a belief, a faith, a credo, a system of thought, nor a category: by its nature art rebels against the urge to classify and instrumentalize. We left the restaurant together and together we boarded the *caique* that would take us back to the European bank.

We were sailing now, before the wind, in no hurry. Now that the audio recorder was off, our conversation languidly flowed in dozens of directions, off track, without a given destination. Our low voices were hardly heard over the backwash of the boat. And it was to Manguel that, eventually, I revealed where I had been the previous nights while in Istanbul and where I would go again, once we parted. "Dancing at a *milonga*? Here in Istanbul? Good on you!" My secret lover was not a man but the Argentine tango, a dance that, by its own nature, tended to go beyond any geographic and cultural barrier. "It's my practice, you know," I explained, "my way to live transculture at a skin level, in the physicality of meeting bodies." The tango was like a slow breath that taught the value of connection, of communication without words, of surrendering to the Other. Everywhere I had been in the world, I had discovered that—even if only for the few minutes of a *tanda* [the sequence of three or four musical pieces usually danced with the same partner in a *milonga*]—one could have access to that dimension that existed right beyond the screen that separated one from the Other. For at least twelve minutes, everything flowed without conflicts, in a melody of notes that anybody—transcending her or his own language, culture, ethnicity, or religion—would be able to recognize and interpret.

"The culture of the embrace," Manguel murmured, looking intensely in front of him, where Istanbul shone in the night, with its millions of possible humanities. "Indeed." Technically either "open" or "closed," the tango embrace offered a way out from the slavery of ourselves, from the cloister of our egos. In an embrace it was possible to forget about our own selves and "to contemplate a beauty . . . aimed at making us forget our moods, our passions and pains, ourselves," as Kundera would say when talking of a Bach fugue (*Testaments* 74). "I'll never be able to consider the tango as something other than from Argentina or from Rio de la Plata," my companion confessed, pondering what I had been telling him. For the first time, I realized how much the years that separated us made us see things in a different light. To me tango seemed no longer—or not only—a cultural manifestation from Argentina. In the last twenty years it had changed and acquired the dimension of a wider global culture: you could dance it in the *milongas* in Osaka or Moscow, Beijing as well as Innsbruck, Auckland or Ottawa, New Delhi as well as Johannesburg. And the more people danced the tango and adapted it to their cultural and present-day contexts, the more its South American origins became blurred, further diluting a cultural purity that historically, by the way, had never belonged to it. I had no difficulty in conceiving the tango as a modern transcultural practice, even as an alternative, purely laic form of shared or collective self-knowledge, perhaps, not dissimilar to the yoga practiced by Baranay, the Zen meditation experienced by Parks, the Sufi rituals in which Trojanow had trained, the immersive reading habits described by Manguel.

Perhaps the tango might also be understood as another way—together with art or certain religious practices—"to move towards a more contemplative rather than purposeful status" (as Parks said talking of Gregory Bateson's views), being aware that indefatigably pursuing an objective inevitably limits one's perceptive abilities. The British anthropologist from whom Parks drew inspiration while writing *Dreams of Rivers and Seas* had also pointed out that a full consciousness cannot separate thought from emotionality, the mind from the body, action from reflection, speed from slowness, harmony from melody. And here was the tango, that humble but passionate conversation through improvised dance steps that allows one to experiment with the complementarity of opposites; to transcend the limitations of the self in the clairvoyance of an embrace; and—even if only for few minutes—to know the stranger, breathe and dance the Other till one gets to imagine him, her, each other. As the tango dancer and writer Kapka Kassabova (born in Bulgaria, raised in New Zealand, currently living in Edinburgh after having lived in Marseille and Berlin) noted: "I feel a stranger among them and yet I am them, with their heartbreaks, fantasies and hopes" ("Diary"). Kapka knew what she was talking about: in the last ten years she had travelled across the globe, from Berlin to Buenos Aires, from New York to Paris, in search for the perfect dance. She had recounted her odyssey in her book *Twelve Minutes of Love*, a creative nonfiction that reads like a novel.

But here I was already treading into new territory, perhaps even into a new book. So I stopped. Once we disembarked, Manguel insisted on escorting me by taxi to the venue where the *milonga* was being held but then refused to enter with me: his chaperon's role did not go beyond that threshold. Bidding our farewell, together we admired for the last time a shining Galata Tower. Pondering on what my five authors had told me in those four days and one night, I felt I appreciated even more what

Borges wrote about saying good-bye to a friend, both knowing that most probably they would never see each other again:

> But beyond any egotistical display, what clamored in my chest was the will to show my soul in its entirety to my friend. I would have wanted to strip myself of it and leave it there, palpitating. We went on talking and debating, on the brink of good-bye, until all at once, with an unsuspected strength of conviction, I understood that this personality, which we usually appraise at such an incompatibly exorbitant value, is nothing. The thought came over me that never would one full and absolute moment, containing all the others, justify my life, that all of my instants would be provisional phases, annihilators of the past turned to face the future, and that beyond the episodic, the present, the circumstantial, we were nobody. ("The Nothingness" 6)

We are but seven billion of nobodies, irreparably lost in the labyrinth of our selves and of our present. Despite all the culture and all the cultures in the world, I thought, we seem to have only one obvious solution ahead of us: to embrace the Other as being reflected in the mirror of our selves. The other nobody . . .

Chapter Five

Multiple Dimensions of the Transcultural

My study is an experiment in creative nonfiction: the interviews with the five author-characters truly happened but the way and the settings in which I chose to report them are imaginary (actually, the places which I chose for my settings exist and I have physically been there but in other circumstances). As a matter of fact, I did not interview Trojanow in the carriage restaurant of a long-distance train headed towards the Golden Horn but in a coffee house in Vienna; I did not meet Castro at the Pera Palas, the historical grand hotel where Agatha Christie used to stay when in Istanbul, but in the city center of Adelaide, in South Australia; Baranay told me about her life and her writing not in a Turkish bathhouse built by a sultan but in Melbourne; Manguel did not organize a passage by *caique* and a dinner on the Anatolian coast for me but received me in his *buen retiro* in the French countryside; finally, Parks answered my questions not in a hypothetical medieval study with a view of the Galata Tower—how much more fascinating it would have been—but in an impersonal office in a modern Milanese university. These were five real meetings which have been reinvented to have as a background setting Istanbul, the harbor city at the confluence of several worlds, religions, cultures; a double, triple city even in its name: Istanbul, Byzantium, Constantinople.

Istanbul, a modern metropolis still redolent with its rich (Greek, Roman, Byzantine, Ottoman) history, soaked in its complex present (with the tensions between Armenian, Kurdish, Turkish Anatolian communities) and at the same time driven towards a roughly European future, straddling two continents, two seas, three monotheisms coexisting in comparative harmony for centuries and dozens of sacred and profane philosophies of life. It represents a physical place made of the same imaginary substance of novels which in the past has embodied repeatedly (and one hopes it will do it again in the future) that concept of "confluence" of cultures, languages, and imaginaries that was so well accounted for by the harbor cities of antiquity. I see today's Istanbul like the mirage of an ancient Byzantium or Alexandria: a hybridized, cosmopolitan, vibrant city that for years nurtured the writing of Orhan Pamuk, who was awarded the Nobel Prize in Literature because "in the quest for the melancholic soul of his native city [he] has discovered new symbols for the clash and interlacing of cultures" (Parks, "The Nobel"). But I was also aware, as Sylvia Ronchey reminds us, that "from a city scintillating with gold and colors at the beginning of the twentieth century suddenly [Istanbul] became grey like a darkened screen, a symbol of the decadence of modernity, of the contradictions between civilizations, of that enigma that today is the meeting/clash between East and West" ("Istanbul" 24). In the same article Ronchey also writes: "Since World War II we have witnessed the consequences of the rending of that veil of tolerance, mediation between civilizations, and cosmopolitan vocation which from the Roman Empire Byzantium passed on to Islam. Without the Ottoman Empire the tensions between ethnic groups, not kept at bay by the West, have become, between the end of the twentieth century and the beginning of the twenty-first century, the biggest problem of our time" ("Istanbul" 24). Some of the tensions that simmered under the surface came into the open in the antigovernment protests of June-July 2013, just a few weeks before this work was completed. Nonetheless, Istanbul is still filled with the geopolitical karma of a Constantinople and a Byzantium which for centuries acted as a physical and metaphorical point of reference between the cultures of the East and the West. It is from this Istanbul that new possibilities might emerge as it happened in the past, when these same possibilities emerged as the product of "the interlacing and the tension between the civilizations of two continents, which here show their indissolubility, their endless interpermeation and shared history" (Ronchey and Braccini xiii).

I could not think of a more suitable and highly symbolic site for my journey across the transcultural dimension of literature than Istanbul. I conceived this journey not only as a personal but also partially as a collective exploration, through which to recount how one lives and writes when one becomes transcultural, either by necessity, fate, or choice and perseverance. That is to say, when the culture in which one is raised becomes a springboard to embrace other cultures and ends up transcending all of them. For this reason, I engaged five more or less internationally renowned writers. When I met them they did not know each other personally (not yet, at least, from what I gathered, except in the case of Manguel and Parks); they were at different ages; they were born and lived in different countries (none of them, like myself, lived in the country in which they were born); they wrote and spoke in different languages (and not necessarily in their mother tongues); only in a couple of cases had they read each other's work. Nonetheless, I had a feeling that they had something in common, both in their transnational experiences and in the transcultural sensibility which emerged from their works. In meeting them individually in deep conversation, I wanted to find out if each of them might represent, in their personal interlacing of lived experience and creative writing, some of the key elements which constitute the multifaceted prism of a transcultural identity.

Inevitably, the subjectivity, or partiality, of each point of view emerged from these meetings. Despite my labeling them as sharing a transcultural way of thinking and feeling, each of these writers is the spokesperson of a relative standpoint, of a personal stance. We cannot escape from that: as much as we can destabilize ourselves, open ourselves to the Other, mix with the Other, we are all children of our own experience and as such we develop a peculiar way of being in the world and in culture. Whether we wish it or not, we are prisoners of our conditioned perspective—as ample, deconstructed, and variegated as this might be—which we have been developing while living. Nonetheless, despite the inevitable differences and the fragmentation which emanates from the individual subjectivities, it was that "commonality" I was keen to investigate and possibly let emerge from these literary dialogues, also with the help of my personal memories and reflections, which are interspersed throughout the text. I thought of this creative nonfiction as a path of discovery which, like any adventure—of the mind, of the body, or of the spirit—I myself did not know where it would lead, or what it would leave as a legacy.

Trojanow, Castro, Baranay, and Manguel are authors who became transcultural by a trick of fate, if we consider that since their childhood their lives were marked by a transnational/(im)migrant condition. On the other hand, I became transcultural out of mere obstinacy, forcefully uprooting myself, out of my own will, as Parks did. If Istanbul/Constantinople offers itself as the ideal place for political-cultural confluences and metamorphoses, this project of creative nonfiction also offers itself, in the way it has been conceived, as another form of confluence. It involves five authors (six, including me) with different backgrounds who are made to mix and combine their ideas, recollections, reflections, and musings like waters from different streams, while chatting on a train, behind a cup of *çay*, among the hot vapor of a *hammam*, aboard a Turkish caique, in the half-light of a private study as if they had gathered in a kind of imaginary literary salon in the Bosphorus. Each chapter reveals an interview with an author, except in the case of Parks, whose sharp comments and provocative answers stud the whole work without coalescing in an interview of its own. This choice was dictated by mere stylistic reasons, in order to give the work a more dynamic slant without burdening it with the excessive reiteration of a formula. In this case, it seemed to me that by "diffusing" my fifth author in the story, in the same way he did with the main character of *Dreams of Rivers and Seas,* he might act on the other interviewees as a witty dialectic stirrer (in his novel Parks draws inspiration on the life and work of Gregory Bateson to depict Albert James, his main character; despite the fact that Albert is already dead at the beginning of the book, his presence nonetheless dominates almost at each page). The comments and observations which Parks made during our interview were thus interspersed throughout the text, either to reinforce or contrast the opinions expressed during the conversations with the other writers. The fact that his views were not held up to scrutiny in an open dialogue with the narrator, as is the case with the other authors, may give the impression that Parks was granted an excessive patina of authority—as if he were a Virgil guiding a postmodern Dante across the multiple dimensions of the transcultural—when in fact his "contrarian" role helps mostly to undermine the excessive and inevitable authority of the author-interviewer. In the spirit of a twenty-first century transcultural work, the discourse was thus kept as much as possible open-ended, multiperspectival, and unregimented.

What I wrote and discovered in my journey across the world of transcultural writing could be read in several ways: from the beginning to the end, but also the other way around from the end to the beginning or by selecting only the passages drawn from my notebooks meant as short *détours,* as fictionalized recollections of my transcultural path, and conceived in such a tight interlacing of reality and imagination, of autobiographical memory and fabrication, that I myself now have a hard time to discern the one from the other. It is explicitly because of this indissoluble intertwining between reality and fiction that in some cases I have preferred to change the names of some people, hide their identity, or confound their identity with that of other people. The interviews with the five writers, five cards in the variegated and borderless deck of cards of transcultural literariness, deal with their life experiences, cultural approaches, sense of identity, and narrative style. They attempt to reveal, through a semifictional lens, to what extent the transcultural elements which permeate their works are a mode of being, sensing, and forming an identity even before being a mode of writing. Using a first-person narrative and looking at the global contemporary literary scene, I described in an imaginary way the emergence of this new species of authors and their transcultural output.

I am well aware that under the umbrella of creative nonfiction there may be a bit of everything: diaries, memoirs, essays, monographs, critical studies, journalistic chronicles with a literary flavor, as well as a plethora of subgenres (writings on nature, cultural critique, travel reports, scientific accounts) which are categorized as such more for their content than their form. As Van Luven remarks, "all sorts of writers commit creative non-fiction . . . I [find] it perfectly logical that poets, novelists, and dramatists also [feel] a need to write non-fiction, perhaps because those three forms draw so heavily on 'real-life bones' to support their inventions" (ii).

Coming from a twenty-five-year experience in journalism, what interested me in particular was the possibility of trying out a much freer form of writing than that—necessarily regimented—within which I had lived through my profession or that—even more stringent—which scholarly writing imposes. In other words, I wanted to confront myself with a more personal voice, using the conventions of fiction also when in fact I was working with nonfictional material (on this see Roorbach, *Contemporary* 304). This would allow me to create out-and-out fictionalized characters (although in front of me I had real writers in their flesh), to adopt the dynamics, pauses, and inflections normally used in the artifice of narrative dialogues rather than inserting quotes in inverted commas, to elaborate imaginary scenes and conversations instead of simply reporting a series of statements, to emphasize a point of view instead of striving for the presumed impartiality of the reporter, to allow when necessary a direct personal involvement instead of displaying the required professional detachment, and possibly to develop although vague the semblance of a plot instead of merely recording the bare facts as they happened. I liked the idea suggested by Van Luven that by operating "on audacity and curiosity," creative nonfiction's "accumulative" and "protean" nature can be approached as "a vehicle of investigation, rumination [and] discovery" (i, ii). I am also aware that in this approach the boundaries between the researcher and the object of the research inevitably tend to blur in the same way in which for transcultural authors the borders between lived and imaginary life, real experience and fictionalized auto/biography, the self and the Other, the writer and the reader tend to blur. It is they who show us that roles, categories of thought, ways of being are increasingly less defined, more fluid and acquire a kind of *créole* transcultural identity in a never-ending process of metamorphosis and (self)transformation.

I thus tried to write each meeting in the same way that an Aboriginal artist would paint, while "singing," on her or his canvas or, in the past, would draw in the sand interpreting the physical and mental spaces of nomadic life. In other words, I tried to detect the underlying *Leitmotiv* (the "totemic essence") of each author's life and body of work and then spin it into a web of correspondences, significant connections, and symbolic meanings. Hence, the emergence of a story "in dots," as in the well-known Aboriginal dot painting: if you get too close to the work, you can only make out the single dots: only when you step away from it can you detect the overall pattern. And only once you get to see the bigger picture can you grasp the underlying connections, the links to similar perspectives. This form of distant writing and reading adapts well to the necessities of a mobile narrative in tune with those peculiarly nomadic aspects of human nature. In this form of writing/reading seen as a whole from a certain distance, the work (as well as a person's life) reveals the essence of a spiritual and aesthetic quest into our unknown where nothing is taken for granted or set and done once and for all, and where everything needs instead to be allowed to grow organically. No longer omniscient, even the narrator does not know where this will lead, since, as David Attwell noted while analyzing the notion of "narrative authority" in Coetzee's writing, "the endless story of the self will be brought to finality only at the point where it is most unaware" (11).

These explorations in contemporary transcultural writing and reading force us to face the sense of the increasing elusiveness of any boundary: not only between cultures or nation-states, but also between lived and imagined lives, the authenticity of a recollection and the dreamed up narration of one's past, the sense of biographical identity and the cultural self, truth and interpretation, writing and reading. As Rushdie reminds us, "Meaning is a shaky edifice we build out of scraps, dogmas, childhood injuries, newspaper articles, chance remarks, old films, small victories, people hated, people loved" ("Imaginary" 12). It is an exercise I attempt although in a different form and with incomparable aesthetic results towards that experimental space so aptly created by Coetzee. Having lived between South Africa, Europe, the United States, and Australia, as well as between the English, the Afrikaans, the German, and the Dutch language, Coetzee has long since sailed transcultural waters. His works seem to invite the reader to accept the fall of any barrier between genres and the loss of any clear-cut distinction between facts and fiction, living and writing, the works of the imagination and the realities of life.

It is as if each one of us, as writer or reader, were nothing but the main character of one's own narrative, lost in a constant play between reality and imagination, between the fictions that we read or write and the lives that we imagine as real, through our writing, reading, and living, in a rhapsody of proliferating selves. As Trojanow would say, "We have many transformations, but not a true story" ("Meeting"). And there is no end in this library of countless "texts," where each book in the end is a book on us—the main characters in a personal novel that changes at each reading. That is why, according to Manguel, "For the ideal reader, every book reads, to a certain degree, as an autobiography" (*A Reader* 152). Thus, from one reading to the next, not only do we rewrite ourselves but we re-make sense of the world: "I believe that we are, at the core, reading animals and that the art of reading, in its broadest sense, defines our species. We come into the world intent on finding narrative in everything: in the landscape, in the skies, in the faces of the others, and, of course, in the images and words that our species creates. We read our own lives and those of others, we read the societies we live in and those that lie beyond our borders, we read pictures and buildings, we read that which lies between the covers of a book" (Manguel, *A Reader* ix).

Postmodern thinkers keep telling us that there is no fixed identity within us which we can offer to the world outside; and that the same idea of our biographical and cultural self depends as much on our personal experiences, with the constraints and conditionings imposed by the social structures, as much as on the interpretation/look that the Other has of/on us, including the Other, the double, the mask which we harbor within ourselves. If we take these considerations seriously, then our biographical and cultural identities are like the ever-changing patterns of light on the sea surface. We are thus pressed to invent fictions of our selves (as nations do with cultures) to offer to others and to ourselves coherent and structured narratives of our lives, while in fact we are but the result of an uncontrolled and involuntary series of constant transformations, complexities, contradictions, and paradoxes. As Bakhtin and poststructuralism teach us, in telling the story of an existence, including our own story, we can no longer linger on notions of stasis or fixity, despite the fact that most of us still seem to do so. According to Bakhtin, each human being becomes "author" of oneself in one's dialogic and simultaneous interaction with the Other, that is, we author ourselves by watching at ourselves from outside, as others might see us. In this way, we become characters in the multiple novels of our lives (*The Dialogic* 28-30).

After Derrida and the legacy of poststructuralism, aiming to capture and convey any absolute truth of another person—or even of ourselves, for that matter—seems out of the question. As Kundera notes, "What do we know of one another? . . . All anyone can do is give a report on oneself . . . Anything else is a lie" (*The Book* 124). But at least we can show how even "facts" are being created, that is, through what kind of psychological and imaginary processes each one of us indulges in the creation of one's and others' cultural and biographical identities. After all, the transcultural authors here represented are at the forefront in showing, in a creative way, that there is no definitive version of one's self but only a constant process of becoming; that the boundaries of the biographical and autobiographical *persona* are being constantly destabilized by the fluctuating phases of life, memory, experience, and self-reflection. In other words, though others (including family members) may cast us in a static role to comfort themselves, "identity and cultural identity . . . [are] an unstable, hybrid and fertile work-in-progress" (Campbell 45). We have reached the diffusion of the self—of the cultural self—through our own and other people's gaze. At each reading, at each new meeting with the Other, we form a new identity, we receive a new reflection of our selves. Is not this what Coetzee insinuates by disseminating his persona in the autobiographical trilogy of *Boyhood, Youth,* and *Summertime*? His sense of becoming is filtered through the gaze of those who have had a meaningful role in his life. In this way, by assuming the multiple versions of how the others (relatives, friends, lovers, readers, colleagues, journalists, biographers, compatriots, strangers) see him, Coetzee becomes plural, dispersed, and, thus, undefinable. Authors are not dead. Authors are alive and become intangible—although inalienable from their writings—presences. As writers, they tend to inscribe themselves in their fictions, like characters inside and outside their work, in that Bakhtinian perspective that sees a fusion between author and character. And now, in this global context of increasing transnational and neo-nomadic experiences, authors are as much psychologically, socially, and culturally fragmented and deterritorialized as their characters.

My objective is to convey glimpses of each of my selected authors' identity (or multiple identities) through a patchwork whose parts have blurred contours. I do so by inserting into the various portraits quotes and ideas drawn from their books, articles, interviews (with me or others); elements of their transnational backgrounds; observations put forward by other critics and researchers; personal notes taken while reading their books. The deliberately frayed pattern which emerges from this collection and organization of voices, facts, and impressions should do justice to the authors and show that any idea of them, their lives, works, opinions, and cultural identities depends not only on their public and intimately private images but also on the personal experience and subjectivity of those who interact with them. Never try to pigeonhole or circumscribe a transcultural writer, never put bars around her changeable identity and cultural traits: this is the message which emerged loud and clear from our conversations. And this I think I have learned: that, like the characters of their fictions, these writers are open-ended agents who operate in a constant state of translation. They translate idioms, worldviews, modes of being, customs, conventions; and at each translation, while they learn a new language and discover a new perspective, a new way of thinking, eating, or seeing things, they nurture the value of confluence. Because it is right in the confluence, in that merging of waters, ebbs, and flows where it is no longer possible to trace back a single origin or envisage a single outlet, that we acquire and are granted the translational—and chameleon like—ability to move in different contexts and adapt to the dynamic quality of cultures. This ability crosses all borders and time frames, as we learn from *Baudolino*, the character born out of the transcultural imagination of Eco and thrown into the medieval

Constantinople at the time of the Fourth Crusade. Here we are again: the circle opens and closes in that Istanbul—or that ancient Alexandria—where we began. In its symbolic circular shape, everything changes, is transformed, and returns: time, waters, symbols, gods, the signs of an open mind, and the dreams of an ancient harbor city.

Part Two

Transcultural Literature in the Age of Multiple Modes of (Post)modernity

Chapter One

Global Nomadism, Multiple Modes of (Post)modernity, and a New Cultural Order

As Bauman suggests, we have entered an age of "global uncertainty" and "liquid times" in which fixed points of reference vanish, boundaries fade, cultural edges blur, and (im)migration (imposed or chosen), movement, and voluntary or involuntary displacement become a common trait for growing numbers of people. In a globalized and interconnected world of "multiple/alternative modernities" (see Eisenstadt, "Multiple"; Gaonkar) and "super-diversity" (see Vertovec), people throughout all layers of society are on the move across the planet and experience the effects of dislocation, deterritorialization, and cross-cultural fertilization. Although the numbers of international (im)migrants are still relatively limited, their transnational work patterns and migratory strategies are impacting on societies at large and are giving birth to new social, political, and lifestyle configurations and conceptualizations (see, e.g., Giddens; Papastergiadis; Tötösy de Zepetnek, Wang, and Sun). As Spivak reminds us, "whatever our view or what we do, we are made by the forces of people moving around the world" (*Death* 3). Indeed, mobility in all its variants—international, professional and leisure travel, diasporas, forced or voluntary (im)migrant labor, elite frequent flying—has become the trope of societies at the beginning of the third millennium (see Cresswell, "Imagining," *On the Move*; Greenblatt; Sturm-Trigonakis; Urry).

It is these increased and increasing migratory flows and transnational dynamics, together with the pressure of economic globalization and the fast growing development of digital communication technologies, that are inciting, as well as enabling, a whole new range of intercultural interactions, transnational social patterns, and neonomadic lifestyles. This, in turn, gives rise to a breed of deterritorialized citizens (more or less educated, more or less well-off and socially advantaged)—what I call the "neonomads" or "global nomads"—who seem to be thriving in the freedom acquired with and the opportunities generated by the contemporary forms of mobility (see Dagnino, *I nuovi*). As Aihwa Ong points out: "While mobility and flexibility have long been part of the repertoire of human behavior, under transnationality the new links between flexibility and the logics of displacement, on the one hand, and capital accumulation, on the other, have given new valence to such strategies of maneuvering and positioning. Flexibility, migration, and relocations, instead of being coerced or resisted, have become practices to strive for rather than stability" (19).

Among this breed of deterritorialized citizens are also culturally and physically mobile writers, and in particular those whom I call "transcultural writers." While moving physically and imaginatively across the globe and across different cultures, these writers find themselves less and less trapped in the traditional (im)migrant/exilic/diasporic syndrome and are more able instead to embrace the opportunities and the freedom that diversity and mobility now bestow upon them. Due to this specific status they are greatly contributing to the development of transcultural literature, which, as we shall see in more detail in chapter 2, may be considered a new member in the cluster of the literatures of mobility within the growing terrain of contemporary world literature(s) (Dagnino, "Global"; "Transcultural").

My argument here is that with the development of this global expression of multiple modernities the creative (literary) outputs connected to this most recent human condition also need to be read, studied, and analyzed through a new interpretive lens and a new vocabulary. Indeed, through a transcultural lens we may elaborate the traditional discourse of modernity by presenting its multiple "modes," steps, and transboundary interconnections in a movement towards an ever-greater complexity of views and cultural horizons. In this light, talking of "multiple modes of modernity" (my term) or, as Shmuel N. Eisenstadt suggests, of "multiple modernities," might be preferable ("Multiple"). Instead of assuming that globalization may lead to a Westernized homogenization of different cultures, Eisenstadt, Jens Riedel, and Dominic Sachsenmaier posit the emergence of a plurality of forms of modernity "shaped by distinct cultural heritages and sociopolitical conditions" (1). Although the Western project launched the premise and established the starting and turning points for the processes that gave birth to and transported humanity into the modern era, they suggest that "the best way to understand the contemporary world—indeed to explain the history of modernity—is to see it as a story of continual constitution and reconstitution of a multiplicity of cultural programs and cultural patterns of modernity" that goes beyond Western-centric models of classification, differentiation, and interpretation (Eisenstadt, Riedel, and Sachsenmaier 27).

Taking a slightly different slant, in his article, "Modernity as History," Dirlik maintains that the "efforts to reformulate modernity" and supersede its Eurocentric perspective are mainly due to the latter developments of "capitalist modernity" itself: "In its globalisation, [it] has had to interiorise cultural difference as part of its very constitution; one fundamental consequence of which has been to compromise its identification with EuroAmerican models of modernity, which provided an earlier modernisation discourse with its teleological power" (16). In any case, as Ong also remarks, it seems no longer possible "to talk about a single modernity within the West" (31). Rather, it sounds more plausible to talk about "multiple interpretations of modernity" (Eisenstadt, "Multiple" 24) which may lead to multiple developments in different political constitutions and geographical areas, away from the essentializing idea of some "master Western prototype" (Ong 31). This way of reasoning resonates with Charles Taylor's "cultural theory of modernity" and, more specifically, with his notion of "alternative modernities" (172-85). In Taylor's view the changes undergone by different societies under the impact of modernity—with their different cultural "understandings of the person, social relations, states of mind, goods and bads, virtues and vices, and the sacred and the profane"—may lead, through a process of "creative adaptation," to different outcomes, including divergence, even in the presence of a convergence of certain main factors (i.e., market-driven industrial economies, bureaucratic forms of administration, popular modes of government). What Dilip Parameshwar Gaonkar is keen to emphasize in Taylor's reasoning is that "creative adaptation" does not mean naively to be able "to freely choose whatever one likes from the offerings of modernity," discarding the bad, the ugly, or the unwelcome; rather, it suggests "the manifold ways in which a people question the present" (18). On the same wavelength, Lawrence Grossberg states that "modernity should be seen as a product of contradictory or [even] conflicting cultural processes" in which the West has lost its centrality: "The West can no longer be thought of as a dominant geographical concept structuring the non-West. Rather, it must be located, immanently within the temporality of a modernity embracing new cultural forms that have been and are still developing in what used to be the non-West and that now offer an occasion for dialectical encounter" (86, 288). In this light, modernity becomes, in all its modes, negotiations, translations, and declinations, "a commonly shared condition" (Eisenstadt, "Multiple" 57). As Venn notes while exploring the possibilities of a theoretical debate that is able to go beyond the postcolonial and the postmodern times: "To begin with, we need to disaggregate the discourse of modernity, recognizing the plural character of the lived experience of modernity. Then we could begin to repose the question of being and of transfiguration" (264). My contention is that a multimodal and transcultural way of looking at modernity is better able to capture the changes in society, critical perspectives, and artistic or literary expressions that often lead to a renegotiation of cultural values and to the acknowledgment of wider "scapes" of interdependence and interconnectedness.

In this chapter I outline the social global arena of contemporary mobility with its growing migratory flows, diasporic movements, transnational relocations, neonomadic lifestyles, and paradigms of culturally pluralist sensibilities in which and through which many authors live and write today. To a certain extent, I accept Tötösy de Zepetnek's invitation to study contextually and through a multipolar lens the processes of globalization, communication, literary production and distribution, and their effects on creative expressions and literature worldwide. I focus on a specific and extremely narrow segment of the mobile global population, that is, those creative intellectuals among the so-called "knowledge workers" (see Drucker; Toffler)—or, in Hannerz's lexicon, people with "decontextualized cultural capital"—who are privileged enough, by census, educational background, life opportunities and circumstances, or expressive abilities, to benefit from and get the most out of their transnational life patterns and imaginations (*Cultural* 246). Having said that, we are all well aware that, as Doreen Massey argues, not everyone is able to benefit equally from the mobility and intensified communication flows generated by late capitalism ("Power-Geometry"). It is also true, however, that several writers—especially the ones once considered "peripheral," emerging from the nonmetropolitan centers—have profited from the increased push towards globalization successfully operated by the publishing industry.

Why should we concentrate on the study of such a tiny portion of the worldly intellectual elite? First, because, as Couldry points out, within the context of cultural studies "more research needs to be done . . . into the cultural experiences of the old, the alienated, those who are on the margins . . . and, paradoxically, those with the highest cultural and/or economic capital" (136), and this is also one of the objectives of comparative cultural studies as framed by Tötösy de Zepetnek. Second, and perhaps more importantly, because it seems it is this tiny self-reflexive and highly knowledgeable (sensitized) segment of society that can express more radically alternative discourses to the still dominant common views which gravitate to the two main master narratives of our present, nationalism and multiculturalism, and that place the deterministic centrality of discrete cultures at their ideological core (for further analyses of nationalism, postcolonialism, and neonomadism within a literary discourse, see e.g., C. Miller; Szeman; Zabus and Nagy). On the one hand we are witnessing all over the world in an assimilationist or realist logic a renewed virulence of nationalist stances and ethnic or religious revanchisms where one culture, often celebrating the values of integrity, the perception of homogeneity and "purity," aspires to or strives to remain dominant over the others or to impose its own particularism (and this is evident in today's Europe as much as elsewhere). On the other we have the paladins of multiculturalism and the risks inherent in cultural ghettoization and extreme conflictuality. As Ulrich Beck points out: "Among the . . . paradoxes of multiculturalism is that it emphatically rejects the essentialism of national homogeneity when defending minority rights, yet itself easily falls into the trap of essentialism . . . Multiculturalist moralism shuts its eyes to the potential for violence which has long since been shown to result from giving free rein to ethnic identities" (67).

Transcultural writers seem to be tuned into a different wavelength and thus are able to capture the first still embryonic, still incoherent, still mostly unexpressed or intercepted symptoms and signals of a different emerging cultural mood/mode, what Burke calls, following Marshall Sahlins and Hannerz, "a new form of cultural order" (115) and Grossberg defines as a "conjunctural shift (or an organic crisis) in which culture itself is rearticulated and relocated" (170). In other words, these writers are developing an alternative discourse, an "oppositional critical consciousness" (Said) that is perceived by both the mainstream (let us call them the assimilationist and the multiculturalist stances) as destabilizing the perceived status quo (*Orientalism* 326; for a discussion on assimilation politics, multiculturalism, and interculturalism, especially in a European context, see Chiro and Vadura). This disruption is being felt even within a purely literary context, where to a certain extent opposing categorizations are advocated: on the one hand, mainstream national/autochtonous writers and on the other hand (im)migrant or minority ethnic writers (see Castan; Gunew and Longley; Jurgensen, *Ethnic*; Orton and Parati); *tertium non datur*: no third (possibility) is given. In both cases, cultural specificity and stressed essentialized difference (in ethnic, national, racial, religious, territorial, or linguistic terms) seem to be the epicenter of social and political organization (and control) at the level both of the nation-state and of the state of literature. As Sewell points out, "The typical cultural strategy of dominant actors and institutions is not so much to establish uniformity as it is to organize difference. They are constantly engaged in efforts not only to normalize or homogenize but also to hierarchize . . . hegemonize, or marginalize practices and populations that diverge from the sanctioned ideal. By such means, authoritative actors attempt, with varying degrees of success, to impose a certain coherence onto the field of cultural practice" (56). With this in mind, I analyze the emergence of an alternative cultural discourse at individual, literary/creative, and theoretical levels versus the two dominant ones. Paraphrasing Ong when explaining why she chose the term "transnationality" instead of globalization to capture "the horizontal and relational nature of the contemporary economic, social, and cultural processes that stream across spaces," we might as well say that transcultural, rather than the term intercultural or cross-cultural, denotes the "transversal, the transactional, the translational, and the transgressive aspects of contemporary behavior and imagination" triggered by the changed and changing dynamics of cultural production and identity building (4).

As it emerges from the interviews reported in the creative nonfiction part of my study, transcultural writers have not necessarily set their mind to diffuse an internationalist ethos. Rather, they may feel more compelled than others to express or uphold the responsibility of the intellectuals' public role and the effects of their creative production on the wide spectrum of cultural discourses: "The resistance to closure, the insistence on permanent openness, partiality, and provisionality so evident in many contemporary cultural and political projects might be seen as part of this commitment to opening multiple paths to the future so as not to foreclose it in advance . . . Such an investigation has even been called one of the most urgent ethical projects that cultural workers can undertake in our altered world" (Berry, "Nomadic" 124-23). In a world more interconnected than ever our shared responsibilities and obligations are a matter for debate.

I emphasize that assimilationism and multiculturalism, nationalism or patriotism, and local interests and affiliations are the conditions and the forms of organization of a society while transculture/ality is an individual condition which is hardly applicable, for obvious pragmatic reasons, at a collective level. Evidently, transcultural policies cannot be imposed by some government agency. Perhaps transcultural societies may only exist if they are made up of increasing numbers of transcultural individuals who are able to reproduce a transcultural mode of being. That is why transculture/ality should be understood neither as an ideology (as the term transculturalism would imply) nor as a political stance, but as a mode of identity formation, as a critical tool, and as a concept for individual (and artistic) cultural resistance to the complex power dynamics expressed on the one hand by global capitalism and on the other by nation-states in this era of increasing mobility. When identifying the estrangement or disinvestment from one's inborn culture as "one of the necessary symptoms" of a neocosmopolitan—and I would add, transcultural—sensibility, Gunew posits that "these perspectives are not majoritarian . . . but instead comprise the stammering pedagogies, the minoritarian interjections that disrupt the business as usual of certain forms of globalization" (*Post-Multiculturalism*). For all these reasons I tend to view transculture/ality as a notion that stems from and can only be fostered by a neonomadic—that is, deterritorialized but at the same time ethically responsible and culturally engaged—approach to life at large (see McLeod, "Sounding Silence"). Much in the same way as Braidotti envisions her neonomadic ethics, "Cultural identities and global capital are the key terms of the current political economy and they need to be turned into active spaces of resistance" (*Transpositions* 2).

In the following pages I define the key terms of the present study, namely, globalization, culture, and identity. I also outline the broad conceptual framework that sustains my thesis, whereby: 1) neonomadism is one and probably the most representative of the social conditions/lifestyles of global modernity, able to inspire alternative forms of critical thinking and ethical considerations based on the concepts of reciprocal autonomy or responsible codependency (Braidotti; Dagnino; D'Andrea; Deleuze and Guattari; Malherbe); 2) transculture/ality is the cultural dimension and orientation (a mode of cultural identity) and the imaginary or literary horizon that characterizes it (Epstein; Welsch); and 3) neocosmopolitanism in its different variants (vernacular, rooted, critical, situated cosmopolitanism) is one of the resulting ideological or political features (Appiah; Beck; Bhabha; Werbner, Pnina).

When talking about globalization I am not referring, or not only, to the narrow notion of neoliberal ideology of free markets, economic deregulation, and total competition, but to the more "multifaceted" concept, "involving a greater historical time depth," where globalization is seen as "a process in which people get increasingly interconnected, in a variety of ways, across national borders and between continents, and in which their awareness of the world and of distant places and regions probably also grows" (Hannerz, "Thinking" 57). This concept is closer to the one expressed by Anthony Giddens: "Globalisation can . . . be defined as the intensification of worldwide social relations which link distant localities in such a way that local happenings are shaped by events occurring many miles away and vice versa" (*The Consequences* 64). This resonates also with the notion of "transnationality," instead of generic globalization, proposed by Ong in *Flexible Citizenship*, in which she analyzes the impact of global cultural forces through the daily practices and border crossing orientations—extremely indicative of shifts in social forms linked to contemporary mobility—of Chinese transnational subjects: "Whereas globalization has been analyzed as consisting of flows of capital, information, and populations, my interest is in the cultural logics that inform and structure border crossings as well as state strategies . . . I seek to bring into the same analytical framework the economic rationalities of globalization and the cultural dynamics that shape human and political responses" (Ong 5).

Within the specific context of comparative literature, Ernst Grabovszki asserts that economic and sociopolitical globalization does not result in an impoverishing process of cultural homogenization ("the flattening or the levelling of culture"), but that on the contrary it bears witness to "an intensification of literary . . . communication and production" ("The Impact"). As Brancato points out, "Far from producing a homogenisation of culture, as was initially feared and forecast, transnationalisation, with the variety of phenomena accompanying it (migration, mobility, circulation of products, ideas, images, knowledge, etc.), is presently manifesting itself in an evident increase in cultural diversity" ("Glocality"). But even if globalizing processes may not produce a flattening or a dull emulsification of the world's cultural diversity, certainly they ask for a reconceptualization, a rerouting, a redirection of critical attention, a "reorganization and refocusing of knowledge," collective/individual imaginaries, and cultural productions (Brydon, "Cracking" 106; for a further discussion of globalization seen as an intertwined development of cultural and economic systems, see Jay; Nederveen Pieterse). We may thus interpret globalization not as a deterministic and rigidly economic process but rather, following Jean-Luc Nancy, in terms of *mondialisation*, that is, as an open-ended "world-forming" process in which our time in the world is, or should be, more concerned with the creation of meaning (enjoyment) and a sense of coexistential community, of being together, than with final destinations, closed essences, and exclusive identities (*The Creation* 1-2).

More than one scholar has been keen to emphasize the difference between the economically restrictive concept of globalization and the wider concept of *mondialisation* or, especially within the discipline of anthropological studies, transnationalization. Derrida as well preferred to use the French term *mondialisation* to distinguish it from the way globalization is interpreted within the framework of neoliberal capitalism and its "homo-hegemonizing" effects (371-76). In *Death of a Discipline* Spivak introduces the counter concept of "planetarity" as a substitute for globalization (72). Paul Gilroy in *After Empire* (xi) and Tariq Jazeel in the article "Spatializing Difference Beyond Cosmopolitanism" also adopt the concept-term "planetarity" (88). Nancy outlines the ontological distinction between globalization and *mondialisation* in his book *The Creation of the World or Globalization*. According to Nancy, the concept of *mondialisation* better captures "the horizon of a 'world' as a space of possible meaning for the whole of human relations (or as a space of possible significance)" which does not necessarily evoke the idea of an indistinct and homogenized totality (*The Creation* 28; for a further investigation on Nancy's use of the term *mondialisation* see Meurs, Note, and Aerts; the use of the concept *mondialisation* within a literary discourse is discussed, among others, by Schoene).

In the present study, I draw specifically on Hannerz's and subsequently Couldry's conceptualization of culture as a notion of "cultural flows," where culture is not seen as a stable, static, and tightly coherent unit resistant to change but as an "ongoing, adaptive, collective activity" (Hannerz, "Thinking" 65). At the global level, in their plurality of manifestations, cultures represent dynamic and polyphonic systems (or flows), ever mutable, "highly permeable" entities affected by processes of "cultural translation" and hybridization, without any specific inner or external hierarchies. As Hannerz emphasizes, "flux, mobility, recombination, and emergence have become favored themes as globalization and transnationality frequently offer the contexts for our thinking about culture" (*Flows* 2). This view of culture—and world cultures—which "listens to, rather than reduces, the complexity of culture" seems particularly suited to investigate issues connected with today's multiple cultural fluxes and interactions, mutable identities, and global cultural changes/exchanges: "Cultures are complex structures of flows whose (relatively ordered) workings have to be gradually pieced together, without assuming their coherence in advance . . . Our primary data are not so much particular meanings, which we imagine to be shared, as patterns of flow and the structural forces which shape them" (Couldry 103, 110). One of the first theorists to speak about cultural hybridization as a process of intersection and transaction able to steer away from the shallows of cultural essentialization, cultural localization, cultural segregation, and, consequently, cultural conflict was García Néstor Canclini, who in 1990 proposed this argument in his book *Culturas híbridas* (*Hybrid Cultures*). In this regard, drawing on Bakhtin, Said suggested that "all cultures are involved in one another; none is single and pure, all are hybrid, heterogeneous, extraordinarily differentiated, and unmonolithic" (*Culture* xxix). More recently, Burke, among others, has taken Said's concept of culture/cultures and further expanded it: "The analysis of our past, present and future culture or cultures that I find most convincing is the one that sees a new order coming into being . . . the crystallization of new forms, the reconfiguration of cultures, the "creolization of the world" (115).

Addressing the issue of cultures and their relation to nations and specific geographies/places, Couldry points out that Gilroy critiqued Williams (with his concept of a common "whole way of life" [*The Long* 63]) and early English cultural studies for attaching a distinctive, shared culture to a particular territory or nation (29-30, 92). In Gilroy's view, this represents a form of "cultural insiderism," "ethnic absolutism," or "crypto-nationalism" that excludes others and prompts the idea that cultural differences are strictly associated to ethnic or even racial, differences (*The Black* 2-4). Couldry remarks that "Williams's whole vision of culture . . . was anchored in a sense of purely local practice" (29), while in his study of Black music and Black Atlantic cultural politics (*The Black*) Gilroy "seeks to transcend the essentialism endemic in cultural description": "He [Gilroy] rejects the idea that cultural forms are ever 'essentially' expressive of one 'race' or tied to one place: an exclusive set of roots. He focuses instead on patterns of movement and exchange, the 'crossroads' rather than the 'centre,' sites of connection rather than boundaries. But like Hannerz, he rejects the naïve idea that cultural flow is free and unconstrained, as if our cultural investments could ever be innocent of the bitter history of conflicts about who belongs and where" (Couldry 106). It is thus clear that in a globalizing world cultures with their inner differentiations and growing complexities tend to become increasingly transcultural and deterritorialized, as Ong shows us by analyzing the culture of Chinese transnationals, in the same way that their individual members—who draw meaning from them and, concurrently, bestow meaning upon them in a dynamic interplay of interpretation and representation—increasingly tend to do. As Couldry remarks, "Wherever we look, cultural life involves adaptations (often very recent ones) of materials from elsewhere: from music, clothing, and food to images and ideas. 'Local' cultures are everywhere made up, in part, from translocal elements; local culture incorporates 'transculturality' . . . if our experiences of culture are increasingly marked by trans-border flows, then the ties of culture to place would seem to be loosened" (95). Culture and the unavoidable influence and confluential dynamics of other cultures appear to be an important element in identity building and, consequently, of creative expression, representation, and interpretation. As Hannerz argues, "The shift between 'culture' and 'cultural identity' may occur almost unnoticeably. One might indeed argue that all identities are cultural insofar as they are constructed from meaningful materials acquired through social life" ("Thinking" 63; on the notion of "cultural identity," "the socio-cultural environments in which selves are constructed," and the importance of a "past personal narrative" as a form of "reflexive and evaluative self-understanding" see Gone, Miller, Rappaport 393-95). For this reason, when I talk of identity I refer to questions of "cultural identities" (in the plural), since, as Jorge González states, "in the contemporary world . . . the complexity of systems of self-reference has increased enormously" (110).

This proliferation of selves, of mutable forms of identity, is fostered by what Gunew and some francophone scholars, especially those active at the Caribbean intersection, describe as the increasing *métissage culturel*, the "intermingling of cultures" (*Transcultural Translations*). In the same vein, Hannerz talks of the contemporary phenomena of cultural contacts, mixings, fusions, and recombinations—both at an individual and at a collective level—in terms of the "creolization" of culture (borrowing the term from sociolinguistics ["Thinking"]), while Homi K. Bhabha (*The Location*), Robert Young, and more recently Burke, among others, prefer to speak of "hybridity" (on this see also Nederveen Pieterse, "Globalization Goes"). In any case, as Gunew notes, in this interconnected world of constant and growing cultural encounters it will be increasingly hard to uphold (and cling to) any essentializing notions of cultural identity: "It is becoming progressively impossible to think in terms of cultural purity or authenticity, although currently revivified national anxieties to produce unified and 'authentic' cultures are on the rise once again . . . over the next few generations it will appear absurd to define identity in terms of one or even two cultural traditions" (*Transcultural Translations*). Jean-Loup Amselle argues that cultures, like societies, have always mixed and "that mixing is the product of entities which are already mixed, thus sending the idea of an original purity to oblivion" (qtd. in Eriksen 108). Kwame Anthony Appiah also warns against the risk of rigidly conceiving cultural identities as a product of biological or historical determinism rather than instances which show to what extent identities are impermanent and polyhedric (*In My Father's* 32-35).

We must be aware, however, that even hybridity can be interpreted as an essentializing category in identity building and group formation. David Parker and Miri

Song, for example, critique the "over-exuberant deployment"—that is, the fetishization and anesthetization—of the notion of hybridity (in this specific case in the context of race, but easily applicable also to culture) in the work of the Chicana writer Gloria Anzaldúa (9). For Parker and Song this approach can lead to an implicit, "uncomfortable" affirmation of the "inherent biological superiority of 'mixed race'" and, one might add indeed, of mixed culture: "However well-intentioned, this eulogy for mixture is problematic. It implies the intermingling of separate streams of blood and genes whose mystical alchemy orchestrates a virtuous medley of mixed cultural practices. Yet such tropes of mixing and blending are predicated on heterosexual reproduction, and an accentuated definition of ancestral loyalty which . . . is still the genealogy of identity being traced . . . these metaphors of intermixing only make sense if you hold a notion of purity constant for at least one of the generations prior to that being designated as 'mixed'" (9).

That is why, together with Trojanow and Hoskoté, when dealing with culture in relation to identity I prefer to talk in terms of "confluence" rather than of "hybridity." The watery, fluid metaphor implies a circulatory process where it is theoretically arduous to identify a single origin, a "pure" initial bloodstream or cultural source, where "becoming" is as relevant as "being," especially in this new world of porous borders: "No great river would reach the ocean without being fed by tributaries: the brooks, streams and rivulets that join its flow . . . By the time the great river has reached the ocean, the source is no more than a faint memory; the flow has been defined by a series of confluences along the way . . . Confluence is to culture what gravity is to nature. Or in other words: No confluence, no culture. When culture is alive, it alters itself through inspirations from near and far, it changes course. Culture is the eternal shape-shifter" (Trojanow and Hoskoté 4-7). This view is not dissimilar to the notion of "cultural translation" expressed by Bhabha, that is, a process in which "the 'original' is never finished or complete in itself; the 'originary' is always open to translation so that it can never be said to have a totalised prior moment of being or meaning—an essence" ("The Third" 210). In Bhabha's reasoning, this means that "cultures are only constituted in relation to that otherness internal to their own symbol-forming activity which makes them decentred structures"; this implies a form of "displacement or liminality" inherent to all cultures that "opens up the possibility of articulating *different* . . . cultural practices and priorities" (210). Further, if in transcultural terms cultures and cultural identities are by their own nature intrinsically hybrid, then, following Jan Nederveen Pieterse's reasoning, hybridity becomes a mere "tautology" (64) and often a stereotype that, by aesthetizing alterity, border zones, and fault lines instead of focusing on connections and the complex interweavings of cultures, leads to new forms of polarization, and to what Joaquín Barriendos Rodríguez calls "the museification of diversity" (328).

What emerges from these scholars' analyses and slightly different interpretations is a feeling that, despite the inherent constraints imposed by one's "habitus" (Bourdieu, *The Logic*; *Outline*) and the different patterns of consumption, individuals—and in particular those who are more deterritorialized and mobile: the neonomads—have started to acknowledge the possibility, and to experience the freedom, of building one's cultural identity in a more personal, complex, integrated—borderless—and less schematic way. This emerging condition had already been identified by Said: "New alignments made across borders, types, nations, and essences are rapidly coming into view, and it is those new alignments that now provoke and challenge the fundamentally static notion of identity that has been the core of cultural thought during the era of imperialism" (*Culture* xxviii). All this implies the shedding of traditional otherizing binaries (us/them; autochtonous/foreigner; pure/mixed; authentic/inauthentic; traditional/modern, ruler/ruled, subject/master) and tends instead to bridge—at a personal, internalized level—social and cultural distances. As Bhabha asserts, "'The people' always exist as a multiple form of identification, waiting to be created and constructed" ("The Third" 210). As David Chaney points out, we are witnessing a cultural shift in our processes of identity and group formation; that is, in our multicultural, postindustrial mass and mass-mediated societies driven by communication and entertainment we have started interpreting culture as "a self-conscious repertoire of styles that are constantly being monitored and adapted" ("From Ways" 81). Using language as a metaphor, Chaney describes contemporary culture as "a polyphony of ways of speaking" ("From Ways" 81). He is suggesting that individuals have now at hand a "proliferation of choices" to create their own "narratives of identity" that they can pick up in fast-growing "virtual cultural supermarkets" or, better, in a global cultural mass market where cultures are no longer seen as constitutive of bounded, stable communities or national identities but are being loosely used and adapted "in a multiplicity of sometimes contradictory ways" ("From Ways" 78, 81, 85-86). Simply put, we both "produce and *consume* identity and culture" (Mhiri 52) and, at the same time, we contribute to the performative "production of identity" (Pennycook, *Global* 71).

It follows that we are all able to creatively use culture and cultural themes not only to come to terms with an increasingly destabilizing world but also to determine our cultural choices as "styles." Lifestyle—meant not as a superficial and passing fashion but rather as one of the possible lifescapes of one's existence—is now a cultural status, where "the self becomes more clearly an object of cultural mapping" (Chaney, "From Ways" 83). In spite of the obvious constraints imposed by the historically and socially situated conditions, this process of "self-construction" from what is on offer out there, simultaneously both at a local and global level, echoes Beck's view: "One constructs a model of one's identity by dipping freely into the Lego set of globally available identities and building a progressively inclusive self-image. The result is the proud affirmation of a patchwork, quasi-cosmopolitan but simultaneously provincial, identity" (5). No doubt, constructing one's identity in the postpostmodern or "protoglobal" (Epstein, "The Unasked) world of cultural confluences and multiple identities implies a very complex process. Tensions, ambivalences, paradoxes invariably become part of the equation: all elements that a scholar, an intellectual, and a self-reflexive diasporic writer like Said was particularly aware of: "Identity—who we are, where we come from, what we are—is difficult to maintain in exile . . . We are the 'other,' an opposite, a flaw in the geometry of resettlement, an exodus" (*After* 16-17). What emerges is that in a more or less marked way we are progressively becoming border crossers, exiles, or neonomads by default, whether we want to or not, errant figures in the ever-changing tapestry of global mobility, mass migration, and mass electronic media/communication where, most of the time, national spaces and traditional boundaries between territories, religions, and cultures are being blurred and transcended. Forced exile or chosen neonomadism are becoming the condition of modern lives lost—or thriving—in a multiplicity of ethnoscapes, mediascapes, and technoscapes. As Appadurai suggests: "This mobile and unforeseeable relationship between mass-mediated events and migratory audiences defines the core of the link between globalization and the modern" ("How" 4).

It is obvious that the kind of imposed or deliberately provoked uprootedness experienced by all those "global souls" (Iyer) who are on the move across physical or virtual borders has radical, sometimes devastating, effects on one's sense of identity and belonging. To the questions "Who am I? Where do I belong?" there is no longer a single answer that remains the same throughout one's life. Instead, there is a variety of possible answers, just as there is a variety of modes of belonging and layers of identity: "Which answer is chosen and which identity is prioritized in a given case depends on external circumstances and on the desires and inclinations of the agent in question" (Beck and Gernsheim qtd. in Beck 26). It is as though we were now constituted by a complex agglomeration of latent selves, waiting to emerge and be expressed at the right time and in the right context. As May Joseph contends, "cultural citizenship is a nomadic and performative realm of self-invention" (357). It is exactly through the intricacies of this experimental "self-making" and "experiential engagement with modernity" that, as Appadurai remarks, new forms of factual or imaginary mobility are emerging, not only among gifted and privileged individuals but also, and more importantly, among postnational collectivities of ordinary people: "More people than ever before seem to imagine routinely the possibility that they or their children will live and work in places other than where they were born . . . They move the glacial force of the habitus into the quickened beat of improvisation for large groups of people" (*Modernity* 3, 6, 10). And it is these postnational collectivities that are fostering the kind of "world culture" announced by Hannerz: "Not a replication of uniformity but an organization of diversity, an increasing interconnectedness of varied local cultures, as well as a development of cultures without a clear anchorage in any one territory. And to this interconnected diversity people can relate in different ways" (*Transnational* 111).

According to Said and in Bill Ashcroft's and Pal Ahluwalia's interpretation of his views, we are all called upon to construct or reconstruct our own identities: "For it is the construction of identity that constitutes freedom, because human beings are what they make of themselves, even if they are subjects of repressive discourses" (Ashcroft and Ahluwalia 112). Thus, in building our own identities we all face the problem of "internalizing" (rather than demonizing) the Other, not to assimilate the Other but to establish an ongoing conversation, since identity is constructed through a constant dynamic and dialectic "interpretation and re-intepretation" of selves and others, both at individual and institutional or collective level (Said, *Orientalism* 332). The solution offered by Said, that is "the essence of liberation and emancipation," as Ashcroft and Ahluwalia explain, "is a consciousness and recognition of a universal self, which is a unification of the self and the other" (115). This overcoming of binary oppositions is not dissimilar to the one proposed by transcultural theorists and to those who reclaim from an ethical standpoint a renewed, inclusive cosmopolitan view: "We do not have a choice: our selves have always sheltered others and their views, which we have used to view and represent ourselves, and stake claims to our identities. We develop a proprietary sense of our being and place as we borrow from others and let them into our lives and thoughts. We shelter them as much as they lend us the shelter of their minds. They allow us to make up our own minds and thus come to terms with the secret of our beings. This is an intellectual and affective process of inclusion, pertaining as it does to psychology, morals, as well as aesthetics" (Moraru 143-44).

In my 1996 book, *I Nuovi Nomadi: Pionieri della mutazione, culture evolutive, nuove professioni,* I analyzed the emergence on the global scene—thanks to the possibilities of global-local interactions opened by the digital communication/information age—of increasingly mobile lifestyles and work patterns, envisaging the social figure of the "neonomad," or "global nomad": "We are talking about individuals who developed a rare transcultural aptitude, who are capable of easily swimming in the waters of ethnic, social, linguistic differences . . . great experts in sudden metamorphoses . . . mutant beings who know how to adapt to a world where, by now and forever, it will no longer be possible to track down a center, a direction, a perpetually steady point of reference" (13-14). Neonomads are postnational subjects whose mobility creates nonlinear, often unpredictable flows of movement, mobile world citizens who inhabit spaces (countries) through an alternative and alternating pattern of temporary deterritorializations and reterritorializations. In this way, they tend to feel at home in more than one country, one place, one culture. Extreme adaptability and a "flexible conceptual schema" are the key features of these "mutants" (in the sense of mutable, ever-changing beings) in a society that, as Craig Bellamy argues, "is rapidly post-industrialising, becoming more complex, 'de-massifying,' 'de-standardising,' globally networking and becoming . . . more 'abstract.'" Nietzsche wrote in 1886 with foreboding that an increasing cultural interbreeding and "independence of any *definite* milieu" would eventually foster the birth of "an essentially supra-national and nomadic type of man which . . . possesses as its typical distinction a maximum of the art and power of adaptation" (153-54). One cannot but emphasize the term used in this case: not a "superhuman" (*Übermensch*), which might have fastidious reminiscences of some kind of super race or master race, but a "supranational" individual, one who goes beyond the nation.

When referring to the status of contemporary nomads, in his book *L'Homme nomade* Jacques Attali prefers to distinguish between "hypernomads" (voluntary nomads) and "infranomads" (involuntary nomads) who can be "nomads by custom" or "nomads by constraint"—the latter term includes refugees, (im)migrant workers, homeless people, and exiles (29-30). In Attali's definition, hypernomads are a constitutionally peripatetic class of creative individuals whose discoveries and art works influence their sedentary counterparts. In addressing the issues of negative globalization and its ambivalences, Bauman makes a somewhat similar distinction when he cites the difference between "tourists," those lured by the privilege and the freedom (for profit or enjoyment) of global mobility and "vagabonds," those underprivileged individuals compelled to be constantly on the move for survival (*Globalization* 94). From an intercultural point of view, Michael Byram also makes a similar distinction between "tourists" and "sojourners" in the way these different subjects relate to different cultural and linguistic contexts. The tourist visits foreign lands with the idea of being "enriched" by encounters with other cultures and traditions "but not [being] fundamentally changed" by them. The sojourner, on the other hand, "produces effects on a society which challenge its unquestioned and unconscious beliefs, behaviours and meanings, and whose own beliefs, behaviours and meanings are in turn challenged and expected to change" (Byram 1).

What we might emphasize and reiterate here is that it is not sufficient to have lived in many countries to acquire a neonomadic penchant; it all depends on one's disposition towards a certain errant status, a certain way of interacting with other people, other cultures, other mental geographies. In this light, neonomadism, meant as a transnational, not-forced movement, may be seen as a twenty-first century form of diaspora, or the further development of more recent diasporic phenomena. As Igor Maver claims: "The concept of the diaspora has been increasingly connected with the constructed and transnational nature of identity formation, diaspora referring to the voluntary and involuntary migrations and movements past and present" ("Post-Colonial" 27). The writer Pico Iyer—born in England of Indian parents, raised between Oxford and California, accustomed to travel extensively around the globe as correspondent, now living in Japan—could be considered the perfect creative representative of this generation of literary neonomads or global souls: "I am simply a fairly typical product of a movable sensibility, living and working in a world that is itself increasingly small and increasingly mongrel. I am a multinational soul on a multinational globe on which more and more countries are as polyglot and restless as airports. Taking planes seems as natural to me as picking up the phone or going to school; I fold up my self and carry it around as if it were an overnight bag" (London and Iyer).

What I highlight here is that neonomads are somewhat different from classical "frequent flyers" (for work or for pleasure) lost in airport shopping malls under a never-ending sequence of departures and arrivals from professional "expatriates" or émigrés, who technically but also conceptually and psychologically live temporarily in a country and culture "other" than that of their upbringing or legal residence or from the fashionable and highly utilitarian "transnationals" of the Chinese trading diaspora described by Ong, whose multiple passports and multiple homes in several countries are mainly a means for capital accumulation and capital management. In this context, the category of the frequent flyers and of the transnationals includes also the fast-lane, privileged mobile lives of what Anthony Elliott and John Urry call the "globals," that is, the new global elite "reconfigured in terms of . . . the speed of mobilities" (65). Neonomads are not simply (im)migrants, who intend to reside permanently in a new country nor sojourners with a preordained and strictly time-framed mission either for professional or educational purposes (international students are usually considered sojourners). In the first book of her trilogy on the "nomadic subject" as a metaphor for contemporary subjectivity and as the prototype of the "man or woman of ideas," Braidotti makes a distinction between the polyglot nomad and the "migrant," a person who in general is the victim of economic global disruptions and tends to be more socially marked (*Nomadic* 22). The migrant "has a clear destination: s/he goes from one point in space to another for a very clear purpose . . . The nomad does not stand for homelessness, or compulsive displacement; it is rather a figuration for the kind of subject who has relinquished all idea, desire, or nostalgia for fixity" (Braidotti, *Nomadic* 22). It must be noted, however, that even migration dynamics have been radically changing in the last twenty years, as well as the idea of migrants as deracinated or displaced people. Nina Glick-Schiller, Linda Basch, and Cristina Blanc-Szanton call for a new reconceptualization and reframing of the notion of migrants and even a new definition, proposing the term "transmigrants," that is, "immigrants whose daily lives depend on multiple and constant interconnections across international borders and whose public identities are configured in relationship to more than one nation-state" (48). In the same way, in the field of literary studies the traditional notion of "migrant writers" is giving way to the emergence of a new category of mobile, postnational, transcultural writers. In the sphere of nomadic becomings and multiple belongings, even writing, both at an imaginary and critical level, acquires specific mobile characteristics. According to Braidotti: "Writing is not only a process of constant translation but also of successive adaptations to different cultural realities . . . I think that many of the things I write are cartographies, that is to say a sort of intellectual landscape gardening that gives me a horizon, a frame of reference within which I can take my bearing, move about, and set up my own theoretical tent . . . each text is like a camping site: it traces places where I have been, in the shifting landscape of my singularity" (*Nomadic* 16-17).

So, who are the neonomads? They may be envisioned as culturalists at heart who, together with the necessary cultural openness and sensibility, have time on their side—"slow" time: the one needed to get to know another culture, another view of the world, another way of doing or feeling things; knowing that the past (its recollections, echoes, and understandings) is as much important as the present to make sense of one's life trajectories and narratives. Drawing on Gilles Deleuze and Félix Guattari (*A Thousand*) as well as Braidotti (*Nomadic*), Michalinos Zembylas and Charalambos Vrasidas also describe the polyglot nomad as "someone constantly on the move, connecting with others, assuming heterogeneous identities, and celebrating plurality, in contradiction to unitary models of Western thought that exclude certain populations . . . who learns to live with the discomfort of uncertainty and multiplicity" (66). To a certain extent, neonomads are "transnational" in the way Beck interprets this category of contemporary mobile people: "The category of the transnational transcends the distinctions between aliens and nations, friends and foes, foreigners and natives. It concerns neither foreigners nor enemies, neither natives nor aliens, and simultaneously both natives and foreigners, both aliens and nationals. The category of the transnational points accordingly to the 'third term' which remains hidden in the distinction between nationals and aliens, between us and the others. In a word, even enemies are in a certain sense less threatening than transnationals, because enemies conform to the established 'us' and 'them' stereotypes" (66; on the concept of neonomadism and the emergence of a nomadic subject see D'Andrea, "Neo-Nomadism"; Zembylas, Vrasidas, and McIsaac). And it is important to point out that such nomads would not be able to experience and explore their spatial and metaphoric neonomadic condition if it were not for the development of the huge array of digital technologies of communication that is now at their full—and truly global—disposal. Their professional and existential errant status, their life in transition, and the ecumenical, sedimented transportable knowledge (digitally available anywhere at any time) they rely upon has been made possible—and, possibly, even augmented—by the internet, the wifi, and the satellite dish. As Pennycook reminds us: "To view culture and language in terms only of reflections of the economic is to miss the point that new technologies and communications are enabling immense and complex flows of people, signs, sounds, images across multiple borders in multiple directions" (*Global* 25). It is thanks to the non-nomads (the sedentary counterparts), who set up, maintain, guard, and cherish territorial—therefore rooted—technological configurations and social organizations that neonomads are allowed to exist and thrive on these terms. It is this technological empowerment that, most of all, distinguishes neonomads from the traditional nomads, the Bushmen of the Kalahari Desert, the shepherds of the Mongolian steppes, the Aboriginal people of Australia. For the first time those who favor—or feel obliged to choose—a mobile status over a sedentary one are now still able to access worldwide heritage knowledge gathered along our common path and, most importantly, to further contribute to it. Because of this, if needed, the last strong tie with the territory as a fundamental defining element of identity and communicative knowledge might be dissolved. In our contemporaneity, even the territory is being dematerialized and the nomadic book of life and knowledge is no longer contained in the unmovability of a physical environment, but in digital portability. We are thus made acutely aware of the vanishing power of the terrestrial landscape to transfer oral histories and foster a sense of belonging. As Anthony D. Smith points out, "Today's emerging global culture is tied to no place or period. It is context-less, a true melange of disparate components drawn from everywhere and nowhere, borne upon the modern chariots of the global telecommunications system" (177).

What probably remains intact of the traditional nomadic attitude—as Patrick Dillon, Phil Bayliss, Ines Stolpe, and Linda Stolpe show us while describing the Mongolian concept of education among mobile pastoralists—is the idea that the world is made of different, ever fluid, both real and abstract, physical and mental landscapes and circumstances. This implies an open-endedness in the nomadic educational process, which must be flexible, adaptive, and capable of accommodating even contrasting stances or methodologies, since "the landscape never behaves as is implied in the static representation of a map" (Dillon, Bayliss, Stolpe, and Stolpe 24). Thus, the goal of education among the Mongolian nomadic tribes "is not 'outcomes-based,' but rather to be imagined as a dynamic balance . . . It is seen as a process, not as a destination" that allows human development as a form of "enlightenment . . . through constant change" (Dillon, Bayliss, Stolpe, and Stolpe 6; on common elements and differences between traditional nomads and neonomads see Dagnino, *I nuovi*; Davidson, "No Fixed"). It is obvious that the kind of imposed or deliberately provoked uprootedness experienced by those on the move simultaneously across physical and cultural (but also virtual, symbolic, and temporal) borders has radical effects on one's sense of identity and belonging: "how to find moorings, foundations, fixed points in a broken, altered time?" asks Iyer of his and his fellow beings' neonomadic condition (34). In other words, where to find one's compass in a world where the sense of home, belonging, and even territory can now prove so elusive? Somehow, it seems that the self is increasingly assuming a rhizomatic nature, without any apparent center or inherent essence, similar to the nomadic "model for culture" visualized by Deleuze and Guattari (*A Thousand*).

On the neonomadic frontier belonging acquires a rhizomatic, decentralized nature: you belong not to a single, terrestrial native root (the one which neatly traces where you come from), but to your emotional and imaginary network of intricately interwoven aerial ramifications and mental cartographies (the ones that link you to lost, living, and digital landscapes, human connections, friends, families, scents, tastes, memories): imaginary roots for "imagined communities" (Anderson). It is indicative of a certain neonomadic attitude the way Appadurai dedicated his book *Modernity at Large*: "For my son Alok, my home in the world." "Home" is now your family, your friends, your close acquaintances, your colleagues, the people with whom you share a passion for certain professional endeavors, hobbies, interests, and activities. Terrestrial, physical roots of belonging are now replaced by ethereal, emotional human bonds, in a system not of hierarchical dependencies but rather of codependencies and mutual ethical relations (see Moraru). Appadurai's dedication synthesizes what can be envisioned as one of the possible antidotes to the "neonomad syndrome" caused by the contemporary "Faustian pact"—unlimited freedom of movement in exchange for ongoing destabilization, in a constant process of disorientation and reorientation. The inner balancing, *la centratura interiore*, would then be anchored not to a place or places, but to people, persons connected to one's family circle, interests, or spheres of influence/expertise (Dagnino, *I nuovi* 122-24). Human relations and interactions become the only possible "home," the only "stable"—although themselves prone to shifting—points of reference a protoglobal neonomadic human may aspire to. It is true that people have always had strong incentives in finding out where they belong, where their roots are, and have the desire for rootedness, that is, for points of orientation and a sense of guidance: "the security of an identity" cannot just simply be ignored or wiped out (Bartoloni, *On the Cultures* 86). However, the dominant model of the *identité-racine*, as Glissant posited, can be challenged by acknowledging the rhizomatic and relational nature of identity (*The Poetics*). From this perspective, identity is no longer conceived as a totalitarian, unique rootstock, but as a network of nonhierarchical, interdependent plurarilities and relations that does not deny the irreducible difference of the Other: "We will change nothing in the situation of the peoples of the world unless we change this imaginary [*cet imaginaire*], unless we change the idea that identity must be a single root, fixed and intolerant" (Glissant qtd. in Zalloua 14).

Accordingly, global nomads have developed their own peculiar, even "augmented," sense of belonging through multiple "imagined" allegiances: not to nations, but to constellations of people, to chosen peers. They teach us—together with "nomadic" critical theorists such as Deleuze and Guattari, Braidotti, Zembylas and Vrasidas—that it is possible to overcome the menace or risk of the loss of identity prompted by a destabilizing, liquefied world of global mobility by adopting a new method of rhizomatic and relational identity formation, one in which we can have added identities, added souls, and multiple allegiances. "As an intellectual style," as Braidotti maintains, "nomadism consists not so much in being homeless, as in being capable of recreating your home everywhere" (*Nomadic* 16). In her second book, *Metamorphoses*, Braidotti deals with the ambivalent cultural representations inherent in the binary distinctions between Self and Other, European and foreign, and human and nonhuman, and in her third volume of the trilogy, *Transpositions,* Braidotti promotes a sustainable nomadic ethics (an "ethics of becoming") attuned to the socioeconomic complexities and the self-constituting, mutating identities of our times, away from the postmodernist risk of relativism, with its "nihilistic defeatism," as well as from the conservative master narratives of liberal individualism.

In the age of global mobility, neonomadism thus represents a deterritorialized lived experience and social condition that in its turn generates not only flexible decentered identities with their specific cultural—transcultural—attitudes and sensibilities, but the premise for alternative critical styles of thinking (Braidotti, *Nomadic*) and ethical meditations based on the concepts of "reciprocal autonomy" (Malherbe). A growing number of those scholars and intellectuals wandering on the global map from one international research center to another like most of the other mobile contemporary knowledge workers seem to fit into the neonomadic lifestyle pattern and attitude. As Gunew suggests in her conversation with Yiu-nam Leung: "I think that increasingly you have the phenomenon of academic intellectuals who don't necessarily call one particular context or national place home. In fact what they are doing is "queering" what we think of as "nation" or home, homeland, mother tongue. All those categories are being questioned by people like that, who function across different kinds of global metropolitan centers" (148). Welsch acknowledges that these intellectuals' lifestyles around the globe are becoming increasingly transient and dynamic and that, more importantly, this is also happening at the grass roots level, not just to some idealized "superhuman" or "superscholar": "The way of life for an economist, an academic or a journalist is no longer German or French, but rather European or global in tone. The new forms of entanglement are a consequence of migratory processes, as well as of worldwide material and immaterial communications systems and economic interdependencies and dependencies . . . What once may have applied only to outstanding persons like Montaigne, Novalis, Whitman, Rimbaud or Nietzsche, seems to be becoming the structure of almost everybody today" ("Transculturality" 198-99).

Recent theorizations of this "neonomadic turn" in the age of global mobility already show several ramifications and adaptations in its critical deployment. As Elspeth Probyn remarks, "The image of the nomad is one response to the critical issue of how to find an adequate symbolic language to describe fractured plural identities in migration and a fractured social world, a messy and disordered geography of plates, continents, or fractal zones slipping, sliding, and skidding into, under, and over one another" (qtd. in Berry and Epstein 125). Deleuze and Guattari anticipated this emerging critical sensibility in their *Anti-Oedipus* in which they pioneered a neonomadic critical discourse and envisioned, as Steven Best and Douglas Kellner point out, "a new . . . mode of existence where individuals overcome repressive modern forms of identity and stasis to become desiring nomads in a constant process of becoming and transformation" (77). Inspired by Deleuze's and Guattari's thought, Braidotti developed her own conceptualization of the "nomadic subject"—not only as a metaphor for contemporary subjectivity but also as a critical and ethical stance: "the kind of critical consciousness that resists settling into socially coded modes of thought and behaviour" (*Nomadic* 5). Braidotti is careful to distinguish her figuration of the nomad from the classical view of the exile or (im)migrant: in terms of her/his displacement, the contemporary nomad finds a position of border crossing with "movable foundations" that cannot be confounded with the often dramatic states of political exiles or refugees, forced out of their countries due to wars, upheavals, or censorship, and thus "too serious to be metaphorized into a new ideal" (*Nomadic* 21-23). Even more importantly, in Braidotti's theorization of contemporary nomadism the constant state of in-process or becoming can only be experienced by the individual if it is grounded in deliberate agency as much as in lived experience (*Nomadic* 5-6). This means that the neonomadic existential condition typical of the kind of subject whose lifestyle is "based on the permanence of temporary arrangements," "in transit and yet sufficiently anchored to a historical position to accept responsibility," needs to be fully, physically and emotionally, lived to be able to become a "form of political resistance to hegemonic and exclusionary views of subjectivity" (Braidotti, *Nomadic* 10-11, 23; and see Vattimo who also developed the concept of nomadic thinking).

When seeking a synthesis for his theory of "reciprocal autonomy" (*autonomie réciproque*)—or what might alternatively be called responsible codependency—Jean-François Malherbe refers metaphorically and idealistically to the contemporary, revised figure of the *nomade polyglotte* as being most representative of a contemporary ethic (30) and describes the polyglot nomad as "the figure *par excellence* of ethics in postmodernity . . . a traveler who, each time, benefits from the gift of hospitality and in return practices hospitality" (10-11). As such, this subject is sensitized to the values of reciprocity and communion. In Malherbe's view, the polyglot nomad is someone who, by knowing more than one language and more than one culture or worldview, is able to relativize her/his own native culture: "Having access to other language-games, he will realize that his mother tongue is nothing but a staging of reality among others [and] he will understand—as if 'from the outside'—why this staging affects him so radically and why it remains for him the only 'original' staging" (206). In so doing, the polyglot nomad develops the required intellectual flexibility and sensibility to feel at ease in a plurality of social and cultural contexts: "To live a culture is to feel 'at home' in a particular social space. The nomad has not got a home or, better, he feels at home in several houses. He can easily slip into a plurality of 'forms of life'" (Malherbe 172). In Malherbe's view this way of being and interacting with others fosters an increased sense of participating and shared autonomy: "In a multicultural context, autonomy means being able to feel at home even outside one's native universe . . . To transform into a synergy what at first was a collision, that is the mode of life of the polyglot nomad, a mode of life through which he increases his autonomy by cultivating the autonomy of his fellow human beings" (173-82). Dialogue in "reciprocal autonomy" is thus the ethical path in the meeting of cultures that ultimately, ideally, would lead to a cosmopolitan outlook, as Appiah also seems to suggest by stressing the role of conversation as a literal and metaphorical "engagement with the experience and the ideas of others," provided it is cleansed of any totalizing or relativizing factors: "Conversation doesn't have to lead to consensus about anything, especially not values; it is enough that it helps people get used to one another" (*Cosmopolitanism* 85). This view leads us to think that people entering a "multidialogue of equal partners" need to shed any preconceived opinion of their values' and ideas' superiority and, at the same time, they need to shun the temptation to believe that any expression of difference is "equally valuable and worthy of choice" and that it "deserves to survive and flourish, simply on account of its difference" (Bauman, *Culture* 60-61). What Bauman is suggesting is that once the principle of mutual respect is established we do not necessarily need to endorse all different views and practices, but are allowed to judge between them. The possible negotiation of different worlds of meaning, instead of the assumption of "an essentialist character of difference," starts from here (Bauman, *Culture* 95).

But what happens when there are social realities in which even the dialogic proposition is being refused, when the cross-interaction is being shunned? When individuals or whole collectivities prefer to "put up the shutters"? According to Malherbe, even in this case one should seek dialogue at any costs, having in mind that there cannot be any dialogue where the following three main pragmatic conditions and fundamental formal principles are not respected: 1) allowing one's interlocutor the freedom to speak, 2) not manipulating the interlocutor, and 3) not lying to the interlocutor (20-30). It is through these values—specific, but not exclusive—to an ethically neonomadic mindset that an act of cultural resistance is made possible, as Ong also suggests within the disciplinary field of contemporary anthropology: "Surely, in an age when the state and capital are directly engaged in the production and destruction of cultural values, we should cultivate a kind of nomadic thinking that allows us to stand outside a given modernity, and to retain a radical skepticism toward the cultural logics involved in making and remaking our worlds" (244). And it is within this emerging social, theoretical, ethical, and political context that transcultural authors/artists and literary/arts critics are called upon to assume a critical neonomadic stance: "Within the nomadic critical aesthetics . . . the critic is redefined as a mobile, flexible subject who follows the flows of the contemporary world . . . The critic as nomad practices hybrid methodologies and engages in trandisciplinary borrowings designed not simply or even primarily to produce answers but rather to provoke previously unforeseen possibilities" (Berry, "Nomadic" 125-29). Indeed, as Berry remarks, a number of scholars and critics have started to employ transcultural nomadic techniques and tropes more attuned to the age of mobility, and these are conceived as: "flexible investigative strategies, a mobile infinity of tactics" that are "contaminated, transgressive, multi-directional, transitive . . . new conjunctive logics capable of thinking the relations between local, regional, national, and international frames of reference and experience" ("Nomadic" 124).

We are living in an increasingly interconnected world where nations tend to loosen their grip on individual and collective identities. Removing thinking and acting from the nation-state, as globalizing forces, transnational patterns, and neonomadic lifestyles enhance their corresponding literary/aesthetic expressions and theoretical/ethical approaches, prompts subjects to remove the nation from the self. As Beck points out, we live "in a world that is becoming increasingly transnational and involves plural attachments that transcend the boundaries of countries and nationality" (26). This kind of physical as well as psychological transpatriation process would lead, eventually, to a renewed interest in cosmopolitanism where now the main focus is on a life experienced and lived both at a global and local level. Indeed, it seems possible to develop a cosmopolitan perspective, a "third eye" in Jennie Germann Molz's terms, "derived through mobility, detachment and multiplicity" (517) that, as Gunew emphasizes, despite "being intensely local and individualized . . . cannot be contained by clichés of identity" (*Post-Multiculturalism*). What counts even more, as Timothy Phillips and Philip Smith remark, is that now "cosmopolitanism is not simply a component of elite life, confined to what used to be called the "jet set," but something fairly mundane which can be traced throughout the social spectrum" (393).

It must be acknowledged, however, that the term "cosmopolitan" is conceptually slippery, highly charged, and over time has acquired a political connotation to the extent that Pheng Cheah and Bruce Robbins prefer to speak of it in terms of "cosmopolitics." Cosmopolitanism as a political ideology that stretches historically from Kant to Habermas is contested: the seemingly covert "neo-imperialist" ideology of capitalist globalization (Brennan, *At Home*) and a "utopian over-idealization of the cosmopolitan virtues of Northern states" (Cheah 494) for some; the resurgence of Western universalist attitudes for others (Calhoun); or the expression of an elitist, postmodern existence for still others (Werbner, "Global"). In this regard, Jonathan Friedman writes that "it is a language of distinction and distantiation from the local which is why it often celebrates the city or even the airport. And while intellectuals may celebrate border-crossing, the lumpenproletariat real border-crossers live in constant fear of the border and express a very different view of the matter" (254). The fact that, despite having been criticized for or accused of representing renewed and elitist forms of Eurocentric/Westernized humanistic universalism and internationalism, new cosmopolitan attitudes triggered by mobility and globalization are alive and kicking has been made manifest by a number of recent studies whose authors attempt to tackle this controversial concept (see, in particular, Braidotti, Hanafin, and Blaagaard, *After Cosmopolitanism*).

In the last decade scholars resorted to a plethora of neologisms to distinguish their conceptualizations—namely, the plurality of "neocosmopolitan" visions—from the historical view of a cosmopolitanism central to the philosophy of the Enlightenment and therefore tainted by its perceived connivance with imperial, colonial, and totalizing logics (see, e.g., Moraru 144). I do not engage here with the theoretical features and the discrepant, privileged, and unprivileged/subaltern practices which distinguish "realistic cosmopolitanism" (Beck) from "vernacular cosmopolitanism" (Bhabha), "critical cosmopolitanism" (Rabinow) from "cosmopolitan ethnicitiy" (Werbner, Richard), "rooted cosmopolitanism" (Appiah) from "micro-cosmopolitanism" (Cronin), "visceral cosmopolitanism" (Nava) from "vulgar" or "demotic" cosmopolitanism" (Gilroy). Suffice it to say that all these apparent oxymorons, as Pnina Werbner calls them, are attempts not to forget, but to acknowledge the inescapable importance of difference, historical trajectories, particularity, locality, and local communities. Local communities are meant, as Craig Calhoun reminds us, as "the solidarities that organize most people's sense of identity and location in the world" (893). In the introduction to the collection of essays dedicated to the arts and popular culture of Asian societies, Edwin Jurriëns and Jeroen de Kloet are mindful of Sun Yat-Sen's view that nationalism is the basis of cosmopolitanism; they thus use the ultra-oxymoronic concept-word "cosmopatriotism" to define the oscillations between regionalism and nationalism, globalism and residual particularism, or patriotic belonging and cosmopolitanism experienced by many artists and intellectuals in Asian societies (9). The fact is that this neocosmopolitan approach does not renounce nurturing, at the same time, "vernacular ethnic rootedness" and "a universalist civic consciousness" (Werbner, "Vernacular" 497)—in short, what Appiah calls "universality plus difference" (*Cosmopolitanism* 151). As Kate McGowan explains, talking about Derrida's concept of *différence*, "the particular will always play within the universal and the universal within the particular, since the possibility and impossibility of each are dependent upon the other" (73). On their part, Sheldon Pollock, Bhabha, Carol A. Breckenridge, and Dipesh Chakrabarty prefer to define this kind of contemporary cosmopolitanism as a "minoritarian modernity," meant "as a source for contemporary cosmopolitical thinking": "Where once we attempted to teach difference by emphasizing areal locality and specificity, today we try to struggle free from the self-fulfilling dialectic of the general and the particular. Instead we attempt to provincialize Europe and we seek cosmopolitical genealogies from the non-Christian Sanskrit world. In each of these cases we are involved, at the same time, in a vernacularization of a great tradition and the amplification of a *pétit recit*" (6). Thus it seems possible to engage in a theoretical debate in which, as Couze Venn envisions, "fundamental issues of epistemology and ontology . . . have a universal bearing, yet avoi[d] the Eurocentrism of the old humanisms" (264). In this way, in poststructuralist terms, the binary universal/particular may be overcome.

In any case, one cannot fail to notice that the contested concept of cosmopolitanism is nonetheless able to trigger, more than ever, the ethical and political responses of growing numbers of individuals. These responses, or cosmopolitan outlooks, are stronger on the neonomadic frontier, where lived cultures are experienced on a daily basis. It is on the neonomadic frontier that people are able or compelled to deploy the greater number of those "cosmopolitan practices"—dealing with strangers, speaking other languages, watching foreign movies, keeping up with global news, and experiencing different lifestyles, religious practices, foods, customs, and art forms—to which neonomads are particularly accustomed (see Phillips and Smith). As Beck and Edgar Grande state, "The cosmopolitan principle heightens awareness of the fact that the apparently sharp ethnic boundaries and territorial bonds are becoming blurred and intermingling at both the national and the transnational levels . . . Hence cosmopolitanism calls for new concepts of integration and identity that enable and affirm coexistence across borders, without requiring that distinctiveness and difference be sacrificed on the altar of supposed (national) equality" (14). Although infused with a high degree of utopianism, neocosmopolitanism is an aim, an intellectual "adventure and an ideal"—consistent with one's neonomadic practices, transcultural orientations, and civic/ethical responsibilities—which feels good to aspire to (Appiah, *Cosmopolitanism* xx). We must not forget, nonetheless, that what may seem a solution is nothing but a challenge (Appiah, *Cosmopolitanism* xv). It is apparent that the "imagined" cosmopolitanism presented by "globalized media cultures and media talk" does not so easily or automatically translate into cosmopolitanism "as lived experience" (Kim 280). In her study on transnational Asian women, Youna Kim points out how, especially when confronted with unequal power relations and with "a world of different visions, hierarchical norms, and values," diasporic and transnational subjects may tend to find refuge instead in the comforting and safe embrace of national and ethno-cultural identity (288).

In sum, transculture/ality is the individual cultural identity mode and imaginary horizon which, together with a neonomadic lifestyle and critical/ethical stance, may lead to a neocosmopolitan political outlook. Transpatriation, that is, the physical deterritorialization and critical distancing from the nation and from one's native culture, is the first stage in this process of becoming transcultural. Transnationality and the concurrent transpatriation process are the first steps towards neonomadic life patterns that, while acknowledging the stabilizing role of nation-states, tend to transcend the rigidity of fixed state boundaries. As Beck explains, "Transnationality signifies forms of life and practice that replace the national either/or with a conational both/and. Conational (hence non-national) forms of life, thought, and practice which do not respect the boundaries between states are transnational . . . although the national and transnational ordering paradigms appear contradictory, they also complement and combine with each other in a variety of ways. Behind the façade of enduring nationality, processes of transnationalization are everywhere taking place" (62-64). Finally, I suggest that this ideal neocosmopolitanism would be better pursued if we accepted the notion that individuals are confluential points through which cultures dynamically flow and meet. This is how Trojanow and Hoskoté describe their "archetypal image of confluence" and propose their view of a culturally confluential (or transcultural, according to the terms of this study) type of individual: "It is the place where the river, the sum of numerous tributaries, meets the ocean.

In our turbulent times, cosmopolitanism and cultural diversity are necessary conditions of existence—of being with others, of meeting the Other. Flowing with confluence, the individual realises gradually that the Other is not an enemy, not a stranger, not an alternative, and at times not even an Other, but just a mirror of the various possible faces, the multiple understandings of human existence, the varied definitions of belonging that can be arrived at. We must look into this mirror, not to lose ourselves in confusion, but to see ourselves and our options with greater clarity" (*Confluences* 18). Emerging states of mind induced by transnational lifestyles, neonomadic attitudes, and transpatriation processes affect societies at large as well as individual transcultural, translingual creative writers such as those examined in this study. These states of mind are induced both by physical, geographic dislocations (which I call transpatriations) and by new cultural attitudes prompted by, and more apt to face the challenges of, the twenty-first century global patterns of mobility. At the forefront of this change of paradigm are those artists and writers who experienced the effects of transnational patterns/neonomadic lifestyles and who in their texts capture and express an emerging mode and outlook of transcultural identity—that is, transculture/ality—whose conceptualization is addressed in the following chapter.

Chapter Two

Transculture, Transculturality, and Transculturalism in the Twenty-First Century

As I argue in the previous chapter, there are important questions raised by the contemporary state of culture and society, and one in particular is that in a rapidly globalizing world cultures, as well as societies and identities, tend to be more fluid and "less irreducibly different," less internally homogeneous, less coherent or self-contained, and less territorially fixed than was expected or thought of them in the past (Schulze-Engler, "Theoretical" 27). They may appear more like loosely bound or confluent streams of meanings and practices than monolithic blocks, or mutually exclusive absolutes; especially at the present time, when cosmopolitan dispositions and pluralistic sensibilities—fostered by (im)migrant, transnational, or neonomadic experiences and modes of being in the world—become ever more relevant.

Appadurai suggests that we look at today's cultural forms as irregular, boundary-less and without any clear structure: "These cultural forms, which we should strive to represent as fully fractal, are also overlapping in ways that have been discussed . . . in biology (in the language of polythetic classifications). Thus we need to combine a fractal metaphor for the shape of cultures (in the plural) with a polythetic account of their overlaps and resemblances. Without this latter step, we shall remain mired in comparative work that relies on the clear separation of the entities to be compared" (*Modernity* 46). Said comes to a similar conclusion stating that "No one can deny the persisting continuities of long traditions, sustained habitations, national languages, and cultural geographies, but there seems to be no reason except fear and prejudice to keep insisting on their separation and distinctiveness, as if that was all human life was about" (*Culture* 408). What has been missing thus far, as Donald Cuccioletta points out, is a "cultural concept of the world" that could match its other conceptualizations in the realms of economy (global capitalism), politics (neo-cosmopolitanism) and socioanthropology (neonomadism/transnationalism) ("Multiculturalism" 9). The development of a transcultural model of analysis and debate, where cultures are read in their organic movements and mutual interactions against the backdrop of contemporary socioeconomic phenomena, creates an opportunity to fill that gap. For this reason, growing numbers of scholars active in the humanities and social sciences study the creative, cultural productions of the twenty-first century global scenario through this newly acquired transcultural lens, "a perspective in which all cultures look decentered in relation to all other cultures, including one's own" (Berry and Epstein 312). In this chapter, I outline a brief historical trajectory of transculture/ality and explain the conceptual differences among the several terms: transculturation, transculturality, transculture, and transculturalism, which are often used alternatively or simultaneously.

Fernando Ortiz first devised the concept of "transculturation" in his 1940 book *Contrapunteo cubano del tabaco y el azúcar*, a historical and cultural examination of Cuban society through the "playful counterpoint" between the two main products of the island, tobacco and sugar (Coronil, "Transcultural" 139). Ortiz developed an understanding of cultural exchange as a complex, often conflictive and contradictive, but mutually transforming form of interaction, even in the case of cultures with unequal negotiating powers. It was through a complex web of "intermeshed transculturations"—namely, processes of combination and recombination of cultural practices, meanings, and influences—that the cultural and racial *méstizaje* of Cuba and, more extensively, of the Americas acquired its distinctive identity traits: "The concept of transculturation is fundamental . . . for an understanding of the history of Cuba, and, for analogous reasons, of that of America in general" (98-103). In proposing his new concept, Ortiz tried to overcome the limits he saw in the existing interpretation of the notion of acculturation: the passive and often unilateral assimilation of a culture or the plain substitution of one culture for another. Instead, in his view, even during processes of "deculturation" (the mutilation or loss of a previous culture) the influences, although uneven, which come to affect both cultures (major and minor, dominant and subaltern) are able to create "new cultural phenomena, which could be called neoculturation" (Ortiz 102-03). Acknowledging his debt to the thought of Bronisław Malinowski, Ortiz concluded his discussion on transculturation by stating that "in the end . . . the result of every union of cultures is similar to that of the reproductive process between individuals: the offspring always has something of both parents but is always different from each of them" (103). In the 1970s, Ángel Rama was among the first to apply Ortiz's concept of transculturation to a literary context for the analysis of texts by Latin American writers, showing the dialectic play of local and imported/imposed dominant cultures (on this see the historical overview by Goulart Almeida).

Over time, some Latin American scholars criticized Ortiz from a postcolonial perspective for not fully acknowledging the colonial dimension and for speaking from a nationalist stance. For example, Walter D. Mignolo puts forward his critique but also his expansion of Ortiz's notion of transculturation in his book *Local Histories/Global Designs*, a "macronarrative" on the "coloniality of power" that relates Western hegemony to the unequal production of knowledge (see also Coronil, "Introduction," "Transcultural"). To counterpose the monolingualism and monoculturalism of "Occidentalism," Mignolo develops a transcultural plurilogical and plurilingual (or at least bilingual) reasoning in which "border thinking," or "bilanguaging," becomes "a way of life between languages: a dialogical, ethic, aesthetic, and political process of social transformation" (264-65). This form of anti-Occidentalism or "postcolonial theorizing," in Mignolo's view, is able to decolonize dominant intellectual thought/knowledge—that is, to disrupt dichotomous concepts by "thinking from dichotomous concepts" (85). Pratt also applies Ortiz's initial concept of transculturation through a postcolonial lens. In her study of travel writing, *Imperial Eyes,* she sees transculturation as "a phenomenon of the contact zone[s]," "social spaces where disparate cultures meet . . . often in highly asymmetrical relations of domination and subordination"; through this lens she examines how the modes of representation from the metropolis are absorbed and then creatively transformed and reshaped by the peripheries (4-6).

Seen from this perspective, transculturation is mainly (if not only) understood as a process of cultural transmutations marked by asymmetrical and unequal relations of power. For this reason, more recently other scholars have noted the limits of Pratt's interpretation of transculturation "solely in terms of the ways that marginalised peoples adopt and adapt the dominant culture" (Dickens). Anne Holden Rønning also points out that Pratt's reasoning is inscribed within a too restrictive and dichotomous paradigm of colonizer versus colonized cultures: "I agree with Pratt that in these 'contact zones' cultures meet but not necessarily in relationships which are binary based, since the very core of transculturation is the ability to move freely from one cultural stance to another and back again" (3). Gunew sums up the different uses and interpretations of the notion of transculturation and the debates regarding cultural hybridization, creolization, and *métissage* which are taking place—often through the Caribbean intersection—in the anglophone North American, Hispanic/Lusitanian, and francophone critical traditions. In particular, Gunew acknowledges the validity of the concept of transculturation in proposing a vision of "cultures and identities [as] heterogeneous rather than homogeneous" through processes that "disrupt[s] national as well as disciplinary borders" (Gunew, *Transcultural Translations*; for a historical analysis of the concept of transculturation and its further developments, see also Hoerder). The specific developments in the transcultural paradigm (namely, Welsch's concept of "transculturality" and Epstein's notion of "transculture") expand its range of action and analysis by transcending the binaries of dominant versus subordinate, mainstream versus minoritarian/marginalized, and colonizer versus colonized cultures overemphasized by the interpretations of transculturation proposed within a postcolonial paradigm.

Almost fifty years after Ortiz's work and around the same time that Mignolo and Pratt formulate their postcolonial interpretations of transculturation, Welsch devises a concept of cultures that might go "beyond the contraposition of ownness and foreignness" ("Transculturality" 196). In Welsch's model of transculturality the classical binaries of center versus periphery, national culture versus local culture, and powerful nations versus weaker nations are erased in favor of a pluralistic understanding of cultural permeation more adherent to "the inner complexity of modern cultures" and to our fluid, liquid times ("Transculturality" 195). As Ong states, with the "emergence of a multipolar world" capitalism is now "distributed across a number of global arenas" and "the complex interweaving relations of domination and subordination by transnational capital . . . blur the division between 'core' and 'peripheral' countries" (29-31). From Welsch's point of view, any separatist vision of cultures as distinct, self-enclosed, and self-sufficient units—which he traces back to Johann Gottfried Herder's view of folk-bound, uniform, and exclusionary single cultures, with its focus on "inner homogenization and outer separation"—is overcome and any divisive (ethnic, geographic, religious, national) barrier is superseded in view of the contemporary dynamics of cultural transformations and "pure cultural interchange processes" ("Transculturality" 195, 204): "The description of today's cultures as islands or spheres is factually incorrect and normatively deceptive. Cultures de facto no longer have the insinuated form of homogeneity and separateness. They have instead assumed a new form, which is to be called transcultural in so far as it passes through classical cultural boundaries. Cultural conditions today are largely characterized by mixes and permeations" ("Transculturality" 197). In a new world of decentered "alternative" (see Appadurai; Gaonkar; Taylor) or "multiple" (see Eisenstadt, "Multiple") modernities, Welsch's transculturality thus combines the concept of the "permeation" of cultures owing to their growing entanglement (a process which he calls "cultures' external networking") and the focus on the commonalities and the urge to connect that all human beings (and cultures) share, despite their intrinsic differences: "It is a matter of readjusting our inner compass: away from the concentration on the polarity of the own and the foreign to an attentiveness for what might be common and connective wherever we encounter things foreign" ("Transculturality" 201).

In this inclusive vision of culture/s, which stresses the power of confluences and interactions rather than that of polarities, Welsch is also keen to point out that any individual has (or should have among his or her own basic rights) the right to freedom in cultural formation and to independence of any predetermined cultural milieu. The focus on individual agency and the right to a personal cultural choice and allegiance appear to be among the central tenets of a transcultural approach keen to acknowledge the proliferation of plural identities, citizenships, affiliations, and nationalities that characterize the lives of increasing numbers of people (see Bosniak). Similarly, Frank Schulze-Engler states that in the emerging complexity of globally interlinked collectives and transnational individuals, "the primary subjects and actors . . . are no longer cultures but people, and the main interest no longer lies in the problem of how cultures shape social groups and their perceptions, but in the question of what individuals and groups do with culture in an increasingly globalised world" ("Theoretical" 28).

Initially through the peculiar perspective of the post-Soviet cultural environment and later through a more global perspective, Epstein proposes his inclusionary notion of "transculture" as "the site of interaction among all existing and potential cultures" and of a transcultural dimension which "lies not apart from, but within all cultures, like a multidimensional space that appears gradually over the course of historical time. It is a continuous space in which unrealized, potential elements are no less meaningful than 'real' ones" (*After* 299). Transculture thus represents, as Epstein elaborates in a subsequent paper: "A transcendence into no culture, a metacultural beyond . . . a newly emerging dimension . . . a process of interaction between cultures in which more and more individuals find themselves feeling outside the ethnic, racial, sexual, ideological, and other limitations imposed by the culture into which they were born" ("The Unasked" 49). It is through this emerging transcultural space that, according to Epstein, the individual is now able to escape the restrictions and essentializing elements imposed by each single culture and access the right to be free from the conditioning and the dependencies of any given, native, or primary culture, thus reaching a full transcultural condition. Pennycook also acknowledges this aspect discussing the transcultural dimension of hip-hop music: "The possibilities of being something not yet culturally imagined mobilizes new identity options. And in these popular transcultural flows, languages, cultures and identities are frequently mixed. Code-mixing, sampling of sounds, genres, languages, and cultures is the norm" ("The Future" 683). In his conversation with Berry, Epstein refers to transculture as to "the process of self-distancing, self-estrangement, and self-criticism of one's own cultural identities and assumptions" (307). He is suggesting—in the same way that Welsch does with his concept of transculturality—that transculture tends to move the focus of cultural identity from the collective to the individual consciousness, where human beings are seen as subjects able to dynamically select from a myriad of different cultural offerings what best suits them depending on the contexts and the circumstances. Epstein maintains that "transculture offers a universal symbolic palette on which an individual can blend colors to produce an expressive self-portrait" while at the same time showing a way to manifest "the freedom of every person to live on the border of one's 'inborn' culture or beyond it" ("The Unasked" 49, "Transculture" 334).

If, according to Welsch, "transculturality" is seen mainly as a new conceptualization of culture or "a specific quality of contemporary cultures" (Schulze-Engler, Introduction xi), for Epstein, "transculture" represents above all a mode of identity building, an existential dimension beyond any given culture (see also Vladiv-Glover). Epstein has further developed his initial theorizations by defining transculture as "a different model of cultural development" that liberates the individual from the tyranny of one's own culture, from the "prison house of language," from unconscious predispositions and prejudices of the "native, naturalized cultures" ("Transculture" 327-30). In Epstein's view, this process marks the next stage of a process of liberation: in the same way that culture liberates us from the constrictions of nature and its biological, preliminary, noncultural world, transculture liberates us—mainly "through interference with other cultures"—from the conditioning effects of culture, with its set of prefixed, imposed habits, customs, assumptions, and dynamics of group identity formation ("Transculture" 339). Although this view of a nature-culture divide may sound somewhat outdated, it helps us to understand the role of a transcultural orientation in our contemporaneity: "To be cultural means to rise above one's inborn identity, such as 'adult white male,' through the variety of self-deconstructions, self-transformations, and interferences with other identities, such as a woman, a black, a child, or a disabled person. For this purpose, books, films, and all works of art and culture are created and consumed: to dissolve the solidity of one's natural identity and to share the experience of 'the other' . . . Culture demystifies and transcends natural identities, whereas transculture demystifies and transcends cultural identities. This process has no limit" (Berry and Epstein 339-40).

This movement beyond predefined horizons, however, as Epstein points out, does not erase the consciousness and relevance of our "primary identity," that is, where we genetically and culturally stem from; we can transcend our origins but we cannot ignore or disregard them: "We cannot simply deny the role of inborn conditions, or genes, in cultural formations. No escape or 'deterritorialization' would be possible without the initial territory occupied by ethnic origins, gender, and so on. We need to state origins clearly in order to transcend them vigorously" ("Transculture" 339). One cannot fail to notice that Epstein is not talking like a poststructuralist but like a Romantic, which, according to Slobodanka Vladiv-Glover, can be "a little irritating to poststructuralist ears . . . In poststructuralism, there is no 'Nature' in discourse and identity issues, and there are no 'origins,' since there is nothing outside the 'text'" ("Transculture"). There is neither a self endowed with agency, for that matter, after "the death of the subject" meant as a centered and unitary whole (see Heartfield). As Epstein acknowledges synthesizing the deconstructionist approach, "what we consider our 'beginnings,' 'origins,' and 'milieu' is but our own constructions" ("Transculture" 337). Despite this, for Epstein origins "are essential"—as are the deconstructionist attempts to demystify them—but instead of insisting on their affirmation or their deconstructive demystification, we should let them go, transcend them ("Transculture" 341-42). Epstein concludes his reasoning stating that the main purpose of culture is, through a creative and historical process of "disorigination and liberation," to make us human beings "a river and not a dam": "I am willing to accept my identity at the beginning of my journey, but I do not agree to remain with it until the end of my life, to be an animal representing the tag on its cage. I do not agree to be determined in terms of race, nation, gender, or class. Culture has any sense only insofar as it makes us dissidents and fugitives from our nature, our sex, or race, or age" ("Transculture" 341-42). It is this "open-endedness," this claim to "not belonging" as the ultimately desirable cultural position, this suspension to any established attachment proposed by Epstein that, according to Vladiv-Glover, makes us accept his way of reasoning: "identification with our 'native' or 'ethnic' culture turned into an ideology tends to reify us and essentialize us as 'ethnics' instead of leaving us the ambience of being open subjects" ("Transculture").

In their introduction to the journal *Transcultural Studies: A Series in Interdisciplinary Research*, Slobodanka Vladiv-Glover and Evert van der Zweerde point out that "the consequence of a critic adopting a position on the *outside* of whatever is conceived as the *inside* of his or her social and cultural domain requires forfeiture of culture-centrism and a conscious resistance to the totalizing effects of ideology. A transcultural critic, like Epstein, or a transcultural philosopher like Merab Mamardashvili, whose concept of nothingness is the ground of Epstein's anti-position, eschews national and cultural identity, identity politics and multiculturalism. Such freedom from ideologically oriented or discipline-bound directions in scholarship requires a conscious effort that is not unlike the job of Socrates: the effort of ridding oneself of prejudices, idols and icons of scholarly fashion" (Vladiv-Glover and Evert van der Zweerde). This transcultural approach to the self as an open-ended process is shared by Couldry, who refers to transcultural positions and theorizations, in particular the ones externalized by Welsch: "What is missing from post-structuralist claims of the death of the subject . . . is any sense of what it is like to be an active, reflexive self. Few would now claim that the self is a simple 'object' rather than an open-ended process; one of the key elements in that process is reflexivity, reflecting back on our past, on the conditions which have brought us to be what we are" (Couldry, *Inside* 119). And Welsch acknowledges that his concept of transculturality can be applied not only at a macro-cultural level but also at "the micro-level of individuals": "For most of us, multiple cultural connections are decisive in terms of our cultural formation. We are cultural hybrids. Today's writers, for example, are no longer shaped by a single homeland, but by different reference-countries. Their cultural formation is transcultural" ("On the Acquisition" 8).

What I assume is that in order to reach this transcultural dimension or "special mode of existence," one needs to undergo a combined process of physical, spatial, or imaginary deterritorialization and of cultural displacement, including linguistic dis/appropriation (Epstein, *After* 304). This is what I synthetically call creative transpatriation, that is, physical, emotional detachment (where detachment means critical distance, not the opposite of commitment) from one's own primordial culture, territory, and roots (the "individual's" motherland) as well as intellectual disalignment from one's own national or ethnic collective fatherland. Indeed, it is increasingly less common, as Welsch is keen to emphasize, that cultural identity automatically coincides with national identity: "It belongs among the mustiest assumptions that an individual's cultural formation must be determined by his or her nationality or national status. The insinuation that someone who possesses an Indian or a German passport must also culturally unequivocally be an Indian or a German and that, if this is not the case, the person is without a fatherland, or a traitor to his or her fatherland, is as foolish as it is dangerous . . . Wherever an individual is cast by differing cultural interests, the linking of such transcultural components with one another becomes a specific task in identity-forming. Work on one's identity is becoming more and more work on the integration of components of differing cultural origin. And only the ability to cross over transculturally will guarantee us identity and competence in the long run" ("Transculturality" 199). A similar view is shared by the writer Lamberto Tassinari: "Transculture implies a vision of displacement, of nomadism, the possibility of setting up one's territory anywhere. That's the force we can set against the dictatorial force of territory. Transcultural territory encompasses the whole planet" (qtd. in Caccia 218).

The transition to a transcultural mode of being, however, is still a rare phenomenon and few people—even in the twenty-first century, when the conditions are most suitable—experience it, are willing to experience it, or are ready to experience it. As Epstein notes, "we acquire transculture . . . at the crossroads with other cultures through the risky experience of our own cultural wanderings and transgressions" ("Transculture" 330). But such freedom, such "continual oscillation between belonging and disorientation," may be perceived as too destabilizing: "Individually and collectively, we still have a deep-seated nostalgia for the reassuring, yet menacing, closure of horizons" (Vattimo 10-11). As Epstein himself reminds us: "Too many people who leave the geographical location of their culture nevertheless remain, for the rest of their lives, prisoners of its language and traditions. Other migrants, having turned their back on their past, become prisoners of a newly acquired culture. Only a small number of people, when acceding to two or several cultures, succeed in integrating them and thus are able to keep their freedom from any of them" ("Transculture" 330).

As I argue in previous chapters, the transcultural transition or metamorphosis—that is, the transpatriation process and its transformational effects—is happening more frequently among those creative individuals who are fortunate enough to benefit from a socioeconomically privileged background and, even more importantly, from a good level of education and exposure to a pluricultural environment. This category of progressive representatives of the mobile, global middle classes includes those imaginative writers whose transcultural orientations become more manifest owing to their self-reflexive attitudes, their ability to articulate the process of transformation they undergo, and their willingness to conceptualize it, put it into words, and share it with their fellow human beings through fictionalized characters and storylines. It is clear that the transcultural path tends to be personalized, inventive, and original. There does not exist a common pattern, a common recipe, a common way of being transcultural. A transcultural constitution—the ability to negotiate between different cultural identities—depends on the specific individual capabilities, attitudes, and experiential backgrounds. Nonetheless, the transcultural path allows a process of transformation—a metamorphosis—that even if played at an individual level can have a collective resonance. This idea of what can alternatively be described as a process of "self-culturation" (the communitarian self-service of cultures for the formation of one's own cultural identity) echoes Schulze-Engler's understanding of Welsch's transculturality with its open notion of cultural identity: "Theories of 'intercultural' communication . . . create the very problem they set out to solve: they posit 'cultures' as separate entities and people as 'belonging' to these separate entities, thereby failing to acknowledge the fact that in an increasingly interconnected world, cultures are increasingly intertwined and people often constitute their cultural identities by drawing on more than one culture" (Schulze-Engler, Introduction xii).

No more "prisoner" of a single traditional culture, nor of any newly acquired one, the transcultural individual consciousness can thus now live diffused in a new dimension—a "continuum," as Epstein calls it, simultaneously "inside and outside of all existing cultures" ("Transculture" 333). It is a way of being and perceiving oneself as highly complex and fluid, where apparent ambiguities and transitoriness are not shunned but espoused in favor of movement, mediation, and ongoing transformation.

This conceptualization of the transcultural continuum as a means of identity and relationship negotiation, where "we may elude the politics of polarity and emerge as the others of our selves," resonates with Bhabha's "third space," the "in-between" space where hybridization occurs, but in many ways it expands it (*The Location* 56; see also Bhabha, "The Third"). More than a liminal or interstitial space, Epstein's transcultural continuum refers to an all-inclusive, nonoppositional point of confluence, an overlapping of cultures, a "fusion of horizons" in Hans-Georg Gadamer's terms, where one cannot really distinguish what belongs to one culture and what belongs to another, where "us" finishes and "them" starts (273). It might rather be understood as an "exo-space" not limited to the "in-between" but external to all cultures: a utopian dimension, not only unreachable but also, literally, without a specific place, without a determinable location. Or it might be conceived as another plane of existence, another state of being, never fully realizable: a conceptual state of "undecidable belonging" or of identity/being-in-the-making (see Venn 263). In a discussion on the process of translating, Bartoloni suggests a further development of the notion of Bhabha's third space in a way not dissimilar to Epstein's conceptualization of the transcultural continuum. Bartoloni envisions a dynamic, "potential zone" of "not belonging" and "wandering" where the individual is allowed to write and speak "in a language . . . that moves in and out of national and cultural borders" through a narrative "which is the result of a combination rather than an exclusion" ("Translation"). In this light transculture and the transcultural self might be seen as "an ongoing process that could by definition never be complete" (Berry and Epstein 312). Accepting this perspective allows a metaphysical, even spiritual, dimension of the transcultural: "There is a spiritual element to transculture but I wouldn't privilege the spiritual over other ways of developing" (Berry and Epstein 312). Chantal Crozet suggests something similar when trying to identify, through her position as a multilingual mediator, that "neutral space" across time and cultures, that state of "being" beyond the mind, generated by the process of disidentification "from the categories of thought within which one is socialised" and "from the immediate identity-related solidarities." In her view, this processual dimension, or trajectory, of self-knowledge is similar to a secular "meditative experience" through which one is able not to eliminate but to transcend one's identity.

In order to envisage and explain this contemporary cultural movement "beyond the horizon of postmodernism," Epstein likens transculture and its transcultural continuum to Borges's *Aleph*, the dimension where symbolically all cultures and noncultures in their infinite possibilities can be active and alive simultaneously: "In Borges's great story 'Aleph,' the brightest point of the universe is described as a place where all times and spaces may be present together, without hiding or overshadowing each other. In the typical terms of physical reality, Aleph is a pure fantasy, but culture is, after all, a symbolic reality that can be condensed indefinitely by the increasing scope of its meanings. We may imagine transculture as the Aleph of the entire cultural world" (*After* 299). In tracing this new trajectory of cultural development, Epstein draws on Bakhtin's views that "every culture is inherently insufficient in itself" ("The Unasked" 48). In the same way that we cannot really know ourselves without taking into account how others see us from their location beyond our personal borders, we need to distance ourselves from a given culture (and its related main verbal system), accepting the viewpoint of another culture to fully grasp it: "The ethical upshot of Bakhtin's view is that each culture, given its natural insufficiency, must develop the quality of humility, an openness to other cultures, rather than revel in the pride (it remains a deadly sin) of self-identity and self-aggrandizement: "Only in the eyes of an alien culture, does another culture open itself in a fuller and deeper way. . . . Being an outsider is an advantageous position for understanding insides" (Epstein "The Unasked" 48). From this perspective, one can better understand the importance that transcultural theorists give to the growing phenomenon of translingualism—that is, the writing between languages or in a language different from the mother tongue. According to Steven G. Kellman, translingual writers are "authors who write in more than one language or at least in a language other than their primary one" (*The Translingual* ix). Subsequently, Kellman further elaborates on this subject pointing out that, "by expressing themselves in multiple verbal systems," such writers "flaunt their freedom from the constraints of the culture into which they happen to be born" (*Switching* ix). Translingualism has also been defined by Ruth Spack as a reinvention of one's identity. Reflecting on students who move between languages, then extending this same concept-process to creative writers and intellectuals "who cross-culturally appropriate a language," Spack argues that "translingualism involve[s] . . . the transformation of their linguistic and cultural identities, for their worldview [is] now being mediated through a new language" (112).

Epstein argues that transculture (or transculturalism) "presupposes 'translingualism'" ("The Unasked" 50). Undoubtedly, in the "globalization of cultures" more and more people are becoming competent in more than one language, and when we talk about languages as systems of meaning making, as Tzvetan Todorov suggests, we talk about accessing other worldviews, other visions of life and life practices: "Language is not a neutral instrument, it is soaked in thoughts, actions, judgments inherited from the past; it cuts out the real in a given manner and it imperceptibly transmits to us a worldview" (13). According to Epstein, this cultural globalizing phenomenon is generating a "multidimensional, multilingual 'culturally curved' discourse" ("The Unasked" 50). It is specifically in this "new layer of imagery" where languages are no longer enclosed within monoethnic and monologic cultures, that according to him new plurilinguistic creative combinations can take form and find an audience through that Bakhtinian process of "'mutual illumination and interanimation of languages'" ("The Unasked" 50-51). In other words, by exploiting the specific untranslatability and nonequivalence among languages, meaning in one language is able to amplify, or even multiply, the meanings in another language: Epstein calls this form of creative expression a "stereo prose," or "stereotextuality" ("The Unasked" 50-51). On a more philosophical and epistemological level, this process may be similar to the one envisioned by Bartoloni when discussing the significance of the translating process to gain access "to the language in-between" (*On the Cultures* 4). Bartoloni suggests that the emergence of "a language-that-comes" with its new meanings is made possible by a synthetic merging of original texts and their translations: "What is arrived at is a language in between—a possible language—indeterminate and yet resounding with a richness that is simply not present in the individual texts and voices from which it derives" (*On the Cultures* 4). This view of cultural expansion, mutual interference, enrichment, creation of potentially new languages and meanings through bilingualism, translingualism, or polyglossia is supported by Kellman: "multilingualism enlarges . . . If identity is shaped by language, then monolingualism is a deficiency disorder. It limits our versions of self, society, and universe" (*The Translingual* viii; see also Sellin). Mary Besemeres and Anna Wierzbicka find themselves on the same wavelength when introducing their edited volume, *Translating Lives,* on common people and writers who live across languages and cultures: "Monolingualism limits people's understanding of the world and of human life in more than one way. It brings about an unconscious absolutisation of the perspective on the world suggested by one's native language. It is only exposure to other perspectives (those suggested by other languages) which shows us that what we, as native speakers of one language, instinctively take for reality is in fact a particular interpretation of reality" (xiv).

I am aware here that attaching a worldview to any specific language might be interpreted as a form of linguistic determinism, as Kellman reminds us mentioning those scholars who, drawing on Noam Chomsky, "insist that universal deep structures subsuming every language are more crucial than superficial differences. For them, translingualism might be . . . not especially a feat of cognitive emancipation or enlargement" (*The Translingual* 23). Theories of linguistic relativity go back to the writings of Wilhelm von Humboldt and Benjamin Lee Whorf via Franz Boas and Edward Sapir. Although over the last century a correlation between linguistic differences and human cognition sparked a wide debate on the risks of linguistic determinism, at present a balanced, nondeterministic view of linguistic relativism is espoused by many linguists (for a historical outlook on the different linguistic theories see Rossi-Landi; for a discussion on the reexamination of linguistic relativity see Casasanto; Gumperz and Levinson). More recently, other researchers have corroborated the idea of a correlation between the language we grew up with (one of our strongest identity markers), our way of thinking, and the way we see the world (see, e.g., Deutscher). Further, what Yamuna Kachru and Larry E. Smith posit is that even though "the relationship between culture and language is not deterministic . . . the two are sensitive to each other and evolve together" (xv; for a further discussion on language as a worldview see Underhill). Thus, we might be tempted to agree with Kellman when he points out that "refusing to be constrained by the structures of any single language, translinguals seem both to acknowledge and to defy the claims of linguistic determinism.

It is precisely because they recognize the power of particular languages that they attempt to transcend them" (*The Translingual* 23-24). Accordingly, it is by transcending linguistic boundaries that transcultural subjects (including writers) tend towards that transcultural continuum, that boundless perspective which allows one, in Epstein's view, to overcome any binary or oppositional thinking. All this implies that languages, together with individuals, cultures, and nations, are no longer seen as monolithic entities or as mutually exclusive absolutes, but through a transcultural lens as hybridizing organisms in constant relation to each other, fluctuating in cultural permeations, amalgamations, and confluences. As Hannerz states, "Rather than being easily separated from one another as the hard-edged pieces in a mosaic, [cultures] tend to overlap and mingle. While we understand them to be differently located in the social structure of the world, we also realize that the boundaries we draw around them are frequently rather arbitrary" ("Cosmopolitans" 239).

If the idea of locating culture and literature exclusively in the context of ethnicities or nations seems more and more anachronistic, the same might be said about national languages, especially if seen through a transcultural prism. In *Global Englishes and Transcultural Flows*, Pennycook examines the spread and use of transnational and transcultural forms of English within processes of globalization and current representations of the world: "these global language uses are not determined by economic relations alone, but rather are part of complex networks of communication and cultural flows" (31). Pennycook's aim is "to understand the role of English both critically—in terms of new forms of power, control, and destruction—and in its complexity, in terms of new forms of resistance, change, appropriation and identity" (*Global* 5). That is why, when discussing the language mixes that result out of the confluential processes fostered by globalization, he prefers to speak of transcultural flows as "the ways in which cultural forms move, change, and are reused to fashion new identities in diverse contexts" (Pennycook, *Global* 6). In the particular case of English, he denies the connection of global Englishes both to linguistic imperialism and to nationalized forms of English (Indian English, Arab English, Singaporean English, etc.), since in his opinion they are "both mired in a linguistics and a politics of the last century, focusing inexorably on languages and nations as given entities, and ill-equipped to deal with current modes of globalization" (Pennycook, *Global* 23). In Pennycook's view, the way global Englishes are used for creative expression by non-native speakers—and I would add also by native speakers/writers who have been exposed to other languages and to the challenges of global postnational or transnational communication—is more hybrid, eccentric, dynamic, and transgressive than had been initially theorized by Braj B. Kachru, the first promoter of the classical "World Englishes" framework with its three concentric circles extending from the core to the periphery. According to Kachru, in the inner circle find their place those countries (Australia, Canada, New Zealand, the United Kingdom, the USA) where English is used as a first language. The outer circle consists of the former colonies (India, Nigeria, the Philippines, Singapore) which adopted English as an additional language. The expanding circle includes those areas (China, Europe,

Japan, Korea, the Middle East) in which English is becoming the preferred language of communication for economic, technological, scientific, and educational purposes.

Focusing on the study of how global Englishes are being employed within the specific context of hiphop music, Pennycook prompts us to shed an outmoded conception of languages and cultures and to focus instead on a transcultural paradigm that draws on Welsch's theorizations: "Notions of the transcultural, transnational, and translocal present a way of thinking about flow, flux, and fixity in relation to location that move beyond both dichotomies of the global and local, and dialectics between global homogenization and local heterogenization . . . This opens up an understanding of cultural movement while never losing sight of the uneven terrain (global economies, the music industry) over which such movements occur" (*Global* 44). What we see at work in our contemporaneity is a combined process of localization and globalization that prompts us to use, where appropriate, either a local idiom (even more so if it is an endangered one that needs to be preserved) or a global language (such as English, but also Spanish, Arabic, Hindi, or Chinese). This process which sees rooted local idioms intertwined with deterritorialized/transnational languages is prompting us to become at least bilingual, able to grasp, albeit superficially, the existence of other worldviews, other perspectives, and other "translingual practices across communities other than those defined along national criteria" (Pennycook, "The Future" 683).

In light of what has been discussed so far, Welsch and Epstein invite us, as a form of intellectual discourse and as a conceptual framework, to replace multiculturalism—what Epstein calls "the pride of minorities" ("Transculture" 329) and Amartya Sen calls "plural monoculturalism" (157)—with transculturale/ality or, in this specific case, with transculturalism. In their view, it is possible to overcome, without denying its historical role and validity, the limitations that growing numbers of critics see in the self-enclosed, at times even racialized and racializing, cultural legacy of multiculturalism—most often adopted by (im)migrant literature—that in Ziauddin Sardar's words "fetishes difference" (qtd. in Xuereb 38; for a further discussion on the otherizing and homogenizing effects underlying the terms "migrant writing" and "multicultural literature" and the assumption of "the centrality of English-language writing" see Huggan, *Australian* 115). Also according to Schulze-Engler "An important dimension of transculturality may be said to reside in a really existing 'transcultural transformation' of lifeworlds, experiences, and cultural practices in Europe and elsewhere that challenges a compartmentalized understanding of 'multicultural' societies in terms of a 'benign cultural apartheid'" (Introduction xiii). Although both advocate mutual understanding, recognition, and tolerance of different cultures, in Welsch's view multiculturality and interculturality "conceptually presuppose" the classical Herderian model of single cultures as autonomous spheres where each culture is defined and is more interested in the relationship of identity to roots and rootedness than to movement and mediation ("Transculturality" 196). For Welsch it is the premise that is wrong: "compared to traditional calls for cultural homogeneity the concept [of multiculturality] is progressive, but its all too traditional understanding of cultures threatens to engender regressive tendencies which by appealing to a particularistic cultural identity lead to ghettoization or cultural fundamentalism" ("Transculturality" 197). Also, Epstein challenges the mosaic multicultural model, which simply recognizes the equal rights and value of self-enclosed cultures and questions the model's ability to address "the contemporary cross-cultural flows" ("Transculture" 329): "Can we move on now from the model of difference (and *différance*) that dominated the humanities from the 1970s to the 1990s?—move on to a model of 'interference,' on the assumption that the most beautiful patterns in culture (as in nature) are made by the overlap of waves coming from various traditions, periods, and disciplines? I do not mean 'interference' as in 'intrusion' or 'intervention.' I am thinking of the use that the word has in physics: the mutual action of two or several waves (of sound, light, etc.) in reinforcing or neutralizing each other" ("The Unasked" 47).

Even if in Epstein's view multiculturalism represents a necessary step in cultural integration, he writes that "multiculturalism paves the way from the dominance of one canon to the diversity of cultures" ("Transculture" 349) and he prompts us to go beyond it "from the diversity of cultures to the even greater diversity of individuals" in order to reach "a broader cultural model capable of appealing not only to specific minorities but to the universal potentials of human understanding" (*After* 306). In this way we may prevent the risk of cultural stagnation and global clashes between oppositional cultural allegiances: "Where there are stiff and 'proud' identities, there are also oppositions fraught with violence. As a rule, violence occurs between groups with firmly established identities, which remain impenetrable for each other and thus aspire to mutual extinction" (Epstein, "Transculture" 347). For this same reason Sardar proposes a vision of "transmodernism"—not dissimilar to the one proposed by the transcultural—based on the notion of "mutually assured diversity" or "mutuality": "Mutuality must be about acculturation—where both sides of the cultural relations equation change, transform, and transcend their own limitations" (qtd. in Xuereb 38).

It is precisely through this process of differentiation, transformation, and cultural metamorphosis that, according to Welsch, the risk of homogenization and cultural uniformity in a globalizing world is shunned and replaced instead by the potential opportunity for a broader production of cultural "manifoldness" and differentiation which, through its network structure with multiple points of affiliation, "favors coexistence rather than combat . . . Diversity, as traditionally provided in the form of single cultures, does indeed increasingly disappear. Instead, however, a new type of diversity takes shape: the diversity of different cultures and life-forms, each arising from transcultural permeations . . . It's just that now the differences no longer come about through a juxtaposition of clearly delineated cultures (like in a mosaic), but result between transcultural networks, which have some things in common while differing in others, showing overlaps and distinctions at the same time. The mechanics of differentiation has become more complex, but it has also become genuinely cultural for the very first time, no longer complying with geographical or national stipulations, but following pure cultural interchange processes" ("Transculturality" 203-04).

Even when there are cultures more prone or fiercely determined to hang onto their particular values, worldviews, traditions, customs, and beliefs, this transcultural process of interaction and identity formation—albeit denied, opposed, or simply ignored—is still under way as a potent, although invisible, undercurrent. Epstein sees in it the chance to escape the homogenizing effects of globalization and its Americanized mass culture and to access instead the "further differentiation of cultures and their 'dissemination' into transcultural individuals" ("Transculture" 328). In this way, Epstein opens up a new perspective towards the future: "Thinking in terms of beginnings and initiations presupposes an open future rather than a consummation of the past" ("The Unasked" 46). This is why he proposes the use of the prefix proto- instead of post- to designate essential traits of new cultural formations and define new theoretical approaches. Proto- expresses a beginning, a development, a generation, an expansion while post- signals death, decline, the end of something, and it has a self-defeating connotation (*The Transformative* 24-28). Analyzing the cultural developments in post-Soviet Russia, Epstein for example talks about "the nascent protoglobal and protouniversalist mentality," which is "another expression of desire for the new intensities of experience possible when horizons broaden" ("The Unasked" 47). He therefore invites us to nurture a proto- instead of a post- mentality, which in his view would "reflect a Bakhtinian transition from finality to initiation as our dominant mode of thinking" (Epstein, "The Unasked" 46; see also Epstein, *After* 280-01, 331-38).

The transcultural approach also seems to point to the "need to move beyond traditional concepts of society that continue to rely on the nation state as the only conceivable frame of reference" (Schulze-Engler, "Theoretical" 27). As Diana Brydon suggests, referring to the Canadian experience, "holding too closely to older notions of national identity may not prove the most effective way to preserve the ability of Canadians [and others] to shape the decisions that affect their daily lives" ("Cross-Talk" 61). Commenting on this remark, Ezra Yoo-Hyeok Lee notes that "the paradigm that focuses too much on a national level . . . does not enable us to deal with changes occurring in our life at this age of globalization, when the global dynamically and dialectically interrelates to the national" ("Globalization"). Thus, right at the moment when national identity appears to be put to the test under the pressure of globalization, growing migratory flows, and cosmopolitan tendencies, the various national and strictly defined cultural imaginaries are offered—through a transcultural perspective—a new way to open up in a process of cultural "dissemination," creating the space for an emerging transcultural imaginary. This process fosters citizens' agency not only at an individual and national level but also at a global (international or transnational) one. This aligns with Tassinari's view: "We can imagine and envision transculturalism as a new form of humanism, based on the idea of relinquishing the strong traditional identities and cultures which in many cases were products of imperialistic empires, interspersed with dogmatic religious values" (qtd. in Cuccioletta 8). Tassinari was for twelve years the editor of *ViceVersa: Magazine Transculturel*, one of the first experiments in transcultural publishing in Montréal

(<http://www.viceversamag.com>). Founded in 1983 by a culturally diverse group of writers, journalists, artists, and intellectuals, *ViceVersa* published articles on literature, arts, culture, and political issues written in English, French, and Italian (its publication ceased in 1996 for lack of funding). For Alessandra Renzi *ViceVersa* represents "a unique example of the emergence of a counter-hegemonic movement questioning identity at its roots" (109; see also Caccia, Ramirez, and Tassinari).

Espousing a transcultural approach does not mean, however, adhering to the "banal" cosmopolitanism denounced by Beck, the kind that unfolds "beneath the surface or behind the façade of persisting national spaces" (19). Epstein in particular is keen to draw a distinction between transculture and cosmopolitanism, which he considers the "older brand" of today's globalism ("Transculture" 342). Epstein argues that as an alternative mode of cultural development, transculture does not disown native cultural or national roots ("biologically and biographically predetermined"), although it tends to transcend them through the "diffusion," "interference," and "dispersion" of inborn cultural identities ("Transculture" 334): "it is precisely this relevance of the primary (ethnic, national) cultures, which the latter [cosmopolitanism] attempts to ignore or bypass. A cosmopolitan, a citizen of the world, claims to belong directly and immediately to the human kind as a whole, disregarding ethnic, racial, and other differences. A transcultural personality fully recognizes hu's roots in a certain cultural ground, though hu does not want to cling to them" ("Transculture" 342; in Epstein's vocabulary "hu" stands for he/she). Further, Welsch states that "transcultural identities comprehend a cosmopolitan side, but also a side of local affiliation . . . Transcultural people combine both" ("Transculturality" 205).

Still, as discussed in the previous chapter, there is another kind of cosmopolitanism, a new vision of liberal humanism (better known as "rooted," "vernacular," or "situated" cosmopolitanism), promoted by thinkers such as Appiah (*Cosmopolitanism* xviii) and Beck, which—philosophically as well as politically and ideologically—seems in sympathy with the transcultural mode proposed by Welsch and Epstein. In this new version, cosmopolitanism does not necessarily need to be "a conflict between local partialities and a universal morality," since in Appiah's view "there are some values that are, and should be, universal, just as there are some values that are, and must be, local" (*Cosmopolitanism* xxi). Interpreting Appiah's way of reasoning, this means that without a strong commitment to the local there cannot be any genuine sense of obligation to the universal, and vice versa. In a transcultural perspective, this also means that both localism and the political and ideological stances of contemporary cosmopolitanism (together with its institutionalized form, nationalism) do not need to be opposed but can instead go together, seeking to balance universals with respect for particulars through an ongoing dialogue between nationalism and cosmopolitanism as a collective human identity including local forms of identity (see Appiah, *The Ethics*).

We are all aware that where there is cultural harmony there can also be at the same time cultural resistance or even cultural conflict, often fueled by a recrudescence of ethnopolitical or religious fundamentalisms, or what Eisenstadt calls the "ideologization of violence, terror, and war" ("Multiple" 25). As Burke writes, "The tendency to assume that cultural exchange is always a reflection of tolerance and open-mindedness is one that historians should resist. It should not be forgotten that cultural interaction in late medieval Spain, the so-called *convivencia*, took place at a time of pogroms, forced conversions, and inquisitors hunting down *moriscos* and *marranos*, crypto-Muslims and crypto-Jews. In other words, cultural "harmony" . . . was apparently combined with social disharmony" (81). In any case, it is always better to promote a mode of interaction with and learn from strangers since, sooner or later, as Appiah reminds us, we will have to deal with them, wherever they are: "Depending on the circumstances, conversations across boundaries can be delightful, or just vexing: what they mainly are, though, is inevitable" (*Cosmopolitanism* xxi). In an increasingly interconnected world, all our destinies seem to be more and more inextricably interlaced, and "even the meanest self-interest suggests we look out for the ones around us" (Iyer 35). In spite of this, as Bauman warns, the opening of the world to globalizing forces also produces, by reaction, new closures, new siege mentalities: "As the polivocality and cultural variegation of the urban environment of the globalization era sets in, likely to intensify rather than be mitigated in the course of time, the tensions arising from the vexing/confusing/irritating unfamiliarity of the setting will probably go on prompting segregationist urges" (*Liquid* 86-87). One way to come to terms—by force or out of sheer curiosity—with our internal or external foreignness, outside or within our societies and ourselves, is precisely through a transcultural approach where we are called upon to look more deeply into ourselves and to put into practice those forms of understanding, translation, negotiation, and interpolation required by our living among culturally different others. As Welsch points out, "Hatred directed towards foreigners is (as has been shown particularly from the psychoanalytic side) basically projected hatred of oneself. One takes exception vicariously to something in a stranger, which one carries within oneself, but does not like to admit, preferring rather to repress it internally and to battle with it externally . . . It is precisely when we no longer deny, but rather perceive, our inner transculturality that we will become capable of dealing with outer transculturality" ("Transculturality" 201).

Most of the time, the terms transculture, transculturality, and transculturalism are used by different scholars interchangeably as synonyms. In the present study I follow Brancato's distinction between transculturality (which in my opinion is somewhat, but not totally equivalent to Epstein's use of the term transculture, hence my coining the term transculture/ality) and transculturalism ("Transculturalità" 45). In the first case we are dealing with a new theoretical framework through which one can describe and analyze the cultural dynamics and the creative expressions in contemporary mobile societies "based on a new conceptualization of culture" and "out of the narrow national and regional boundaries" (Brancato, "Transculturalità" 45). Transculturalism, on the other hand, is better understood as the new operative and ideological mode of cultural interaction and represents, as Brancato suggests, "an answer . . . to the menace of cultural homogenisation on the one hand and of fundamentalist essentialisms on the other" ("Transculturalità" 45). Brancato also suggests that the analytical model and the ideological mode need to work together: "There where transculturality becomes the analytical model which allows us to read the present cultural reality, transculturalism (the two terms are often used as synonyms) could be a more suitable term to describe the ensuing ideology, a will to interact starting from the intersections rather than from the polarities and differences, a consciousness of the transcultural that is in us to better comprehend and accept what is outside of us, a vision that privileges flexibility and fluidity, movement and ongoing exchange, the constant re-negotiation of identity" ("Transculturalità" 44).

Understood in its broader and nonideological sense, transculture/ality is deployed within a literary context as a mode for individual identity building and, most importantly, as an analytical and critical tool able to capture the interplay between culture, the different modes of (post)modernity, and the works of a globalizing imagination and sense of belonging (see also Hoerder, Hébert, and Schmitt). Even if in itself this position may betray a Western individualist point of view, the accent on the individual and the respect for individuality emerging from a transcultural perspective should not be conflated with US-American-style liberal individualism. On the contrary, in this book I am talking about a socially mediated "process of subjectivity" that disengages itself from the conventional concept of individualism and asserts the undeniable singularity, fluidity, but also interrelatedness of any self-constituting being as part of a "collective enterprise" (Braidotti, *Metamorphoses* 7; see also Nancy's theorizations on "singularity" and "being singular plural").

I thus summarize the central tenets of transculture/ality as a new theoretical paradigm and as a mode of cultural investigation as follows. 1) A nonessentialized, inclusive approach to culture. A refusal to think of cultures as pure and holistic essences: cultures are not seen as fixed (stable), autonomous, and insular (separate) entities located exclusively or mainly in the context of ethnicities or nations but as hybrid formations characterized by interconnectedness, permeation, and ongoing transforming dialogues between or among them; 2) the idea of blurred, fluctuating, and overlapping cultural borders within and outside societies or nations—what Eugen Banauch calls "the deconstruction of national cultures as stable and clear entities" (187); 3) the idea of culture and cultural individual formation as a dynamic process; 4) the focus on human agency "with an affirmative position by the individual" (Banauch 188) and the right to personal cultural choices, allegiances, plural affiliations, and multiple, multilayered identities; 5) a cosmopolitan approach which does not deny the relevance of one's primary cultural and national origins but does not accept the oppositional dynamics of fixed, self-enclosed, cultural, ethnic, and national identities or allegiances; 6) a humble cultural disposition. Epstein remarks how a transcultural orientation is prone to adopt "the moral value of humility that makes one culture open to other cultures" ("Transculture" 334); and 7) the relevance of translingualism (and polyglossia) for the transcultural constitution.

I emphasize that in the present study the concept of transculture/ality is confined within a literary, artistic, or critical discourse where creativity and identity are expressed at a personal and individual level. In other words, it is not my objective to investigate its implications within a broader sociopolitical/collective or ideological/psychoanalitical context. And I refer to Brancato's vision of transculturality within a literary context: "Within a literary context, transculturality must be conceived as a theoretical framework that includes phenomena of cultural interactions (from post-colonial intertextuality to cross-cultural hybridization and creolization up to the multiple modernities of the global world) and that allows us to pull out the new literatures from the narrow boundaries of the national and the regional as well as to revise the local and the diasporic from a global point of view" ("Transculturalità" 46).

Chapter Three

Transcultural Literature in the Global Ecumene

Thomsen illustrates, in his 2010 *Mapping World Literature,* that with the denationalizing wave of globalization even national literatures are under pressure to find new arrangements of form and content to adapt to a changed cultural and social paradigm. In other words, a mutation is under way within the global ecumene of letters, where new notions of belonging, as well as definitions of selfhood and identity, are being externalized through new creative artistic and literary processes. Within this emerging social, cultural, and literary scenario, scholars—especially when dealing with the so-called New Literatures in English (represented by the works of, e.g., Zadie Smith, Hanif Kureishi, Kamila Shamsie, Michael Ondaatje, Maxine Hong Kingston, or Joy Kogawa)—feel the urge to identify new literary paradigms. This is why transcultural and transnational theorizations conducted in the past two decades in cultural anthropology, philosophy, and cultural studies are now being introduced in literary studies and quickly gaining scholarly currency (see, e.g., Helff, "Shifting" 77).

Particularly in Germany a group of scholars (Schulze-Engler, Helff, and Brancato, among others) initiated the field of Transcultural English Studies and in northern Europe another group of scholars—drawing mainly on Ortiz's concept of "transculturation"—now engage in similar work in The Nordic Network for Literary Transculturation Studies (<https://www.uib.no/rg/nnlts>). Although both of these groups focus on the study of anglophone literatures, the same approach can be adopted for the study of any work of literature in any other language whose nature can be defined as intrinsically "transcultural." Here is Schulze-Engler's definition: "Transcultural English Studies . . . stands for a genuinely transnational and transcultural perspective that is capable of encompassing both the literary practice of writers who can no longer be related to one particular 'national literary space' and the complex articulations that link individual works of literature not only to local or regional modernities with their specific social, linguistic, and cultural constellations, but also to the world-wide field of English-language literatures and specific forms of communicative interaction and political conflict engendered by it" (Introduction xvi).

On a more general level, since its inception in 2006 the Centre for Transcultural Writing and Research <http://www.transculturalwriting.com> at the University of Lancaster created a transnational environment for scholars interested in "writing across cultures" and in "studying the work of writers from a wide range of social and cultural contexts." Something similar is being offered through the Institut d'Etudes Transtextuelles and Transculturelles at the University Jean Moulin Lyon 3 <http://www.iett.eu>, a founding partner of the International Institute for Diasporic and Transcultural Studies with Liverpool Hope University, the University of Cyprus, and Sun Yat-sen University in Guangzhou. Through transcultural and historicized approaches, they promote studies on the specificities and changes of sociocultures and localities in a globalized world, as well as on questions of textual and cultural representations—but also self-representations—of diasporic, (im)migrant, and transnational communities. Active since 2007 at the University of Heidelberg is the program Asia and Europe in a Global Context: The Dynamics of Transculturality <http://www.asia-europe.uni-heidelberg.de/en/about-us.html>, whose objective is the study and discussion of cultural interactions between and within Asia and Europe through the development of a strong interdisciplinary and transcultural research approach. In the US is the Center for Transcultural Studies <http://www.sas.upenn.edu/transcult> at The Pennsylvania State University, where since the mid-1980s "new forms of cultural understanding for a rapidly internationalizing world" have been studied with interdisciplinary approaches. In Canada transcultural studies applied to literary works were initiated in the mid-1990s by Janice Kulyk Keefer, a critic, novelist, and poet of Ukrainian and Polish descent. Keefer was born in Toronto, studied literature in England and France, and in the early 1990s returned to Canada where she started her literary and academic career. Confronted with the problematics of multiculturalism to foster a kind of self-imposed ghettoization with its ethnic, immigrant, and marginalized literary productions, Keefer suggested revisiting the notion of multiculturalism through a transcultural lens and a transcultural form of writing that can cross the borders of different ethnic and cultural groups (studies on transcultural writers and the concept of transculturalism applied to a Canadian literary context have also been conducted by Mårald).

Eva Darias Beautell acknowledges that Keefer's way of writing, in conjunction with the writing of other Canadians that do not belong to the dominant culture, "seem[s] to undermine traditional concepts of (ethnic) identity as something unitary and fixed . . . Together they defy a concept of identity in terms of nation and/or national language" (31-32). Keefer's transcultural approach resonates with the one proposed around the same time by Fulvio Caccia, an Italian-Canadian poet, writer, and cofounder of the transcultural Québécois magazine *Vice Versa,* who, in Gunew's words, "like a number of us . . . identifies 'transculturalism' as the latest term in a continuum to which multiculturalism belongs; a continuing quest to capture the hybrid realities of diaspora and globalisation" (*Haunted* 127). Gunew herself, a literary scholar of Bulgarian descent who moved from Australia to Canada in the early 1990s, has been instrumental in fostering a transcultural approach within the field of literary scholarship and cultural studies. In 2001, while teaching at The University of British Columbia, she was asked by the International Council for International Studies to coordinate a team of scholars, artists, and performers—with a sister team based in Brazil—for an international project devoted to investigating transculturalism, the intermingling of cultures (*métissage*), cultural hybridity, and their impact on Canadian and other national identities.

But what exactly is transcultural literature? Different scholars have come up with different definitions. For example, As'ad E. Khairallah maintains it consists of works which are: "Either: (a) intentionally' transcultural in vision and scope (e.g., *The Waste Land*), regardless of [their] ability to reach or impact other cultures than [their] own, or (b) originally not transcultural by intention, vision or scope, but acquire . . . this characteristic through [their] ability to cross cultures and to play an active part in their literary worlds, e.g. *The Iliad*" (233). Others argue that transcultural literature explores the formation of identities in a process of cross-cultural communication and immersion in modern diasporas (Haberkorn); that it delves into the "cultural complexity" (emerging from a network of multiple modernities) while "engag[ing] in a renegotiation of cultural norms and values" (Schulze-Engler, "Theoretical Perspectives" 29); and that it is made of cultural products of a multicultural society which assert, explore, or allude to their creators' liminal position between two or more different countries, communities, or cultures (Keefer, "Writing" 193). I posit that transcultural literature engages with and expresses the confluential nature of cultures, overcoming the different dichotomies between North and South, the West and the Rest, the dominator and the dominated, the native and the immigrant, the national and the ethnic. I also infer that the genesis of transcultural literature lies as much in the ever increasing globalizing forces that are reshaping our cultural, economic, and social landscapes as in the literary discourse related to mobility at large, including its (im)migrant, diasporic, postcolonial, and transnational variants (on this see Ascari and Corrado; Walkowitz, "The Location").

There is no doubt that at the forefront of the change of paradigm under discussion are those artists, writers, and sometimes scholars who experienced the effects of global mobility, transnational patterns, and neonomadic lifestyles and who in their texts capture and express an emerging transcultural mood. In this sense, transcultural literature records the reshaping of national collective imaginaries in their efforts to adjust to a new age of transnational and supranational economic, political, social, and cultural processes. All this keeping in mind that a text's visibility in the global literary arena can be amplified or undermined by the "dominant discourses and their control over the circuits of communication" as well as by the market forces behind any decision to publish or not to publish, to translate or not to translate, or to distribute globally or not to do so (Khairallah 242). If, on the one hand, we can infer that to some extent the modes of narration of transcultural writing are a direct expression of their creators' transcultural realities and sensibilities, then, on the other hand what makes this kind of writing different is first and foremost its resistance to appropriations by one single national canon or cultural tradition. Speaking about the New Literatures in English, Schulze-Engler claims that "The idea of 'locating' culture and literature exclusively in the context of ethnicities or nations is rapidly losing plausibility throughout an 'English-speaking world' that has long since been multi- rather than monolingual . . . The New Literatures in English themselves have long since become a transcultural field with blurred boundaries" (Introduction x, xvi). This same assumption refers to any of those literary expressions in any other language whose features may fit into a transcultural paradigm.

Transcultural literature can be considered the youngest representative of the literatures of mobility, and these literatures include those works of fiction which are affected and shaped by migratory flows, wanderlust, travel experiences, diasporic, exile, or postcolonial conditions, expatriate statuses, and, more recently, the multiple trajectories of transnational and neonomadic movements (see, e.g., Ette). In *The Location of Culture* Bhabha notes that "where, once, the transmission of national traditions was the major theme of a world literature, perhaps we can now suggest that transnational histories of migrants, the colonized, or political refugees—these border and frontier conditions—may be the terrains of world literature" (12). This view is shared by Ottmar Ette, who in his analysis of travel literature as "the point of departure for examining a bordercrossing literature on the move," envisions that "the literatures of the twenty-first century will be literatures without a fixed abode, literatures that evade attempts at clear territorialization" (9-13; see also Tötösy de Zepetnek and Wang; Tötösy de Zepetnek, Wang, and Sun; for a bibliography of travel studies see Salzani and Tötösy de Zepetnek). More importantly, the transcultural perspective marks an attempt to overcome the limits that a growing numbers of scholars find in postcolonial and multicultural approaches. Once cultures are no longer seen as monolithic entities but are perceived as hybridizing organisms in constant dialogue with each other, it is easier, as Brancato points out, to delink literatures from their national, territorial, or ethnic belongings and at the same time to offer "an alternative to the dichotomic paradigm of postcolonialism" ("Transculturalità" 44).

Postcolonial approaches in particular, as Schulze-Engler points out, tend to understand cultural dynamics in terms of classical binaries such as "colonizer vs. colonized or centers vs. peripheries" (Introduction xi) and in Helff's view remain "obsessively . . . tied to notions of difference," dissidence, subalternity, alterity, opposition, and marginality, which invariably imply subversive stances ("Shifting" 78). Paradoxically, in this respect, even the "loose use of the term "postcolonial," as Ong remarks, "has had the bizarre effect of contributing to a Western tradition of othering the Rest" (34). Aijaz Ahmad points out that "in at least one of the many nuances, 'postcolonial' is simply a polite way of saying not-white, not-Europe, or perhaps not-Europe-but-inside-Europe" (8). Similarly, Grabovszki acknowledges that in the postcolonial discourse "we have the implicit and explicit differentiation between a 'home' culture and a culture of the 'Other'" ("The Impact"). We should not forget, however, that Spivak admitted the importance and validity, when needed and judiciously applied, of a "strategic use of positivist essentialism," that is, the advantage for those in subaltern positions to essentialize themselves, bring forward their group identity and provide a perspective from below in order to subvert hegemonic narratives or to reveal how truths are being produced (Introduction 13). Spivak has nonetheless disputed the misuse by other scholars of her concept (see Landry and MacLean). Similarly, Ashcroft does not dispute the influential role of postcolonialism in devising a "language to describe the diversity of cultures and the intersecting global range of cultural production"; however, he also warns about the peril of the transformation of postcolonialism into yet another dominant narrative: "The challenge for post-colonial theorists is to avoid the temptation to view 'post-colonialism' as a master-discourse" ("Introduction" xvi, xvii).

The postcolonial outlook seems less and less appropriate in a world where the thus far misconceived perception of a "monocultural" Western imperialism (as we all know, Western imperialism is hardly monocultural, since we have different countries and cultures involved: England, France, Spain, Portugal, the Netherlands, Germany, the US, etc.) is being replaced by a plurality of centers of techno-economic power, cultural creativity, and extended knowledge. As Schulze-Engler stresses, not only do "many postcolonial debates today seem increasingly irrelevant to literary studies" but, even more importantly, "some of the chief tenets of postcolonial theory developed in the last two decades now seem hard to reconcile with the literary and cultural dynamics of a rapidly globalising world" ("Theoretical" 20). In the same vein, Sandra Ponzanesi argues that "the pressing reality of new global dynamics challenges postcolonial intellectuals to think beyond the premises of their original quest" (xiii). Indeed, more than one scholar has noticed that even Spivak, one of the pioneers and main theorists of the postcolonial paradigm, "distances herself from mainstream postcolonial literary theory" (Maver, "Post-Colonial" 27; on Spivak's concept of "planetarity" see also Moore and Rivera). Instead, Spivak proposes a move towards "transnational cultural studies" (see *A Critique*) and a model of planetary cultural studies (see *Death*). Spivak's call for a death of traditional ways of doing comparative literature through a canonical (and to a certain extent exhausted) postcolonial lens leaves no space for doubt: "The old postcolonial model—very much 'India' plus the Sartrian 'Fanon'—will not serve now as the master model for transnational to global cultural studies on the way to planetarity" (*Death* 85).

By highlighting cultural "permeation" and "blending" (Welsch, "Transculturality"), the new transcultural paradigm in literary scholarship and criticism appears more suitable for describing and analyzing transcultural literature of transforming societies in an increasingly globalized world made of "multiple modernities" (Eisenstadt, "Multiple"). For Bernd Peter Lange and Dirk Wiemann, "transculturality . . . does not have to be minoritarian, diasporic, or dissident, but rather is a constitutive feature of the culture at large" (6). Obviously, this does not mean discounting the important contribution of postcolonial thinking to the debate on issues concerning mutual exploitation and subalternity, the machinations of power, and the renewed prejudices fostered by the enforced globalized proximity. The question here is that, in John McLeod's words, "we are urged to think instead across and beyond the tidy, holistic entities of nations and cultures—transnationally, transculturally—if we hope to capture and critique the conditions of our contemporaneity" ("Sounding" 1). A similar critique might be extended to the literary criticism of (im)migrant/diasporic literature seen from the perspective of multiculturalism (on multicultural literature see, e.g., Gunew, *Framing*). As it has already been argued, multiculturalism has been an important step in the development of a consciousness and sensibility of difference, but by overstressing the value of difference and territorial nostalgia for lost geographies and broken identities (with the negative disruption of "displacement" seen as a main trope), it seems unable to foster togetherness and solidarity beyond ethnic, religious, national, or cultural borders and to envision alternative modes of belonging for a new kind of derooted and denationalized generation of citizens. Hence it can be better viewed as a step in the movement towards the complexity and multiplicity of cultures that might eventually lead to a transcultural mode of being, writing, reading, and critiquing.

My point is that in these fluid, neonomadic global times there exists a possibility of a transcultural literature and a critical perspective that can be better attuned to the changes in contemporary cultural horizons (see Thomsen, "Migrant") and can convey a sensibility towards new forms of cultural pluralism and "diversity" triggered by a growingly heterogeneous social composition and more variegated migratory flows (see Faist; Vertovec). Owing to a number of globalizing, trans/postnational phenomena which characterize transcultural literature, transculturality can offer a profound and responsible approach to cultural encounters and their inevitable tensions or even clashes. Seen in this light, transcultural literature corresponds to some extent to a third moment of imaginative transformation in addition to the two moments proposed by Manfred Jurgensen (see "Transformative"). Starting from the perspective of the primary/native culture (first moment) and the need for mediation in regard to the host culture (second moment), the third moment can be understood as a cross-cultural experimentation with the development of "a language of creative cultural transformation" (Hopfer 27). The literature and adjoined literary scholarship and criticism emerging from this third moment seem more aligned to the sensibilities of a new breed of writers, as well as to a physically and mentally growing dislocated readership. Commenting on Mark Stein's writing about the emergence of a transcultural imagination, Schulze-Engler notes that "The 'location of transculture' is not only to be found in realities outside texts or in the texts themselves, but also in audiences that make sense of them according to 'new regimes of reference, norm, and value' drawing upon several cultural backgrounds; the transcultural potential of texts thus lies in their impact on the reader as well as in the modes of representation required to approximate the cultural complexity they engage with" (Introduction xiv).

So where does transcultural literature stand in relation to postcolonial and multicultural literature? To a certain extent, it delineates itself from the previous domains while still being permeated by them. In other words, it marks a further literary "wave," in Moretti's terms, in the cultural and geographical dislocation of narratives from the center towards the periphery—or better still, it signals the nullification of the dichotomy between centers and peripheries ("Conjectures" 66-68).

Potentially, every periphery can now become the center and vice versa in a performance of construction and deconstruction where it is no longer possible to identify a single, permanent, and hegemonic center. According to Margareta Petersson, "the concept of transculturation, with its denial of centre-periphery binarism, is seen as a way of overcoming difficulties of linearities, or postcolonial reversed linearities" (156). This does not deny, nonetheless, the reality that in ways similar to the economic system of globalization in liberal capitalism the "planetary system" of literature—that is, the "one world literary system (of inter-related literatures)"—is "profoundly unequal" (Moretti, "Conjectures" 54). Hence we can say that transcultural literature is outgrowing the (im)migrant, exile, diasporic, ethnic forms of writing conceived within the context of postcolonialism and multiculturalism to inscribe itself in the theoretical context of transculture/ality. Despite sharing a common constellation of theoretical languages and modes of reasoning, transcultural literature is pursuing a literary narration and discourse that is branching away from the tradition of (im)migrant and postcolonial literatures. It is true that in most cases transcultural literature may have its roots in migration, as well as in postcolonial, diasporic, exile conditions and in identity displacement and the cultural dislocation that ensues; but then it detaches (or flows out) from them in a process of metamorphosis. However, this does not imply that these conditions and modes of writing are opposed to each other nor that they are subject to a linear, temporal pattern of development with unwanted evolutionist, progressive, or teleological undertones. Instead, these specific modes of writing tend to coexist, interact, and often overlap (see, e.g., Sturm-Trigonakis).

This leads us to think that if in the field of the literatures of mobility, the twentieth century may be identified as the century of exile, (im)migrant, postcolonial, and diasporic writing par excellence, the early twenty-first century of neonomadic lifestyles and transnational patterns may be conducive to a transcultural way of writing, reading, and analysis. With the transcultural we now have not only a theoretical and methodological framework, but also a literary model to relate to modes of writing (and of reading) produced within the transnational circuits of global communication and movement. We might thus say that transcultural literature is more in tune with the perspective referred to by Ashcroft in his discussion of the cultural and hence the literary multipolar and decentered system of the "transnation" ("Transnation" 73). In this way the local and the global, the national and the transnational are inextricably intermeshed and engaged with each other through new, though often unequal or disjunctive, configurations and heterogeneous temporalities: "If we think of the 'transnation' extending beyond the geographical, political, administrative and even imaginative boundaries of the state, both within and beyond the boundaries of the nation, we discover it as a space in which those boundaries are disrupted, in which natural and cultural affiliations are superseded, in which binaries of centre and periphery, national self and other are dissolved. This is because, most noticeably in the case of China and India, the nation is already a migratory and even diasporic aggregation of flows and convergences, both within and without state boundaries" (Ashcroft, "Transnation" 73). In other words, if the balances of economic power are rapidly changing, the same is happening to cultural and literary production. As Paul Jay puts it: "The stress . . . ought to be on the multidirectionality of cultural flows, on the appropriation and transformation of globalized cultural forms wherever they settle in, with close attention to how those forms are reshaped and sent off again to undergo further transformations elsewhere" ("Beyond" 42).

Anticipating one of the arguments that will be developed in the following two chapters, we can thus say that transcultural creative works are born in multiple spaces at once, and that they already belong to more cultural landscapes. Baranay's *Neem Dreams*, for example, was written in English while the author was living in Queensland and on an island (Muralag) in the Torrens Strait, but was first published in India, which is also the main setting of the novel. Manguel wrote his novel *Todos los hombres son mentirosos* (set in Madrid and revolving around a mysterious South American author) in Spanish while living in France (although he had started writing it in English while in Canada) and he first published it in Spain. Parks wrote *Dreams of Rivers and Seas*, his novel set in India with Indian and British characters, in English while living in Italy. Trojanow wrote *The Collector of Worlds*, set between India, Tanzania, and the Middle East, in German while moving from Cape Town to Vienna. It is these writers' transcultural, as well transnational (or, even better, postnational) nature that inscribes these works of fiction within the wider context of world literature. Rebecca Walkowitz makes a similar statement when analyzing Kazuo Ishiguro's transnational body of work: "Kazuo Ishiguro's novels function as world literature in two principal ways. As objects, they are written, printed, translated, circulated, and read in several places. As narratives, they organize local anecdotes into global networks and then consider the ethical consequences of that process" ("Unimaginable" 219). Despite the inevitable issues raised by categorization and the desire of most, if not all, imaginative authors to escape unwanted definitions, we may thus classify transcultural literature in the context of the other subclusters of the literatures of mobility—that is, (im)migrant, exile, expatriate, ethnic, refugee, diasporic, or postcolonial literatures—within the wider domain of world literature(s).

The concept of "world literature" has undergone a steady revision since it was first theorized by Goethe in 1827 (see, e.g., Birus; Juvan, "Worlding"; Sturm-Trigonakis). In the nineteenth century and for most part of the twentieth century it was mainly attached to the notion of a Eurocentric canon of literary works belonging to different national landscapes. Since the 1970s poststructuralism, postcolonial approaches, and cultural studies contributed to the easing of the Eurocentric grip and to the expansion of the canon to a wider international, possibly truly planetary dimension. In its broad generalization, world literature encompasses literary texts which come from different cultural and linguistic traditions and are able to cross national and cultural borders. Damrosch views world literature as constituted by "all literary works that circulate beyond their culture of origin, either in translation or in their original language" (*What Is* 4). From the perspective proposed by Debjani Ganguly, this also means thinking of world literature(s) as a literary territory "where the journeys are multi-linear and where literary capital can be found in works that are locally inflected and have both regional and global purchase" (26). In this light, the terrain of world literature has grown to progressively include a greater number of those works that are able to go beyond their country of origin and thus challenge a way of studying literatures grounded in national traditions. The latest theorizations, however, induce us to take a further step: they prompt us to see world literature(s) as "a mode of circulation and of reading" applicable to "established classics and new discoveries alike," taking into account the complexity of the present cultural and economic globalization, with its distinctive traits and its narrations of transnational interactions (Damrosch, *What Is* 5). I hope to contribute to this more expanded and open-ended vision of world literature(s), seconding Ascari's remark that "what we need today are tools rather than lists" (7), and Thomsen's claim that "the *future* of world literature is . . . the idea of a change in the way that literature will be taught and criticized. It is based on a belief that cultural globalization will and should influence the way literature is selected and studied" ("Migrant" 246). That is why, seconding this more pluralist notion of world literature, growing numbers of scholars now prefer to talk about "world literatures" in the plural (Boruszko and Tötösy de Zepetnek; Juvan, "Introduction"; Wang).

If scholars acknowledge that now there are texts which seem to "ask to be read across several national and political scenes," accordingly, there seem to be readers who increasingly tend to read across several cultural and territorial landscapes, in the original or—even when English is not their native language—in English translation (Walkowitz, "Unimaginable" 223). Talking in this particular case about a prominently European readership, Parks contributes the following comment: "There appears to be a tension, or perhaps necessary balance, between evasion and realism in fiction, between a desire to read seriously about real things—to feel I am not wasting my time, but engaging intelligently with the world—and simultaneously a desire to escape the confines of one's immediate community, move into the territory of the imagination, and perhaps fantasize about far away places" ("Most"). On a similar note, but taking into consideration the rest of the world, Kanaka Bashyam Sankaran argues that "modernization and globalization have brought about enormous social and economic changes in postcolonial societies, producing a new Third-World generation of cosmopolitan readers and learners" (412). Not only has the readership changed in the West as well as in the Rest, but owing to the growing influence of global mobility on people's lifestyles it has also started to transcend national borders and become more international, if not transcultural. Trojanow among others recognizes this trend, aware that whoever reads his books in German, even before they are translated into English or other languages, now sends him feedback from various parts of the world and often even sooner than those geographically closer.

It is specifically with this global readership in mind that Kazuo Ishiguro, who was born in Japan but since the age of five was raised in England by his Japanese parents, feels the necessity to focus on "shape, structure, and vision" or "architecture" rather than on "sentences" and "phrases" (qtd. in Walkowitz, "Unimaginable" 219). As noticed by Walkowitz, it is as if Ishiguro's and other major transnational or postnational authors' books were from the moment of their conception already meant either to be read in English by readers whose native language is not English or to be translated into other languages and thus to become part of a wider literary context ("Unimaginable"). Talking specifically about literature produced in English away from the traditional national centres of the US and the UK, Jay shows us how this literature is increasingly becoming postnational "defined less by a nation than by a language, in which authors from a variety of cultural and ethnic backgrounds write" ("Beyond" 33).

One cannot deny there still exists a manifest predominance of the Anglo-American cultural sphere in contemporary literary production and distribution: writers who achieve international visibility are selected and "created" by publishing houses and reviews remain concentrated in the metropolitan centers of the West. As Coetzee remarked in a private e-mail correspondence, "one cannot treat writers as free agents, when in fact the publication of their books is in the hands of an industry that is far from transcultural—that, at least in its Anglo-American manifestation, I would call an arm of cultural imperialism" (e-mail correspondence 13 December 2011). But even when channeled by a predominantly Anglo-American book market, this trend towards literary globalization achieves a positive impact. As Armando Gnisci maintains, there is a world literature that "begins to form a planetary network of knowledge and acknowledgements, of translations and multiple reciprocities . . . a poetics of the future" (qtd. in D'Angelo 177; see also Gnisci, "Littérature"; and Gnisci, Sinopoli, and Moll). What is questionable, as Parks points out, is the mix of international commercialization and literary celebrity created by globalization: "Today, a first draft, a first chapter, by Jonathan Franzen can be emailed to a score of publishers worldwide. It can be translated while it is still being written then published simultaneously in as many countries, supported by an international promotional campaign, not unlike those used to launch a new electronic gadget" ("The Nobel").

This eager commercialization of books and the celebrity industry surrounding their creators on a global scale is also responsible for a parallel and contested phenomenon, the carefully marketed push towards "ethnicized" authors and the growing fashion of inserting transnational settings in so-called global novels. In other words, we are witnessing an attempt to sell to a global audience novels with the ethnic and exotic flavor of India, China, or the deep African South (see Parks, "A Game"). Talking about the international success of a number of authors from the Indian subcontinent, Kai Friese warns that they all belong to a type of fiction he calls "Hinduistic realism," or what Baranay calls the novel "with an eye on international consumption" ("Multiculturalism" 125). Here is Friese's description of the genre: "An excess of 'authentic' detail . . . This is India by numbers. Hinduism 101 . . . books . . . peppered with set pieces on spicy food, master-servant dynamics and redeeming vignettes on the possibility of romance in an arranged marriage. Reincarnation. Mighty Avatars, Spicy Food, Servants, Arranged Marriage. Sound familiar?" (qtd. in Baranay, "Multiculturalism" 126).

Despite flattening commercial rules, the simplistic search for ethnic color and the alluring traps of the "postcolonial exotic" hovering over the contemporary international literary market, transcultural literature—which de facto belongs to world literature(s)—tends toward that "transpace" (my term) that lies beyond the divides, often commercially or ideologically emphasized, of cultures (see Huggan, *The Postcolonial*). It is there, in that "potential zone," to use Bartoloni's words, that we can "experience the interaction of cultures and languages as they fluidly intermingle" ("Translation" 9). It is clear that transcultural literature is not immune to the competitive dynamics of the international literary scene characterized by "rivalry, struggle, and inequality," as Pascale Casanova highlights (*The World* 4). Nonetheless, paraphrasing J. Hillis Miller, who speaks of contemporary world literature in general, transcultural works help us "to understand and to live productively in the new uncomfortable world of global intercommunication and global wandering that Nietzsche calls 'nomadism'" ("Globalization" 264).

World literature thus encompasses all those literary works which "circulate beyond their culture of origin, either in translation or in their original language." For those who see it in a slightly more stringent—and probably more pragmatic—perspective, it encompasses only those works that are "actively present within a literary system beyond that of its original culture" (Damrosch, *What* 4). For this reason Damrosch comes to the conclusion that world literature is both "a mode of circulation" as well as "a mode of reading" whose parameters are constantly shifting: "Just as there never has been a single set canon of world literature, so too no single way of reading can be appropriate to all texts, or even to any text at all times" (*What Is* 5). Further, Damrosch proposes to include in the broad definition of world literature also those works which, instead of going out in the world, bring in the world: this usually happens, for example, when "writers draw on foreign literatures in order to intervene within their own culture" ("World" 307). Following this line of reasoning, I see as an integral part of world literature(s) those literatures of mobility, including transcultural literature, whose authors—in one way or another, freely or forcefully, consciously or subconsciously, physically or virtually—make the voyage out of their national, linguistic, homeland, ethnic, or cultural boundaries. This is why in their texts they negotiate and inspire new border-crossing imaginaries and, in some instances, either create entirely imaginary homelands or reimagine the world at large. It is also important to note that the previous literary configurations/expressions (i.e., [im]migrant, exile, diasporic, postcolonial literature) are instrumental in generating a transcultural awareness. It is thus clear that the "fuzzy" category of transcultural literature, with its blurred boundaries and fluid nature, tends to overlap—if not at times coincide—with the adjacent categories of postnational, cosmopolitan, transnational, and global/ized writing.

As forms of cultural practices and producers of meaning, the creative works inscribed in the constellation of the literatures of mobility express and at the same time affect the imaginary, emotional states, and attitudes both of people who are on the move across (or beyond) nations, languages, cultural borders and of their more sedentary counterparts. Like all creative/artistic manifestations functioning in conjunction with economies and other sociotechnological factors or contexts, they may too have contrasting functions: more or less intentionally they may support or challenge dominant cultural discourses or counterdiscourses. As Jay points out, "culture is a set of material practices linked to economies, and economic and material relations are always mediated by cultural factors and forms" (*Global* 45). Only by taking into account all the different situations, perspectives, outlooks, social dimensions, and creative manifestations of human activity, creativity, and imagination are we able to catch a glimpse of the whole fluctuating, ever-changing pattern in the global tapestry. There appear to be no teleological forces (or theories) at work in the emerging picture, nor plans for large-scale projects of social engineering, only the dialogic interaction of contending, and mutually qualifying, multiple social voices and modes of discourse (in Bakhtin's terms)—what Appadurai calls "the everyday cultural practice through which the work of the imagination is transformed" (*Modernity* 9). Within this framework of reference, one can more easily acknowledge also the dialectical tension between the autonomy of art and its status as a *fait social* proposed by Theodor W. Adorno (*Aesthetic Theory* 311-14; see also Adorno, *Essays*). Despite being a cultural aesthetic product related to a particular society, economic circumstance, or political contingency, and despite having a social history attached to it, art can still have a degree of autonomy, freedom, and power to affect prevailing discourses: "By the inherent tendency of art to cast different lights on the familiar, artworks correspond to the objective need for a transformation of consciousness that could become a transformation of reality" (Adorno, *Aesthetic* 317). This allows writers and their readers engaged with the texts as active interpreters to think critically and imagine in ways which do not correspond to the dominant understanding of the world with its political agendas and social conditioning.

What emerges from this open-ended tapestry of (post)modern conditions is that with globalization even the creative (literary) outputs need to be read, studied, and analyzed through a new interpretive lens and its adjoined new vocabulary. As Liam Connell and Nicky Marsh point out: "One obvious reason why critics have been slow to engage with the theories of globalization as they were being developed in other disciplines is the fact that literary studies seemed to possess, in postcolonialism and postmodernism, two prior modes of thinking about transnationalism . . . However, while this kind of approach to globalization is obviously attractive for postcolonial scholars it may cloud our awareness of what is distinctive or new about globalization as a way of organizing international inequalities and a mode of narrating transnational interactions" (94-96). With transculture/ality we have a new perspective from which to address critically the cultural impact of globalalization and its creative expressions away from the "continuing influence of the nation as a structure for the study of literature" (Connell and Marsh 97). As Jay makes clear: "We need to find a way to accommodate the transnational and postnational perspectives of globalization studies in our programs and curricula without subordinating the heterogeneous literatures we deal with to outdated critical paradigms" ("Beyond" 44). It is this crystallization of national paradigms in the study of literatures which, as Connell and Marsh highlight, "has served as an impediment to the engagement with globalization as a critical idea" (97).

What I am arguing for contributes to suggesting the definition of a heuristic model within literary studies that might be called "transcultural comparativism." If we wanted to represent graphically this specific analytical framework, we would probably end up with a kind of 5D model in which the five dimensions are: 1) time (that is, the historical dimension); 2) context (in terms of socioeconomic realities, technological developments, political processes, geographical locations); 3) practice (in terms of lived experience, language, communication, interaction); 4) meaning (in terms of dominant ideologies, worldviews, cultural constructs); and 5) agency (in terms of self-reflexivity, critical thinking, innovation, imagination, creative outputs). From this perspective, transcultural comparativism shows affinities with—and might be inscribed within—the contextual (systemic and empirical) approach Tötösy de Zepetnek has been developing since the 1990s and has first described in 1998 in his book *Comparative Literature: Theory, Method, Application*. Drawing on existing and emerging theories in the disciplines of comparative literature and cultural studies, Tötösy de Zepetnek has formulated a theoretical and methodological framework that he refers to as "comparative cultural studies" ("From Comparative" 2). In his view, this framework facilitates the pluralistic, inclusionary, and interdisciplinary study of literature and culture while emphasizing the connections and the dialogic realities and practices between cultures, languages, literatures, and disciplines. Starting with these assumptions, I see transcultural writers as a direct creative expression of the emerging social and economic patterns of globalization, of people's increased mobility across the planet, and of the cultural complexities and interactions that these combined factors generate. In the first three chapters of the critical exegesis I identify the global, social, critical, and theoretical arenas in which these authors and their writing practices thrive and explain in which context I use words like "culture," "identity," "transnationalism," "neonomadism," "cosmopolitanism," "transculturalism," "world literature(s)," and "literatures of mobility." Further, I outline the concepts of (transculture/ality) and the analytical framework (transcultural comparativism) I propose. In the following chapters I proceed to analyze the results of my research, outline a profile of transcultural writers, and identify the main features of their creative outputs, namely transcultural novels. What emerges through the analytical and comparative process—in particular with regard to issues of identity, dislocation and rootlesseness, belonging, home, allegiance, translingualism, relation with the Other—are the fluid patterns and "fuzzy" contours which characterize these authors' cultural identities, orientations, and their imaginative texts.

Chapter Four

Transcultural Writers, Creative Transpatriation, and Transcultural Fiction

In this study I argue that transcultural writers undergo a creative transpatriation process similar to the processes of cultural transformation that, on a broader social scale, the neonomads experience. Neonomadism—even more so than (im)migration, exile, expatriation, or other kinds of travel experiences—is a social condition which can lead to a transcultural orientation and which at the literary level can promote the creation of transcultural texts. By creative transpatriation I mean the process generated by life circumstances, attitudes, imposed or self-imposed rootlessness, cultural dislocations, and physical deterritorializations by which writers attain a transcultural orientation. More precisely, it is a combined process of defamiliarization with one's primary culture and of de-ethnicization, detribalization, delocalization, and denationalization of one's sense of identity, belonging, and allegiance. This condition had already been recognized and envisaged at the end of the twentieth century by Henry James, who described it by coining the term "dispatriation," meaning "a kind of detachment in viewpoint of, not severance of interest in, the birthland" (Edna Kenton qtd. in Izzo and O'Hara 33; see also Palandri; Sinopoli and Tatti). The same term would be later used with a similar meaning by Luigi Meneghello in his book *Il dispatrio*. Talking about Meneghello's own dispatriation (in 1947 he left Italy to live in the UK), Frederika Randall writes that he was "not an expatriate, nor an exile longing for his native ways and language. Not an emigrant driven by economic forces, or a refugee fleeing political chaos. But someone who had taken a good, hard look at his mother culture even as he was adopting a second one. Someone who had moved abroad not only physically but also psychologically and intellectually, 'who had taken apart and remade his cultural and national identity'" (xvi).

It is through the above described process that the writers I interviewed—and who have among their forerunners and contemporaries expatriate, (im)migrant, exile, or neonomadic authors such as Bowles, Rushdie, Maalouf, Ondaatje, and Iyer—show to have developed a transcultural disposition and mode of being. I prefer to call this process of becoming transcultural "transpatriation" in order to emphasize the importance not only of moving away from one's own native or primary culture but also of overcoming—or, better, "unlearning"—ways of identity formation which rely on ethnicity, nationality, locality, tribal affiliation, or religious allegiance (somewhat similarly, drawing on Ortiz, Alessandra Renzi talks about a "process of transculturation" [111]; on the influence of processes of transculturation on transcultural writers, see also Rosalía Baena). Through this process, which is often set in motion by physical dislocation and by multiple cultural encounters, the Other becomes "a fundamental reality, yet not as a presence evaluated in opposition to the 'self' but as part of it" (Renzi 111). This kind of creative transpatriation, therefore, allows one to experience the Other in a way that is conducive to the integration of a plurality of differences and viewpoints within one's self. It is through integral and integrated differences or an interpenetration of multiple cultural selves that one gets to "embrace 'Otherness' by occupying the standpoint of different cultures" or to imagine oneself in the mindset of a different cultural world (Renzi 111). We are not in front of a new form of undesirable "appropriation" or presumptuous knowledge of the Other, but are witnessing an enriching and fruitful experience of—or dialogic encounter with—the Other. In Glissant's terms, it is this relationship with the Other which is able to foster a cultural and imaginative expansion of the self (*Traité* 248-51). Trojanow and the other writers I interviewed do not seem to attach any negative connotations to the process of transpatriation except for a shared dissociation from the patriotic idea of nation. As Enrico Palandri, who lived for many years in England, puts it,

> There will be more and more people who will find it natural to move, who no longer perceive "dispatriation" as a national identity crisis . . . If we look at the ancient world, the Middle Ages, our Renaissance or the Age of Enlightenment, we might think that it is precisely in the era between Leopardi and Meneghello that we have *dispatriation.* After all, before the Romantics this unity of language, culture, and geography from which we trace the idea of national identity was incomprehensible and one that perhaps tomorrow will no longer concern us. What idea of . . . *dispatriation* is there in Da Ponte, Casanova or Goldoni? In Shakespeare or even in Milton? In Rabelais, Rousseau or Voltaire? In Ovid or in Martial? . . . it is rather what Foscolo, imbued with nationalist ideals, would call exile in his autobiographical sonnet *A Zacinto*. ("Seminario")

Creative transpatriation thus represents a psychological threshold, a membrane one has to walk through to access a transcultural dimension and thus become a "transpatriate" (my term), that is a transcultural dispatriate. Divesting oneself of the primordial identity cornerstones of one's primary culture, ethnicity, and nationality is not an easily accomplished task. We are all too aware of that little corner of our inner social, and not only cultural, identity that gets upset when we hear someone criticize our own ethnicity, cultural background, or national character. There seems to be a primeval urge to identify with and to defend certain allegiances and paradigms. Particularly when associated with the adjective "creative," however, transpatriation signals the assertion of the subject's (in this case, the writer's) freedom from the ties of rooted cultural affiliations and national traditions. It also represents the overcoming of all those traumatic and distressing feelings (nostalgia, estrangement, loss of memory, loss of one's sense of identity, loss of native language) associated with the experience of (im)migration and displacement. Seen in this light, transpatriation rehabilitates through its imaginative and creative—or generative—power, that attitude of the polyglot writers *sans patrie* of the Enlightenment or even pre-Enlightenment evoked by Palandri.

In the interviews with the five authors selected for the present study, it emerges that one can undergo a transpatriation process and attain a transcultural orientation for several reasons and in different ways or circumstances. One can be the son or daughter of (im)migrant, exile, refugee, or expatriate parents (Baranay, Castro, Trojanow, Manguel). One can decide to "uproot" oneself in one's youth or choose a transnational career/expatriate status (Parks). One can even reach or earn a deep sense of transculture/ality after having started from a monocultural background, deeply rooted in one's particular history, culture, and location: this is for example the case of Cesare De Marchi, who went to live in Germany, immersed himself in German culture and started publishing novels with transcultural elements only later in life. All such writers with their different ways of getting to and living through transpatriation show a positive attitude towards their dislocation. Instead of considering it a hindrance, a displaced condition of alienation, fragmentation, and insecurity (although most of them have also experienced these feelings), they come to realize and acknowledge that the process of dislocation and of cultural rootlessness of their own self can be an intriguing and insightful creative device, a portal to infinite possibilities of being and imagining. Simply put, they have reached that peculiar attitude or transcultural dimension of being that frees them from the necessity of constantly interrogating their sense of identity (I acknowledge the forerunners of creative transpatriation such as Rushdie who regard exile and [im]migration not so much as a state of deprivation, but as a privileged condition that generates multiple perspectives). For them, identity, like culture, is not stable, but an ongoing expansion, a process, a work in progress that does not need to be kept at bay or monitored in order to define its centers and borders.

This generation of transcultural writers shares the fact that their creative transpatriations may have been acquired more ore less consciously. "At what point is such a tool sought?" asks the Australian author of Hungarian origin Baranay. Following in the steps of earlier analyses, personal accounts, and creative representations linked to concepts of "hybridity" (on this see, e.g., Papastergiadis; Young) and to certain forms of travel writing (for example the works of Chatwin and Kapuściński), we might even expect that other writers could become interested in experimenting with the transcultural by consciously transpatriating themselves in order to use this form of cultural *depaisement* as a potentially creative tool. According to Welsch, the future seems to encourage a growing number of transcultural authors: "For most of us, multiple cultural connections are decisive in terms of our cultural formation. We are cultural hybrids. Today's writers, for example, emphasize that they're shaped not by a single homeland, but by differing reference countries, by Russian, German, South and North American or Japanese literature. Their cultural formation is transcultural (think, for example, of Naipaul or Rushdie)—that of subsequent generations will be even more so" ("Transculturality" 198). We should be aware, however, that dislocation is a condition which is necessary but not sufficient to the achievement of a transcultural perspective. As Alexa Weik reminds us, lived experience and practices are essential aspects of any "actually existing" cosmopolitanism, which means that "pure imaginative engagement" is not enough (3). Yet, dislocaton alone cannot guarantee the experience of a transpatriation process nor the attainment of a more open, culturally multifaceted mindset. The expatriate US-American writers of the so-called Lost Generation are a good case in point in this regard. They indeed roamed Europe in the 1930s and were "widely traveled and intellectually sophisticated" (Weik 3); however, they never renounced their US-American view of the Other and "rarely did they get personally involved in ways that shifted their loci of identification" (Weik 3-4). Being on the move is not enough if there is not the willingness, the curiosity, the disposition, the (cultural/material) means, the sensibility, and, in general, an "expansive orientation" to open oneself to the Other and participate in, be involved with the culture/s of the Other (Hannerz, "Cosmopolitans" 249). Transposing Hannerz's reasoning and Weik's views on literary cosmopolitanism into a transcultural practice and discourse, it is clear that physical, effective immersion in the cultures, languages, and geographies of the Other is vital for engendering the transpatriation process that can lead to a transcultural mode of being and possibly mold the creative mindsets and imaginary landscapes from which transcultural fiction emanates. As Jarmila Očkayová argues, "to know the Other, it is necessary to step through the mirror, like Lewis Carroll's Alice . . . we need to run the risk, if we do not want to know only the clichés, the stereotypes, the commonplaces, the abstracts judgments that are prejudices—still so frequent, so present in thousand and thousand minuscule but widespread daily barbarities" (27). Evidently, all this may be possible—as Martine Bovo Ramoeuf writes referring to the life and work of Carmine Abate, a contemporary Italian author whom she believes to be well on the path towards a full transcultural orientation—once the identity quest (more than its assertion) is addressed "under the sign of fluidity, of becoming, of transformation" ("Rhapsodie").

One of the recurrent themes in conventional (im)migrant fiction is the search for identity. In the past, most (im)migrant writers expressed the urge to wonder about their own identity and problematize it. To a lesser or greater extent, it appeared that (im)migrant writers and their fictionalized characters were "haunted by some sense of loss, some urge to reclaim, to look back" (Rushdie, "Imaginary" 10). Unlike the past, these contemporary transcultural authors do not seem at odds with their destabilized, decentred sense of cultural, racial, ethnic, or national sense of self. They have outgrown, perhaps "transcended," the problem having developed a somewhat relaxed, fluid, neonomadic attitude towards issues of identity, nationality, rootlessness, and dislocation: "They ask me about my roots, but I am not a tree. Identity is rather something dynamic, a fluid concept, even if many people tend to think only in terms of belonging. At the beginning I suffered from this not belonging of mine.

Now I have understood that all this constitutes a richness" (Trojanow, "Le identità"). On the same note, Manguel writes that "our identity, and the time and place in which we exist, are fluid and transient, like water" (*A Reader* 42). Maalouf also rejects the motionless—and paralyzing—vegetal metaphor of roots to describe identity: "Others but not me would talk about 'roots.' It is not in my vocabulary. I do not like the word 'roots,' let alone the image that it evokes. Roots sink into the ground, twist in the mud, grow in the darkness; they keep the tree captive from its birth; they feed it but the price is an extortion: 'If you get free, you die!'" (*Origines* 9).

A founding critique of nation-based identities already emerged in the field of anthropology from James Clifford's *Routes*, in which he outlines new forms of belonging which, in Ursula K. Heise's words, "would transcend exclusive commitments to a particular nation, culture, race, or ethnicity in favor of more global modes of awareness and attachment" (57). He did so by showing the way in which local cultures form and manipulate their identity "from connections to a variety of places ('routes') rather than their anchoring in just one locale ('roots')" (Heise 57). Instead of roots, Maalouf also prefers to talk about "routes," where the concept of identity stemming from a single totalizing origin (root) is discarded in favor of the idea of a plurality of paths (routes) not dissimilar to the Deleuzian rhizome or the concept of confluence and confluential identities expressed by Trojanow and Hoskoté: "Contrary to trees, routes do not emerge from the soil . . . Like us, they have an origin. Illusory origin, since a route never has a real beginning. Elusive origin, since at any intersection other routes, that came from other origins, meet" (Maalouf, *Origines* 9; for a further discussion of "roots" and "routes" in identity see Gilroy; with regard to the concept of identity in Maalouf's writings see Negro). To a certain extent, for these authors the essence of culture (identity) is represented by the paradoxical—or narrative—coherence of a transformational and constantly dynamic process of becoming, with its starting points, multiple entries, and lines of flight. As Berry points out: "The goal becomes to 'mutate' beyond any singular or bounded mode of cultural identity—even a hybridized identity—in order to 'become transcultural'" ("Nomadic" 130).

Drawing on the interviews I conducted, what distinguishes such writers as transcultural appears to be their relaxed, neonomadic attitude when facing issues linked to displacement, rootlessness, nationality, cultural allegiance, and identity. Contrary to the past, they do not dwell nostalgically upon a perceived sense of loss or displacement. Instead, they aim at being culturally or geographically dislocated or "transpatriated"; they self-induce and somewhat indulge in their diasporic or exilic state in order to gain a new perspective on the world, on different cultures, on humanity, and, ultimately, on themselves. As Mootacem Bellah Mhiri remarks analyzing the poetics of Ameen Rihani, a Lebanese-born US-American writer and translator of English and Arabic: "The nomad, as a trope for the transcultural and transnational subject/consciousness, thrives on this state of movement and flux that s/he finds him/herself in" (50). In the same vein, Rushdie writes in "Imaginary Homelands": "It is normally supposed that something always gets lost in translation. I cling, obstinately, to the notion that something can also be gained . . . If literature is in part the business of finding new angles at which to enter reality, then . . . our distance, our long geographical perspective, may provide us with such angles" (15-17). These are no longer writers "out of place," but "in place" wherever they happen to be: "someone like me, I figured, could (for worse as much as better) fit in everywhere," writes Iyer (258). Transcultural authors adapt, change in accordance with the language and the customs of the place, metamorphose as they blend in. They are ready to do it, willing to surrender, not afraid to lose themselves in the process. And by adapting they spur their creativity along a path which is not already set, or clear-cut, but which tends to attract writers and readers who share certain life patterns, experiences, views, and sensibilities.

In the opinion of Castro, "Hybridity, a mixture of forms, a mixture of character types and ethnicities, is what I bring to writing. It is what the 'I' is. A proliferation of selves. A juxtapositioning of differences. I am not only Portuguese, English, Chinese, and French, but I am writing myself out of crippling essentialist categorisations, out of the control exerted over multiplicities" ("Auto/Biography" 115; for a further distinction between enforced exile and the mode of voluntary exile or "poetic isolation," that is, literary and philosophical exile, perceived and lived as a "mental flight" able to foster new conditions of belonging, see Bartoloni; in the same vein, dealing with the relationship between migration, transcultural transplantation, and artistic identity, or as "displacement as an artistic device" see also Grauby, "A Transcultural" 71). Transcultural writers are confluentially imaginative beings whose cultural make-up consists of more than one culture, one language, one worldview. Hence, they tend neither to exhibit nor to creatively express or interpret a fixed identity, their own are a blend of all their metamorphoses. Once they transpose this pluralistic cultural attitude into their writings, they become bridges: connectors of ideas, cultures, and stories; imaginative and linguistic translators of different ways of perceiving life and human relationships. In acting as bridge people, as cultural ambassadors able to negotiate among multiple cultural landscapes, transcultural writers may play a special role in a world where belligerent and clashing views of cultural identity and allegiance still prevail. Maalouf has come to the conclusion that it is this kind of people who, "by forging links"—although imaginary ones—can act as "go-betweens, mediators between the various communities and cultures" (*In the Name* 5).

By straddling boundaries, physically shifting location, learning new languages, and being exposed to different worldviews, transcultural writers acquire different mindsets which they then adapt to the different cultural conditions they might find themselves in. They change in order to adapt and every adaptation further transforms them, making them eternal chameleons, champions of an individualized, metamorphic sense of identity which nonetheless allows them to maintain intact the multifaceted integrity of their selves. In other words, transcultural writers never get lost in translation. Even in the most fluid of cultural states, there still is the possibility and perhaps the need (a very human need) to maintain one's peculiar—and unique—sense of self, even when this may no longer be represented by an inner core surrounded by concentric rings (like an onion that can be peeled) of identitarian clues and attachments. As the writer Mario Barenghi remarks in his conversation with Palandri:

> There is a very strong assumption, that is that identity is a concentric structure, a hard core that constitutes the essence of each one's identity, and that this should be identified with a national label. For some time I asked myself if it wasn't possible to imagine identity as a concentric structure, according to which I am Milanese, Lombard, Italian, European, and so on. This is a misleading image, because anyhow this spatial metaphor implies a hierarchy. What stays in the middle counts more, and I don't think it is so.

Maalouf is keen to stress this same point when noting that there is a widespread, and in his opinion "dangerous," "view of humanity" that presupposes that "'Deep down inside' everyone there is just one affiliation that really matters, a kind of 'fundamental truth' about each individual, an 'essence' determined once and for all at birth, never to change thereafter. As if the rest, all the rest—a person's whole journey through time as a free agent; the beliefs he acquires in the course of that journey; his own individual tastes, sensibilities and affinities; in short his life itself—counted for nothing . . . Anyone who claims a more complex identity is marginalized" (*In the Name* 2-3).

Instead, transcultural authors tell us that one can still build one's own cultural identity like an ever-changing puzzle or a fluid web of interconnections choosing from different cultures what suits one best and at which moment or under which circumstance it is most appropriate to express specific elements, without necessarily renouncing the cultural framework within which one feels most at ease. This way of reasoning sustains the view that people—and writers—can effectively construct culture, and even spiritual or religious inclinations, in a highly personalized fashion, as was apparently the case in Richard Francis Burton's nineteenth-century India, a place where, again according to Trojanow, "You had a lot of religious mobility; where you had a huge cultural and spiritual confluence . . . where you had a lot of merging . . . To believe that only one path is true for me it's actually a form of blasphemy" ("Meeting").

In *The City of Words* Manguel tells the story of Cassandra who, together with her brother, had been forgotten by their mother: "Cassandra's individuality is thrust upon her in her infancy . . . Alone, she must define herself and her attachments . . . alone she must imagine what 'home' will be and what stories will take place in this 'home'—all this not based on what she is told is hers but on what she chooses to identify as hers" (21). This way of getting to establish one's own identity resonates with the transcultural writers' path towards self-culturation. Getting to know other places, different cultures, languages, worldviews, and then integrating them into their own sense of being, choosing—despite the inevitable structural constraints—which elements of these cultures to keep and what to leave out is a selection process and a sort of cultural self-making. As humans living in a decentered, deregulated, individualized global modernity of melting societies, omnipresent fluidity, and pervasive precariousness, these writers are also left bereft of their institutional parental guidance (the traditional commanding authority—the nation-state, the clergy, the party, the local community) as Cassandra was of hers. So they too, perhaps driven by voluntary enthusiasm and curiosity, need to find by themselves the interpretive keys of their own identity. And, sometimes, the vision of the world which is conjured up by this hybrid mix, this open-minded choice, is not what other people want to see, in the same way as Cassandra's own vision of the world "is not the one her fellow Trojans want to see" (Manguel, *The City* 22). The role of Cassandra, as well as of the writer, however, "is not to convince but merely to say . . . This is the great richness and difficulty of literature: that it is not dogma. It states facts, but it gives no definitive answers, declares no absolute postulates, demands no unarguable assumptions, offers no labelling identities" (Manguel, *The City* 22). In the same way, we might say that the identity of such transcultural writers acquires a Deleuzian rhizomatic nature, with multiple, nonhierarchical entry and exit points: for "a rhizome has no beginning or end; it is always in the middle, between things, interbeing, intermezzo" (Deleuze and Guattari, *A Thousand* 27). Following Haberkorn's view of transcultural literature and its connection to the neonomadic identities of its authors, we can perceive transcultural writers as travellers between worlds who reinvent their identities. This view is not dissimilar to the one envisioned by McLeod when talking about Kureishi's sense of place in the world. Drawing upon Gilroy's transnational models of identity and close to Maalouf's way of thinking, McLeod heralds the advent of a transcultural, dispatriate subject for whom *roots* are exchanged with *routes*: "[Kureishi] does not have secure roots which fix him in place, in a nation or an ethnic group; rather, he must continually plot for himself itinerant cultural routes which take him, imaginatively as well as physically, to many places and into contact with many different people . . . The grounded certainties of roots are replaced with the transnational contingencies of routes" (*Beginning* 215).

A strong consciousness of life's impermanence is a common feature among the transcultural writers I have interviewed. Trojanow, for example, recounts how "everything we think important in life can change" (Dagnino and Trojanow). "Nothing is permanent," echoes Baranay, who is also keen to emphasize that "I like to have a private peaceful pleasant place to sleep and write in for long enough to get something done . . . I have recently spent over three years living in temporary places and most of them suited me fine. I found sub-let apartments or stayed in artists' colonies. I like to have a home of my own but not necessarily the same one for very long . . . and anyway, there's an uncertain line in my life between 'living' somewhere and just 'staying' there a while. A combination of my research/creative interests and the opportunity to pursue them decides a lot" (Dagnino and Baranay). In this light one might see dispatriate transcultural writers as liquid people, fluid characters flowing in their stories as much as they do in their lives—impermanent as water is impermanent; protean as water is, taking the shape of things it encounters along its path. Water people. Fluid people. Transcultural writers are as slippery and difficult to grasp as flowing water; nonetheless, like water, capable of great memory. They form patterns in their lives, but once the pattern is formed, it can also be easily dissolved. Their lives and their characters' lives are like those *mandalas* made of sand or dry flower petals which, once they have been patiently completed, are then blown away or burned by their own creators. To a certain extent, these writers resemble

Albert James, the free spirit anthropologist in Parks' novel *Dreams of Rivers and Seas*: "He was deliberately dispersing himself, distracting himself, not following a thread, disappearing, as it were, into other people's thoughts so as to weave connections between them, spread his mind across them" (225-26). This emphasized sense of impermanence, like other features which define transpatriate writers also allows identification with and is shared among an increasing number of those nomadic global citizens I discuss in chapter 1. With their innovative and positive attitudes towards their dislocations these mobile early twenty-first century writers belong to the category of those fortunate few who enjoy an "availability of surpluses—of money-capital or cultural capital, or both" (Ahmad 18). This realization does not contradict what Maver posits: "A body of major international authors in English has emerged who, refusing to be spokespersons for any ethnic or national group, deliberately seek to go beyond the colonial in their 'transcolonial' or transcultural cross-border literary texts, aimed at a global audience" ("Post-Colonial" 12).

Although their creative transpatriations and transcultural attitudes may be seen as a niche or elitist phenomenon, transcultural writers affect and at the same time reflect and express the specific sensitivities and collective imaginaries of growingly wider sections of global societies. What I am suggesting is that the cultural and creative mindsets of these writers emerging from contemporary transnational movements and neonomadic life patterns are already geared up to face the social and literary identity challenges posed by the globalizing and supranational pressures of the early twenty-first century: these writers are already able to reach that transpace between integration and disintegration, expatriation and transpatriation, local and global. It is as if the transcultural experience expressed creatively and narrated by these writers were an amplified version of the ones lived by any one of those new nomads and transnational individuals (including more or less privileged artists, academics, intellectuals, and knowledge workers) who are roaming the planet at this moment in time. By voluntarily living abroad or by consciously choosing to be culturally dislocated, the transcultural writers of the present study thus appear to outgrow their own ethnic, racial, religious, territorial identity and transcend the domestic concerns and interests of just one nation and one culture in favor of a broader, more complex transcultural identity. It is precisely on such cultural interactions and permeations that their creative works are built. Their novels are literary expressions of what it means to understand the nuances in cultural transactions and transformations. It is not only a question—or not any more—of how Westerners see Others, but also of how Others see Westerners and the rest of the world. That is why transcultural writers seem artistically committed to the comprehension of other cultures, other worldviews.

We may thus infer that transcultural writers are celebrating that dialogic form of being and of the self theorized by Bakhtin, where, according to Michael Holquist, the self and the Other do not exist as separate entities but as two necessary interacting ongoing, and shared, "events" (21). Holquist explains that for Bakhtin, who was particularly influenced by Albert Einstein's theory of relativity, the dialogic self stems from a relation of simultaneity between self and Other, where the "observer is also, simultaneously, an active participant in the relation of simultaneity" (21). This implies that reality is being experienced from a specific position in "cognitive time/space," since "dialogism, like relativity, takes for granted that nothing can be perceived except against the perspective of something else" (Holquist 22; Holquist explains "dialogism," a term that Bakhtin himself never used, as "basically a theory of knowledge, an architectonics of perception" 35). From this perspective, if "consciousness is otherness," that means that "dialogism is the name not just for a dualism, but for a necessary multiplicity in human perception" and that usually it is the artist's role and ability to perceive, experience, and represent the Other "not only as an other, but as a self" (Holquist 18-34). In other words, paraphrasing Heartfield when explaining the relationship between the subject and the object in Derridean terms, the self and the Other "are not opposed, but mutually supporting" entities (20). "Because of the intervention of that otherness," this means, as Bhabha remarks, that the subject is "always ambivalent" ("The Third" 211).

Transcultural writers show an ethical motivation in recognizing and representing Others—not to invade, ingest, annihilate, or violate them nor to trap them "within the prisons of their own fantasies and fears" (Black, *Fiction* 32), instead to establish a possible, even though arduous and sometimes uncomfortable, conversation with them. Bakhtin insists on this point: "Only a dialogic and participatory orientation takes another person's discourse seriously, and is capable of approaching it as both a semantic position and another point of view" (*Problems* 64). Discussing Bakhtin's approach, Wilfred L. Guerin, Earle Labor, Lee Morgan, Jeanne C. Reesman, and John R. Willingham remark that it is specifically "through such orientation that one can come into "intimate contact with someone else's discourse" and yet not "fuse with it, not swallow it up, not dissolve in itself the other's power to mean" (367). This implies, as Shameem Black suggests, that "even in a world marked by radical inequality, oppression, and violence, not all imaginative acts are doomed to be invasive"; on the contrary, she shows us how border crossing fiction can positively address the ethics of representing Others "without falling into familiar forms of discursive domination" (*Fiction* 20). In this light and if I interpret Baranay's reasoning correctly, the Other is no longer the postcolonial subject nor the colonial master: "The point is the idea of the Other often relies on stereotypes and ideological constructs, those of post-colonial correctitude as much as those of earlier Orientalising; and a novelist is, I believe, well advised to disengage from any discourse based upon ideas of the Other that prohibit or inhibit the characters that desire to be written" ("It's the Other").

Taking into account premises and imaginary dispositions, Baranay explains that in her novel *Neem Dreams* she created the Indian female character of Meenakshi without drawing on the postmodernist aesthetic of what is "appropriate" ("It's the Other"). She drew instead on what Frank Moorhouse defines as the "cosmopolitan position" (a concept not dissimilar to the transcultural orientation), namely, "the capacity of the imagination [to] go across centuries, genders, ages, and cultures with the only limitation being the self-recognized limitations of the writer . . . It was from a sense of wanting to extend the way imagination can reveal the necessary knowledge. It is to what Moorhouse calls 'cosmopolitanism'—being a citizen of the world—finally, that Meenakshi and I give highest value. It was what made her feel at home in the mongrel city of New York; and it was what made me able to imagine her there, and follow her home to India" ("It's the Other"). This might explain why transcultural writers resist judging other cultures from the standpoint of just one culture, since in themselves they aim to the multidimensional and to incorporate several other cultures in their own cultural make up, assuming the perspectives of Others. It is through this layered, pluralist, and permeable sense of identity they make their own judgments. What most counts for them is their commitment to an open conversation with the Other's cultures and the acknowledgement that cultures need to be dealt with and understood—we cannot allow ourselves not to try to comprehend them or, even worse, disrespect them, ignore them, feign they do not exist. This does not mean that transcultural writers inevitably fall prey to a basic cultural relativism. On the contrary, they do not consider all cultures by the same standard and they do not restrain themselves from giving their critical opinions or value judgments.

Being open to the Other, as Manguel claims, is neither totally relativistic nor aprioristic: "The fact that it simply is another culture, another important culture, another rich culture does not mean that necessarily I will take it on board and that I become more transcultural than before" (Dagnino and Manguel). So, while still holding competing ideas in the mind, transcultural writers can accept, but also refute what the Other proposes or in some cases tries to impose: "People often recommend relativism because they think it will lead to tolerance. But if we cannot learn from one another what is right to think and feel and do, then conversation between us will be pointless. Relativism of that sort isn't a way to encourage conversation; it's just a reason to fall silent" (Appiah, *Cosmopolitanism* 31). Neither does this mean that despite their nonfixed, nonready-made and often unpredictable identity mode, transcultural writers become unreliable Zeligs (like Leonard Zelig, the main character in Woody Allen's movie, who out of a desire to be accepted assumes the characteristics of others), mock humans affected by some sort of chameleon disorder, incapable of finding an inner point of reference or cultural framework. Being transcultural does not mean not having a latitude, a set of cultural coordinates, an angle of vision through which to establish one's position in a metaphoric human and ethical cartography where maps and points of reference are "entirely oriented toward an experimentation in contact with the real"; according to them, "the map," like the rhizome, "is open and connectable in all of its dimensions; it is detachable, reversible, susceptible to constant modification . . . has multiple entryways" (Deleuze and Guattari, *A Thousand* 12).

There is a space, although malleable and open-ended, for self-determination, even within a certain level of indeterminacy. The borders—fluid, porous, or expanded as they might be—of one's transcultural dimension are to a great extent affected, but not totally dictated, by a complex agglomeration of elements, including one's origins (here intended not as a mythical static starting point imbued in tradition, but as an initial bundle of experiences, genetic traits, teachings), biography, learned knowledge, contingencies, personal characteristics, social contexts, and political events. As Bhabha posits: "The 'originary' is always open to translation so that it can never be said to have a totalized prior moment of being or meaning—an essence" ("The Third" 210). It is within and through these fluctuating borders and life trajectories that an expanded and permeable transcultural form of identity establishes its parameters and levels of interconnectedness, in a way not dissimilar to the "metaphor for subjectivity" represented by the "crowded self" envisioned by Black: "Although many theories of subject formation suggest that a self consolidates its own identity by expelling unwanted others or defining itself against them, the crowded self expands to include diverse, sometimes contradictory, and occasionally even threatening points of view . . . it is not an exercise in literary narcissism, in which perspective taking is only valued as means to heightened self-knowledge or self-completion. Instead, this expansive concept of selfhood helps visualize a subject that is always already multiple, flexible, and open to future metamorphosis" (*Fiction* 47). Black's crowded self resonates also with Derrida's personal sense of plural self, as he describes it in a conversation with Elisabeth Roudinesco: "Nothing matters for me as much as my Jewishness, which, however, in so many ways, matters so little in my life. I know very well that such statements seem contradictory, lacking in common sense. But they would be so only in the eyes of someone who could say 'I' only in one whole piece, only by expelling from himself all alterity, all heterogeneity, all division, indeed all altercation, all 'explication' or 'coming to terms' with oneself. I am not alone with myself, no more that anyone else is—I am not all-one. An 'I' is not an indivisible atom" (*For What* 112).

If transcultural writers give us a new direction, a new solution to the problem of identity—with the development and acquisition of a plural, flexible identity capable of metamorphosis—they also show us what it means to live with a multiple sense of belonging made of plural affiliations and a somewhat dispersed sense of allegiance (and of place/home), where again the borders of a single nation are transcended in favor of a planetary, cosmopolitan view of humanity (and community). In this specific attitude transcultural writers are not dissimilar to the "genuine" cosmopolitans described by Hannerz, for whom cosmopolitanism more than a charged political ideology or ideal is "first of all an orientation, a willingness to engage with the Other ("Cosmopolitans" 239). It is an intellectual and aesthetic stance of openness toward divergent cultural experiences, a search for contrasts rather than uniformity. To become acquainted with more cultures is to view them as works of art.

Discussing the North American literary landscape, Aitor Ibarrola-Armendariz acknowledges the emergence of a new breed of postnational authors "characterized by their rootlessness and sense of transcultural identity . . . Rather than seeing their existence divided between their old home and indigenous heritage and a new home in a post-imperial order, they prefer to (un)define themselves as belonging to two—or more—half-homes simultaneously" ("Boundary" 37-38; Ibarrola-Armendariz refers in particular to Kingston and Marshall in the United States and Kogawa and Ondaatje in Canada). And here is how Manguel expresses this mode of being: "Even when declaring allegiance to one place, we seem to be always moving away from it . . . Nationalities, ethnicities, tribal, and religious filiations imply geographical and political definitions of some kind, and yet, partly because of our nomad nature and partly due to the fluctuations of history, our geography is less grounded in a physical than in a phantom landscape. Home is always an imaginary place" (*The City* 144-45). For the same reason, an author in Arabic and French like Maalouf—born in Lebanon, Christian rather than Muslim, Malachite rather than Maronite, now resident in Paris—when asked about his identity and allegiances whether he feels "more" French or "more" Lebanese, replies "Both! . . . I am poised between two countries, two or three languages and several cultural traditions" (*In the Name* 1). His position is not a subtraction or a denial, but an addition and an inclusive one: "The notion that reduces identity to one single affiliation . . . encourages people to adopt an attitude that is partial, sectarian, intolerant, domineering, sometimes suicidal, and frequently changes them into killers or supporters of killers" (Maalouf, *In the Name* 30).

Apart from a handful of exceptions, in the past most exile writers tended to maintain their national traits, only rarely would they "open up." Instead of stepping out of their national linguistic and cultural environments most "sealed themselves off in order to maintain the purity of their mother tongue . . . retained the national mentality of their youth" (Neubauer 1). Today, transcultural writers are aware that the conventional narratives about nation, allegiance, and belonging firmly rooted in a particular community, location, or tradition no longer work in a world where transnational experiences and neonomadic trajectories tend to disrupt the cohesive sense of belonging of clearly defined and homogenized groups. As Iyer points out, "Even the man who never leaves home may feel that home is leaving him, as parents, children, lovers scatter around the map, taking pieces of him wherever they go" (27). Brancato as well notes that transcultural subjects show "a determination to make a home of any place the self inhabits" ("Transcultural" 245). Thus, Iyer provides an exemplary model when he explains that to him home is not identified as a country, but as a private space no matter where it is, where one feels comfortable: "I am not rooted in a place, I think, so much as in certain values and affiliations and friendships that I carry everywhere I go; my home is both invisible and portable" (qtd. in Brenner). Similarly, Silke Catharine Schade writes about a writer's personal sense of home, maintaining that "new and particular perspectives . . . come out of allegiances to multiple localities, and from real and imagined 'double locations'" (167). For Baranay, "asking what constitutes belonging is like asking how many ways there are to tell a story; there are infinite possibilities" (Dagnino and Baranay). This has also been pointed out by Brancato: "A transcultural subject is also a person strongly connected with a culture other than the one dominant in his/her place of birth or residence, a person, in other words, with multiple belongings" ("Transcultural" 241). But perhaps the best description of this new fluid attitude towards the sense of belonging and allegiance comes from Manguel: "We live in a world of fluid borders and identities. The slow movements of migration and conquest that defined the shape of the earth for thousands of years have, in the past few decades, accelerated a hundredfold so that, as in a fast-forwarded film, nothing and no one seems to remain fixed in one place for long. Attached to a certain site through birth, blood-ties, learned affection or acquired need, we relinquish or are forced to relinquish these attachments and shift into new allegiances and devotions that in turn will shift again, sometimes backward, sometimes forward, away from an imagined centre" (*The City* 143). Manguel, however, is aware that this liquefaction of national borders and of collective as well as individual identities is counterweighted by a renewed virulence of nationalisms, religious fundamentalisms, and ethnic tensions. The daily flow of global news and events cannot but contribute to the acknowledgment that, as Manguel remarks, "after the dissolution of most of the imperial powers, nationalism, both political and religious, seems more virulent than almost ever before" (*The City* 145).

In the same way as with their adaptable fluid identities, it is mainly through a process of extreme cultural personalization, in which any kind of possible group affiliation is necessarily overcome (or, better, transcended), that transcultural writers obtain their transpatriate condition. Castro, for example, "opposes the myth of nationality as a singular construct" and substitutes it with "a hybrid notion of nationality that does not delimit a person" (Deves 79). Indeed, Castro is not sympathetic to those Australians who are "obsessed with their 'national identity' . . . instead of defining themselves in terms of their own, individual accomplishments and desires" (Deves 79). Drawing on Welsch's concept of the subject as multitude, Brancato also remarks that transcultural writers show a tendency to overcome "notions of group identity . . . focusing instead on the multifaceted nature of the individual subject" ("Transcultural" 244). If for Manguel, echoing Castro, the pressures of (post)modernity, political fragmentation, and economic globalization "make it almost impossible to hold for long on to a shared definition of nationality" (*The City* 143), for Trojanow any feeling of "we" is a constructed one and thus hardly acceptable (Dagnino and Trojanow). The extent to which such writers have lost all sense of belonging to a nation, to an ethnic group, to a religion, to a political movement, to any kind of ideologized and essentialized "we" is all the more apparent. For them there is no "we" construction as a singular institutionalized identity; cultural identity is always plural, even when it is an individual affair, as Iyer points out outlining the portrait of Rushdie: "He soars beyond all traditions and religions and lives in the spaces between cultures (his book on India offends the Indians and his book on Pakistan outrages the Pakistanis). Belonging nowhere, he's beholden to nowhere, and, settled in no faith, he underestimates, perhaps, the extent to which many people remain fiercely rooted in an older order, of doctrine and heritage and the past . . . The great spokesman of the people who lives everywhere becomes literally a man with no address" (32-33). Obviously, here the "we" feeling is meant as the sense of group belonging attached to notions of race, gender, ethnicity, class, nation; it is altogether different from the Nancean concept of "we" as being "within" the world together which I discuss in chapter 1.

It is true that this kind of uprootedness and lack of affiliation can lead to a perceived lack of accountability and commitment, as Iyer acknowledges: "Displacement can encourage the wrong kinds of distance, and if the nationalism we see sparkling up around the globe arises from too narrow and fixed a sense of loyalty, the internationalism that's coming to birth may reflect too roaming and undefined a sense of belonging. The Global Soul may see so many sides of every question that he never settles on a firm conviction: he may grow so used to giving back a different self according to his environment that he loses sight of who he is when nobody's around" (24-25). However, this is a critique that can hardly be applied to transcultural subjects. Transcultural writers eschew a socially preordained path as it used to be in the past, where "his or her values were prescribed by the hierarchies and expectations of society" (Grimshaw and Sears 269). They have nevertheless challenged themselves to overcome the limits and negative effects of postmodern relationships, whose essential traits are "fragmentariness and discontinuity, narrowness of focus and purpose, shallowness of contact" (Bauman, "From Pilgrim" 34).

The path transcultural writers have chosen is a more laborious one since they cannot rely upon the reassuring enclosure of any preexisting group (see Nancy, *Being*). On this path the only compass, the only fixed destination, and the only form of affiliation is the relationship with Others (strangers, as well as colleagues, friends, or family). Given that the chosen community is not subject to any exterior or preexistent definition, the mutual exposure to one another does not hinder the freedom and the attainment of a transcultural sense of identity. These forms of noncodified human attachments, these intimacies-in-community (see Nancy, *Being*)—or these "networks," as Welsch prefers to call them—are per se transcultural, transversal, polyhedric, and nonmutually exclusive, since any one of them does not necessarily deny or efface the others: "Transcultural identities, despite their differences in some respects, will in most cases also have a couple of elements in common. So there is overlap between them, and this allows for exchange, understanding and transitions between those [transcultural identity] networks. Hence identities of this transcultural type are altogether more capable of affiliation amongst one another than the old cultural identities ever were" ("Rethinking" 3). Nonetheless, some might still be induced to see transcultural writers in the same way Timothy Brennan sees cosmopolitan writers, as a well-heeled class of international globe-trotters or of competent and perhaps not less privileged "consumers" of cultural (mainly in terms of food and music) folklore ("Cosmopolitans" 16). In Brennan's view, these elitist literati with a "'picturesque' attachment to a cultural miscellany" more or less contribute naively to strengthening, imaginatively and ideologically, a US-American neo-imperialist supranational project ("Cosmopolitans" 16; see also Brennan, "Cosmo-Theory"). Others might see transcultural writers merely as an expression of the *longa manus* or in this case the *longa mens* of global capital, going opportunistically where they can to maximize their individual interests and transnational opportunities without committing to furthering the national, regional, or local interests of any place.

What I argue is that transcultural writers have an accentuated sense of engaged responsibility to land (now meant as any land) and people (any people). If any residual attachment to the territory exists, it is through the communities who inhabit it:

"One of the things that has given me professional pleasure is to see some of my students succeed in their work as translators. This gives me a sort of grounding in the territory. I like to feel that you do get a sense of responsibility and because of that responsibility, because you have done the job seriously, people would appreciate what you've done for them" (Dagnino and Parks). Through their works, lived experiences, cultural dispositions, and ways of reasoning, transcultural writers show us that their commitment towards land and people transcends the tribal, national, or even imperial dimension and acquires a much wider scope: "Identity would then be seen as the sum of all our allegiances, and, within it, allegiance to the human community itself would become increasingly important, until one day it would become the chief allegiance, though without destroying our many individual affiliations" (Maalouf, *In the Name* 100). In other words, with "deterritorialization and eco-cosmopolitanism" transcultural writers share "not so much a sense of place as a sense of planet . . . A sense of how political, economic, technological, social, cultural, and ecological networks shape daily routines. If the concept of deterritorialization foregrounds how cultural practices become detached from place, it also points to how these practices are now imbricated in such larger networks" (Heise 55).

Further, Epstein associates the transcultural condition to the translingual mode and the way it is creatively expressed through the forms and modes of what he calls "stereo prose," where at least two languages or the fusion of two languages are needed to convey a particular concept, emotion, or way of reasoning or simply to "savor precisely the discrepancies among languages" ("The Unasked" 51). Indeed, most of the selected authors of my study speak or know more than one foreign language and in some cases they write in a language different from their native one (translingualism); in others, they introduce in their works terms, expressions, or whole sentences in another language or other languages from the one used to tell the story, thus conveying their linguistic or cultural hybridization (Kellman, *The Translingual*; on this see also Francuski). When asked about his relationship with languages, this is how Trojanow replies: "I slide into the different languages that I know. I wear them depending on where I am" (Dagnino and Trojanow).

This easiness and plasticity towards speaking and "wearing" different languages reflects itself also in the way of writing, as Michael I. Deves points out, stressing the effect of multilingualism on Castro's writing in English: "He is competent in Cantonese, which makes Chinese settings convincing, not just because he understands the language but because he understands the culture associated with it . . . His French gives him access to European modes of speech and thought, and his Portuguese to both European and colonial modes. But most importantly, his multi-lingualism acquaints him with the shifting world of the traveller and the migrant, swapping between 'identities' and inhabiting several at a time" (80-81). More than their bilingualism or polyglossia, which appear to be two of their distinctive traits, what is important is the significance these writers give to the knowledge of languages. As we have seen in chapter 2, knowing a second or third language means acquiring additional perspectives and increases the possibility of entering in a relationship with the

Other, to experience—and appreciate—the value of difference. Talking about Glissant, a precursor of early twenty-first century transcultural sensibility, Micla Petrelli writes that "the reality is that, according to the Caribbean author, it is no longer possible to write in a monolingual way, much less to defend one's language in a monolingual manner. In the contemporary context, the chaos-world, the totality-world, is a poetic dimension that imbues literatures" ("L'Arte").

Transcultural writers show an uncommon fascination for foreign languages as well as the utmost respect and deference towards what they represent: the doors to other worldviews, other cultural horizons, other ways of perceiving reality, human relationships, ethical and cultural values, and modes of being and thinking. The acquisition of each new language is not only the acquisition of a new communicative and expressive instrument, but also the conquest of a new dimension, mental and psychological. As the German-Canadian writer Henry Kreisel experienced in person, to get to know a new language implies "an alteration of basic parts of one's identity" (120). This does not however imply—in any essentialist way—giving up one's identity to favor another one, instead it is experienced as a process that adds on and dynamically, progressively transforms that initial identity. In other words, identities, like languages, can travel: "A language that travels is always made of many languages since a language that *really* travels is always an open language, porous, inclusive, and willing to disappear into another language, from within which its very own singularity will resurface more fully" (Bartoloni, *On the Cultures* 87). As Conrad recounted in the second preface to *A Personal Record*, once he "was adopted by the genius of the language"—an intimate process "too mysterious to explain"—the new language, English—"had a direct action on [his] temperament and fashioned [his] still plastic character" (5). Sabina Hopfer, who wrote the translingual novel *Moulin Rouge* mixing English and German, describes the process as follows: "When I translate into English, I go back and forth between the German and the English text, between two ways of thinking and seeing the world, and I make changes not only in the English translation, but also in the German original, until . . . I can no longer see the boundaries—until the two languages begin to flow into one another . . . Blending two languages on the page . . . creates a new voice, a new layer or world of meaning, in which the cultures of two individual languages begin to merge, reconcile, and bring about change—cutting through any nationalist claims attached to each language" (54-61).

By adopting any language other than the native one, we are confronted with an extremely laborious conquest—especially if one decides to use it as a new tool for creative expression—which demands an act of great humility. Transcultural/translingual writers seem to aspire to that disorienting, humbling experience and suspended dimension created by immersing themselves in another language, which—by not being their mother tongue (the language of their childhood)—will never be intimately possessed. In Castro's view, "Language marks the spot where the self loses its prison bars—where the border crossing takes place, traversing the spaces of others. When one speaks or translates Chinese, one metaphorically becomes Chinese; when one speaks Japanese one 'turns' Japanese. Each language speaks the world in its own way . . . When we translate from one language to another we not only reinvent ourselves but we free up the sclerotic restrictions of our own language. We feel free to transgress, to metamorphose, to experience the uncanny, where we are receiving what Wilson Harris has called the *quantum immediacy* of another culture. Other cultures and languages reinforce and enrich us by powerfully affecting and destabilising our familial tongue. We gain by losing ourselves" ("Writing" 152-53).

Taken all together, these reflections emphasize the power of self-transformation that exists along—or beyond—linguistic/cultural boundaries. They show us that temporary linguistic/cultural outsidedness, situated ethical nonbelongings, or located singular desires to belong "outside the divisiveness of categorizing" (Probyn, *Outside* 10) are conditions which nurture a transcultural imaginary and understanding. This concept is indebted to Bakhtin's idea of intercultural "creative understanding" among human beings, which Ludmila Marchenkova interprets as "the culminating moment for the sake of which dialogue exists," built on the dynamic equilibrium of intersecting worldviews and values (162). As Bakhtin maintained when talking of the interaction between cultures, "in the realm of culture, outsidedness is a most powerful factor in understanding . . . A meaning only reveals its depths once it has encountered . . . another, foreign meaning: they engage in a kind of dialogue which surmounts the closedness and one-sidedness of these particular meanings, these cultures. We raise new questions for a foreign culture, ones that it did not raise itself; we seek answers to our own questions in it; the foreign culture responds to us by revealing to us its new aspects and new semantic depths" (*Speech* 7).

Even if transcultural writers see cultures as mobile, movable, transitory, and as plural and hybridized as their identities, they are still aware of the significant role that history, memories, and the past play in the formation of their biographical and literary identities. As Baranay notes, "Still, a writer is aware of antecedents and influences, a history from which we emerge" (*Sun* 99). At the same time, they reject the conditioning and the restrictions imposed by a "cultural tradition" or by those (critics, academics, literary agents, publishers, judges in national literary juries) who insist that writers need to write "within a tradition." If I appear keen on calling them transcultural, it is because in my view these mobile writers distance themselves and go beyond the politically and culturally constructed categories of the "(im)migrant writer," "ethnic writer," "multicultural writer," "Commonwealth writer," "Writer of New Literatures in English," or "francophone writer" that dominated the critical discourse of the late twentieth century. "So many of us at Binger were pressed to answer unanswerable questions about our identity and our work, did we feel more this or more that, where did we really belong, that kind of thing," as Baranay writes recalling her last stay in Amsterdam as a participant in the Writers Program at Binger Film Laboratory, "Here I was among hyphenates and hybrids, and some of us now refused the available categories" (*Local* 1).

Transcultural writers hardly adhere to any conventional forms of categorization and, as Chad Habel notes, even the hyphenated stratagem usually does not work with them: "Indeed, a focus on diaspora and globalisation rules out simplistic hyphenations suggested by terms like 'Asian-American' or 'Asian-Canadian,' and this problem in itself is a point of discussion for many authors . . . acknowledging, analysing and even encouraging a diversity which disputes not only binaries such as East/West, but even the dominance of terms such as 'diaspora' and the easy hyphenations which pigeonhole authors, texts, and ultimately individuals" (*Local* 2). Rushdie, who might be inscribed within a transcultural discourse despite his having being alternatively and indiscriminately defined by critics and scholars as an (im) migrant, exile, diasporic, or postcolonial writer, has commented in "Commonwealth Literature Does Not Exist" on his annoyance about his invariably being ethnically labeled: "In my own case, I have constantly been asked whether I am British, or Indian. The formulation 'Indian-born British writer' has been invented to explain me. But . . . my new book deals with Pakistan. So what now? 'British-resident Indo-Pakistani writer?' You see the folly of trying to contain writers inside passports. One of the most absurd aspects of this quest for national authenticity is that . . . it is completely fallacious to suppose that there is such a thing as a pure, unalloyed tradition from which to draw" (67). Rushdie's viewpoint is shared by Castro: "I was referred to as a Chinese author, an Asian-Australian, a foreigner who didn't subscribe to the Australian ethos, whatever that meant, and finally . . . misplacing the facts, as an Australian-born Chinese. It is interesting to see how the cross-cultural writer in other societies has also had to go through this frustrating assimilation. Salman Rushdie is sometimes an English writer but mostly an English-Indian writer or a writer from India who writes in English" ("Writing" 158). It is worth noting that Rushdie also refuses to be categorized under the postimperial umbrella of "Commonwealth literature," a term that in his view "is not used simply to describe . . . but also 'to divide'": at best, he writes, "what is called 'Commonwealth literature' is positioned below English literature 'proper' . . . it places Engl. Lit. at the center and the rest of the world at the periphery" ("Commonwealth" 66). In the same tone Casanova deplores those British critics who, ignoring the ambiguity implicit in the notion of Commonwealth literature, did not take into consideration, or merely overlooked, Rushdie's refusal "to be treated as a post-imperial product," and were instead ready to annex him under the British aegis in an act of literary misappropriation driven by the new postcolonial "vogue for exoticism" (120-21). The wider and more neutral realm of transculture/ality allows writers, as Claudia Esposito states, to finally "share a fundamental critique of narrow identitarian labeling" (3).

Any category is constructed but at least, despite the limitations inherent in any categorization, the one relating to transculture/ality tries to overcome the ethnic, national, cultural, imperial, or religious boundaries imposed by previous categorizations. Although this remark is most valid for those writers of mobility active in the realm of Anglophone literature (being the most widely diffused), it also applies to any other transcultural writer writing in any other language. Furthermore, this approach allows us to reread through a new lens, as Esposito's study on the Maghreb francophone writers shows us, those transnational authors who, despite having been alternatively labeled as migrant, exile, diasporic, ethnic, or refugee "operate outside the confines of a nation and consequently address questions of multiple forms of cultural, political, sexual and existential belonging" (5).

Transcultural writers tend to eschew their ethnic and national categorizations because these categories are not dissimilar from those preexisting, essentialized constructions of gender, race, class, sexuality, family relation, or other such biological and biographical classifications that have been defied and refused by the postmodern literary discourse in an age when, as Michael Herzfeld claims, "just about every other category has been deconstructed and reconstructed, or at least has self-destructed" (46). This is how Baranay, who first published most of her works in Australia (while her last two novels were published first in India), addresses this issue: "What's happened is that the multicultural in Ozlit has been given its own territory, its own separate colour in the mosaic. When the mosaic not the melting pot became the slogan it was the 1980s and multiculturalism was the intellectual, sociological and social-engineering fashion . . . Then I declined the advice: 'Write about your family, go find your roots, write about the old country with communism coming to an end and your life in the new country' . . . Multiculturalism in Australian writing has become a useful term to identify migrant narratives and the explorations of identity related to that. It's as if Australian writing is divided into the multicultural and the mainstream" ("Multiculturalism" 127-28).

As we have seen, the main element that distinguishes transcultural writers from previous categorizations is the fact that in their lives, as well as in their writing, they have transcended any intimation of a fixed national identity and of any specific culture they were born into: "When we have this idea of being an Australian writer, I am tempted to say that we are writers first of all . . . our material is writing, we are not a nationality" (Castro qtd. in Deves 79). These writers feel they have multiple belongings and that their sense of cultural identity rests on contingency. In other words, we are not dealing here with the infatuations of twenty-year-olds who feel they are children of the world, or flower children; we are instead talking about a much more serious development, matured over the course of many years (if not generations)—the fruit of an intellectual and life journey in which much time has been spent introjecting and creatively analyzing what has been experienced, emotionally felt, and, ultimately, understood. As Maalouf explains, "Anyone who sets out, as I have done, a number of affiliations, is immediately accused of wanting to 'dissolve' his identity in a kind of undifferentiated and colourless soup. And yet what I'm trying to say is exactly the opposite: not that all human beings are the same, but that each one is different" (*In the Name* 21). That is why in reading Manguel, Trojanow, Castro, Baranay, or Maalouf it is difficult to locate them nationally, as well as culturally. This feature marks also the main difference between transnational literature, which is mainly a reading across different national literatures, and transcultural literature, a literary creation, not only a reading, across different cultures, where the national and cultural identity of a text—as well as of its author—has been transcended.

By its own nature, each transcultural path is highly individualized and cannot be assimilated to a collective experience. We should thus avoid the temptation to make of transculture/ality a phenomenon shared by and associated with a specific and well identifiable group of people (or creative authors). Pauline T. Newton acknowledges that "the process of achieving transculturality" as a means of negotiating multiple cultures "is a long journey, perhaps one that continues without end from generation to generation" (149). There is no handbook showing how to become a transcultural subject, let alone a transcultural writer. There can be some shared or distinctive traits, but nothing more than that. It is for this reason that I argue for a concept of transculture/ality as an individual, existential condition more than some sort of cultural category, ideological standpoint, or literary affiliation. To a certain extent, culture is transmittable—thus shareable—while the individual condition is not: it is unique. That is why each of my selected authors expresses and represents him/herself in a transcultural dimension utterly peculiar to him/herself and by no means repeatable under those same terms. Otherwise, it would be like implying that someone else can replicate another's life. For this reason it becomes unrealistic to aspire to gather this multiplicity of personal experiences under a minimal common denominator, or worse, under a single literary movement or canon. Here we are confronted more by a state of thinking (and being) rather than by a current of thought.

The transcultural condition is still a rare and privileged phenomenon, no doubt, which implies a series of detachments and abstractions from social, economic, psychological, and identity ties or bonds that people can hardly do without and that, most of the times and in specific stages of one's life, appear unavoidable. In forming our personalities and developing our identities, we might find a chance to progressively loosen the bonds and ties within which we were raised or that were/are imposed upon us. We are all born within the boundaries of specific cultures (as much transcultural as any culture might be) and not by our choice, which means that we are not born transcultural—we can become such only by subsequent approximations, enriching our multilayered, metamorphic cultural identity, made of a plurality of affiliations, cultural practices, linguistic immersions, and emotional sensibilities. In this sense, paraphrasing Braidotti when suggesting the cultivation of a "nomadic consciousness," the transcultural consciousness "combines coherence with mobility" (*Nomadic* 31).

While being aware that they require further definition, I am also aware that these authors living and being creatively active outside their own native cultures or homelands tend to defy any conventional pigeonholing. Their same complex and fluid nature seems to dispel any attempt to pin them down, to fit them in any kind of definitional box, even the most flexible and academically sophisticated one. As Castro states, "It is precisely by classifying that we demolish nuances, tones and flows . . . the very dynamics of being" ("The Private" 92). To echo the notion of indeterminacy expressed by Ien Ang when talking about the precariousness of cultural construction in diasporic subjects, "positive indeterminacy" is woven into the identity fabric of transcultural writers (66). There are no prescriptions or fixed definitions for them, only incommensurable propositions. Thus, to define these authors transcultural is mainly to differentiate them from their "(im)migrant" or "postcolonial" predecessors and contemporaries, with whom they still share some aspects of the transpatriation process, even if not the same attitude towards it and, perhaps, as we have seen in this chapter, not the same outcomes in terms of cultural approaches and literary expressions. Affected by their cultural dispositions and imaginations, transcultural writers are able to share with us the nature of contemporary encounters emerging from biographies and lifestyles which are—through changes, chances, or deliberate choice—no longer located in relatively stable or fixed cultural frameworks and where individuals find themselves to be negotiating, compromising (or in conflict with) several cultures on a daily basis.

In summary, I would conclude that the main characteristics that might define transcultural writers—given the previous caveats regarding stringent and often arbitrary categorizations—and that, more or less explicitly, also manifest themselves in their literary outputs, are: 1) a flexible mental disposition and fluid, metamorphic sense of identity; 2) the knowledge that the process of dislocation and rootlessness of one's own self can be an intriguing and insightful creative device—a portal towards infinite possibilities of being and of imagining; 3) the development of new ways of belonging and the lack of imposed/fixed allegiances; 4) a mindset similar to the one developed by their contemporary social counterparts—the "neonomads," alternatively understood as "global nomads" (in this case, the notion of neonomadism suggests that mobile lifestyles may be conceptualized as a form of cosmopolitan diaspora); 5) a willingness to be "open" to and be "transformed" by the experience of the Other, in this way acting as cultural mediators or intercultural ambassadors; 6) knowledge of other languages (with accentuated forms of bilingualism, trilingualism, or even polyglossia) recognized as one of the main tools for an enriching and transforming transcultural experience; and 7) a transpatriation process which can be either self-induced or utterly random, as aleatoric as their creative processes.

In sum, it is evident that the same characteristics which define transcultural writers to a large extent are reflected also in their creative outputs. In this respect, Castro's reflection is particularly illuminating: "The generic function I've used most of all is a form which is not only unstable in itself and which has undergone intense transformation, but which has the potential to transgress the furthest. This is the auto/biographical form. The slash is already an implosion of multiple forms, dividing the conjunction of prefixes and yet allowing the crossing over between self, life, and writing" ("Auto/Biography" 105-06).

Chapter Five

The "Fuzzy" Nature of Transcultural Novels

In *Transcultural Writers and Novels in the Age of Global Mobility* I focus on early twenty-first century transcultural writers and their creative output—the transcultural novel—because the novel represents historically one of the earliest examples of a global cultural literary product related to the modern age. In its planetary travels, the novel has become a literary mutant in the transnational arena or, as Eileen Julien would say, "a global *forma franca,* the privileged and prestigious form beyond the nation's border" (130). What is even more impressive is that in its long history not only has the novel always crossed geographical borders (well before the nation-states were formed), but it has also gone beyond the boundaries imposed by genres and subgenres incorporating all of them along the way. In the course of time and in different locations, it has mutated and picked up from epic poetry, pastorals, chivalric romances, and the picaresque, the parodic and the burlesque, historical and travel accounts, nonfiction, film scripts, memoirs, war reporting, autobiography, philosophical reasoning, epistolary forms, and melodrama: "At times [its] endless flexibility borders on chaos . . . but thanks to it, the novel becomes the truly planetary form: a phoenix always ready to take flight in a new direction, and to find the right language for the next generation of readers" (Moretti, *The Novel* ix).

The history of the novel has always been intrinsically "transnational" (better, "supranational"), transcontinental, and transoceanic from the beginning. This happened well before its influence expanded "below the thirty-fifth parallel," especially with its "tropicalization" and subtropicalization, fostered by writers such as Patrick Chamoiseau, Carlos Fuentes, Gabriel Garcia Marquez, Chinua Achebe, Yukio Mishima, and Kenzaburo Oe: "The French novel, the English novel, the Hungarian novel, are in no position to create autonomous histories of their own but are all part of a common, supranational history that provides the only context capable of revealing both the direction of the novel's evolution and the value of particular works" (Kundera, *Testaments* 29-30). This view is shared by Rushdie, who stresses the transcultural nature of novelistic intertextuality: "We are inescapably international writers at a time when the novel has never been a more international form (a writer like Borges speaks of the influence of Robert Louis Stevenson on his work; Heinrich Böll acknowledges the influence of Irish literature; cross-pollination is everywhere)" ("Imaginary Homelands" 20). The novel truly represents the most exemplary cultural "product of a global dynamic," although "it may have been put to paper first in Spain, France, and Britain, [it] has reached its full potential, has become a commanding presence on the global stage, thanks to its enormous success at the 'edges' of the 'world system'" (Julien 127-28). This is especially evident at this moment in time when binary oppositions between center and periphery, East and West, North and South, postcolonizer and postcolonized, majorities and minorities are deconstructed and superseded. As Eva Hoffman remarks, "We are no longer the norm or the center . . . there is no geographic center pulling the world together and glowing with the allure of the real thing . . . we are always simultaneously in the center and on the periphery . . . every competing center makes us marginal" (274-75).

From this perspective, transcultural fiction transcends the borders of a single culture or nation in choice of topic, scope, location, language, and characters and resonates with the notion of minor literature as argued by Deleuze and Guattari (*Kafka*; see also Deleuze, Guattari, and Brinkley) and subsequently interpreted by Castro thus: "Minor literatures flow . . . into social, national and linguistic dissociations and disconnections. It is because this expression unsettles one, startles one with the residues of bilingualism and trilingualism, that the traditional mind wants to suppress it, to prevent the rhapsodic and avoid change . . . to restore the everlasting monument to sovereign power" ("The Private" 90-91). As Ibarrola-Armendariz acknowledges in his analysis of postnational authors and transcultural identities, "their literary production is . . . affected by this change in self-perception . . . A remarkable number of these writers' achievements need to be sought precisely in their eclecticism and their ability aesthetically to amalgamate materials coming from quite different cultures . . . Although several scholars have detected traces of a postcolonial split in their novels, it is more accurate to speak of their creations as representations of the international culture that has developed since the late 1960s" ("Boundary" 38). Vera Alexander makes a similar observation when exploring the transcultural elements in the novels by Romesh Gunesekera (*The Sandglass*) and Shyam Selvadurai (*Cinnamon Gardens*): "Some of the spatial and temporal border crossings evident in the authors' biographies are reflected on the level of the novels' plot lines . . . Both novels . . . describe . . . characters living on the shifting border between several identities and cultures" (142).

I note again that precursors and representatives of a transcultural sensibility may be found in all ages, from ancient times (let us just think of Ovid or Martial) to the nineteenth and twentieth century, without mentioning the polyglot authors *sans patrie* of the Enlightenment. However, the emergence of the transcultural novel in the early twenty-first century is considered a phenomenon still in its infancy (see, for example, Löschnigg, "Trans-culturalism" and Ertler, "Trans-culturalism"). Although most contemporary literary critical exploration is still focused on the well-established categories of (im)migrant and postcolonial writings, more than one scholar seems to have embarked on the task to define the main elements that characterize a transcultural novel, since, as David Lodge maintains, "the effort to generalize, to classify, has to be made; for without some conceptual apparatus for grouping and separating literary fictions criticism could hardly claim to be knowledge, but would be merely the accumulation of opinions about one damn novel after another" (25). Furthermore, "not only do we have to compartmentalize," as Mohamed Bakari has stated during a private conversation, but "at every decade we also need new categories" (Bakari and Dagnino, private conversation, July 2012).

According to Helff, the transcultural novel seems to have already developed its own main general features, although obviously we should be aware that "a neat categorization of transcultural literature is hardly feasible . . . because categories will always be prone to lose their apparent rigidity and leak into each other" ("Shifting" 82). It is specifically this element of indeterminacy that characterizes—together with its blurred boundaries—the intrinsically metamorphic and to a large extent indistinct "fuzzy" nature of trancultural novels (and of their authors). I extend the use of the term "fuzzy" applied in mathematics and computer science to those elements or data which have uncertain, amorphous, or blurred boundaries. Such qualities may indeed be inherent in the nature of transcultural novels. Rather than a new subgenre then, it would be more appropriate to define the transcultural novel, following Mieke Bal's conception of narratology, as "a perspective on culture," as an alternative "cultural mode of expression" emerging from the way of experiencing the early twenty-first century globalized world (21). The prefix trans- (meaning going across or beyond) implies by itself a transcending of every possible categorization, or the capacity or willingness of not letting itself/oneself be grasped. Castro addresses this issue in his lecture "Auto/Biography": "You can begin to see what terrible things genres are; they imprison every situation within the expected. Genre categorisation exerts a disproportionate power over books" (104-05). All this shows that it is in the intrinsic nature of novels to mix genres and even more so in transcultural novels, where—using what Helff calls the stratagem of "transcultural narrative unreliability" ("Signs" 277-78)—authors blend facts and fiction, reality and imagination, novelistic storytelling and auto/biographical accounts, while at the same time combining "cultural performances" ("Indian"). In line with Coetzee's auto/biographical narrative trilogy, the creative component of the present study also demonstrates to what extent fiction and nonfiction can be "fused" into each other, further expanding and blurring the already "fuzzy" contours and nature of transcultural literature.

Having put forward these initial precautionary clarifications about the still young and amorphous nature of transcultural novels, I concur with Helff when she defines a transcultural novel as having at least one of the following aspects: 1) "The narrator and/or the narrative challenge(s) the collective identity of a particular community," 2) "Experiences of border crossing and transnational identities characterize the narrators' lifeworld," and 3) "Traditional notions of 'home' are disputed" ("Shifting" 83). Trojanow talks of his own work *The Collector of Worlds* as a novel "which basically deals with the capacity of a human being to overcome cultural boundaries, the capacity to redefine themselves as a very hybrid creature," thus unintentionally giving his own definition of a transcultural novel ("Meeting"). Khairallah suggests a more generic definition of transcultural works of fiction, that is, works whose characters are "endowed with a cross-cultural destiny," whose authors write "between cultures," belong to more than one culture, and "compel us to revise our understanding of cultural belonging" (242). Similarly, when talking about the transcultural identity of a new breed of postnational authors, Ibarrola-Armendariz points out that their novels have an international scope and takes Michael Ondaatje's *The English Patient* as one of the early examples of this new boundary-erasing literature ("Boundary"). Referring to the main four characters of the novel (a Hungarian wounded man with an English accent, his Canadian nurse, an Italian-Canadian thief, and an Indian sapper in the British Army), he writes: "This quartet shares with the author who conceived them a highly nomadic nature and an incredible ease in traversing geographical, racial and cultural boundaries . . . these four 'dislocated' people try to invent new forms of . . . reconstituting . . . their selfhood . . . It is self-evident that representing such a global meeting and evoking these new modes of identity-building are far from easy undertakings. However, it is these two ingredients that give the novel the universal quality that has enthralled so many readers . . . the author's mastery in creating a remote microcosm in which national or ethnic identities seem no longer relevant . . . allows their complex interrelationships to occur" (Ibarrola-Armendariz, "Boundary" 40-41).

I note that although early scholars of transcultural literary studies have been focusing on the specific context of the New Literatures in English (see in particular Schulze-Engler and Helff), transcultural works of fiction do not necessarily depend on a specific language: in any given language, they still tend to show the same features which have been partially already identified. It is also true that some of the literary characteristics which define transcultural novels, where "the narrative and the reader are constantly crossing and shifting boundaries between . . . transcultural spaces," do not necessarily differ from the general tropes of modern and postmodern writing, with its presence of "self-doubting characters," its challenges to "essentialist modes of identity construction," an often fragmented plot structure, and a mixing of genres (Helff, "Shifting" 82-83). However, the key characteristic of the transcultural novel is the accentuated physical and cultural mobility and transformative nature of its fictional characters—together with their ability to re-envisage common situations from alternative points of view—which mainly reflects that of its authors.

It is precisely by exploring how the specific creative and cultural attitudes and lived experiences of transpatriate writers manifest themselves in and inform the textual characteristics of their works of fiction that it is possible to identify an initial general set of common features that might best apply to early twenty-first century transcultural novels. This aspect is also what at present distinguishes, in broader terms, a transcultural novel from a cosmopolitan novel, at least in the way Schoene envisions the latter as "the novel that imagines the world" instead of the nation (28). It is true that in both cases one might detect a tendency to capture the complex destabilizing realities and effects of contemporary globalization, with its growing presence of diasporic, transnational, or postnational characters, changing geographies, and "complex enmeshment" of global and local realities (Schoene 130). But in the case of the cosmopolitan novel there does not seem to be (or at least Schoene does not expressly underlines this point) a direct link between the lived experience of a writer, her propensity to adhere to the sensibilities of a distinct "British cosmopolitanism" and her literary imagination or mode of expression. Schoene suggests that "what matters in the end is a particular stance towards the world" (16). But how does one acquire that particular stance? Ashcroft raises the same issue when he asks: "But who is 'the cosmopolitan'? Within the cultural space of 'the cosmopolitan city,' which category of its citizens may be constituted by cosmopolitan subjects? Which narrative of identity in the transitional, open and exogenous space of the world city frames a cosmopolitan subject?" ("Transnation" 76). D'Andrea goes to the core of the question when he critiques a limited conception of cosmopolitanism that does not sufficiently delve into the analysis of how new forms of reflexive subjectivities—with their embodiments, desires, perspectives, social dispositions, imaginaries—are being engendered under conditions of cultural, spatial, geographical deterritorialization, and complex global environments: "This conception virtually ignores the impact of affective and visceral engagements with radical alterity in reshaping personhood" (*Global* 16).

In light of this, transcultural writers cannot imagine a transcultural state of mind nor creatively express a transcultural orientation which may also be conducive to a neocosmopolitan outlook unless they have experienced these conditions in their minds, tongues, and bones through that kind of transpatriation process outlined in the previous chapter. In other words, they need to have "gone through" the monocultural mirror and "been there," in the transcultural continuum. It is expressly this process and a newly acquired (trans)cultural dimension which they now narrativize and make manifest in their creative works. As Castro states, "There is no complexity to the extent of just playing with technique, no complexity without the encounter with the world" (Dagnino and Castro). That is why, when discussing contemporary transcultural narratives, Ascari also emphasizes the fact that their "various linguistic and cultural declinations . . . are often rooted in the hybrid identities of their authors" (11). Thus, he points out for example that the Japanese writer Haruki Murakami was exposed to Western culture having lived in the United States and worked as a translator or that the Iranian-born writer Azar Nafisi studied in London before moving to live in the U.S. Further, Barbara Schaff suggests that the contradiction emerging from the desire to delink from fixed, essentialist notions of identity (based on the idea of nation, origins, and roots) and at the same time the contrasting need to belong (by sharing cultural values with the people who surround us) may be resolved by developing a notion of identity constructed via a fluid form of transcultural narration, "told and retold according to changing circumstances" (291). Schaff's view resonates also with Couldry's reasoning on this issue: "The self is best understood as an open-ended practice of *narration* whose coherence is not that of an object but 'a narrative unity,' which, if it succeeds as a narrative, can integrate contradictions into a complex and distinctive perspective on the world" (119).

We are thus now witnessing the narrativization of never ending processes of cultural contamination and metamorphosis. By interpolating or mixing the narratives of their lives with those of their imaginary works, these writers creatively and more or less consciously share with us what it means to have transcended and negotiated the boundaries of any previous rooted or primary categorizations and how we might then read or live even our personal stories if we acquired that same mindset. Not only do they open new imaginaries but they also show us their applicability in practice. It happens for example with Coetzee's fictionalized auto/biography, the trilogy represented by *Childhood*, *Boyhood*, and *Summertime*. There he extricates himself from his various cultural belongings as a South African author born within an Afrikaner speaking context, educated in the English language, and grown up to experience life in the United Kingdom, the U.S., back in South Africa, and, later on, in antipodean Australia.

What is important to notice here is also the fact that the development from a monocultural, migrant, diasporic, or postcolonial experience to a transcultural one can be sometimes traced in the same lives of the authors as well as in their corresponding outputs. For example, although in his earlier works (*Birds of Passage*, *After China*) Castro may have displayed many of the traits of (im)migrant or exile writing (characters feeling "out of place," homesickness, nostalgia of lost place, disorientation, cultural alienation, loss of language, muted characters), in his later works he has progressively used distinct transcultural elements. In *The Bath Fugues,* for example, we have a pluralization of points of view, the decentering of the narrative voice, the interplay and intermingling of different cultural perspectives, the increased use of foreign words and foreign concepts, a transnational choice of settings that involves narrative detours—or lines of flight—from Paris to Macao, from Portugal to the Australian Queensland, and, most importantly, characters who dispute traditional concepts of home, identity, and belonging. All this allows the imagining of wider or alternative cultural horizons, while at the same time enriching the cultural linkages provided by the endless concatenation of literary creations and intertextuality.

From a narratological point of view, the way transcultural novels develop their narratives does not affect the final result. They may display a more traditional linear plot or be extremely experimental, giving preference to a fragmented text, where the storyline (or, in many cases, a storyboard particularly adaptable to our ever growing visual imaginations and cinematic transpositions) is exploded in multiple layers of meaning. If we take the debut novel *Ilustrado* by Miguel Syjuco, for example, we are confronted with an amorphous mass where different and fragmented forms of writing are being used: blog entries, personal recounts in first person, memoirs, biographic paragraphs, newspaper articles, and interviews interspersed with the excerpts from an imaginary Filipino author in exile in the U.S. who writes in different genres. The book starts off as a crime mystery fiction, becomes a coming of age novel, and subsequently transforms itself into an examination of the broader mysteries of life, thus also blurring the boundaries between different genres. Only in the end does the reader realize that all these elements and their underlying themes—the Filipino diaspora, the guilt of belonging to the upper class (like the author himself), exile, expatriation, the responsibility to the family and allegiance to the country, the search for identity, the escape from the search for identity—are held together, understood, and metabolized by a main thread intertwined throughout the book: the acquired transcultural orientation of the author. We might say the same thing of Baranay's *Neem Dreams*, of Parks's *Dreams of Rivers and Seas*, of Manguel's *Todos los hombres son mentirosos* and, of Castro's *The Bath Fugues*. In writing their novels and through their characters—often a plurality of fictionalized selves, thus further hybridizing fiction with autobiography—these writers manifest their transcultural state of mind first to themselves and then to us. In this context, Parati's view that she considers "autobiography as fiction, as a narrative in which the author carefully selects and constructs the characters, events, and aspects of the self that she or he wants to make public in order to convey a specific message" is appropriate (*Public* 4). By tracing imaginatively in their lives and in their writing a web of narrative transcultural routes, transcultural authors help us realize that as citizens of a globalized world we can develop and expand our sense of cultural identity and, possibly, reach a transcultural dimension.

I return now to my point of how the writers' transcultural attitudes affect the writing of their transcultural novels and to what extent they define their common elements. Having this in mind and considering mainly, but not only the works of fiction of the writers selected in the present study, I posit that these writers tend to: 1) set their novels in more than one country or change the country in which they set their novels for each novel. Furthermore, the foreign settings (but "foreign" to whom? we might provocatively ask) are not used as exotic stereotypes meant to allure the growing market of global mass fiction or what others call postcolonial exoticism (Huggan; Maver); 2) create characters coming from more than one cultural background and who tend to live transnational lives; 3) display a proliferation of narrating voices and tell a story from "a multiplicity of perspectives" (Stein 257); 4) use foreign words and expressions, thereby creating texts characterized by a mix of linguistic or cultural spaces and promoting a kind of blended or "fusion" idiom, be it English, German, French, Spanish, Hindi, or Chinese. For these writers the only limit, the only line of demarcation can only be linguistic, not certainly geographic, social, or political; as Castro asserts: "The territory can only be language" (qtd. in Barker 243); and 5) write in a way and express things in such a way that it is difficult for a reader to understand or infer, without knowing anything about their complex biographies, to what nationality, cultural community, or ethnic group they belong. In other words, they tend to "undermine habitual classification of literary texts in terms of national or regional literatures" (Stein 251). All these aspects contribute to showing that transcultural novels are often conceived in what Braidotti calls a "nomadic," "de-territorializing," or "rhizomatic"style of thinking and writing which renders and in itself generates processes of becoming and "flows of connection" out of "mutual contamination of states of experience" (*Metamorphoses* 8). Obviously, not all these elements need necessarily to be present at the same time in the same novel to define it as "transcultural," but they tend to be common features of transcultural prose fiction.

I therefore identify the traits and elements of distinctive transcultural narrative and techniques of representation as follows:

1) Multiple foreign settings, not exotic stereotypes. As stated, transcultural authors tend to use multiple locations either in the same novel or throughout their body of work and this aspect reflects their own transnational experiences. For example, Castro's *The Bath Fugues* is set mainly in Australia, but his characters then move to and from other countries and have experiences or remember things from having lived in Shanghai, Macao, Paris, and Portugal. Parks has set his different novels either in Italy, his adopted country (*Goodness*), in England, his native country (*Family Planning*), in South Tyrol (*Cleaver* and *Rapids*), or in the broader imaginary space of Strasbourg (*Europa*) while his last work, *Dreams of Rivers and Seas*, as he describes, is set in the "pullulating enigma of India" ("Novels"). Similarly, Baranay has set her stories in Australia (*Pagan*), Indonesia (*The Edge of Bali*), India and Australia (*With the Tiger*), India (*Neem Dreams*), and Europe (*Always Hungry*). By the same token, in the novel by Kamila Shamsie *Burnt Shadows* the characters depicted belong to a plethora of seemingly disparate cultures (Japanese, English, Indian, Pakistani, Afghan, and US-American) which reveal their shared and interwoven history while the action shifts—together with the characters' life trajectories—from Nagasaki to New Delhi, from Karachi to Istanbul, and from New York to Guantánamo. Despite this territorial heterogeneity in their settings, transcultural authors are not prone to use foreign countries as exotic stereotypes, but as loci best suited to the issues they intend to address and the themes they want to develop, which most of the time are independent even of geographic connotations. As Deves remarks analyzing Castro's *Stepper*: "Although nominally set in Tokyo, [it] deals not with 'Asian' questions but problems of identity, honesty/duplicity, multiple selves, loyalty . . . Stepper is attracted by the 'Japaneseness' of Reiko, but he himself is an exotic, hybrid character. Ishigo Isaku is a man torn between Japanese traditions and his desire for Western life styles. The novel is an existential examination of identity, in which race plays a co-incidental role" (82). Another example is *Neem Dreams*, a novel Baranay set in India, a country in which she lived intermittently for extensive periods of time: "The writer does not use India as an exotic backdrop . . . Its location in India is not your usual outsider's perspective on India. Rather it strikes a chord in the completely familiar way both natural landscapes and those of the human mind are painted in verbal pictures . . . the author in no way adheres to the stereotype of India as the land that helps to ease pain" (Pal). As Baranay admits, "Setting a novel elsewhere gives a writer the possibility of the necessary perspective that enables the creation of fictive truth" ("Multiculturalism" 128). And this truth, sometimes, does not correspond to the conventional vision of a country that only partially emerges from the breaking news realm of today's mass media. In *Neem Dreams* Baranay is keen to illustrate the fact that despite "the daily news of communal violence, caste wars, [and] ethnic

tensions," India is thriving in the plurality of its cultures, idioms, religions, ethnicities, castes, and classes: "There have been enormous successes in this: migratory movements and mixed marriages resulting in content and stability. The tolerance of difference in India is so deep and widespread and natural that it is an effort to bring it to conscious attention. But this is not always noticed by the outsider's gaze upon India, with the domination of the daily news . . . and the ways they are manipulated for political purposes . . . As an Australian author including this phenomenon in a novel set in India, I might have been looking for a way to understand it in my own country and in the world, to expose it, to register my own refusal to ignore or endorse it" ("Multiculturalism" 128). Also when the Western characters (Pandora, Andy, and Jade, respectively Australian, British, and Australian-American) of Baranay's novel interact with their Indian counterparts the risk of stereotyping is kept at bay. As Swati Pal is keen to emphasize, what emerges is that despite "cultural barriers and national boundaries, notwithstanding Kipling's poetically expressed beliefs on this subject, [these barriers] do not prevent the meeting of minds."

2) Characters with a transnational/transcultural background or experience. Often, in Baranay's, as well as in Trojanow's and Castro's novels, we encounter characters who come from different cultural backgrounds or reflect transnational and transcultural experiences. Let's take, for example, the novel *With the Tiger* by Baranay, who grew up in Australia of Hungarian parents, lived for extensive periods of time in India and now resides in Istanbul. The novel is a tribute to Somerset Maugham's *The Razor's Edge*. In it, Elliott, the main character created by Maugham and revisited by Baranay in the Australia of the 1970s, explains himself and his charismatic young companion, Larry, in this way: "Our communities are not geographically based, we don't live where we were born, we don't have a single workplace, we are global souls" (Baranay, *With the Tiger* 225). In Castro's *The Garden Book*, on the other hand, a poetess living with her Chinese father first marries an Australian man who dreams of his time in Shanghai and subsequently falls in love with a US-American architect who is hired to build her husband's mansion in the Australian bush. Again, in her Indian novel *Neem Dreams* Baranay weaves her story around four main characters: Pandora, an Australian eco-scientist interested in self-sustainable rural projects and "knowledgeable about cultural sensitivity"; Meenakshi, a middle-class young Indian lady who studied and lived in New York and moved back to India with her husband to help him run the family business and, on the side, initiate her own project of rural development; Andy, an English lawyer looking for the healing powers of the *neem tree*; and Jade, an Australian living in the United Stated in search of trendy indigenous skin-care products for an exclusive New York store (5). In changing geographies and locations, these characters find themselves having more chances to be exposed to Others and "be transformed," as Couldry suggests, drawing on Elspeth Probyn's views, "by sharing [their] self-reflections with others": "The self is not an end in itself, it is the opening of a perspective, one which allows us to conceive of transforming ourselves with the aid of others" (qtd. in Couldry 123).

3) Plural identities through a plurality of voices. Transcultural novels tend to display a plurivocal perspective: they look at the different, often complex aspects or concerns of life from a multiplicity of angles by interweaving in their texts a plurality of voices or by exposing the subtle interplay of their characters' multiple identities, where any rigid notions of self and other have collapsed. For example, Castro writes that "most of my novels deal with two or three 'voices' and move through several different spaces, rather in the manner of a hologram. That is when one sees things in depth, and when one abandons the notion of a fixed, two-dimensional reality" ("Writing" 150). In these novels, usually there is not an omniscient narrator through whom all the characters are kept at arm's length, nor a single viewpoint protagonist, but rather a multiplicity of characters endowed with multiple viewpoints or able to elaborate different points of view. For example, in the first part of Trojanow's *The Collector of Worlds,* Burton's experiences in India, Arabia, Africa, and Europe are relived not only through the voice of his Indian servant Naukaram—who sometimes expresses his independent views together with the critically interiorized way of reasoning of his master—but also contextualized through the voice and point of view of the *lahiya*, the professional letter writer to whom Naukaram goes to have his story written down in the hope to find a new employment after having being discarded by Burton. The second section, which deals with Burton's pilgrimage to Mecca and Medina disguised as a pilgrim, is split between a third-person interior account and accounts of his journeys given by several Arab officials. In the last section, which covers Burton's African explorations, we "listen" to the narrating voice of Sidi Mubarak Bombay—a Black slave who after having been brought in chains to India came back to Africa as a free man and took part in Burton's and Speke's expedition in the African interior: "With its radical code-switching, shifts of perspective and ahead-of-his-time hero who himself knew how to turn barriers into through-ways, *The Collector of Worlds* triumphantly shows us one method" (Foden, "Bwanas"). In most of the transcultural novels considered in this study, the technique of the rotation of points of views is amplified by multiple views expressed by each character, although some characters may have predominating experiences and considerations. In other words, not only do several protagonists express different points of views, but often they say or think things in a deeply self-reflexive or self-doubting manner: in this way they contribute to enriching the inner complexity and contradictory nature of the narrative and to generating a decentering or destabilizing effect. It is as if the same authors' plural cultural identities and points of view were dispersed among their characters with their plurality of equally relevant voices, making it impossible to distinguish a single authorial reliable standpoint. This is an aspect that Helff emphasizes with regard to Oonya Kempadoo's *Tide Running* as an early example of transcultural fiction: "On the level of storytelling the text introduces the narrative phenomenon of polyphony. This latter term denotes the narrative strategy of multivoiced storytelling, and it is the tension created by the clash of voices that is crucial to [this] multiperspectival narrative structure" ("Shifting" 85). Helff's comment resonates with Castro's reasoning when discussing the voice assumed by his culturally hybridized

characters: "Their *métissage* opens up a multiplicity of views and worlds which are not only new to homogenous cultures but which embody an open secret, an overt mystery which is ungraspable by those cultures, not because it is a mystery *per se* in the end, but because uniform cultures are so blind" (Castro qtd. in Barker 246). This proliferation of points of view happens also in Parks's *Dreams of Rivers and Seas*: in it the voice of the main protagonist, already dead since the beginning of the story, mingles with and is often juxtaposed, in a subtle and complex dialogue without a master voice, to the voices of his wife, his forgotten son, his young Indian lover, and his bewildered and at times reluctant US-American biographer. Further, Castro's *The Bath Fugues* is composed like a contrapuntal polyphony of voices competing for attention, as he himself acknowledges and as the title of his novel evokes: "I write in a kind of fugal way and I'm a great admirer of Bach. It's this sort of counterpoint and that sense of voices chasing each other and yet able to come back to the point of origin. This babble of voices in other words, but all making very clear sense, is what I like about it. There's a purity about it, when the obvious thing to say is that it's a confusion" (qtd. in Deves 55). In these transcultural novels, as Nadia Butt remarks, even the characters' mnemonic processes tend to be as plural and self-reflexive as their voices, resonating with their "experiences in heterogeneous cultural landscapes" (294). Analyzing in particular the novel of the Indian writer Zulfikar Ghose, Butt writes that "these experiences begin to take the form of contradictory stories once he [the protagonist] recollects them in a new country and continent, leaving him in a state of constant doubt about the reality of his past. Hence memory and fiction are not only indispensable to his tales of multiple cultural encounters, but also pervade his perception of self and identity throughout the novel" (294). According to Butt, this mode of "transcultural memory" is fostered by the multiple belongings and multiple identities that individuals tend to generate and perceive in their increasing cultural crisscrossings: "We may realize amidst global flows that our memory of any given situation is now more and more multiform, because plurality tends to characterize the practice and act of memory in contemporary times . . . in the wake of movement and migration as well as of political and social change, memories of today's individuals are no longer an outcome of a singular world but are rooted in 'multiple times' and 'contact zones'" (295-96).

4) Engagement with foreign words or expressions. One peculiar trait of transcultural fiction is the intentional engagement with the experience of foreign languages, concepts, and expressions. There is a tendency in transcultural authors who, as we have seen, are usually bilingual and more often than not multilingual, to introduce in their novels terms, expressions, or whole sentences in another language or other languages from the one used to tell the story, thus conveying their linguistic and cultural plurality. As Deves remarks, analyzing Castro's work, "Language is also culturally a specific system, and Castro's characters are cultural hybrids crossing linguistic-cultural boundaries" (56). This choice reveals a psychological enfranchisement from the dominant language in which these writers write their works, as well as the openness and lack of inhibition to think, imagine, and communicate through

other linguistic codes and worldviews. Further, this way of approaching the learning or the acquired knowledge of other languages is not dissimilar to the way Braidotti envisions the aesthetic or ethical practices of the nomadic polyglot: "Writing is, for the polyglot, a process of undoing the illusory stability of fixed identities, bursting open the bubble of ontological security that comes from familiarity with one linguistic site" (*Nomadic* 15). And Castro's view seems to directly echo Braidotti's reasoning: "The polyglot is a freer person, a person capable of living in words and worlds other than the narrow and the confined one of unimagined reality" ("Writing" 153). Not dissimilarly, and opening the vision on a larger picture, Beck remarks that "the Babylonian heart of world society beats in the hubbub of languages and identities" (qtd. in Schulze-Engler, "Theoretical" 27). If Besemeres and Wierzbicka point out that "there is a world of human experience which is closed to speakers of one language," the same might be said of those who dwell in only one cultural landscape, even when one does not theoretically accept the deterministic view of a too tight a correspondence between language and culture, where language becomes another form of essentializing ethnocentrism (xv). Besemeres and Wierzbicka are among scholars who emphasize that "a monolingual perspective on the world is also a monocultural one" and take as their main example a contemporary Australia that, despite its multicultural policies to accommodate increasing streams of linguistically diversified immigrants, still remains locked in its English monolingualism and, correspondingly, "in an Anglocentric view of the world" (xiv-vi). To a certain extent it is as if within the same dominant language it were now possible to create a destabilizing and decentralizing form of polyglossia. Nora Moll, for instance, emphasizes the unusual ability—she talks of "great creativity and courage"—of the contemporary German model of writing to transform its own language "not only necessarily towards the low codes of the 'scum' (Kanaken), but towards spaces in which a plurality of imaginaries, languages, and worlds react mixing themselves among each other" (Moll). This point of view is shared by Braidotti: "In this respect, writers can be polyglots within the same language; you can speak English and write many different Englishes . . . Writing in this mode is about disengaging the sedentary nature of words, destabilizing commonsensical meanings, deconstructing established forms of consciousness" (*Nomadic* 15). While in *The Bath Fugues* Castro plays with foreign words taken from French, Portuguese, Italian, and Latin, in *Ilustrado* Syjuco decides not to italicize the Spanish or Tagalog words which Filipinos use when speaking Filipino English, which is the English normally spoken among the local cultured upper class. In doing so, he gives us a powerful example of what translingualism really means when used "live" in a contemporary transcultural context. It is as if Syjuco had listened to and accepted the Indian writer Kamala Markandaya's more radical invitation and suggestion: "The thing to do is to use local words with brio(u), as the Americans do: that is to say simply to go ahead and use Indian words without italics, or footnotes, or glossaries, or apologies . . . These devices seem to me to interrupt the natural flow, and to introduce an unfortunate ethnic note. Novels, after all, are not and should not be regarded as ethnic studies . . . When I read an American novel there are any number of words I don't know. I have to work for the meaning, and it is a rewarding experience in a way that discovery by footnote could never be" (31). One must concede, however, that in this connection it is still fairly unusual—especially when dealing with the Anglo-American literary market—to find writers who are given the opportunity to assert their freedom to mix languages, use "native" expressions, do away with "ethnic" footnotes, etc. As Coetzee on the contrary points out in an exchange of emails with me, "it is a much more common experience that metropolitan publishers compel writers to walk a fairly narrow linguistic path" (13 December 2011). It is also true that now more than ever, with the advent of the internet and of easily accessible free online dictionaries, even the practice of "working for the meaning" of a foreign word may start to be perceived as less of a hurdle and instead a cultural discovery. A whole new world of cultural signs is there to be imaginatively written and interpreted by a new generation of transcultural authors and, possibly, readers.

5) Neither nationally nor culturally identifiable. Transcultural novels have at least one common feature: it is not easy to fit them within a single national geography. In other words, it is difficult to identify to which cultural or national environment their authors and sometimes their characters belong. It is as if they were set and as if the action took place in a sort of metaphorical or mental transplace, a transcultural territory or continuum, which can be the homeland, the new country of residence, another nation, but where one has the feeling of a sort of intellectual or imaginary "detachment" from that reality. Even when writing within an explicit Western canon, transcultural authors narrate from a different perspective as if they were thriving "on the fascination of the stranger's gaze" (Thomsen, "Migrant" 248). We might say that this is another reflection of the authors' physical, cultural, and identity mobility, of their transient or "not belonging" state. In reading these novels no one would easily discern the nationality of their authors. At the most, readers can make out that these writers are somewhat linked to an imagined—and perhaps questionable or questioned—Western literary tradition, but cannot really detect their ethnicity, nationality, cultural belonging, or religious views.

In sum, to a certain extent the transcultural novel "demonstrates the ways in which artistic and literary spaces blur the boundaries between home and away, familiarity and foreignness" (Schade ii). As Castro also writes, "I feel that contemporary writing must create a defamiliarization with the world, and with one's place in it" ("Writing" 150). That is why a transcultural novel may be best understood as the creation, re-creation, and interlacing of diverse cultural landscapes through which the author and the readers are able to see things from different perspectives and through which, as Braidotti would say, they may convey or generate states of "empathic proximity" and "intensive interconnectedness" (*Metamorphoses* 8). Transcultural novels show us the strengths and at the same time the limits and the illusory perception of single bounded cultures/civilizations and monocultural/monological identities. Through them, we are rewarded with the pleasure of stepping into different cultural landscapes and being exposed to the "virtues and shortcomings" in all of them (Ibarrola-Armendariz, "Native"

68). At the same time, as readers we may also be led towards a path of deconstruction and personalization of our cultural identity. It is on this path of cultural self-knowing and self-creation that cultural conditionings can be reflected upon and transcended. Through this process of transcendence comes also the acknowledgement of the hidden reality of our inner pluralities, cultural confluences, and constant becomings.

As we have seen in part 1, chapter 5, Trojanow and Hoskoté describe the harbor city, be it the ancient Alexandria or an imaginary Istanbul of the near future, as the archetypal image of cultural confluence: the place where the river, the sum of numerous tributaries, meets the ocean. In our turbulent times, neonomadism, cultural diversity, and a cosmopolitan outlook are necessary conditions of existence—of being with others, of meeting the Other. Flowing within the confluence, within the transcultural continuum, the individual gradually realizes that the Other is not an enemy, not a stranger, not an alternative, and most of the time not even an Other, but just a mirror of the various possible faces, the multiple understandings of human existence, the varied definitions of belonging that can be grasped, refuted, or internalized. We must look into this mirror, not to lose ourselves in confusion, but to see our selves, our options, and our choices with greater clarity. The harbor novel might thus represent that mirror, that opening of new cultural imaginaries and of their practicability. In this sense, it represents a transcultural fiction able to envision future cultural landscapes and at the same time to reconcile different, centuries-old cultural perspectives. As Rushdie warned us in his contribution to a seminar about Indian writing held in London in 1982: "The largest and most dangerous pitfall would be the adoption of a ghetto mentality. To forget that there is a world beyond the community to which we belong, to confine ourselves within narrowly defined cultural frontiers, would be . . . to go voluntarily into that form of internal exile which in South Africa is called the 'homeland'" ("Imaginary Homelands" 19). Rushdie's words seem to echo those of Kapuściński, one of the twentieth century's transcultural authors, forerunner of those who would follow the wake of his ever moving pen, of the many Trojanows, Castros, Manguels, Baranays, Parks dispersed in the world: "We now know that the immensity and the cultural richness of the world are infinite. After over forty-five years of constant travelling, and despite knowing this earth better than those who have not travelled, I am convinced I still know nothing. My main ambition is to show Europeans that our mentality is quite Eurocentric and that Europe, or better a part of it, is not the whole world. That Europe is surrounded by an immense and ever increasing variety of cultures, societies, religions, and civilisations. Life on a planet covered by a growing number of interconnections must have this consciousness and adapt itself to a radically new global condition" (Kapuściński, *Autoritratto* 12).

Conclusion

Cultural transformations and interactions have always been part of human history, but as we have seen in the course of this study, what we are facing today is an exponential growth in their dynamics and practices. Whether we like it or not, whether we embrace these influences or resist them, the thrust of globalization and the complexities of our (post)modern, liquid, transnational times are leading towards that new "global cultural order" suggested by Burke (115). As it has emerged both in the creative section and the critical exegesis of *Transcultural Writers and Novels in the Age of Global Mobility*, writers position themselves—by chance, life circumstances, intellectual curiosity, or sheer determination—at the forefront in trying to interpret and creatively express the power of these changes and their effects on people's lives and imaginations. The writers whose texts I analyze work at an international or transnational level with a manifest transcultural sensibility that allows them to adopt cultures, be transformed by them, and, ultimately, write about them. These writers have been affected by their personal experiences of traversing cultural territories, of living in different cultures, or between different cultures, and they are writers without borders whose geographic, cultural, national, or homeland borders are self-identified, self-chosen. By transcending their primary culture and loosening or even abandoning their ties with ethnic or national forms of identification, these writers, almost by a process of osmosis, undergo both an identity and cultural metamorphosis. Through what I call a creative transpatriation process, they acquire that distinctive and complex transcultural orientation towards the world at large so essential in the creation of transcultural literary expressions, namely, those works which, together with their authors, are intrinsically border crossers, that is, able to go beyond the limits of any one culture or national landscape. These transcultural—or transpatriate—writers are thus both here and there, both one thing and another, "diffused" in a transcultural continuum. Being physically and imaginatively on the move across geographical and cultural borders and literary categories they defy conventional pigeonholing. If once they might have been labeled as (im)migrant, ethnic, diasporic, exile, or postcolonial writers, now they may be referred to as "transcultural."

It is important to note that transcending one's primordial culture and affiliations does not mean repudiating them or disavowing their relevance in terms of the cultural provenance of the subject. In other words, one may stretch the umbilical cord with one's native cultural heritage (that is, with one's personal and intersubjective historicity), but not eliminate it. Nonetheless, according to transcultural discourse and practice one can transcend any residual or rigid sense of national or ethnic affiliation by exploring alternative and more encompassing modes of belonging or not belonging. By transposing this attitude into the aesthetic and creative realm, imaginative writers and artists are able to challenge the perceived dominance of ethnic or national forms of identification and the potency of territorial, native, and cultural roots. Emerging from this process is a transcultural literature which enriches a growing transcultural imaginary in the world and of the world. As Sinopoli and Tatti write, the various forms of the contemporary literary "dispatriation" (*dispatrio*)—or what I call creative transpatriation—are able to "show us a new and significant world level of contemporary literature, the one that makes it universally indispensable . . . to build for oneself a new identity through other territories, languages, cultures" (18).

I conducted my research project with the intent of getting to know better who transcultural writers are or might be, what characterizes them, how they face their processes of transpatriation and how they creatively exploit them. In part 1 I present interviews with selected writers meant to have an illuminating effect on the course my critical exegesis takes. This occurs by creatively speculating on these literary conversations and my personal transcultural background. In the process I also capture and mature an understanding of the interconnections between the writers' lived experiences, transpatriation processes, cultural outlooks, and ways of writing. Taken all together, the findings which emerge show to what extent the transcultural perspective and a transcultural mode of writing can perhaps, in Epstein's words, "open . . . a possibility for globalization not as homogenization but, rather, as further differentiation of cultures and their 'dissemination' into transcultural individuals" ("Transculture" 328). In a similar tone, Welsch suggests that "we can transcend the narrowness of traditional, monocultural ideas and constraints, we can develop an increasingly transcultural understanding of ourselves" ("Transculturality" 201).

It is no longer a question of being a Camus-like stranger, of looking at things with the detachment of the outsider. Instead, what is pressing against the pages of these writers of contemporary mobility is the awareness of being in a hybridized state, of having accepted the osmosis, the constant process of dilution, and crossing over of cultural elements, of always introducing in any context a more open, complex, and thus more elusive and less classifiable perspective: "The hybrid threatens the stability of society and State, subverts the gospel truth of "one people, one nation, one culture" (Trojanow and Hoskoté, *Confluences* 5). It is the perspective of the "outlier" rather than of the "outsider," not of the one being kept (or willing to be) out of the group, but of the one who having transcended any cultural, ethnic, religious, or territorial line of demarcation and not belonging to anything ends up feeling she or he belongs to everything. Only if conceived in this new light can we aspire to be citizens of neither country in order to be citizens of every country. Only then, as

Hélène Cixous—born in French Algeria, raised in Germany, educated in France, and dedicated to English literature—writes, "foreignness becomes a fantastic nationality" (*Three Steps* 80). It is from this perspective and within a literary context that transcultural writers may also develop an aesthetic sensibility together with an engaged and ethical responsibility thus able to inspire and nurture transcultural conversations across all borders, both physical and imaginary. In Epstein's words, such writers would help us "to go beyond our biographical identity in an attempt to speak (and listen) on behalf of cultures other than our own" ("Transculture" 345). Rorty was convinced that, among other reasons, we read literary texts in order to find "more resourceful ways of describing [our]selves or altering [our] vocabularies for a variety of purposes," and thus give us the chance "to enlarge ourselves by enlarging our sensitivity and our imaginations" (*Take Care* 124). We might thus infer that by opening up new worlds transcultural novels make us—writers and readers from different backgrounds alike—conscious of the imaginative presence of a transcultural sphere of experience, perception, identity building, and self-knowledge. The following is therefore a synthesis of the main elements of a transcultural orientation and its correlated transcultural narrative expressions:

1) Individuals (characters as well as writers and readers) thriving in, or at least positively challenging, the feeling of precariousness of one's existence; 2) Movement experienced as freedom—an opening of new possibilities, beginnings, and becomings; 3) A feeling of being "in place," not "out of place"—no longer guests, at home anywhere, despite the difficulties inherent in any process of adaptation and translation; 4) The perception of the boundaries between cultures and geographic entities as mobile, liquid, and changeable; 5) Identity conceived as a fluid process: no need for self-affirmation or categorical reference to ethnic roots; 6) Enrichment through interaction with, and immersion in, multiple cultures; 7) The perception of the annulment, weakening, or supersession of traditionally conceived hegemonic centers; 8) The playful and creative engagement with the experience of foreign idioms, concepts, meanings, geographies, and verbally empowered characters, fluent in more than one language; 9) The blurring of the boundaries between self and Other, and; 10) The sense of becoming experienced and understood as an empowering, although sometimes distressful, dialogic process of mutual transformation and cultural confluence.

Where there is cultural harmony there can also be, at the same time, cultural asymmetry, resistance, suspicion, or even conflict. As Monica Juneja reminds us, "global phenomena . . . generate their own forms of exclusion and violence": "A close look at transregional circulation and communication invariably brings forth a vast amount of material making assertions of difference—cultural, ethnic, linguistic, and religious—which become central to the construction of identities" (qtd. in Kravagna 8-9). Huntington's critics have perhaps too easily dismissed his bleak view of a future and logic "of unbridgeable civilizational differences" (Ong 26). We should not forget that well into the twenty-first century people kill and die to oppose or affirm their ideas of cultural identity and cultural differences. Lack of comprehension, poor communication, ignorance, and prejudices are not the only causes of cultural clashes.

Challenging Huntington's view does not imply disregarding it as morally unacceptable or not coinciding with one's political views. Unfortunately, as Said makes clear, a lurking fear of the unknown and of the stranger can be hardly ignored: "No one finds it easy to live uncomplainingly and fearlessly with the thesis that human reality is constantly being made and unmade, and that anything like a stable essence is constantly under threat. Patriotism, extreme xenophobic nationalism, and downright unpleasant chauvinism are common responses to this fear" (*Orientalism* 333).

Despite the fact that a transcultural and individualistic approach to globalization may sound idealistic, it may also reveal itself as the most pragmatic as well as ethically sound. What would happen if growing numbers of global citizens started to adopt Epstein's freely accepted "rule of thumb": "Oppose yourself to nobody, identify yourself with nothing" ("Transculture" 350)? Otherwise, we might suggest: Always identify yourself with an impermanent plurality of affiliations. For this reason even cultures often associated with centuries-old religions, as Huntington emphasizes in the case of the Hindu or Islamic civilizations, might be understood more as "spheres of influence" rather than rigidly bound concepts or entities doomed to endless forms of conflict. Cultures do not need to be seen as replicas of cultural identifications transposed to a macro level. As Sen remarks, "to see any person preeminently as a member of a civilization . . . is already to reduce people to this one dimension" (41). On the same wavelength, Gilroy proclaims that "today's civilizationism shamelessly represents the primary lines of antagonism in global politics as essentially cultural in character" (*After* 25). Sen also states that "the insistence . . . on a choiceless singularity of human identity not only diminishes us all, it also makes the world much more flammable . . . the main hope of harmony in our troubled world lies in the plurality of our identities, which cut across each other and work against sharp divisions" (16).

But how do we attain such a state of mind, such a cultural outlook, such a freedom of choice? In his book *Cosmopolitanism*, an ethical manifesto for a planet shared by seven billion strangers, Appiah suggests that "we should learn about people in other places, take an interest in their civilizations, their arguments, their errors, their achievements, not because that will bring us to agreement, but because it will help us get used to one another" (78). By creating and interlacing diverse cultural landscapes, transcultural novels have an ability to familiarize us with other lifeworlds: through them we can reflect upon and transcend those cultural conditionings that "in most contemporary societies . . . encourage a conformity of cultural judgement," warping the use of reason and choice (Couldry 50). If stories may transform us by helping us to emotionally and affectively imagine the lifeworlds of others, then literature may certainly contribute, as Rorty maintains, "to the widening of the moral imagination" (*Take Care* 67). Indeed, Ascari prompts us not to discount as irrelevant "the performative power of literature to cross cultural barriers and weave a network of connections, for in a way all good works of literature are transcultural . . . as is proved by the importance translation has had over the millennia in the development of human civilization" (6). In our best interests, we cannot ignore other cultures, and the more we comprehend them and—most importantly—interact and engage with them, the better. By dealing with them not only might we find it harder "to think of the world as 'divided between the West and the Rest'; between locals and moderns; between a bloodless ethic of profit and a bloody ethic of identity"; we might even find new paths and inspirations for our creativity, knowledge, and human development (Appiah, *Cosmopolitanism* xxi). As Welsch seems to suggest, "in meeting with other life-forms there are always not only divergences but opportunities to link up, and these can be developed and extended so that a common life-form is fashioned which includes even reserves which hadn't earlier seemed capable of being linked in. Extensions of this type represent a pressing task today" ("Transculturality" 200-01).

I am prone to think that cultural conflicts are always part of the same equation where cultural harmonization appears: cultures can clash and not only, or not always, intermingle and even before they have a chance to flow into one another, they may spend some time fiercely breaking against each other before finding a more peaceful, unifying course. As Sachsenmaier points out, "In the near future, it will be a major intellectual, political, and also economic challenge to harmonize claims to diversity with global commonalities and responsibilities" ("Multiple" 42). Hence, the significance of a transcultural transforming approach (and experience) in writing, reading, and critiquing. Instead of heightening conflicts and culture clashes, this transcultural approach promotes the value of confluence, fruitful encounters, and mutual respect. Rather than erecting new barriers, it encourages a new sense of communality through "the possibility of other logics of difference" and of cultural—albeit asymmetric—exchanges (Grossberg 89). Instead of devaluing the enriching presence of countless permeations, it acknowledges more complex and multifaceted forms of self-identity. As Trojanow prompts us, "If we want to be armed for the future, we have to understand that our frontiers are confluences which in the past have fertilised us, the playgrounds of mixed cultures which have been and still are of capital importance for our evolution. What divides us is nothing but an ephemeral difference, a blink of an eye of history" (*Un Voyage* 130).

I conclude that, in order to advance our understanding of the current literary production prompted by global mobility, it seems necessary to acknowledge the presence and identity, the fluid nature, and the transforming role of transcultural works. Further, by examining these works through a transcultural lens we might be able to grasp and interpret in a more profound way what Hannerz describes as the inescapable and often unpredictable influence of other cultures in our contemporaneity. Most importantly, transculture/ality and its creative expressions and practices promote a new understanding of cultural encounters, revealing the often asymmetrical but always multidirectional flows of cultural circulation, which are marked by ruptures, disjunctures, and mutual tensions but also by commonalities and shared ventures, affects, and outlooks. The significance of a transcultural transforming approach (and experience) in writing, reading, and critiquing has been highlighted by Gilles Dupuis when marking the differences between transculturalism and interculturalism within a literary context: "The discourse of transculturalism . . . does not limit itself to two cultures facing each other, trying to work out what they assume to be their intrinsic discrepancies. Transculturalism takes place when at least two—and sometimes three or more—cultures are not only engaged in dialogue, but partake in a more profound and often contradictory process, in which enlightenment, misunderstanding, and continuous reassessment of identity are at play. The ultimate aim is to transform each other's identity through a long, arduous, and sometimes painful negotiation of Otherness" (500).

With transculture/ality and away from the "continuing influence of the nation as a structure for the study of literature," we now have a new discursive field from which to critically address the cultural impact and the creative expressions of global modernity (Connell and Marsh 97). Through this lens, which extends our view well beyond national or cultural frontiers, disciplinary boundaries, and literary canons, it is possible to promote a type of transcultural comparativism for the global age. This analytical model can show a relationship between literary works that appear in different countries and in the context of multiple cultural and linguistic expressions, revealing, exemplifying, or emphasizing the complex and ever-present dynamics of cultural encounters, transformations, and negotiations. In tune with theoretical approaches in comparativism and in particular in tune with comparative cultural studies, the conceptual framework I present for the study of transculture/ality appears to be endowed with the kind of dynamic nonlinear nature and flexibility needed in dealing with the changing patterns and transformations in cultures and literatures. My framework also creates the premise for a new "borderless"—rather than border crossing—comparative methodology. In doing so, the framework marks an attempt to move away from the nationalist stances and agonistic dichotomies (core/periphery, empire/colony, mainstream/minority, pure/hybrid, self/Other, dominant/subaltern) with which comparative literary studies, especially within a postcolonial perspective, have lately been associated: "A transcultural lens might open up new avenues of coming to terms with the complex category of national literature" (Helff, "Locating" 140). It also offers the possibility of overcoming—or better, integrating—the self-defeating nature of anything "post-" to embrace instead the "visionary power" (Braidotti), "neo-vitalist" possibilities, and new beginnings inherent in an approach that accepts the prefix "proto-" starting with "protoglobal" (Epstein) or protoplanetary when dealing with our contemporaneity (Librett). As Rorty argues, there is no inspiration and spiritual change without hope, enthusiasm, utopian thinking, and originality ("The Inspirational" 133-39). "Proto-" expresses a start, a generation, the early development of a new phase characterized by its open-endedness, by the unpredictability of the transformation and "post-" signals decline, the end of something, and it has a self-defeating connotation. It also seems important to point out that transculture/ality does not imply a dismissal of questions of power and hierarchy; rather, it opens the path towards alternative—but not exclusivist or essentialist modes of interpretation—approaches and practices based on notions of alterity and subversion.

As global citizens of a communal Earth, we need a temporal perspective from the past tense to the distant future, as well as a spatial one from our insignificantly small planet to the infinite vastness of the cosmos to make a different sense of who we are, where we come from, and who we might become. To do so, we might need to distance ourselves from our globe, to look at ourselves as a cosmonaut would do watching humanity from the silent, dark depths of outer space. We might do this not with the self-satisfied, self-centered Apollonian eye of the past, as Jazeel warns us ("Transatlantic" 89), but—in Massey's words—with a multiplicity of humble, centerless "we"-gazes turned towards a planet spatially imagined as a fluid grid of multirelational, non-"settled" and non-"pre-given" places that demand "the negotiation of multiplicity" (*For Space* 141). In Jazeel's view, "thinking place as relational is one way of grounding the challenge of the unexpected, the discontinuous, that planetarity poses" ("Transatlantic" 93).

We live our daily lives with our noses close to the ground and we forget, lest someone reminds us, to look outside, above, beyond. That is what artists usually do: they "extend the reach of our imagination about the potential of real life" (Phillips 149). And they do so regardless of Adorno's bitter but justifiable consideration that "in a society that has disaccustomed men and women from thinking beyond themselves, whatever surpasses the mere reproduction of their life and those things they have been drilled to believe they cannot get along without, is superfluous" (*Aesthetic* 317). As literary artists, transcultural writers might thus be part of a new constellation of creative "cosmonomads" (my term) who with their mix of cosmopolitan ethical stances, neonomadic lifestyles, and "cosmodern" (Nicolescu) or "planetist" (Ellyard) views remind us to transcend the limitations of our ingrained given cultures, biographies, and identities and to look beyond. Even beyond the limits of time and geography, there where lies our naked humanity stripped of its constructed masks, structural constraints, and superficial, false representations—thus finally deconstructively universal. As Masao Miyoshi suggests, "literature and literary studies now have one basis and goal: to nurture our common bonds to the planet—to replace the imaginaries of exclusionist familialism, communitarianism, nationhood, ethnic culture, regionalism, 'globalization,' or even humanism, with the ideal of planetarianism. Once we accept this planet-based totality, we might for once agree in humility to devise a way to share with all the rest our only true public space and resources" (295-96). Miyoshi's reasoning resonates with Peter Ellyard's "planetism," the new paradigm for the globalized society of the twenty-first century which "will play a role similar to the role nationalism played in the nineteenth and twentieth centuries" (38). People then gave their first allegiance to their tribe or nation. In the twenty-first century they will give their first allegiance to the planet, to Spaceship Earth, which they share with the rest of humanity.

I think that what counts in a text, as Richard Bales argues when talking about the sublime in Proust's and Sebald's works is what "transports us," sometimes with "rapture," into "unfamiliar verbal worlds" and disconcerting territories, allowing us to experience the power of defamiliarization, border crossing, and transcending—transcending one's culture, others' cultures, one's self or all one's selves, one's language, others' languages, one's identity or all of our identities (470). We transcend in order to become, change, metamorphose. As Sinopoli and Tatti remind us: "Each literature, perhaps since the remotest origins, is animated by a pressure to get out of oneself, to confront oneself with something else, with a non-belonging, with a difference . . . In writing there is like an elective push to commensurate oneself with what brings far away from the origin, from the nest, from the identitarian closure" (11). If transcultural fiction has a role in the context of early twenty-first century world literature(s), it is to show us and let us discover and appreciate the process of this eternal cultural becoming while attempting to surpass our limits, without fear of losing something essential in the process: "If we want to know anything beyond ourselves . . . if we want to transcend our limited capabilities, we have to edge just a little towards chaos. Fall off our horse. Go beyond measure" (Castro, *The Bath* 107). Castro's intimation resonates with Berry's thought: "The goal becomes to 'mutate' beyond any singular or bounded mode of cultural identity—even a hybridized identity—in order to 'become transcultural' ("Nomadic" 130). This means to inhabit a decentered imaginary space on the border of all cultures encompassing yet distinct from any of them. Moreover, it is mainly by sharing our self-reflections with others that we may be communally and mutually transformed: "The self is not an end in itself, it is the opening of a perspective, one which allows us to conceive of transforming our selves with the aid of others" (Probyn, *Sexing* 145).

Glossary of Concepts for the Study of Transculturality

In *Transcultural Writers and Novels in the Age of Global Mobility* neologisms, expressions, phrases, and personally designated terms are used in order to convey the sense of argumentation and to contribute to the definition of a new taxonomy for the field of transcultural comparative literary studies. For references consult the works cited.

bird's eye view. A form of comparative analysis based on Moretti's ("Conjectures") model of "distant reading." It promotes the comparative study of a collection of literary texts by privileging a kind of panoptic analysis of the overall works at a conceptual and macro-structural level rather than a finely detailed formalist analysis of single texts or brief passages. This mode of proceeding seems particularly apt to capture new literary "waves" (Moretti, "Conjectures") or "constellations" (Thomsen, Mapping).

confluence. The effect of processes of amalgamation, overlapping, and permeation in the ongoing meeting, creation, and re-creation of cultures. The liquid metaphor implies a circulatory process where it is theoretically arduous to identify a single origin, a "pure" initial bloodstream, or cultural source.

continuum. See *transcultural continuum*

cosmonomads. Those who, with their mix of cosmopolitan ethical stances, neonomadic lifestyles, cosmonautic perspectives, and planetarian views, have transcended the limitations of their ingrained given cultures, ethnic identities, biographies, or sedentary states of mind/being. Transcultural writers may represent creative cosmonomad subjects.

creative transpatriation. See *transpatriation*

distant reading. One of the possible analytical tools of "transcultural comparativism" modelled on Moretti's concept of "distant reading," that is, the analysis not of particular texts but of the aggregated data coming from others' studies and analyses of those texts ("Conjectures"). This approach does not substitute close reading but strategically integrates it. In this study, Moretti's model of "distant reading" has been adapted to the needs of a comparative "bird's eye view."

fuzzy. A concept used in mathematics and computer science to describe those elements or data which have uncertain, amorphous, or blurred boundaries. Such qualities may indeed be inherent in the nature of transcultural novels.

harbor novel. Another way of defining a "transcultural novel." A harbor novel is a transcultural work of fiction able to open up new cultural imaginaries and at the same time reconcile metaphorically different cultural perspectives.

language. In the context of the present study, language is understood in the way Bakhtin envisages it, that is, "not as a system of abstract grammatical categories, but rather . . . as ideologically saturated, language as a world view, even as a concrete opinion" (*The Dialogic* 271). Bakhtin also reminds us that language, by living and developing in an interrelated, elastic environment, "is never unitary" (*The Dialogic* 288).

literatures of mobility. The cluster—or in Thomsen's terms the "constellation"—of works affected by or dealing with migratory flows, exploratory/travelling experiences, diasporic/exile conditions, transnational movements, and neonomadic trajectories (*Mapping*; see also Dagnino, "Global"). It includes, among others, the subclusters of expatriate literature, (im)migrant literature, exile literature, postcolonial literature, transcultural literature, and cosmopolitan literature.

mondialisation. See *planetarity*

multilingualism. See *polyglossia*

multiple modes of modernity. The understanding and elaboration, through a transcultural lens, of the traditional discourse of modernity by presenting its multiple declinations, steps, and transboundary interconnections in a movement towards an ever-greater complexity of views and cultural horizons (see Dagnino, "Global").

neonomadism/global nomadism. The contemporary social condition/lifestyle emerging from the transnational and deterritorialized patterns produced by global mobility and by the intense digitalization of information and communication technologies. This social condition in its turn may generate flexible decentered identities with specific transcultural attitudes and sensibilities.

outlier. Unlike the "outsider," the "outlier" is not the one being kept (or willing to be) out of the group, but the one who, having transcended any cultural, ethnic, religious, or territorial line of demarcation, not belonging to anything ends up feeling he or she belongs to everything.

planetarity/planetary. This concept is borrowed from Spivak (*Death*). It relates to the state of interdependence among fellow human beings, as well as to their bond with earth. It expresses a mode of being in the world that emphasizes the convivial, communitarian, and sustainable aspects of our shared humanity, rather than the conflicting and belligerent ones. It moves away from the economically and commercially restrictive concept of globalization as it is understood within the framework of neoliberal capitalism and tends instead towards the wider concept of mondialization (*mondialisation*) devised, among others, by Nancy and Derrida.

polyglossia/multilingualism. The coexistence and interplay of more than two languages in one subject or in one area/discipline/culture. The term is drawn from the concept of "polyglossia" by Bakhtin by which he meant the interaction of two or more national languages within a given culture. Bakhtin differentiated between "polyglossia" and "heteroglossia," the latter meaning the copresence and stratification of dialects and informal or "extraliterary" languages within any given national language (*The Dialogic* 67). Polyglossia should not be confused with Bakhtin's notion of "polyphony," the multivoiced nature of any dialogic event from human social interactions to literary works.

polyphony. See *polyglossia*

protoglobal. A concept by Epstein to designate postpostmodern culture by stressing the importance of thinking in terms of "beginnings and initiations" ("The Unasked" 46). In my study, "protoglobal" refers to our contemporary, increasingly globalizing hypermodernity and it indicates the neovitalist early development of a new phase, characterized by an open-endedness "rather than a consummation of the past" ("The Unasked" 46).

transcultural comparativism. The analytical framework that promotes the comparative study of texts and their formalist literary elements (such as plot, character, setting) through the combined interplay of socio-techno-economic realities, cultural constructs (ideologies, worldviews, language patterns), time (the historical dimension), and lived experience.

transcultural continuum/transpace/transplace. An all-inclusive space of subjective consciousness and cultural possibilities which does not deny the formative importance of native cultures (and, to some extent, their accompanying worldviews) but at the same time allows an openness to the reception, integration, negotiation, and permeation of other cultures, languages, worldviews. This notion of a transcultural continuum draws directly from the one formulated by Epstein.

transcultural literature. A type of literature that not only transcends the borders of a single culture in its narrative choices, but that also promotes and engages with a wider global literary perspective not attached to any single national paradigm.

transcultural memory. A plural, self-reflexive, and self-narrative mnemonic process which is generally fostered by the multiple belongings and multiple identities that individuals tend to generate and perceive in their ever growing cultural criss-crossings. Butt describes it as "the fictional(izing) nature of memory in the face of our 'moving world'" (293).

transcultural narrative unreliability. A "narrative device" and mode of aesthetic expression that "reflects transcultural practices, modern homeworlds and transcultural lifestyles by consciously conflating fact with fiction, reality with imagination," fictionalized characters with auto/biographical personas (Helff, "Signs" 277-78).

transcultural novel. A novel whose main characteristics include the creation, re-creation, and interweaving of diverse cultural landscapes through which the writer and readers are able to see things from different perspectives and through which empathic and mental states of proximity and interconnectedness are being generated (Braidotti, *Metamorphoses* 8). See also harbor novel.

transcultural orientation. An inclusive vision of culture(s), which stresses the power of confluences, overlappings, and interactions rather than of polarities. While fostering an imaginary and a sensibility by which "all cultures look decentered in relation to all other cultures, including one's own," this perspective promotes and witnesses a more encompassing and open-ended way of imagining and living one's and others' cultural identity (Berry and Epstein 312).

transcultural writers/transpatriate writers. Writers who have experienced a creative transpatriation process and thus express a transcultural orientation through their writing.

transculturation. An understanding of cultural exchange as a complex, often conflictive, and contradictive, but mutually transforming form of interaction even in the case of cultures with unequal negotiating powers (see Ortiz).

transculture/ality. A conceptual framework that expands the original notion of "transculturation" by combining Epstein's concept of "transculture" and Welsch's concept of "transculturality" ("Transculturality").

translingua franca. According to Pennycook (*Global*, "The Future"), a flexible, polycentric world idiom used from a multilocal and non nation-based perspective, such as contemporary practices of "global English/es."

translingualism. The writing between languages or in a language different from the native language (Kellman, *The Translingual*). It defines the phenomenon of cultural expansion, mutual interference, enrichment, and creation of potentially new languages and meanings through bilingualism or polyglossia.

transpace/transplace. Another way of defining the transcultural continuum. Transpace/transplace is the transcultural dimension that lies beyond the divides, often commercially or ideologically emphasized, of cultures. It represents a nonoppositional point of confluence or overlapping of cultures that in many ways expands Bhabha's notion of the third space, the in-between space where hybridization occurs. It may be conceived as an exo-space or a "potential zone" (Bartoloni, "Translation" 9) not limited to the in-between but external to all cultures.

transpatriate (adjective, noun, verb). A transcultural dispatriate subject: someone who undergoes a transpatriation process. A transpatriate writer is used as a synonym of transcultural writer. To transpatriate oneself, as a verb, means to undergo a transpatriation process.

transpatriation/creative transpatriation. The process that by moving physically, virtually, imaginatively, and emotionally outside one's cultural and homeland/national borders allows individuals, including artists and writers, to adopt new ways of self-identification and consequently new creative approaches and modes of expression through the acquisition of a transcultural lens. It is not seen as a loss, but as an enrichment (Dagnino, "Transculturalism"). The neologism "transpatriation" comes from the combination of the words "transcultural" and "dispatriation."

undecidable belonging. The condition typical of a transcultural state of being/identity, where the feeling of belonging and sense of home is constantly negotiated, renegotiated, and open to new or more extensive possibilities, as if the transcultural self were an expression of "creative becoming" (Braidotti, Transpositions), "an ongoing process that could by definition never be complete" (Berry and Epstein 312).

world literature(s). World literature—although growing numbers of scholars now prefer to talk about "world literatures" in the plural (see Boruszko and Tötösy de Zepetnek; Juvan)—is a mode of literary circulation, as well as of reading and writing (see Damrosch). It includes texts printed, translated, and distributed in several places and thus acquire an international dimension. Usually these texts propose narratives which even when dealing with local anecdotes engage with wider global and ethical perspectives, thus inspiring new border crossing imaginaries (see Walkowitz). In its multiple border crossings (through cultures, national boundaries, and literary genres), transcultural literature belongs in every respect to the ever growing realm of world literature(s) (see Dagnino, "Transcultural").

Works Cited

Adorno, Theodor W. *Aesthetic Theory*. Trans. Robert Hullot-Kentor. London: Continuum, 2004.

Adorno, Theodor W. *Essays on Music*. Ed. Richard Leppert. Trans. Susan H. Gillespie. Berkeley: U of California P, 2002.

Ahmad, Aijaz. "The Politics of Literary Postcoloniality." *Race & Class* 36.3 (1995): 1-20.

Alexander, Vera. "Investigating the Motif of Crime as Transcultural Border Crossing: *Cinnamon Gardens* and *The Sandglass*." *Postcolonial Postmortems: Crime Fiction from a Transcultural Perspective*. Ed. Christine Matzke and Susanne Mühleisen. Amsterdam: Rodopi, 2006. 139-60.

Anderson, Benedict. *Imagined Communities: Reflections on the Origin and Spread of Nationalism*. London: Verso, 1983.

Anderson, Laurie. *A Story about a Story*. Adelaide: Anne & Gordon Samstag Museum of Art (1 March-19 April 2013).

Ang, Ien. "Migrations of Chineseness." *Journal of the South Pacific Association for Commonwealth Literature and Language Studies* 34-35 (1993): <http://wwwmcc.murdoch.edu.au/ReadingRoom/litserv/SPAN/34/Ang.html>.

Appadurai, Arjun. "How Histories Make Geographies: Circulation and Context in a Global Perspective." *Transcultural Studies* 1 (2010): 4-13.

Appadurai, Arjun. *Modernity at Large: Cultural Dimensions of Globalization*. Minneapolis: U of Minnesota P, 1996.

Appiah, Kwame Anthony. *Cosmopolitanism: Ethics in a World of Strangers*. New York: Norton, 2006.

Appiah, Kwame Anthony. "The Cultural Turn and the Civilizational Approach." *European Journal of Social Theory* 13.1 (2010): 67-82.

Appiah, Kwame Anthony. *The Ethics of Identity*. Princeton: Princeton UP, 2007.

Appiah, Kwame Anthony. *In My Father's House: Africa in the Philosophy of Culture*. Oxford: Oxford UP, 1992.

Apter, Emily. "Literary Readings." *Literature and Globalization: A Reader*. Ed. Liam Connell and Nicky Marsh. London: Routledge, 2011. 147-55.

Ascari, Maurizio. *Literature of the Global Age: A Critical Study of Transcultural Narratives*. Jefferson: McFarland, 2011.

Ascari, Maurizio, and Adriana Corrado, eds. *Sites of Exchange: European Crossroads and Faultlines*. Amsterdam: Rodopi, 2006.

Ashcroft, Bill. "Introduction. A Convivial Critical Democracy: Post-Colonial Studies in the Twenty-first Century." *Literature for Our Times: Postcolonial Studies in the Twenty-First Century*. Ed. Bill Ashcroft, Ranjini Mendis, Julie McGonegal, and Arun Mukherjee. Amsterdam: Rodopi, 2012. xv-xxxv.

Ashcroft, Bill. "Transnation." *Rerouting the Postcolonial: New Directions for the New Millennium*. Ed. Janet Wilson, Cristina Sandru, and Sarah Lawson Welsh. London: Routledge, 2010. 72-84.

Ashcroft, Bill, and Pal Ahluwalia. *Edward Said*. London: Routledge, 2001.

Ashcroft, Bill, Gareth Griffiths, and Helen Tiffin, eds. *The Empire Writes Back: Theory and Practice in Post-Colonial Literatures*. London: Routledge, 1989.

Attali, Jacques. *L'Homme nomade*. Paris: Fayard, 2003.

Attwell, David. "Editor's Introduction." *Doubling the Point: Essays and Interviews*. Ed. David Attwell. Harvard: Harvard UP, 1992. 1-13.

Baena, Rosalía. "Transculturing Auto/Biography: Forms of Life Writing." *Transculturing Auto/Biography: Forms of Life Writing*. Ed. Rosalía Baena. London: Routledge, 2006. vii-xiii.

Bail, Murray. *Eucalyptus*. London: Harvill, 1998.

Bakhtin, Mikhail M. *Problems of Dostoyevsky's Poetics*. Trans. Caryl Emerson. Minneapolis: U of Minnesota P, 1984.

Bakhtin, Mikhail M. *Speech Genres and Other Late Essays*. Ed. Michael Holquist and Caryl Emerson. Austin: U of Texas P, 1986.

Bakhtin, Mikhail M. *The Dialogic Imagination: Four Essays*. Trans. Caryl Emerson and Michael Holquist. Ed. Michael Holquist. Austin: U of Texas P, 1981.

Bal, Mieke. "Close Reading Today: From Narratology to Cultural Analysis." *Grenzüberschreitungen. Narratologie im Kontext / Transcending Boundaries: Narratology in Context*. Ed. Walter Grünzweig and Andreas Solbach. Tübingen: Gunter Narr, 1999. 19-40.

Bales, Richard. "Homeland and Displacement: The Status of the Text in Sebald and Proust." *W. G. Sebald: Schreiben ex patria / Expatriate Writing*. Ed. Gerhard Fischer. Amsterdam: Rodopi, 2009. 461-74.

Banauch, Eugen. "Inter- and Transcultural Writing." *Fluid Exile: Jewish Exile Writers in Canada 1940-2006*. By Eugen Banauch. Heidelberg: Winter, 2009. 185-211.

Baranay, Inez. *Always Hungry*. Melbourne: Australian Scholarly Publishing, 2011.

Baranay, Inez. *The Edge of Bali*. Pymble: Collins Australia, 1992.

Baranay, Inez. "It's the Other Who Makes My Portrait: Writing Self, Character and the Other." *Text* 8.2 (2004): <http://www.textjournal.com.au/oct04/baranay.htm>.

Baranay, Inez. *Local Time: A Memoir of Cities, Friendships and the Writing Life*. Unpublished Ms.

Baranay, Inez. "Multiculturalism, Globalisation and Worldliness: Origin and Destination of the Text." *Journal of the Association for the Study of Australian Literature* 3 (2004): 117-32.

Baranay, Inez. *Neem Dreams*. New Delhi: Rupa, 2003.

Baranay, Inez. *Pagan*. Pymble: Collins Australia, 1990.

Baranay, Inez. *The Saddest Pleasure*. Sydney: Imprint, 1989.

Baranay, Inez. *Sun Square Moon: Writings on Yoga and Writing*. Moorooka: Sun Square Moon, 2005.

Baranay, Inez. *With the Tiger*. New Delhi: HarperCollins India, 2008.

Baranay, Inez. "Writing Lessons: Settings." *Griffith Review* 26 (2009): <https://griffithreview.com/edition-26-stories-for-today/writing-lessons-settings>.

Baranay, Inez "Writing Self, Character and the Other." *Text* 8.2 (2004): <http://www.textjournal.com.au/oct04/baranay.htm>.

Barbieri, Francesco Eugenio. "Dove comincia l'Europa. La scrittura transculturale di Tawada Yōko." *Scritture Migranti* 4 (2010): 65-88.

Barker, Karen. "Theory as Fireworks: An Interview with Brian Castro." *Australian Literary Studies* 20.3 (2002): 241-48.

Bartoloni, Paolo. *On the Cultures of Exile, Translation, and Writing*. West Lafayette: Purdue UP, 2008.

Bartoloni, Paolo. "Translation Studies and Agamben's Theory of the Potential." *CLCWeb: Comparative Literature and Culture* 5.1 (2003): <http://dx.doi.org/10.7771/1481-4374.1179>.

Bauman, Zygmunt. *Culture in a Liquid Modern World*. Cambridge: Polity, 2011.

Bauman, Zygmunt. "From Pilgrim to Tourist—Or a Short History of Identity." *Questions of Cultural Identity*. Ed. Stuart Hall and Paul Du Gay. London: Sage, 1996. 18-36.

Bauman, Zygmunt. *Globalization: The Human Consequences*. Cambridge: Polity, 1998.

Bauman, Zygmunt. *Liquid Times: Living in an Age of Uncertainty*. Cambridge: Polity, 2007.

Beautell, Eva Darias. "Postcoloniality, Multiculturalism and Ethnicity in the Canadian Context." *Tricks with a Glass: Writing Ethnicity in Canada*. Ed. Davis G. Rocío, and Rosalía Baena. Amsterdam: Rodopi, 2000. 19-36.

Beck, Ulrich. *The Cosmopolitan Vision*. Trans. Ciaran Cronin. Cambridge: Polity P, 2006.

Beck, Ulrich, and Edgar Grande. *Cosmopolitan Europe*. Trans. Ciaran Cronin. Cambridge: Polity, 2007.

Bellamy, Craig. "The Death of Mr Practical: The Practical Man and Globalisation." *craigbellamy.net* (13 November 2003): <http://www.craigbellamy.net/2003/11/13/the-death-of-mr-practical-the-practical-man-and-globalisation/>.

Berry, Ellen E. "Nomadic Desires and Transcultural Becomings." *Transcultural Experiments: Russian and American Models of Creative Communication*. Ed. Ellen E. Berry and Mikhail N. Epstein. New York: St. Martin's, 1999. 121-40.

Berry, Ellen E., and Mikhail N. Epstein. "In Place of a Conclusion: Transcultural Dialogue." *Transcultural Experiments: Russian and American Models of Creative Communication*. Ed. Ellen E. Berry and Mikhail N. Epstein. New York: St. Martin's, 1999. 302-22.

Besemeres, Mary, and Anna Wierzbicka. *Translating Lives: Living with Two Languages and Cultures*. St. Lucia: U of Queensland P, 2007.

Best, Steven, and Douglas Kellner. *Postmodern Theory: Critical Interrogations*. New York: Guilford, 1991.

Bhabha, Homi K. *The Location of Culture*. London: Routledge, 1994.

Bhabha, Homi K. "The Third Space: Interview with Homi Bhabha." *Identity: Community, Culture, Difference*. Ed. Jonathan Rutherford. London: Lawrence & Wishart, 1990. 207-21.

Bhabha, Homi K. "Unsatisfied: Notes on Vernacular Cosmopolitanism." *Postcolonial Discourses: An Anthology*. Ed. Gregory Castle. Oxford: Blackwell, 2001. 38-52.

Birus, Hendrik. "The Goethean Concept of World Literature and Comparative Literature." *Comparative Literature and Comparative Cultural Studies*. Ed. Steven Tötösy de Zepetnek. West Lafayette: Purdue UP, 2003. 11-22.

Black, Shameem. *Fiction across Borders: Imagining the Lives of Others in Late Twentieth-Century Novels*. New York: Columbia UP, 2010.

Black, Shameem. "Is There a Global Literature?" *insights.som.yale.edu* (April 2009): <http://insights.som.yale.edu/insights/there-global-literature>.

Borges, Jorge Luis. *The Aleph and Other Stories, 1933-1969*. New York: E. Dutton, 1970.

Borges, Jorge Luis. "The Nothingness of Personality." *The Total Library: Non-Fiction 1922-1986.* Harmondsworth: Penguin, 2001. 3-9.Borges, Jorge Luis. "A Profession of Literary Faith." *The Total Library: Non-Fiction 1922-1986*. By Jorge Luis Borges. Harmondsworth: Penguin, 2001. 23-27.

Boruszko, Graciela, and Steven Tötösy de Zepetnek. "Introduction to *New Work about World Literatures*." *CLCWeb: Comparative Literature and Culture* 15.6 (2013): <http://dx.doi.org/10.7771/1481-4374.2353>.

Bosniak, Linda. "Multiple Nationality and the Postnational Transformation of Citizenship." *Virginia Journal of International Law.* 42 (2001-2002): 979-1004.

Bourdieu, Pierre. *The Logic of Practice*. Cambridge: Polity, 1990.

Bourdieu, Pierre. *Outline of a Theory of Practice*. Trans. R. N. Cambridge: Cambridge UP, 1977.

Bourelle, Andrew. *Creative Nonfiction in the Composition Classroom*. Ph.D. Diss. Reno: U of Reno, 2009.

Bovo Romoeuf, Martine. "Rhapsodie italo-albanaise de Carmine Abate." *Kumà* (11 April 2006): <http://www.dislet.uniroma1.it/kuma/critica/kuma11romoeuf.html>.

Braidotti, Rosi. *Metamorphoses: Towards a Materialist Theory of Becoming*. Cambridge: Polity, 2002.

Braidotti, Rosi. *Nomadic Subjects: Embodiment and Sexual Difference in Contemporary Feminist Theory*. New York: Columbia UP, 1994.

Braidotti, Rosi. *Transpositions: On Nomadic Ethics*. Cambridge: Polity, 2006.

Braidotti, Rosi, Patrick Hanafin, and Bolette B. Blaagaard, eds. *After Cosmopolitanism.* London: Routledge, 2013.

Brancato, Sabrina. "Transcultural Perspectives in Caribbean Poetry." *Transcultural English Studies: Theories, Fictions, Realities*. Ed. Frank Schulze-Engler and Sissy Helff. Amsterdam: Rodopi, 2009. 233-47.

Brancato, Sabrina. "Transculturalità e transculturalismo. I nuovi orizzonti dell'identità culturale." *Le Simplegadi* 2.2 (2004): <http://all.uniud.it/simplegadi/wp-content /uploads/2004/Brancato_Simplegadi_2.pdf>.

Brennan, Timothy. *At Home in the World: Cosmopolitanism Now*. Cambridge: Harvard UP, 1997.

Brennan, Timothy. "Cosmopolitans and Celebrities." *Race & Class* 31.1 (1989): 1-19.

Brennan, Timothy. "Cosmo-Theory." *South Atlantic Quarterly* 100.3 (2001): 659-91.

Brenner, Angie. "Pico Iyer: Global Writer, Heart & Soul." *wildriverreview.com* (19 November 2007): <http://www.wildriverreview.com/INTERVIEW/Pico-Iyer/PEN/angie-brenner/2-10>.

Brydon, Diana. "Cracking Imaginaries: Studying the Global from Canadian Space." *Rerouting the Postcolonial: New Directions for the New Millennium*. Ed. Janet Wilson, Cristina Sandru, and Sarah Lawson Welsh. London: Routledge, 2010. 150-65.

Brydon, Diana. "Cross-Talk, Postcolonial Pedagogy, and Transnational Literacy." *Home-Work: Postcolonialism, Pedagogy, and Canadian Literature*. Ed. Cynthia Sugars. Ottawa: U of Ottawa P, 2004. 57-74.

Bulgakov, Mikhail. *The Master and Margarita*. Trans. Diana Burgin and Katherine Tiernan O'Connor. London: Vintage, 1995.

Burke, Peter. *Cultural Hybridity*. Cambridge: Polity, 2009.

Butt, Nadia. "Fictions of Transcultural Memory." *Transcultural English Studies: Theories, Fictions, Realities*. Ed. Frank Schulze-Engler and Sissy Helff. Amsterdam: Rodopi, 2009. 293-308.

Byram, Michael. *Teaching and Assessing Intercultural Communicative Competence*. Clevedon: Multilingual Matters, 1997.

Byrnes, Paul. Review of *Wake in Fright*. *smh.com.au* (29 June 2009): <http://www.smh.com.au/news/entertainment/film/film-reviews/wake-in-fright/2009/06/29/1246127466590.html>.

Caccia, Fulvio. "Lamberto Tassinari." *Interviews with the Phoenix: Interviews with Fifteen Italian-Québécois Artists*. Trans. Daniel Sloate. Ed. Fulvio Caccia. Toronto: Guernica, 1998. 211-22.

Caccia, Fulvio, Bruno Ramirez, and Lamberto Tassinari, eds. *La transculture et ViceVersa*. Toronto: Triptyque, 2010.

Calhoun, Craig J. "The Class Consciousness of Frequent Travelers: Toward a Critique of Actually Existing Cosmopolitanism." *The South Atlantic Quarterly* 101.4 (2003): 869-97.

Calvino, Italo. *If on a Winter's Night a Traveler.* New York: Harcourt, 1981.

Calvino, Italo. *The Invisible Cities.* New York: Harcourt, 1974

Campbell, Marion. "Dismantling the White Picketfence: Reclaiming Multiplicity in Kim Scott's *Benang* and Brian Castro's *Shanghai Dancing*." *Les Cahiers du CICLaS* 11 (2007): 45-57.

Canclini, García Néstor. *Hybrid Cultures: Strategies for Entering and Leaving Modernity*. Trans. Christopher L. Chiappari and Silvia L. López. Minneapolis: U of Minnesota P, 1995.

Cantle, Ted. *Interculturalism: The New Era of Cohesion and Diversity*. Basingstoke: Palgrave Macmillan, 2012.

Casanova, Pascale. *The World Republic of Letters*. Trans. M. B. DeBevoise. Cambridge: Harvard UP, 2004.

Casasanto, Daniel. "Who's Afraid of the Big Bad Whorf? Crosslinguistic Differences in Temporal Language and Thought." *Language Learning* 58.1 (2008): 63-79.

Castan, Con. "Terms of Engagement: Multiculturalism, Nation and Literature." *And What Books Do You Read? New Studies in Australian Literature*. Ed. Irmtraud Petersson and Martin Duwell. St. Lucia: U of Queensland P, 1996. 76-86.

Castro, Brian. *After China*. North Sydney: Allen & Unwin, 1992.

Castro, Brian. "Auto/Biography." *Looking for Estrellita*. By Brian Castro. St. Lucia: U of Queensland P, 1999. 98-123.

Castro, Brian. *The Bath Fugues*. Artarmon: Giramondo, 2009.

Castro, Brian. *Birds of Passage*. Sydney: Allen & Unwin, 1983.

Castro, Brian. *Double-Wolf*. Sydney: Allen & Unwin, 1991.

Castro, Brian. *Drift*. Melbourne: Heinemann, 1994.

Castro, Brian. *The Garden Book*. Artarmon: Giramondo, 2005.

Castro, Brian. *Looking for Estrellita*. St. Lucia: U of Queensland P, 1999.

Castro, Brian. "Memoirs of a Displaced Person." *Looking for Estrellita*. By Brian Castro. St. Lucia: U of Queensland P, 1999. 39-58.

Castro, Brian. "The Private and the Public." *Looking for Estrellita*. By Brian Castro. St. Lucia: U of Queensland P, 1999. 75-97.

Castro, Brian. *Shanghai Dancing*. Artarmon: Giramondo, 2003.

Castro, Brian. *Stepper*. Sydney: Random House, 1997.

Castro, Brian. "Writing Asia." *Looking for Estrellita*. By Brian Castro. St. Lucia: U of Queensland P, 1999. 139-71.

"Center for Transcultural Studies." *sas.upenn.edu* <http://www.sas.upenn.edu/transcult>.

"Centre for Transcultural Writing and Research." *transculturalwriting.com* (2004): <http://www.transculturalwriting.com>.

Chaney, David C. "Cosmopolitan Art and Cultural Citizenship." *Theory, Culture & Society* 19.1-2 (2002): 157-74.

Chaney, David C. "From Ways of Life to Lifestyle: Rethinking Culture as Ideology and Sensibility." *Culture in the Communication Age*. Ed. James Lull. London: Routledge, 2001. 75-88.

Chatwin, Bruce. *Anatomy of Restlessness: Selected Writings 1969-1989*. London: Jonathan Cape, 1996.

Cheah, Pheng. "Cosmopolitanism." *Theory, Culture & Society* 23 (2003): 486-96.

Cheah, Pheng, and Bruce Robbins, eds. *Cosmopolitics: Thinking and Feeling Beyond the Nation*. Minneapolis: U of Minnesota P, 1998.

Chiro, Giancarlo, and Katherine Vadura. "Whither European Integration? The Impact of Multicultural Identities in a Globalising Context." *New Europe, New World? The European Union, Europe and the Challenges of the Twenty-First Century*. Ed. Alfonso Martínez Arranz, Natalie J. Doyle, and Pascaline Winand. Bern: Peter Lang, 2010. 35-47.

Cixous, Hélène. *Three Steps on the Ladder of Writing*. New York: Columbia UP, 1993.

Clayton, Cherry. "Janice Kulyk Keefer Interviewed by Cheery Clayton." *The Journal of Commonwealth Literature* 34 (1999): 183-97.

Clifford, James. *Routes: Travel and Translation in the Late Twentieth Century*. Cambridge: Harvard UP, 1997.

"Cluster of excellence 'Asia and Europe in a Global Context: The Dynamics of Transculturality.'" *asia-europe.uni-heidelberg.de* <http://www.asia-europe .uni-heidelberg.de/en/about-us.html>.

Code 46. Dir. Michael Winterbottom. London: BBC Films, 2002.

Coetzee, J. M. *Boyhood: Scenes from Provincial Life*. London: Secker & Warburg, 1997.

Coetzee, J. M. *Summertime*. London: Harvill Secker, 2009.

Coetzee, J. M. *Youth*. London: Secker & Warburg, 2002.

Connell, Liam, and Nicky Marsh. *Literature and Globalization: A Reader*. London: Routledge, 2011.

Conrad, Joseph. *A Personal Record*. Ed. Zdzisław Najder and J. H. Stape. Cambridge: Cambridge UP, 2008.

Cook, Kenneth. *Wake in Fright*. Melbourne: Text Publishing, 2009.

Cornis-Pope, Marcel. "Transnational Approaches in Post-1989 Comparative Literary History: Writing the History of East Central European Literary Cultures." *Studying Transcultural Literary History*. Ed. Gunilla Lindberg-Wada. Berlin: Walter de Gruyter, 2006. 197-208.

Coronil, Fernando. "Introduction. Transculturation and the Politics of Theory: Countering the Center." *Cuban Counterpoint: Tobacco and Sugar*. By Fernando Coronil. Trans. Harriet De Onís. Durham: Duke UP, 1995. ix-lvi.

Coronil, Fernando. "Transcultural Anthropology in the Américas." *Cuban Counterpoints: The Legacy of Fernando Ortiz*. Ed. Mauricio A. Font and Alfonso W. Quiroz. Lanham: Lexington Books, 2005. 139-56.

Cosic, Miriam. "Location, Location, Location. The Bulgarian-Born Writer Ilija Troyanov Is a Man of the Globalised World." *theaustralian.com* (20 February 2010): <http://www.theaustralian.com.au/arts/books/location-location-location/story-e6frg8nf-1225834841196>.

Couldry, Nick. *Inside Culture: Re-Imagining the Method of Cultural Studies*. London: Sage, 2000.

Cresswell, Tim. "Imagining the Nomad: Mobility and the Postmodern Primitive." *Space and Social Theory: Geographical Interpretations of Post-Modernity*. Ed. Ulf Strohmayer and George Benko. Oxford: Blackwell, 1997. 360-82.

Cresswell, Tim. *On the Move: Mobility in the Modern Western World*. London: Routledge, 2006.

Cronin, Michael. *Translation and Identity*. London: Routledge, 2006.

Crozet, Chantal. "Spiritual Dimensions of Identity for Intercultural Language and Culture Education." *unisa.edu.au* (18 April 2012): <http://lrs.unisa.edu.au/ess/echo/presentation/403dbec9-150b-4b51-b05d-ced02463c2b9>.

Cuccioletta, Donald. "Multiculturalism or Transculturalism: Towards a Cosmopolitan Citizenship." *London Journal of Canadian Studies* 17 (2001-2002): 1-11.

Dagnino, Arianna. "Comparative Literary Studies in the Twenty-First Century: Towards a Transcultural Perspective?" *unisa.edu.au* (2012): <http://www.unisa.edu.au/Research/International-Centre-for-Muslim-and-non-Muslim-understanding/Publications/CSAA-conference-proceedings/>.

Dagnino, Arianna. "Global Mobility, Transcultural Literature, and Multiple Modes of Modernity." *Transcultural Studies* 2 (2013): <http://archiv.ub.uni-heidelberg.de/ojs/index.php/transcultural/article/view/9940>.

Dagnino, Arianna. *I Nuovi Nomadi. Pionieri della mutazione, culture evolutive, nuove professioni*. Roma: Castelvecchi, 1996.

Dagnino, Arianna. "Transcultural Literature and Contemporary World Literature(s)." *CLCWeb: Comparative Literature and Culture*. 15.5 (2013): <http://docs.lib.purdue.edu/clcweb/vol15/iss5/7/>.

Dagnino, Arianna. "Transculturalism and Transcultural Literature in the 21st Century." *Transcultural Studies: A Series in Interdisciplinary Research* 8 (2012): 1-14.

Dagnino, Arianna. "Transcultural Writers and Transcultural Literature in the Age of Global Modernity." *Transnational Literature* 4.2 (2012): <http://dspace.flinders.edu.au/jspui/bitstream/2328/25881/3/Transcultural_Writers.pdf>.

Dagnino, Arianna, and Mohamed Bakari. Private Conversation. Istanbul: Fatih U (9 July 2012).

Dagnino, Arianna, and Inez Baranay. Interview with Inez Baranay. Melbourne (16 July 2011).

Dagnino, Arianna, and Brian Castro. E-mail correspondence (6-7 September 2012).

Dagnino, Arianna, and Brian Castro. Interview with Brian Castro. Adelaide (10 December 2010).

Dagnino, Arianna, and J. M. Coetzee. E-mail correspondence (13 December 2011).

Dagnino, Arianna, and Nicola Lecca. Interview with Nicola Lecca. Innsbruck (9 January 2011).

Dagnino, Arianna, and Alberto Manguel. Interview with Alberto Manguel. Mondion (28 September 2011).

Dagnino, Arianna, and Tim Parks. Interview with Tim Parks. Milano (5 October 2011).

Dagnino, Arianna, and Ilija Trojanow. Interview with Ilija Trojanow. Wien (8 January 2011).

Damrosch, David. "Toward a History of World Literature." *New Literary History* 39.3 (2008): 481-95.

Damrosch, David. *What Is World Literature?* Princeton: Princeton UP, 2003.

Damrosch, David. "World Literature as Alternative Discourse." *Neohelicon: acta comparationis litterarum universarum* 38.2 (2011): 307-17.

Damrosch, David. "World Literature in a Postcanonical, Hypercanonical Age." *Comparative Literature in an Age of Globalization*. Ed. Haun Saussy. Baltimore: The Johns Hopkins UP, 2006. 43-53.

Damrosch, David, and Gayatri Chakravorty Spivak. "Comparative Literature/World Literature: A Discussion with Gayatri Chakravorty Spivak and David Damrosch." *Comparative Literature Studies* 48.4 (2011): 455-85.

D'Andrea, Anthony. *Global Nomads: Techno and New Age as Transnational Countercultures in Ibiza and Goa*. London: Routledge, 2007.

D'Andrea, Anthony. "Neo-Nomadism: A Theory of Post-Identitarian Mobility in the Global Age." *Mobilities* 1.1 (2006): 95-119.

D'Angelo, Carmela. "La dimensione transculturale della letteratura in lingua italiana di scrittori afferenti alla cultura ebraica del Novecento postbellico." *Scrittori italiani di origine ebrea ieri e oggi. Un approccio generazionale*. Ed. Raniero Speelman, Monica Jansen, and Silvia Gaiga. Utrecht: Igitur, 2007. 167-83.

Davidson, Robyn. "No Fixed Address: Nomads and the Fate of the Planet." *Quarterly Essay* 24 (2006): 1-52.

Deleuze, Gilles, and Félix Guattari. *Anti-Oedipus: Capitalism and Schizophrenia*. Trans. Robert Hurley, Mark Seem, and Helen R. Lane. Minneapolis: U of Minnesota P, 1983.

Deleuze, Gilles and Félix Guattari. *Kafka: Toward a Minor Literature*. Trans. Dana Polan. Minneapolis: U of Minnesota P, 1986.

Deleuze, Gilles, and Félix Guattari. *A Thousand Plateaus: Capitalism and Schizophrenia*. Trans. Brian Massumi. Minneapolis: U of Minnesota P, 1987.

Deleuze, Gilles, Félix Guattari, and Robert Brinkley. "What is a Minor Literature?" *Mississippi Review* 11.3 (1983): 13-33.

Derrida, Jacques. *Negotiations: Interventions and Interviews 1971-2001*. Trans. Elizabeth Rottenberg. Stanford: Stanford UP, 2002.

Derrida, Jacques, and Elisabeth Roudinesco. *For What Tomorrow . . . A Dialogue*. Trans. John Fort. Stanford: Stanford UP, 2004.

Deutscher, Guy. "Does Your Language Shape how You Think?" *nytimes.com* (26 August 2010): <http://www.nytimes.com/2010/08/29/magazine/29language-t.html?_r=1&pagewanted=all>.

Deutscher, Guy. *Through the Language Glass: Why the World Looks Different in Other Languages*. New York: Henry Holt, 2010.

Deves, Michael I. *"Apart from the Expected": The Novels of Brian Castro*. Ph.D. Diss. Adelaide: Flinders U, 1999.

D'haen, Theo, David Damrosch, and Djelal Kadir, eds. *The Routledge Companion to World Literature*. London: Routledge, 2012.

Dickens, Lyn. "Transcultural Horizons and the Limitations of Multiculturalism in *The World Waiting to Be Made*." *Australian Studies* 3 (2011): <http://www.nla.gov.au/openpublish/index.php/australian-studies/article/viewFile/2128/2519>.

Dillon, Patrick, Phil Bayliss, Ines Stolpe, and Linda Stolpe. "What Constitutes 'Context' in Sociocultural Research? How the Mongolian Experience Challenges Theory." *Transtext(e)s Transcultures: Journal of Global Cultural Studies* 4 (2008): 18-31.

Dirlik, Arif. *Global Modernity: Modernity in the Age of Global Capitalism*. Boulder: Paradigm, 2007.

Dirlik, Arif. "Modernity as History: Post-Revolutionary China, Globalization and the Question of Modernity." *Social History* 27.1 (2002): 16-39.

Driver, Dorothy. "Zoë Wicomb and the Cape Cosmopolitan." *Current Writing: Text and Reception in Southern Africa* 23.2 (2011): 93-107.

Drucker, Peter F. *The Landmarks of Tomorrow*. New York: Harper and Brothers, 1958.

Drucker, Peter F. *Management Challenges for the Twenty-First Century*. Oxford: Butterworth-Heinemann, 1999.

Dupuis, Gilles. "Transculturalism and *Ecritures Migrantes*." *History of Literature in Canada: English-Canadian and French-Canadian*. Ed. Reingard M. Nischik. Rochester: Camden House, 2008. 497-508.

Eckstein, Lars. *English Literatures across the Globe: A Companion*. Paderborn: Wilhelm Fink, 2007.

Eco, Umberto. *Baudolino*. Trans. William Weaver. Orlando: Harcourt, 2002.

Eco, Umberto. "When the Other Appears on the Scene." *Five Moral Pieces*. By Umberto Eco. Trans. Alastair McEwen. Orlando: Harcourt, 2002. 19-30.

Eisenstadt, Shmuel N. "Multiple Modernities." *Daedalus* 129.1 (2000): 1-29.

Eisenstadt, Shmuel N. "Some Observations on Multiple Modernities." *Reflections on Multiple Modernities: European, Chinese and Other Interpretations*. Ed. Dominic Sachsenmaier, Jens Riedel, and Shmuel N. Eisenstadt. Leiden: Brill, 2002. 27-41.

Eisenstadt, Shmuel N., Jens Riedel, and Dominic Sachsenmaier. "The Context of the Multiple Modernities Paradigm." *Reflections on Multiple Modernities: European, Chinese and Other Interpretations.* Ed. Dominic Sachsenmaier, Jens Riedel, and Shmuel N. Eisenstadt. Leiden: Brill, 2002. 1-25.

Elliott, Anthony, and John Urry, eds. *Mobile Lives*. London: Routledge, 2010.

Ellyard, Peter. *Designing 2050. Pathways to Sustainable Prosperity on Spaceship Earth.* N.d.: TPN TXT, 2009.

Epstein, Mikhail N. *After the Future: The Paradoxes of Postmodernism and Contemporary Russian Culture.* Trans. Anesa Miller-Pogacar. Amherst: U of Massachusetts P, 1995.

Epstein, Mikhail N. "Response: 'Post-' and Beyond." *The Slavic and East European Journal* 39.3 (1995): 357-66.

Epstein, Mikhail N. "Transculture: A Broad Way between Globalism and Multiculturalism." *American Journal of Economics & Sociology* 68.1 (2009): 327-51.

Epstein, Mikhail. *The Transformative Humanities: A Manifesto.* Trans. and ed. Igor Klyukanov. New York: Bloomsbury, 2012.

Epstein, Mikhail N. "The Unasked Question: What Would Bakhtin Say?" *Common Knowledge* 10.1 (2004): 42–60.

Eriksen, Thomas Hylland. *Globalization: The Key Concepts*. Oxford: Berg, 2007.

Ertler, Klaus-Dieter. "Trans-Culturalism and the Contemporary French-Canadian Novel." *Global Realignments and the Canadian Nation in the Third Millennium*. Wiesbaden: Harassowitz, 2010. 187-98.

Esposito, Claudia F. "Mediterranean Imaginaries: Writing Transcultural Subjectivities in Contemporary Francophone Literature." Unpublished paper. Providence: Brown U, 2007.

Ette, Ottmar. *Literature on the Move*. Trans. Katharina Vester. Amsterdam: Rodopi, 2003.

Faist, Thomas. "Diversity: A New Mode of Incorporation?" *Ethnic and Racial Studies* 32.1 (2009): 171-90.

Fallaci, Oriana. *Interview with History*. Boston: Houghton Mifflin, 1976.

Fallaci, Oriana. *Nothing, and So Be It*. New York: Doubleday, 1972.

Foden, Giles. "Bwanas, Banyans and Bhang." *guardian.co.uk* (28 June 2008): <http://www.guardian.co.uk/books/2008/jun/28/saturdayreviewsfeatres.guardianreview30>.

Fowers, Blaine J., and Barbara J. Davidov. "Dialogue as the Interplay of Otherness and Shared Humanity." *American Psychologist* 62.7 (2007): 705-06.

Francuski, Biljana Djorić. "Multilingual Literature, Translation, and Crnjanski's *Роман о Лондону* (A Novel about London)." *CLCWeb: Comparative Literature and Culture* 15.7 (2013): <http://dx.doi.org/10.7771/1481-4374.2383>.

Friedman, Jonathan. "The Hybridization of Roots and the Abhorrence of the Bush." *Spaces of Culture: City-Nation-World*. Ed. Mike Featherstone and Scott Lash. London: Sage, 1999. 230-56.

Gadamer, Hans-Georg. *Truth and Method*. Trans. Garrett Barden and John Cumming. London: Sheed & Ward, 1975.

Ganguly, Debjani. "Global Literary Refractions: Reading Pascale Casanova's *The World Republic of Letters* in the Post-Cold War Era." *Literature for Our Times: Postcolonial Studies in the Twenty-First Century*. Ed. Bill Ashcroft, Ranjini Mendis, Julie McGonegal, and Arun Mukherjee. Amsterdam: Rodopi, 2012. 15-35.

Gaonkar, Dilip Parameshwar. "On Alternative Modernities." *Alternative Modernities*. Ed. Dilip Parameshwar Gaonkar. Durham: Duke UP, 2001. 1-23.

Germann Molz, Jennie. "Getting a 'Flexible Eye': Round-the-World Travel and Scales of Cosmopolitan Citizenship." *Citizenship Studies* 9.5 (2005): 517-31.

Ghosh, Bishnupriya. *When Borne Across: Literary Cosmopolitics in the Contemporary Indian Novel*. New Brunswick: Rutgers UP, 2004.

Giddens, Anthony. *The Consequences of Modernity*. Stanford: Stanford UP, 1990.

Giddens, Anthony. *Runaway World: How Globalisation is Reshaping Our Lives*. London: Profile Books, 1999.

Gilroy, Paul. *After Empire: Melancholia or Convivial Culture?* London: Routledge, 2004.

Gilroy, Paul. *The Black Atlantic: Modernity and Double Consciousness*. Cambridge: Harvard UP, 1993.

Gilsenan Nordin, Irene, Julie Hansen, and Carmen Zamorano Llena. "Introduction: Conceptualizing Transculturality in Literature." Amsterdam: Rodopi, 2013. ix-xxvii.

Glick-Schiller, Nina, Linda Basch, and Cristina Blanc-Szanton. "From Immigrant to Transmigrant: Theorizing Transnational Migration." *Anthropological Quarterly* 68.1 (1995): 48-63.

Glissant, Edouard. *The Poetics of Relation.* Trans. Betsy Wing. Ann Arbor: U of Michigan P, 1997.

Glissant, Edouard. *Traité du tout-monde*. Paris: Gallimard, 1997.

Gnisci, Armando. "Littérature globale et littérature des mondes." *Neohelicon: acta comparationis litterarum universarum* 29.1 (2002): 113-22.

Gnisci, Armando, Franca Sinopoli, and Nora Moll, eds. *La letteratura del mondo nel XXI secolo*. Milano: Bruno Mondadori, 2010.

Goethe, Johann Wolfgang von. *Essays on Art and Literature.* Ed. John Gearey. Trans. Ellen von Nardroff and and Ernest H. von Nardroff. Princeton: Princeton UP, 1986.

Gone, Joseph, Peggy J. Miller, and Julian Rappaport. "Conceptual Self as Normatively Oriented: The Suitability of Past Personal Narrative for the Study of Cultural Identity." *Culture & Psychology* 5.4 (1999): 371-98.

González, Jorge A. "Cultural Fronts: Towards a Dialogical Understanding of Contemporary Cultures." *Culture in the Communication Age*. Ed. James Lull. London: Routledge, 2001. 106-31.

Goulart Almeida, Sandra Regina. "Transcultural Fictions and Travels in Cultural Criticism." *Estudos Literários* 4 (2004): 9-27.

Grabovszki, Ernst. "The Impact of Globalization and the New Media on the Notion of World Literature." *CLCWeb: Comparative Literature and Culture* 1.3 (1999): <http://dx.doi.org/10.7771/1481-4374.1040>.

Grauby, Francoise. "A Transcultural Becoming: The Cultural Immigrants in Paris." *Literature & Aesthetics* 20.1 (2010): 69-80.

Greenblatt, Stephen. *Cultural Mobility: A Manifesto.* Cambridge: Cambridge UP, 2010.

Grimshaw, Trevor, and Coreen Sears. "Where Am I From? Where Do I Belong?" *Journal of Research in International Education* 7.3 (2008): 259-78.

Grossberg, Lawrence. *Cultural Studies in the Future Tense*. Durham: Duke UP, 2010.

Guerin, Wilfred L., Earle Labor, Lee Morgan, Jeanne C. Reesman, and John R. Willingham. *A Handbook of Critical Approaches to Literature*. Oxford: Oxford UP, 2005.

Gumperz, John J., and Stephen C. Levinson, eds. *Rethinking Linguistic Relativity*. Cambridge: Cambridge UP, 1996.

Gunesekera, Romesh. *The Sandglass*. New York: New Press, 1998.

Gunew, Sneja. *Framing Marginality: Multicultural Literary Studies*. Carlton: Melbourne UP, 1994.

Gunew, Sneja. *Haunted Nations: The Colonial Dimensions of Multiculturalisms*. London: Routledge, 2004.

Gunew, Sneja. *Post-Multiculturalism: Immanent Cosmopolitanism. A Future Anterior*. Unpublished Ms, 2011.

Gunew, Sneja. "Stammering 'Country' Pedagogies: Sickness for and of the Home." *Journal of Australian Studies* 86 (2006): 73-82.

Gunew, Sneja. *Transcultural Translations: Performative Pedagogies*. Unpublished Ms, 2002.

Gunew, Sneja, and Kateryna O. Longley. *Striking Chords: Multicultural Literary Interpretations*. London: Allen & Unwin, 1992.

Gupta, Suman. *Globalization and Literature*. Cambridge: Polity, 2009.

Habel, Chad. Rev. of A. Robert Lee, ed., *China Fictions/English Language: Literary Essays in Diaspora, Memory, Story* (Rodopi, 2008). *Transnational Literature* 2.2 (2010): 1-2.

Haberkorn, Michaela. "Treibeis und Weltensammler: Konzepte nomadischer Identität in den Romanen von Libuše Moníkovà und Ilija Trojanow." *Von der nationalen zur internationalen Literatur Transkulturelle deutschsprachige Literatur und Kultur im Zeitalter globaler Migration*. Ed. Helmut Schmitz. Amsterdam: Rodopi, 2009. 243-61.

Hage, Ghassan, *White Nation: Fantasies of White Supremacy in a Multicultural Society*. London: Routledge, 2000.

Hannerz, Ulf. "Cosmopolitans and Locals in World Culture." *Theory, Culture & Society* 7 (1990): 237-51.

Hannerz, Ulf. *Cultural Complexity: Studies in the Social Organization of Meaning*. New York: Columbia UP, 1992.

Hannerz, Ulf. "Flows, Boundaries and Hybrids: Keywords in Transnational Anthropology." *transcomm.ox.ac.uk* (2 October 2001): <http://www.transcomm.ox.ac.uk/working%20papers/hannerz.pdf>.

Hannerz, Ulf. "Thinking about Culture in a Global Ecumene." *Culture in the Communication Age*. Ed. James Lull. London: Routledge, 2001. 54-71.

Hannerz, Ulf. *Transnational Connections: Culture, People, Places.* London: Routledge, 1996.

Heartfield, James. *The "Death of the Subject" Explained.* Sheffield: Sheffield Hallam UP, 2002.

Heise, Ursula K. *Sense of Place and Sense of Planet: The Environmental Imagination of the Global.* Oxford: Oxford UP, 2008.

Helff, Sissy. "Indian Diasporic Literature from Down Under." *museindia.com* (March-April 2009): <http://www.museindia.com/viewarticle.asp?myr=2009&issid=24&id=1438>.

Helff, Sissy. "Locating Indo-Australian Fiction in Multicultural Australia." *Australian Made: A Multicultural Reader.* Ed. Sonia Mycak and Amit Sarwal. Sydney: Sydney UP, 2010. 137-57.

Helff, Sissy. "The Missing Link: Transculturation, Hybridity, and/or Transculturality?" *Literature for Our Times. Postcolonial Studies in the Twenty-First Century.* Ed. Bill Ashcroft, Ranjini Mendis, Julie McGonegal and Arun Mukherjee. Amsterdam: Rodopi, 2012. 187-202.

Helff, Sissy. "Shifting Perspectives: The Transcultural Novel." *Transcultural English Studies: Theories, Fictions, Realities.* Ed. Frank Schulze-Engler and Sissy Helff. Amsterdam: Rodopi, 2009. 75-89.

Helff, Sissy. "Signs Taken for Truth: Orchestrating Transcultural Aesthetics through Transcultural Unreliable Narration." *Proceedings of the Annual Conference of the German Association of University Teachers of English.* Ed. Sabine Volk-Birke and Julia Lippert. Trier: Wissenschaftlicher, 2007. 277-88.

Herzfeld, Michael. "Practical Mediterraneanism: Excuses for Everything, from Epistemology to Eating." *Rethinking the Mediterranean.* Ed. William V. Harris. Oxford: Oxford UP, 2005. 45-63.

Hoerder, Dirk. "Transculturalism(s): From Nation-State to Human Agency in Social Spaces and Cultural Regions." *Global Realignments and the Canadian Nation in the Third Millennium.* Ed. Karin Ikas. Wiesbaden: Harassowitz, 2010. 197-206.

Hoerder, Dirk, Yvonne Hébert, and Irina Schmitt. *Negotiating Transcultural Lives: Belongings and Social Capital among Youth in Comparative Perspective.* Toronto: U of Toronto P, 2005.

Hoffman, Eva. *Lost in Translation: A Life in a New Language.* Harmondsworth: Penguin, 1989.

Hokenson, Jan Walsh. "The Culture of the Context: Comparative Literature Past and Future." *Comparative Literature and Comparative Cultural Studies.* Ed. Steven Tötösy de Zepetnek. West Lafayette: Purdue UP, 2003. 58-75.

Holquist, Michael. *Dialogism: Bakhtin and His World.* London: Routledge, 1990.

Hopfer, Sabina. *Der Traum vom Moulin Rouge: Transnational Literature and Words in Flight.* Ph.D. Diss. Adelaide: U of Adelaide, 2004.

Howells, Coral Ann. "Not Belonging, but Longing: Shifts of Emphasis in Contemporary Diasporic Writing in English Canada." *Diasporic Subjectivity and Cultural Brokering in Contemporary Post-Colonial Literatures.* Ed. Igor Maver. Lanham: Lexington Books, 2009. 1-16.

Hrabal, Bohumil. *Too Loud a Solitude.* Orlando: Harcourt, 1990.

Huggan, Graham. *Australian Literature: Postcolonialism, Racism, Transnationalism.* Oxford: Oxford UP, 2007.

Huggan, Graham. *The Postcolonial Exotic: Marketing the Margins*. London: Routledge, 2001.

Huntington, Samuel. *The Clash of Civilizations and the Remaking of World Order*. New York: Simon & Schuster, 1996.

Ibarrola-Armendariz, Aitor. "Boundary Erasing: Postnational Characterization in Michael Ondaatje's *The English Patient*." *Tricks with a Glass: Writing Ethnicity in Canada*. Ed. Davis G. Rocío and Rosalía Baena. Amsterdam: Rodopi, 2000. 37-58.

Ibarrola-Armendariz, Aitor. "Native American Humour as Resistance: Breaking Identity Moulds in Thomas King's *Green Grass, Running Water*." *Miscelánea: A Journal of English and American Studies* 42 (2010): 67-90.

Institut d'Etudes Transtextuelles and Transculturelles. *iett.eu* <www.iett.eu>.

Iyer, Pico. *The Global Soul: Jet Lag, Shopping Malls and the Search for Home*. London: Bloomsbury, 2001.

Izzo, David Garrett, and Daniel T. O'Hara. *Henry James Against the Aesthetic Movement: Essays on the Middle and Late Fiction*. Jefferson: McFarland, 2006.

James, Henry. "The Storyteller at Large: Mr. Henry Harland." *Fortnightly Review* April 1 (1898): 650-54.

Jay, Paul. "Beyond Discipline? Globalization and the Future of English." *PMLA: Publications of the Modern Language Association of America* 116.1 (2001): 32-47.

Jay, Paul. *Global Matters: The Transnational Turn in Literary Studies*. Ithaca: Cornell UP, 2010.

Jazeel, Tariq. "Spatializing Difference Beyond Cosmopolitanism: Rethinking Planetary Futures." *Theory, Culture & Society* 28 (5): 75-97.

Jose, Nicholas. *Chinese Whispers*. Kent Town: Wakefield, 1995.

Joseph, May. "Transatlantic Inscriptions: Desire, Diaspora, and Cultural Citizenship." *Talking Visions: Multicultural Feminism in a Transnational Age*. Ed. Ella Shohat. Cambridge: MIT P, 2001. 357-67.

Julien, Eileen. "Arguments and Further Conjectures on World Literature." *Studying Transcultural Literary History*. Ed. Gunilla Lindberg-Wada. Berlin: Walter de Gruyter, 2006. 122-32.

Jurgensen, Manfred. *Ethnic Australia*. Brisbane: Phoenix, 1981.

Jurgensen, Manfred. "Transformative Identities of Literary Multiculturalism." *Southerly* 59.3-4 (1999): 267-76.

Jurriëns, Edwin, and Jeroen de Kloet. "Introduction. Cosmopatriots: On Distant Belongings and Close Encounters." *Cosmopatriots: On Distant Belongings and Close Encounters*. Ed. Edwin Jurriëns and Jeroen de Kloet. Amsterdam: Rodopi, 2007. 9-18.

Juvan, Marko. "Introduction to World Literatures from the Nineteenth to the Twenty-First Century." *CLCWeb: Comparative Literature and Culture* 15.5 (2013): <http://dx.doi.org/10.7771/1481-4374.2333>.

Juvan, Marko. "Worlding Literatures between Dialogue and Hegemony." *CLCWeb: Comparative Literature and Culture* 15.5 (2013): <http://dx.doi .org/10.7771/1481-4374.2343>.

Kachru, Braj B. "Standards, Codification, and Sociolinguistic Realism: The English Language in the Outer Circle." *English in the World: Teaching and Learning the Language and Literatures*. Ed. Randolph Quirk and Henry G. Widdowson. Cambridge: Cambridge UP, 1985. 11-30.

Kachru, Braj B. "Teaching World Englishes." *The Other Tongue: English Across Cultures*. Ed. Braj B. Kachru. Urbana: U of Illinois P, 1992. 355-66.

Kachru, Braj B. "World Englishes and English-Using Communities." *Annual Review of Applied Linguistics* 17 (1997): 66-87.

Kachru, Braj B., Yamuna Kachru, and Cecil L. Nelson, eds. *The Handbook of World Englishes*. Malden: Wiley-Blackwell, 2009.

Kachru, Yamuna. "World Englishes: Approaches, Issues and Resources." *Language Teaching* 25 (1992): 1-14.

Kachru, Yamuna, and Larry E. Smith. *Cultures, Contexts, and World Englishes*. London: Routledge, 2008.

Kapuściński, Ryszard. *Autoritratto di un reporter*. Milano: Feltrinelli, 2006.

Kapuściński, Ryszard. *Imperium*. Trans. Klara Glowczewska. New York: Knopf, 1994.

Kassabova, Kapka. "Diary." *scottishreviewofbooks.com* 6.4 (2010): <http://www.scottishreviewofbooks.org/index.php?option=com_content&view=article&id=368:diary-kapka-kassabova&catid=37:volume-6-issue-4-2010&Itemid=86>.

Keefer, Janice Kulyk. "From Dialogue to Polylogue: Canadian Transcultural Writing during the Deluge." *Difference and Community: Canadian and European Cultural Perspectives*. Ed. Peter Easingwood, Konrad Groß, and Lynette Hunter. Amsterdam: Rodopi, 1996. 59-70.

Keefer, Janice Kulyk. "From Mosaic to Kaleidoscope." *Books in Canada* 20.6 (1991): 13-16.

Keefer, Janice Kulyk. "Writing, Reading, Teaching Transcultural in Canada." *Multiculturalism in North America and Europe: Social Practices-Literary Visions*. Ed. Hans Braun and Wolfgang Kloos. Trier: Wissenschaftlicher, 1995. 189-97.

Kellman, Steven G. *Switching Languages: Translingual Writers Reflect on their Craft*. Lincoln: U of Nebraska P, 2003.

Kellman, Steven G. *The Translingual Imagination*. Lincoln: U of Nebraska P, 2000.

Kempadoo, Oonya. *Tide Running*. London: Macmillan, 2001.

Khairallah, As'ad E. "The Story of Majnūn Laylā in Transcultural Perspectives." *Studying Transcultural Literary History*. Ed. Gunilla Lindberg-Wada. Berlin: Walter de Gruyter, 2006. 232-44.

Kim, Youna. "Female Cosmopolitanism? Media Talk and Identity of Transnational Asian Women." *Communication Theory* 21.3 (2011): 279-98.

Kravagna, Christian. "Monica Juneja Interviewed by Christian Kravagna." *Mapping Transcultural Modernism*. Ed. Christian Kravagna. Berlin: Sternberg Press, 2013. 1-9.

Kreisel, Henry. "Language and Identity: A Personal Essay." *Another Country: Writings by and about Henry Kreisel*. Ed. Shirley Neuman. Edmonton: NeWest Press, 1985. 119-34.

Kundera, Milan. *The Book of Laughter and Forgetting*. Trans. Aron Asher. New York: HarperCollins, 1996.

Kundera, Milan. *The Curtain: An Essay in Seven Parts*. Trans. Linda Asher. New York: HarperCollins, 2006.

Kundera, Milan. *Slowness*. Trans. Linda Asher. New York: HarperCollins, 1997.

Kundera, Milan. *Testaments Betrayed: An Essay in Nine Parts*. Trans. Linda Asher. New York: HarperCollins, 1995.

Landry, Donna, and Gerald MacLean, eds. *The Spivak Reader*. London: Routledge, 1996.

Lange, Bernd Peter, and Dirk Wiemann. 2008. "Transcultural Britain: An Introduction." *Journal for the Study of British Cultures* 15.1 (2008): 3-10.

Lee, Ezra Yoo-Hyeok. "Globalization, Pedagogical Imagination, and Transnational Literacy." *CLCWeb: Comparative Literature and Culture* 13.1 (2011): <http://dx.doi.org/10.7771/1481-4374.1705>.

Leung, Yiu-nam, and Sneja Gunew. "From Australia to Canada: A Conversation with Sneja Gunew." *Tamkang Review* 35.2 (2004): 141-60.

Librett, Jeffrey S. "The Finitude of Method: Mourning Theory from the New Criticism to the New Vitalism." *Comparative Literature* 64.2 (2012): 121-49.

Lodge, David. *After Bakhtin: Essays on Fiction and Criticism*. London: Routledge, 1990.

London, Scott, and Pico Iyer. "Postmodern Tourism: A Conversation with Pico Iyer." *scottlondon.com* (1996): <http://www.scottlondon.com/interviews/iyer.html>.

Löschnigg, Martin. "Trans-Culturalism and the Contemporary English-Canadian Novel." *Global Realignments and the Canadian Nation in the Third Millennium*. Ed. Karin Ikas. Wiesbaden: Harassowitz, 2010. 177-86.

Loti, Pierre. *Aziyadé*. Brussels: UltraLetters, 2013.

Maalouf, Amin. *In the Name of Identity*. Harmondsworth: Penguin, 2003.

Maalouf, Amin. *Origines*. Paris: Grasset, 2004.

MacRae, Ian J. "American Incunabula: 'Grotesque Genesis' and the Genealogical Genre." *Ameriquests* 5.1 (2008): 1-25.

Malherbe, Jean-François. *Le nomade polyglotte. L'excellence éthique en postmodernité*. Montréal: Bellarmin, 2000.

Manguel, Alberto. "A 30,000-Volume Window on the World." *nytimes.com* (15 May 2008): <http://www.nytimes.com/2008/05/15/garden/15library.html?pagewanted=all&_r=0>.

Manguel, Alberto. "Borges in Love." *A Reader on Reading*. By Alberto Manguel. New Haven: Yale UP, 2010. 47-61.

Manguel, Alberto. *The City of Words: Understanding Civilisation Through Story*. London: Continuum, 2007.

Manguel, Alberto. "On the Footsteps of My Grandfather." Text provided by author.

Manguel, Alberto. *A Reader on Reading*. New Haven: Yale UP, 2010.

Manguel, Alberto. *Stevenson under the Palm Trees*. Edinburgh: Canongate, 2004.

Manguel, Alberto. *Todos los hombres son mentirosos*. Barcelona: RBA, 2009.

Manguel Alberto. *Una vita immaginaria. Conversazioni con un amico*. Milano: Rosellina Archinto, 2011.

Mårald, Elisabeth. *In Transit: Aspects of Transculturalism in Janice Kulyk Keefer's Travels*. Uppsala: Swedish Science Press, 1996.

Marchenkova, Ludmila. "Language, Culture, and Self: The Bakhtin-Vygotsky Encounter." *Dialogue with Bakhtin on Second and Foreign Language Learning: New Perspectives*. Ed. Joan Kelly Hall, Gergana Vitanova, and Ludmila Marchenkova. Mahwah: Lawrence Erlbaum Associates, 2005. 160-76.

Markandaya, Kamala. "One Pair of Eyes: Some Random Reflections." *The Commonwealth Writer Overseas: Themes of Exile and Expatriation*. Ed. Alastair Niven. Brussels: Librairie Marcel Didier, 1976. 23-32.

Massey, Doreen. *For Space*. London: Sage, 2005.

Massey, Doreen. "Power-Geometry and a Progressive Sense of Place." *Mapping the Futures: Local Cultures, Global Change*. Ed. Jon Bird, Barry Curtis, Tim Putnam, and Lisa Tickner. London: Routledge, 1993. 59-69.

Maugham, Somerset. *The Razor's Edge*. London: Random House, 2000.

Maver, Igor. "Canadian New Diasporic Writing and Transnational/Borderland Literary Identities." *Diasporic Subjectivity and Cultural Brokering in Contemporary Post-Colonial Literatures*. Ed. Igor Maver. Lanham: Lexington Books, 2009. 17-26.

Maver, Igor. "Post-Colonial Literatures in English *ab origine ad futurum*." *Critics and Writers Speak: Revisioning Post-Colonial Studies*. Ed. Igor Maver. Lanham: Lexington Books, 2006. 11-33.

McDonald, Peter D. "Thinking Interculturally: Amartya Sen's Lovers Revisited." *Interventions* 13.3 (2011): 367-85.

McGowan, Kate. *Key Issues in Critical and Cultural Theory*. Maidenhead: Open UP, 2007.

McLemee, Scott. "Literature to Infinity." *insidehighered.com* (4 January 2006): <http://www.insidehighered.com/views/mclemee/mclemee193>.

McLeod, John. *Beginning Postcolonialism*. Manchester: Manchester UP, 2000.

McLeod, John. "Sounding Silence: Transculturation and Its Thresholds." *Transnational Literature* 4.1 (2011): 1-13.

Meneghello, Luigi. *Il dispatrio.* Milano: Rizzoli, 1993.

Meurs, Pieter, Nicole Note, and Diederik Aerts. "This World without Another: On Jean-Luc Nancy and *la mondialisation*." *Journal of Critical Globalisation Studies* 1 (2009): 31-46.

Meyer-Kalkus, Reinhard. "World Literature Beyond Goethe." *Cultural Mobility: A Manifesto.* Ed. Stephen Greenblatt. Cambridge: Cambridge UP, 2010. 96-121.

Mhiri, Mootacem Bellah. *A Study in Self-Writing and Identity: The Transcultural and Transnational Poetics of Ameen Rihani and Paul Smaïl*. Ph.D. Diss. University Park: The Pennsylvania State UP, 2005.

Mignolo, Walter D. *Local Histories/Global Designs: Coloniality, Subaltern Knowledges, and Border Thinking*. Princeton: Princeton UP, 2000.

Milech, Barbara H., and Ann Schilo. "'Exit Jesus': Relating to the Exegesis and Creative/Production Components of a Research Thesis." *Text* 3 (2004): 1-13.

Miller, Christopher L., ed. *Nationalists and Nomads: Essays on Francophone African Literature and Culture*. Chicago: U of Chicago P, 1998.

Miller, J. Hillis, "Globalization and World Literature." *Neohelicon: acta comparationis litterarum universarum* 38.2 (2011): 251-65.

Miller-Pogacar, Anesa. "Introduction: Mikhail Epstein's Transcultural Visions." Mikhail N. Epstein, *After the Future: The Paradoxes of Postmodernism and Contemporary Russian Culture*. Trans. Anesa Miller-Pogacar. Amherst: The U of Massachusetts P, 1995. 1-16.

Miyoshi, Masao. "Turn to the Planet: Literature, Diversity, and Totality." *Comparative Literature* 53.4 (2001): 283-97.

Moll, Nora. "La letteratura della migrazione in Italia e in Europa: Modelli a confronto." *Kúmá* (15 June 2008): <http://www.dislet.uniroma1.it/kuma/kuma15.html>.

Moore, Stephen D., and Mayra Rivera, eds. *Planetary Loves: Spivak, Postcoloniality, and Theology*. Bronx: Fordham UP, 2011.

Moraru, Christian. "The Forster Connection or, Cosmopolitanism Redux: Zadie Smith's *On Beauty*, *Howards End*, and the Schlegels." *The Comparatist* 35 (2011): 133-47.

Moretti, Franco. "Conjectures on World Literature." *New Left Review* 1 (2000): 54-68.

Moretti, Franco. *Graphs, Maps, Trees: Abstract Models for a Literary History*. New York: Verso, 2005.

Moretti, Franco. *The Novel*. Princeton: Princeton UP, 2006.

Nancy, Jean-Luc. *Being Singular Plural*. Trans. Robert D. Richardson and Anne O. Byrne. Stanford: Stanford UP, 2000.

Nancy, Jean-Luc. *The Creation of the World or Globalization*. Trans. François Raffoul and David Pettigrew. Albany: State U of New York P, 2007.

Nancy, Jean-Luc. *The Sense of the World*. Trans. Jeffrey S. Librett. Minneapolis: U of Minnesota P, 1997.

Nava, M. *Visceral Cosmopolitanism: Gender, Culture and the Normalisation of Difference*. Oxford: Berg, 2007.

Nederveen Pieterse, Jan. *Globalization and Culture: Global Mélange*. Boulder: Rowman & Littlefield, 2004.

Nederveen Pieterse, Jan. "Globalization as Hybridization." *Global Modernities*. Ed. Mike Featherstone, Scott Lash, and Roland Robertson. London: Sage, 1995. 45-68.

Nederveen Pieterse, Jan. "Globalization Goes in Circles: Hybridities East-West." *Hybridising East and West: Empirical Contributions to the Debates on Hybridity*. Ed. Dominique Schirmer, Gernot Saalmann, and Christl Kessler. Münster: LIT, 2007. 21-32.

Negro, Maria Grazia. "Il buco nel muro e il gioco degli avi: *Origines* di Amin Maalouf." *La storia nella scrittura diasporica*. Ed. Franca Sinopoli. Roma: Bulzoni, 2009. 19-52.

Neubauer, John. "Voices from Exile: A Literature for Europe?" *European Review* 17.1 (2009): 133-48.

Newton, Pauline T. *Transcultural Women of Late-Twentieth-Century U.S. American Literature: First-Generation Migrants from Islands and Peninsulas*. Aldershot: Ashgate, 2005.

Nicolescu, Basarab. *From Modernity to Cosmodernity: Science, Culture, and Spirituality.* Albany: State U of New York P, 2014.

Nietzsche, Friedrich, Wilhelm. *Beyond Good and Evil: Prelude to a Philosophy of the Future*. Trans. Reginald J. Hollingdale. Harmondsworth: Penguin, 1973.

"The Nobel Prize in Literature 2006: Orhan Pamuk." *nobelprize.org* (2006): <http://www.nobelprize.org/nobel_prizes/literature/laureates/2006/>.

Nordic Network for Literary Transculturation Studies. *uib.no* (2010-): <http://www.uib.no/rg/nnlts/research/framework-and-objectives>.

Očkayová, Jarmila. "Dispatrio e Scrittura." *I confini della scrittura: Il dispatrio nei testi letterari*. Ed. Franca Sinopoli and Silvia Tatti. Isernia: Cosmo Iannone Editore, 2005. 25-31.

Ong, Aihwa. *Flexible Citizenship: The Cultural Logics of Transnationality*. Durham: Duke UP, 1999.

Ortiz, Fernando. *Cuban Counterpoint: Tobacco and Sugar*. Trans. Harriet de Onís. New York: Knopf, 1947.

Orton, Marie, and Graziella Parati, eds. *Multicultural Literature in Contemporary Italy*. Jefferson: Fairleigh Dickinson UP, 2007.

Pal, Swati. "*Neem Dreams*. A Review." *The Sunday Pioneer* (14 September 2003): <http://www.inezbaranay.com/?reviews=swati-pal-the-sunday-pioneer-september-14-2003>.

Palandri, Enrico. "Seminario itinerante di Enrico Palandri (Bordeaux, 20 Marzo 2005)." Ed. Stefania Ricciardi and Martine Bovo-Romoeuf. *unibo.it* (2007): <http://www3.unibo.it/boll900/numeri/2007-i/Bordeaux.html>.

Papastergiadis, Nikos. *The Turbulence of Migration: Globalization, Deterritorialization, and Hybridity*. Cambridge: Polity, 2000.

Parati, Graziella. "Introduction: Studying Cultures. Definition, Theory and Accented Practices." *New Perspectives in Italian Cultural Studies: Definitions, Theory, and Accented Practices*. Ed. Graziella Parati. Jefferson: Fairleigh Dickinson UP, 2012. ix-xxii.

Parati, Graziella. *Public History, Private Stories: Italian Women's Autobiography*. Minneapolis: U of Minnesota P, 1996.

Parker, David, and Miri Song. *Rethinking "Mixed Race."* London: Pluto, 2001.

Parks, Tim. *Cleaver*. London: Vintage, 2007.

Parks, Tim. *Dreams of Rivers and Seas*. London: Harvill Secker, 2008.

Parks, Tim. *Europa*. London: Secker & Warburg, 1997.

Parks, Tim. *Family Planning*. London: Collins, 1989.

Parks, Tim. "A Game Without Rules." *nybooks.com* (8 November 2012): <http://www.nybooks.com/blogs/nyrblog/2012/nov/08/game-without-rules/>.

Parks, Tim. *Goodness*. London: William Heinemann, 1991.

Parks, Tim. "Most Favoured Nations." *nybooks.com* (11 June 2012): <http://www.nybooks.com/blogs/nyrblog/2012/jun/11/literary-globalization-europe-translation/>.

Parks, Tim. "The Nobel Individual and the Paradoxes of 'International Literature.'" *timparks.com* (20 April 2011): <http://tim-parks.com/the-nobel-individual/>.

Parks, Tim. "Novels." *timparks.com* (2014): <http://tim-parks.com/novels/>.

Parks, Tim. *Rapids*. London: Secker & Warburg, 2005.

Patteson, Richard F. "Paul Bowles/Mohammed Mrabet: Translation, Transformation, and Transcultural Discourse." *The Journal of Narrative Technique* 22.3 (1992): 180-90.

Pennycook, Alastair. "The Future of Englishes: One, Many, Or None?" *The Routledge Handbook of World Englishes*. Ed. Andy Kirkpatrick. London: Routledge, 2010.

Pennycook, Alastair. *Global Englishes and Transcultural Flows*. London: Routledge, 2007.

Petersson, Margareta. "The Practice of Writing Transnational and Translingual Literary History." *Studying Transcultural Literary History*. Ed. Gunilla Lindberg-Wada. Berlin: Walter de Gruyter, 2006. 155-57.

Petrelli, Micla. "L'arte pura in tutte le lingue del mondo (Luis Cernuda)." *Confluenze* 1.2 (2009): <http://confluenze.unibo.it/article/view/1647>.

Pettersson, Anders. "Introduction: Concepts of Literature and Transcultural Literary History." *Literary History: Towards a Global Perspective: Notions of Literature across Times and Cultures.* Vol. 1. Ed. Anders Pettersson. Berlin: Walter De Gruyter, 2006. 1-35.

Pettersson, Anders. "Transcultural Literary History: Beyond Constricting Notions of World Literature." *New Literary History* 39.3 (2008): 463–79.

Phillips, Mike. "Broken Borders: Migration, Modernity and English Writing—Transcultural Transformation in the Heart of Europe." *Transcultural English Studies: Theories, Fictions, Realities*. Ed. Frank Schulze-Engler and Sissy Helff. Amsterdam: Rodopi, 2009. 133-49.

Phillips, Timothy, and Philip Smith. "Cosmopolitan Beliefs and Cosmopolitan Practices." *Journal of Sociology* 44.4 (2008): 391-99.

Pirsig, Robert. *Lila: An Inquiry into Morals.* New York: Bantam, 1991.

Pollock, Sheldon, Homi K. Bhabha, Carol A. Breckenridge, and Dipesh Chakrabarty. "Cosmopolitanisms." *Cosmopolitanism.* Vol. 4. Ed. Carol A. Breckenridge, Sheldon Pollock, Homi K. Bhabha and Dipesh Chakrabarty. Durham: Duke UP, 2002. 1–15.

Ponzanesi, Sandra. *Paradoxes of Postcolonial Culture: Contemporary Women Writers of the Indian and Afro-Italian Diaspora.* Albany: State U of New York P, 2004.

Pratt, Mary Louise. *Imperial Eyes: Travel Writing and Transculturation.* London: Routledge, 1992.

Probyn, Elspeth. *Outside Belongings*. London: Routledge, 1996.

Probyn, Elspeth. *Sexing the Self: Gendered Positions in Cultural Studies*. London: Routledge, 1993.

Rabinow, Paul. *Essays on the Anthropology of Reason*. Princeton: Princeton UP, 1996.

Randall, Frederika. "Translator's Introduction: The Dispatriate." *Deliver Us.* By Luigi Meneghello. Evanston: Northwestern UP, 2011. vii-xviii.

Rama, Ángel. *Transculturación narrativa en América latina*. Romero de Terreros: Siglo XXI, 1982.

Renzi, Alessandra. "Identity and Transculture in *Vice Versa*." *Collegium Antropologicum* 28.1 (2004): 109-13.

Rodríguez, Joaquín Barriendos. "Global Art and Politics of Mobility: (Trans)Cultural Shifts in the International Contemporary Art-System." *Thamyris/Intersecting: Place, Sex and Race* 23.1 (2011): 313-34.

Ronchey, Silvia. "Istanbul la polis." *Ulisse* 1 (2011): 18-29.

Ronchey, Silvia, and Tommaso Braccini, eds. *Il romanzo di Costantinopoli. Guida letteraria alla Roma d'Oriente.* Milano: Einaudi, 2010.

Rønning, Anne Holden. "Literary Transculturations and Modernity: Some Reflections." *Transnational Literature* 4.1 (2011): 1-10.

Roorbach, Bill, ed. *Contemporary Creative Nonfiction: The Art of Truth*. Oxford: Oxford UP, 2001.

Root, Robert. *The Nonfictionist's Guide: On Reading and Writing Creative Nonfiction*. Lanham: Rowman & Littlefield, 2008.

Rorty, Richard. *Achieving our Country: Leftist Thought in Twentieth-Century America.* Cambridge: Harvard UP, 1998.

Rorty, Richard. *Contingency, Irony, and Solidarity*. Cambridge: Cambridge UP, 1989.

Rorty, Richard. *Take Care of Freedom and Truth Will Take Care of Itself: Interviews with Richard Rorty*. Stanford: Stanford UP, 2006.

Rossi-Landi, Ferruccio. *Ideologies of Linguistic Relativity*. The Hague: Mouton, 1973.

Rushdie, Salman. "Commonwealth Literature Does Not Exist." *Imaginary Homelands: Essays and Criticism 1981–1991*. London: Granta Books, 1991. 61-70.

Rushdie, Salman. "Imaginary Homelands." *Imaginary Homelands: Essays and Criticism 1981-1991*. London: Granta Books, 1991. 9-21.

Rushdie, Salman. *Midnight's Children.* London: Vintage, 1995.

Sachsenmaier, Dominic. "Multiple Modernities: The Concept and Its Potential." *Reflections on Multiple Modernities: European, Chinese and Other Interpretations.* Ed. Dominic Sachsenmaier, Jens Riedel, and Shmuel N. Eisenstadt. Leiden: Brill, 2002. 42-67.

Sachsenmaier, Dominic, Jens Riedel, and Shmuel N. Eisenstadt, eds. *Reflections on Multiple Modernities: European, Chinese and Other Interpretations.* Leiden: Brill, 2002.

Şafak, Elif. "Pulled by Two Tides." *elifsafak.us* (August 2006): <http://www.elifsafak.us/yazilar.asp?islem=yazi&id=408>.

Said, Edward W. *After the Last Sky*. New York: Pantheon, 1986.

Said, Edward W. *Culture and Imperialism*. London: Vintage, 1993.

Said, Edward W. *Orientalism*. London: Penguin, 1995.

Said, Edward W. *Representations of the Intellectual: The 1993 Reith Lectures*. London: Vintage, 1996.

Said, Edward W. *The World, the Text and the Critic.* Cambridge: Harvard UP, 1983.

Salzani, Carlo, and Steven Tötösy de Zepetnek. "Bibliography for Work in Travel Studies." *CLCWeb: Comparative Literature and Culture* (*Library*): <http://docs.lib.purdue.edu/clcweblibrary/travelstudiesbibliography>.

Sankaran, Kanaka Bashyam. "A New Dialogue at the Periphery?" *Transcultural English Studies: Theories, Fictions, Realities*. Ed. Frank Schulze-Engler and Sissy Helff. Amsterdam: Rodopi, 2009. 409-18.

Schade, Silke Katharine. *Rewriting Home and Migration: Spatiality in the Narratives of Barbara Honigmann and Emine Sevgi Özdamar*. Ph.D. Diss. Cincinnati: U of Cincinnati, 2007.

Schaff, Barbara. "Trying to Escape, Longing to Belong: Roots, Genes and Performativity in Zadie Smith's *White Teeth* and Hari Kunzru's *The Impressionist*."

Transcultural English Studies: Theories, Fictions, Realities. Ed. Frank Schulze-Engler and Sissy Helff. Amsterdam: Rodopi, 2009. 281-92.

Schindhelm, Michael. *Dubai High: A Culture Trip.* Oxford: Arabian Publishing, 2011.

Schoene, Berthold. *The Cosmopolitan Novel*. Edinburgh: Edinburgh UP, 2009.

Schulze-Engler, Frank. Introduction. *Transcultural English Studies: Theories, Fictions, Realities*. Ed. Frank Schulze-Engler and Sissy Helff. Amsterdam: Rodopi, 2009. ix-xvi.

Schulze-Engler, Frank. "Theoretical Perspectives: From Postcolonialism to Transcultural World Literature." *English Literatures across the Globe: A Companion*. Ed. Lars Eckstein. Paderborn: Wilhelm Fink, 2007. 20-32.

Schulze-Engler, Frank, and Sissy Helff, eds. *Transcultural English Studies: Theories, Fictions, Realities*. Amsterdam: Rodopi, 2009.

Sellin, Eric. "Translingual and Transcultural Patterns in Francophone Literature of the Maghreb." *Transcultural Identities in Contemporary Literature*. Ed. Irene Gilsenan Nordin, Julie Hansen, and Carmen Zamorano Llena. Amsterdam: Rodopi, 2013. 223-44.

Selvadurai, Shyam. 1998. *Cinnamon Gardens*. Toronto: McClelland and Stewart, 1998.

Sen, Amartya. 2007. *Identity and Violence: The Illusion of Destiny*. Harmondsworth: Penguin, 2007.

Sewell, William H., Jr. "The Concept(s) of Culture." *Beyond the Cultural Turn: New Directions in the Study of Society and Culture*. Ed. Victoria E. Bonnell and Lynn Hunt. Berkeley: U of California P, 1999. 35-61.

Seyhan, Azade. *Writing Outside the Nation*. Princeton: Princeton UP, 2000.

Shamsie, Kamila. *Burnt Shadows*. London: Bloomsbury, 2009.

Shankman, Steven. *Other Others: Levinas, Literature, Transcultural Studies*. Albany: State U of New York P, 2010.

Sinopoli, Franca, and Silvia Tatti. *I confini della scrittura. Il dispatrio nei testi letterari*. Isernia: Cosmo Iannone, 2005.

Smith, Anthony D. "Towards a Global Culture?" *Global Culture: Nationalism, Globalization and Modernity*. Ed. Mike Featherstone. London: Sage, 1990. 171-92.

Spack, Ruth. *America's Second Tongue: American Indian Education and the Ownership of English, 1860–1900*. Lincoln: U of Nebraska P, 2002.

Spitta, Silvia. *Between Two Waters: Narratives of Transculturation in Latin America*. Houston: Rice UP, 1993.

Spivak, Gayatri Chakravorty. *An Aesthetic Education in the Era of Globalization*. Cambridge: Harvard UP, 2012.

Spivak, Gayatri Chakravorty. *A Critique of Postcolonial Reason: Toward a History of the Vanishing Present*. Cambridge: Harvard UP, 1999.

Spivak, Gayatri Chakravorty. *Death of a Discipline*. New York: Columbia UP, 2003.

Spivak, Gayatri Chakravorty. "Introduction. Subaltern Studies: Deconstructing Historiography." *Selected Subaltern Studies*. Ed. Ranajit Guha and Gayatri Chakravorty Spivak. Oxford: Oxford UP, 1988. 3-32.

Spivak, Gayatri Chakravorty. "Rethinking Comparativism." *New Literary History* 40.3 (2009): 609-26.

Stein, Mark. "The Location of Transculture." *Transcultural English Studies: Theories, Fictions, Realities*. Ed. Frank Schulze-Engler and Sissy Helff. Amsterdam: Rodopi, 2009. 251-66.

Steinby, Liisa. *Kundera and Modernity*. West Lafayette: Purdue UP, 2013.

Sturm-Trigonakis, Elke. "Comparative Cultural Studies and the *New Weltliteratur*." *Companion to Comparative Literature, World Literatures, and Comparative Cultural Studies*. Ed. Steven Tötösy de Zepetnek and Tutun Mukherjee. New Delhi: Cambridge UP India, 2012. 93-99.

Sturm-Trigonakis, Elke. *Comparative Cultural Studies and the* New Weltliteratur. West Lafayette: Purdue UP, 2013.

Syjuco, Miguel. *Ilustrado*. London: Picador, 2010.

Szeman, Imre. *Zones of Instability: Literature, Postcolonialism, and the Nation*. Baltimore: The Johns Hopkins UP, 2003.

Taylor, Charles. "Two Theories of Modernity." *Alternative Modernities*. Ed. Dilip Parameshwar Gaonkar. Durham: Duke UP, 2001. 172-96.

Thomsen, Mads Rosendahl. *Mapping World Literature: International Canonization and Transnational Literatures*. London: Continuum, 2010.

Thomsen, Mads Rosendahl. "Migrant Writers and Cosmopolitan Readers." *Studying Transcultural Literary History*. Ed. Gunilla Lindberg-Wada. Berlin: Walter de Gruyter, 2006. 244-50.

Todorov, Tzvetan. "Il multiculturalismo non è il vero pericolo." *Vita e pensiero* 11.2 (2011): 12-22.

Toffler, Alvin. *Powershift: Knowledge, Wealth, and Violence at the Edge of the Twenty-First Century*. New York: Bantam, 1990.

Tötösy de Zepetnek, Steven. *Comparative Literature: Theory, Method, Application*. Amsterdam: Rodopi, 1998.

Tötösy de Zepetnek, Steven. "Configurations of Postcoloniality and National Identity: Inbetween Peripherality and Narratives of Change." *The Comparatist: Journal of the Southern Comparative Literature Association* 23 (1999): 89-110.

Tötösy de Zepetnek, Steven. "From Comparative Literature Today toward Comparative Cultural Studies." *CLCWeb: Comparative Literature and Culture* 1.3 (1999): <http://dx.doi.org/10.7771/1481-4374.1041>.

Tötösy de Zepetnek, Steven. "The New Humanities: The Intercultural, the Comparative, and the Interdisciplinary." *Globalization and the Futures of Comparative Literature*. Ed. Jan M. Ziolkowski and Alfred J. López. Thematic Section *The Global South* 1.2 (2007): 45-68.

Tötösy de Zepetnek, Steven, and Tutun Mukherjee, eds. *Companion to Comparative Literature, World Literatures, and Comparative Cultural Studies*. New Delhi: Cambridge UP India, 2013.

Tötösy de Zepetnek, Steven, and Louise O. Vasvári. "About the Contextual Study of Literature and Culture, Globalization, and Digital Humanities." *Companion to Comparative Literature, World Literatures, and Comparative Cultural Studies*. Ed. Steven Tötösy de Zepetnek and Tutun Mukherjee. New Delhi: Cambridge UP India, 2013. 3-35.

Tötösy de Zepetnek, Steven, and I-Chun Wang, eds. *Mapping the World, Culture, and Border-Crossing*. Kaohsiung: National Sun Yat-sen UP, 2010.

Tötösy de Zepetnek, Steven, I-Chun Wang, and Hsiao-Yu Sun, eds. *Perspectives on Identity, Migration, and Displacement.* Kaohsiung: National Sun Yat-sen UP, 2010.

"Towards a Global Literature." *iulm.it* (2011): <http://www.iulm.it/wps/wcm/connect/iulmit/iulm-it/ricerca/progetti-di-ricerca/progetti-di-ateneo/letteratura-globalizzata>.

Trojanow, Illija. "Adelbert von Chamisso Prize." Acceptance speech. Frankfurt: Frankfurt Book Fair, 2000.

Trojanow, Ilija. *The Collector of Worlds.* Trans. Will Hobson. London: Faber and Faber, 2008.

Trojanow, Ilija. "Le identità in movimento. Incontro con Ilija Trojanow." *infinitestorie.it* (20 April 2007): <http://www.infinitestorie.it/frames.speciali/speciali.asp?page=15&ID=568&searchString=>.

Trojanow, Ilija. "Location, Location, Location." *theaustralian.com* (20 February 2010): <http://www.theaustralian.com.au/arts/books/location-location-location/story-e6frg8nf-1225834841196>.

Trojanow, Ilija. "Meeting with the Author: Questions and Answers Time." Adelaide: Adelaide Writers Week 2010. Unpublished Transcript.

Trojanow, Ilija. *Un Voyage Mystique*. Paris: Buchet Chastel, 2009.

Trojanow, Ilija, and Ranjit Hoskoté. *Confluences: Forgotten Histories from East and West*. New Delhi: Yoda Press, 2012.

Tsiolkas, Christos. "On the Concept of Tolerance." *Tolerance, Prejudice and Fear*. Ed. Christos Tsiolkas, Haigh Gideon, and Alexis Wright. London: Allen and Unwin, 2008. 1-56.

Underhill, James. *Creating Worldviews: Metaphor, Ideology, and Language*. Edinburgh: Edinburgh UP, 2011.

Underhill, James. *Humboldt, Worldview, and Language*. Edinburgh: Edinburgh UP, 2009.

Urry, John. *Mobilities*. Cambridge: Polity, 2007.

Van Luven, Lynne. *Going Some Place: Creative Nonfiction Across Canada*. Regina: Coteau Books, 2000.

Vattimo, Gianni. *The Transparent Society*. Baltimore: The Johns Hopkins UP, 1992.

Venn, Couze. "Narrating the Postcolonial." *Spaces of Culture: City-Nation-World*. Ed. Mike Featherstone and Scott Lash. London: Sage, 1999. 257-81.

"Venti d'Australia." *Three of Us* (17 November 2009): <http://www.di-noi-tre.blogspot.ca/search/label/aussie%20life-%20intorno%20a%20me>.

Vertovec, Steven. "Super-Diversity and Its Implications." *Ethnic and Racial Studies* 30.6 (2007): 1024-54.

ViceVersa: Magazine Transculturel <http://www.viceversamag.com>.

Vladiv-Glover, Millicent. "Transculture: Mikhail Epstein's Theses on Culture/Culturology/Transculture. Position Paper." *artsonline.monash.edu.au* (February 2003): <http://artsonline.monash.edu.au/slavic/files/2013/02/trans-2003-epstien-position.pdf>.

Vladiv-Glover, Slobodanka, and Evert van der Zweerde. "Introducing TransCultures." *artsonline.monash.edu.au* (2005): <http://artsonline.monash.edu.au/slavic/transcultural-studies-a-series-in-interdisciplinary-research/>.

Wake in Fright [*Outback*]. Dir. Ted Kotcheff. Sydney: NLT Productions, 1971.

Walkowitz, Rebecca L. *Cosmopolitan Style. Modernism Beyond the Nation*. New York: Columbia UP, 2006.

Walkowitz, Rebecca L. "The Location of Literature. The Trasnational Book and the Migrant Writer." *Immigrant Fictions. Contemporary Literature in an Age of Globalization*. Ed. Rebecca L. Walkowitz. Madison: U of Wisconsin P, 2006. 527-45.

Walkowitz, Rebecca L. "Unimaginable Largeness: Kazuo Ishiguro, Translation, and the New World Literature." *Novel* 40.3 (2007): 216-39.

Wang, Ning. "On World Literatures, Comparative Literature, and (Comparative) Cultural Studies." *CLCWeb: Comparative Literature and Culture* 15.5 (2013): <http://dx.doi.org/10.7771/1481-4374.2336>.

Weik, Alexa. *Beyond the Nation: American Expatriate Writers and the Process of Cosmopolitanism*. Ph.D. Diss. San Diego: U of California, 2008.

Welsch, Wolfgang. "On the Acquisition and Possession of Commonalities." *Transcultural English Studies: Theories, Fictions, Realities*. Ed. Frank Schulze-Engler and Sissy Helff. Amsterdam: Rodopi, 2009. 3-36.

Welsch, Wolfgang. "Rethinking Identity in the Age of Globalization: A Transcultural Perspective." *Aesthetics & Art Science* 1 (2002): 85-94.

Welsch, Wolfgang. "Transculturality: The Puzzling Form of Cultures Today." *Spaces of Culture: City-Nation-World*. Ed. Mike Featherstone and Scott Lash. London: Sage, 1999. 194-213.

Welsch, Wolfgang. "Transkulturalität. Lebensformen nach der Auflösung der Kulturen." *Information Philosophie* 2 (1992): 5-20.

Werbner, Pnina. "Global Pathways: Working Class Cosmopolitans and the Creation of Transnational Ethnic Worlds." *Social Anthropology* 7.1 (1999): 17-35.

Werbner, Pnina. "Vernacular Cosmopolitanism." *Theory Culture Society* 23.2-3 (2006): 496-98.

Werbner, Richard. "Cosmopolitan Ethnicity, Entrepreneurship and the Nation: Minority Elites in Botswana." *Journal of Southern African Studies* 28.4 (2002): 731-53.

Williams, Raymond. "Literature in Society." *Contemporary Approaches to English Studies*. Ed. Hilda Schiff. New York: Barnes & Noble, 1977. 24-37.

Williams, Raymond. *The Long Revolution*. Harmondsworth: Penguin, 1961.

Wood, James. "Bohumil Hrabal." *lrb.co.uk* (23 January 2001): <http://www.lrb.co.uk/v23/n01/james-wood/bohumil-hrabal>.

Xuereb, Karsten. "European Cultural Policy and Migration: Why Should Cultural Policy in the European Union Address the Impact of Migration on Identity and Social Integration?" *International Migration* 49.2 (2011): 28-53.

Yee, Danny. "*Eucalyptus*, Murray Bail." *dannyreviews.com* (April 2003): <http://dannyreviews.com/h/Eucalyptus.html>.

Yoko, Tawada. *Where Europe Begins*. New York: New Directions, 2002.

Young, Robert. *Colonial Desire: Hybridity in Theory, Culture, and Race*. London: Routledge, 1995.

Zabus, Chantal J., and Silvia Nagy, eds. *Perennial Empires: Postcolonial, Transnational, and Literary Perspectives*. London: Cambria, 2011.

Zalloua, Zahi. "The Future of an Ethics of Difference after Hardt and Negri's *Empire*." *symplokē: a journal for the intermingling of literary, cultural and theoretical scholarship* 16.1-2 (2008): 127-52.

Zelig. Dir. Woody Allen. New York: Orion, 1983.

Zembylas, Michalinos, and Charalambos Vrasidas. "Globalization, Information and Communication Technologies, and the Prospect of a 'Global Village': Promises of Inclusion or Electronic Colonization?" *Journal of Curriculum Studies* 37.1 (2005): 65-83.

Zembylas, Michalinos, Charalambos Vrasidas, and Marina S. McIsaac. "Of Nomads, Polyglots, and Global Villagers: Globalization, Information Technologies, and Critical Education Online." *Distance Education and Distributed Learning*. Ed. Charalambos Vrasidas and Gene V. Glass. Charlotte: Information Age Publishers, 2008. 201-24.

Index